Machine Vision and its Applications

Machine Vision and its Applications

Edited by **Martha Lesley**

CLANRYE INTERNATIONAL

New Jersey

Published by Clanrye International,
55 Van Reypen Street,
Jersey City, NJ 07306, USA
www.clanryeinternational.com

Machine Vision and its Applications
Edited by Martha Lesley

International Standard Book Number: 978-1-63240-332-2 (Hardback)

Printed in the United States of America.

Contents

Preface

Machine Vision is exactly what it entails, the ability of a machine to 'see', though the process might differ according to type and application. Distantly related to computer vision, machine vision is increasingly used to provide services equivalent to that of a human supervisor and analyst, that is, using technology to provide image based applications for processes like automatic inspection and robotic guidance in industries. As machines are increasingly becoming part and parcel of our daily lives, the scope of machine vision in ever-increasing. Though standardization is slowly becoming the norm, there are still various methods of using machine vision. As digital image processes are used to extract information, different types of lenses, cameras and lighting are used as required. Machine is not just restricted to 2D images but also infrared bands and X-ray imaging as well as 3D images. Such differentiated methods speak for the ever changing instruments of machine vision. Such an essential part of the industrial process has a constantly increasing market for its varied applications. The future is limitless for machine vision, from agriculture to robotics. But there is also trepidation about such advanced uses as it can potentially take away jobs from the workforce.

The book focuses on the various applications, markets and changing technology in the field known as machine vision. I would like to thank those who have contributed to this field of work for making this book possible and my family for their constant support.

Editor

A New Scheme for the Polynomial Based Biometric Cryptosystems

Amioy Kumar, M. Hanmandlu, and Hari M. Gupta

Biometrics Research Laboratory, Department of Electrical Engineering, Indian Institute of Technology Delhi, Hauz Khas, New Delhi 110 016, India

Correspondence should be addressed to Amioy Kumar; amioy.iitd@gmail.com

Academic Editors: M. Leo and N. A. Schmid

This paper presents a new scheme for the fuzzy vault based biometric cryptosystems which explore the feasibility of a polynomial based vault for the biometric traits like iris, palm, vein, and so forth. Gabor filter is used for the feature extraction from the biometric data and the extracted feature points are transformed into Eigen spaces using Karhunen Loeve (K-L) transform. A polynomial obtained from the secret key is used to generate projections from the transformed features and the randomly generated points, known as *chaff points*. The points and their corresponding projections form the ordered pairs. The union of the ordered pairs from the features and the chaff points creates a fuzzy vault. At the time of decoding, matching scores are computed by comparing the stored and the claimed biometric traits, which are further tested against a predefined threshold. The number of matched scores should be greater than a tolerance value for the successful decoding of the vault. The threshold and the tolerance value are learned from the transformed features at the encoding stage and chosen according to the tradeoff in the error rates. The proposed scheme is tested on a variety of biometric databases and error rates obtained from the experimental results confirm the utility of the new scheme.

1. Introduction

Intrusions in the secret data protection arena pose potential threat to the information security. In the recent trends of the data protection, biometrics based cryptosystems are emerging as promising technologies. Biometric cryptosystems can be broadly divided into two main schemes: (a) *Key binding mode*, in which the secret key is integrated with the biometric template. In this mechanism, both the biometric template and the key are so locked that it is very difficult to retrieve any one without the information of other [1–4]. (b) *Key generation mode*, in which the biometric template generates the keys used in any cryptographic algorithm for the encryption and decryption of secret messages [5–8]. Both the approaches are secure and computationally very difficult for the intruder to attack. However, these approaches pose implementation problems as it requires the encryption key to be exactly same as the decryption one. But the biometric data acquired at different times is substantially different, due to the intraclass variations, necessitating a different key every time.

The implementation of key binding mode is greatly affected by the cryptographic construct called fuzzy vault, investigated by Juels and Sudan [9]. This fuzzy vault can tolerate the intraclass variability in the biometric data, which has inspired several researchers [1–4] to pursue the biometrics based fuzzy vaults. This paper proposes another attempt on using fuzzy vault scheme in key binding mode by presenting a new scheme which exploits textural features from biometric traits.

1.1. The Prior Work. Both the key binding mode [1–4, 10] and the key generation mode [5–8, 11] of biometric cryptosystem have been addressed in the literature. Moreover, prevention of the attacks on the biometric templates is also addressed by using the nonrevocable biometrics [12–14] and BioHashing [11, 15–18]. One widely accepted solution to the intrusion of the stored biometric templates is the reissuance of biometric features.

The key generating mode of the biometric cryptosystem is of particular interest in [6–8, 11, 19]. Hao et al. [6] select iris for generating the cryptographic keys with the help of the hybrid Reed & Solomon and Hadamard error correcting codes. Sauter et al. [7] resort to the key generation using the fingerprints and their work has resulted in the product, *Bioscrypt*. Instead of generating a key directly from biometrics, they have devised a method of biometric locking using the phase product. A fuzzy extractor based approach is suggested by Dodis et al. [8] to generate a strong cryptographic key from the noisy biometric data. This scheme is modified by Boyen [19] by generating multiple keys before hashing.

The basic idea of a key binding was borrowed from the work of Juels and Sudan [9] which was an extension of the work in [20]. They introduce the polynomial construction to hide the secret key with integration of an unordered set and modify the fuzzy vault scheme of Davida at el. [13] by invoking Reed and Solomon error correcting code [21]. However, Uludag et al. [1] were among the first to investigate the fuzzy vault using the fingerprint biometric as an unordered set. The difficulties associated with the minutiae point alignment are significantly reduced in [4] with the *helper data* during the minutiae point extraction. A modified fuzzy vault is suggested in [22] where the secret key and the biometric features are hidden in separate grids with chaff points added to make the grids fuzzy. The same scheme makes its way in a palmprint based vault [23].

1.2. The Motivations. Note that fingerprint has been utilized as a biometric trait [1–4] in most of the published work on polynomial based fuzzy vault. In the context of fingerprint authentication, minutiae points are widely accepted as the most significant features [4]. The minutiae points are the specific locations in a finger and can be considered as ordered triplet (x, y, θ) [4]. But since the points are associated with their locations and saved accordingly, they become an unordered set which can be shuffled without losing its significance and can be matched with original set in any order. Despite the current popularity of other biometric traits like palmprint, iris, and hand veins, there are less attempts to use them in the polynomial based fuzzy vault. In this direction, iris [24], palmprint [25], and handwritten signature [26] based cryptosystems merit a mention. Here, the work in [24] made use of clustering method to make iris features unordered while the other two cryptosystems operate on key generation mode. The reason for lack of interest could be the orderliness of the features extracted from these traits. The orderliness of these features implies that any change in their order will result in a new set of features that can affect the authentication process.

1.3. The Proposed Work. This paper devises a new scheme for the polynomial based fuzzy vault, in the key binding mode, by employing the textural features generated using Gabor filters of the biometric traits [27]. In the proposed approach, Karhunen Loeve (K-L) transform [28] to transform the features into the Eigenspace through the transformation matrix (Eigenvector matrix). The projection of the transformed features is taken on the polynomial and chaff points are added to form the fuzzy vault. The original and the transformed features are discarded after creating the vault. However,

the transformation matrix is stored along with the vault to be used during the decoding process. Essentially, a query feature vector is transformed using the stored transformation matrix. Each point of the transformed query feature vector is subtracted from all the stored vault points, and the differences are matched against a cutoff threshold. If the difference is less than this threshold, the corresponding biometric feature point is supposed to be the original feature vector. However, only $N + 1$ features are required to reconstruct a polynomial of degree N and an original feature set may have more points than N. Thus, total count of such feature points should be greater than a tolerance value for the claimed identity to be true. The cutoff threshold and tolerance value are learned from the transformed features (before being discarded) at the time of encoding. The reconstruction of the polynomial of any query takes place only when these two thresholds are validated. These values can also be compared with the decision thresholds in the traditional biometric authentication, chosen according to the tradeoff between the error rates (false acceptance/rejection).

The usage of the Gabor filter based features in the vault allows this scheme to be generalized for many biometric traits. The proposed scheme is tested on variety of publicly available databases, that is, FVC 2004 DB2, Hong Kong PolyU V2, and CASIA V1 of fingerprint, palmprint, and iris, respectively, including the hand vein database of IIT Delhi with the textural features extracted using Gabor filters. The experimental results show that the presented approach operates on lower error rates and can be acceptable for any security applications. It is remarked that no existing biometric cryptosystem is tested on such a variety of publicly available databases. The block diagram of the complete approach is shown in Figure 1.

The rest of the paper is organized as follows. Section 2 presents an overview on implementation of the earlier proposed fuzzy vault and the modifications done in our scheme. Section 3 details the proposed scheme of the fuzzy vault. The experimental results are presented in Section 4, and some security-related issues are discussed in Section 5. Finally, a summary of the overall work is outlined in Section 6.

2. An Overview on Fuzzy Vault

2.1. The Fuzzy Vault. The fuzzy vault introduced by Juels and Sudan [9] contains a secret key integrated with an unordered set using polynomial projections. The key can be accessed through the polynomial reconstruction using another unordered set, if the set is much similar to the original one. The fuzzy vault is used as biometric cryptosystem in [2] with the minutiae points of the fingerprint as an unordered set. In this work, the polynomial coefficients are computed from the secret key and the projections of the minutiae points are taken on this polynomial. The added chaff points are such that they do not lie on the generated polynomial. Let secret key S (e.g., cryptographic key) be hidden using a biometric feature set $T = \{t_1, t_2 \cdots t_r\}$ of length r. Error correcting bits are added to the secret key S to form $S1$ to tolerate the errors created at the time of decoding. The coefficients of the polynomial are generated using $S1$. Let

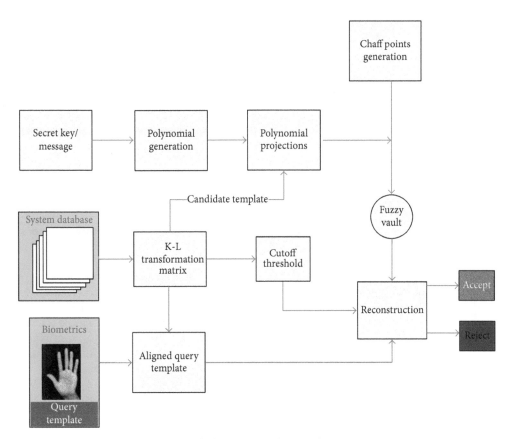

FIGURE 1: Block diagram of the complete system.

$P(x) = a_0 + a_1 x + \cdots + a_{(n-1)} x^{N-1}$ be the polynomial of degree $N - 1$ formed from S1. The projection of each element of T on the polynomial P together with element itself forms a couplet $(t_k, P(t_k))$. The chaff couplet (u_i, v_i) is generated such that $P(u_i) \neq v_i$. The union of feature couplet $(t_k, P(t_k))$ and chaff couplet (u_i, v_i) creates the vault **V**. The secret key S and the feature T are thus integrated and bind in the fuzzy vault.

At the unlocking step, the user provides a query template denoted by $T' = \{t'_1, t'_2 \cdots t'_r\}$ of "r" elements. If T' overlaps substantially with T, the user can retrieve many original points from **V** that lie on the polynomial. These overlaps help reconstruct the polynomial coefficients and thereby the secret key S. If the number of discrepancies between T and T' is less than $(r - n)$, n overlaps are needed to interpolate the polynomial. Error checking is one way to check whether the set of overlaps chosen is appropriate to decode the vault. On the other hand, if T and T' do not have a sufficient overlap, P cannot be reconstructed; hence the authentication fails. The vault is called *fuzzy* because the added chaff points to the original biometric features make them so vague that it cannot be separated without the presence of original features.

The crucial parameters in the vault implementation are R, N, and C, where R is the number of features used in the vault encoding, N is the degree of the polynomial chosen according to the length of the secret message in the vault, and C is the number of chaff points added to the vault for concealing the original data points from an attacker.

2.2. Modifications in the Earlier Approach.

The new scheme for fuzzy vault, presented in this paper, has the following main differences from the earlier schemes [2–4, 29].

(1) The textural features extracted using Gabor filters are attributed as one of the most significant features in palmprint [27], iris [30], and even fingerprint [31]. Note that the use of these features is made for the first time in the polynomial based fuzzy vault. To separate out the original points from the chaff points, a cutoff threshold and a tolerance value are learned empirically at the encoding phase of the vault. A novel scheme for the generation of the polynomial coefficients from the secret key is also developed.

(2) One parity check bit is added to each binary string of the secret message/key. The binary strings are formed from the secret key by splitting the key into N parts, where N is the number of coefficients of the polynomial. The reconstruction of the polynomial is successful only if the parity check bit is unaltered. Otherwise, this gives rise to the false acceptance/rejection error.

(3) At the learning phase, the biometric features are employed to construct the transformation matrix of Eigenvectors. The original feature vector is then transformed and the transformed feature vector is used for the polynomial projection. The cutoff threshold is also learned at this phase using the transformed feature

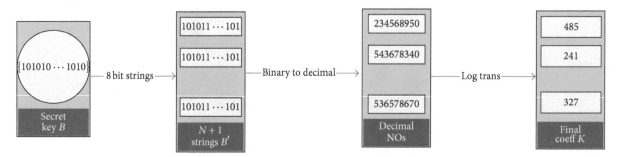

vector. After the vault is generated, both the original and transformed feature vectors are discarded for the security reasons. However, the transformation matrix (i.e., Eigen vector matrix) is retained for the assessment of the query features toward the access to the authentication system.

3. The Proposed Scheme for the Fuzzy Vault

3.1. Generation of the Polynomial Coefficients. A secret key S of lengths B bits is randomly generated. For a polynomial of degree N, a total of $N + 1$ number of coefficients should be generated from the random bits B. So, B is divided into $N + 1$ binary strings denoted as B'. With each B', a cyclic redundancy check (CRC) bit is added to every string. At the authentication stage, these bits are checked after the reconstruction of the polynomial coefficients and any discrepancy in these bits is declared as an unsuccessful attempt to the access of the vault.

Each of bit strings B' is converted to a decimal number and then the logarithmic transformation is applied on the decimal numbers to bring them into the lower range of values that become the polynomial coefficients K. The block diagram in Figure 2 shows the stages in the generation of the polynomial coefficients. We have 384 randomly generated bits B, which are split into $B' = 8$ strings of equal length. One bit of CRC is added to each B' and converted into its decimal equivalent, which is subjected to the logarithmic transformation (base 2) to yield the coefficients of the polynomial.

In the proposed scheme, a polynomial of degree 7 is chosen to hide the secret key of 384 bits. Any secret key of more than this length can be hidden by choosing a polynomial of higher degree. The method in [4] uses an 8 degree polynomial to hide a secret of 128 bits.

3.2. Significant Features for Encoding. K-L transform, also known as PCA (principal component analysis), is used to extract the significant features [28]. In the proposed scheme, the transformation matrix arising out of the K-L transform facilitates the determination of the subspace of the original feature vector for encoding the vault. The same transformation matrix is applied on the query feature vector to convert it into the same subspace for aligning (matching) with the fuzzy vault.

Let $\{S\}_{N1 \times 1}$ denote the feature vector of size $N1$ extracted from the biometric trait. The covariance matrix $\{M\}_{N1 \times N1}$ is constructed from S. The Eigenvector matrix $\{V\}_{N1 \times N1}$ corresponding to the Eigenvalues $\{\lambda\}_{N1 \times 1}$ of M spans the feature subspace. The extracted features sometime contain redundant data which can increase the error rates (FAR/FRR) in the vault implementation. Hence S has to be reduced to the chosen dimension k and $\{\delta\}_{k \times 1}$ can be made up of Eigen vectors corresponding to the dominant Eigen values $\{\lambda\}_{k \times 1}$ by multiplying the transformation matrix $\{V\}_{k \times N1}$ as follows:

$$\{\delta\}_{k \times 1} = \{V\}_{k \times N1} \times \{S\}_{N1 \times 1}. \tag{1}$$

The transformed feature vector is used to learn the cutoff threshold (α) and the tolerance value (β). The cutoff threshold is taken as the maximum of the pointwise differences between the training feature vectors. The tolerance value is determined from the ROC curve for each modality. The cutoff threshold and tolerance value are fine-tuned as per the specified error rates to be achieved.

3.3. Encoding of the Vault. Let the transformed feature vector $\{\delta\}_{k \times 1}$ be represented by $\{\theta_1, \theta_2 \cdots \theta_k\}^T$, whose projections on the polynomial P of degree N form the projection set $P_r = \{P(\theta_1), P(\theta_2) \cdots P(\theta_k)\}^T$. Next, $N + 1$ coefficients of P computed using the secret key (detailed in Section 4.1) are saved as $K = \{C_0, C_1, C_2 \cdots C_N\}$. The elements of the projection set are obtained as

$$P(X) = C_N X^N + C_{N-1} X^{N-1} + \cdots + C_0. \tag{2}$$

The ordered pairs $\{\theta_i, P(\theta_i)\}$; $i = 1, 2, 3, \ldots, k$, are made up of point θ_i and its corresponding projection $P(\theta_i)$.

The next task is to generate the chaff points that do not satisfy P. In the proposed scheme, the random numbers are generated by fitting a U-distribution [32] having the mean and variance of the feature point. Any number of chaff points can be generated using this distribution corresponding to each data point δ_i; $i = 1, 2, 3, \ldots, k$, and the generated random numbers do not coincide with any of the original k features. For example, considering δ_i as mean and $[\delta_{i+1} - \delta_i]$ as variance, we can generate 10 random numbers for each data point δ_i resulting in 900 chaff points corresponding to 90 transformed feature points.

Let the chaff points $\{\mu_{i1}, \mu_{i2}, \ldots, \mu_{ig}\}$, g, be the random numbers for a feature point θ_i. The ordered pairs (μ_{it}, η_{it}) arise

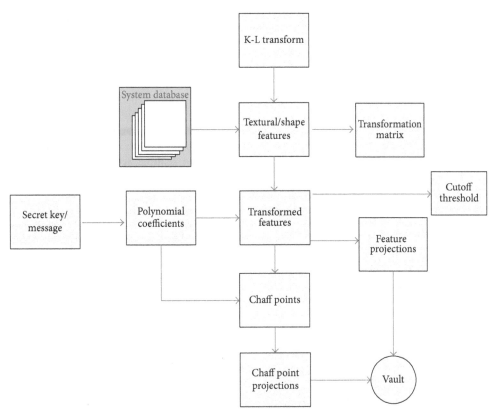

FIGURE 3: Encoding of the vault.

from μ_{it} such that $P(\mu_{it}) \neq \eta_{it}$. The union of the two ordered pairs $\{\theta_i, P(\theta_i)\}$ and $\{\mu_{it}, \eta_{it}\}$ for all θ_i's creates the fuzzy vault, V, given by

$$V = \{\theta_{i+k}, P(\theta_{i+k})\} \cup \{\mu_{it}, \eta_{it}\}. \tag{3}$$

As mentioned above, the original feature vector $\{S\}_{N1 \times 1}$ and the transformed feature vector $\{\delta\}_{k \times 1}$ are removed from the database. The transformation matrix $\{V\}_{k \times N1}$, the cutoff threshold (α), tolerance value (β), and the vault V are stored for decoding. The block diagram in Figure 3 shows the modules required in encoding the fuzzy vault.

3.4. Decoding of the Vault. The decoding of the vault involves alignment of a query template with the stored one. This alignment of query template helps in separating the chaff points from the stored template points in the vault. In the fingerprint based fuzzy vault in [4] the minutiae features are aligned using an adaptive bounding box, which counters the distortions in the minutiae features more effectively than the approach in [2]. The approach in [4] resorts to a threshold to separate the original minutiae points from the chaff points. The basic idea is to cash in on a parameter to differentiate between the genuine and the imposter templates. In the proposed scheme, the successful decoding of the vault depends upon two parameters: the cutoff threshold (α), learned from the transformed features $\{\delta\}_{k \times 1}$, and the tolerance value (β) which is fixed according to the tradeoff in the error rates (FAR/FRR).

The query feature vector $q = \{q_1, q_2, q_3 \cdots q_{N1}\}$ undergoes the K-L transformation $\{V_k^T\}_{k \times N1}$, to yield the transformed query feature vector $Q = \{Q_1 Q_2 \cdots Q_k\}$ of length k at the encoding. Let the ordered pairs of the vault V be denoted as $\{\mu, \eta\}$. Subtraction of Q_k from all the abscissas of the ordered pairs in V provides $(g + 1)k$ differences stored in an array A as the matching score. The scores below the cutoff threshold α is assumed to be from original feature points, otherwise from chaff points. The ordered pairs corresponding to these scores are separated out from the vault V. Let H of the set of ordered pairs be separated from the vault V. To reconstruct the polynomial coefficients $K = \{C_0, C_1, C_2 \cdots C_N\}$ only $N+1$ original (genuine) ordered pairs are needed. If $H < N + 1$ then it results in the authentication failure. If $H \geq N + 1$ the polynomial can be successfully reconstructed. However, H may also exceed $N + 1$ due to the noisy biometric data. The task of tolerance value (β) is to prevent the imposter attempts to open the vault. Even if $H = N + 1$ is sufficient to reconstruct the polynomial the condition $H \geq \beta$ is enforced for the access. But the high values of β can restrict the genuine users from decoding the vault. Hence, the choice of β must be made to achieve the requisite error (FAR/FRR) in the authentication system.

In case $H > \beta$ and $H > N+1$ as well, any $N+1$ points from H can be taken for the reconstruction of the polynomial. Let $\{\theta_H, P(\theta_H)\}$ be the set of ordered pairs corresponding to the points with $H > \beta$ and let $\{\theta_{N+1}, P(\theta_{N+1})\}$ be the candidate points selected for the reconstruction of the polynomial p.

The reconstruction is done using Lagrange's interpolation and the reconstructed polynomial $P^*(x)$ is obtained as

$$P^*(x)$$

$$= \frac{(x - \theta_2)(x - \theta_3) \cdots (x - \theta_{N+1})}{(\theta_1 - \theta_2)(\theta_1 - \theta_3) \cdots (\theta_1 - \theta_{N+1})}$$

$$\times P(\theta_1) + \frac{(x - \theta_1)(x - \theta_3) \cdots (x - \theta_{N+1})}{(\theta_2 - \theta_1)(\theta_2 - \theta_3) \cdots (\theta_2 - \theta_{N+1})}$$

$$\times P(\theta_2) + \cdots \frac{(x - \theta_1)(x - \theta_3) \cdots (x - \theta_N)}{(\theta_{N+1} - \theta_1)(\theta_{N+1} - \theta_3) \cdots (\theta_2 - \theta_N)}$$

$$\times P(\theta_{N+1}).$$

$$(4)$$

The reconstructed polynomial $P^*(x)$ using Lagrange's interpolation in (4) can also be represented as

$$P^*(X) = C_N^* X^N + C_{N-1}^* X^{N-1} + \cdots + C_0^*. \quad (5)$$

The reconstructed coefficients $\{C_0^*, C_1^*, C_2^* \cdots C_N^*\}$ help recover the secret binary bits by applying the method in reverse order as discussed in Section 3.1. The Antilog (base 2) transformation of all the coefficients will yield the decimal representations which are converted to binary equivalents. Each of the binary equivalents C^* is of length 49 with the first bit being the CRC parity bit.

A check is made to see whether the parity bit is changed during the reconstruction of the polynomial. This check is about finding whether the binary equivalent is equal to the original one. If this check fails, it may be due to the noisy biometric data or due to the coefficient approximation by Lagrange's interpolation in (5). In this case, we examine other candidates in the set $\{\theta_H, P(\theta_H)\}$ and reconstruct the coefficients $\{C_0^*, C_1^*, C_2^* \cdots C_N^*\}$ again using (5). If none of the candidates is unable to reconstruct the original coefficients the authentication failure occurs and the user is identified to be an imposter. Finally, the converted bits (the binary equivalent) are concatenated to form the original secret key. The decoding of the vault is shown in Figure 4.

4. Experiments and Results

The performance of the proposed vault is ascertained by making rigorous experiments on several standard databases of different biometrics. A random binary string of 392 bits is generated as the random key (or message), which is used to calculate the polynomial coefficients. As the minutiae points of the fingerprint have been employed already for the fuzzy vault, the motivation of the proposed scheme is to evaluate the fuzzy vault on other biometric modalities using the textural features. We will enumerate the following strategies for the implementation of our fuzzy vault:

(1) Only one impression from the enrolled images of each user in the database is employed for encoding the vault and the rest are used for testing. In all the experiments the parameters of the vault are taken as

follows: 392 randomly generated secret binary bits, 8 coefficients chosen for the 7 degree polynomial, 90 features selected from K-L transform for encoding of the vault, and 910 chaff points added to the original projections.

(2) Having done the encoding with one sample, other enrolled samples of the same user are recalled to encode the vault and other enrolled samples of the same user are recalled to open the vault for testing the genuine access and those of the different users are recalled to open the vault for testing the imposter access. The authentication failure of the genuine cases is marked as false rejection (FR) whereas the successful attempts of the imposter cases are marked as false acceptance (FA). For example, a 100 user database with 6 genuine attempts per user (two from each 3 enrolled samples) a total of 600 (100 × 6) genuine attempts can be made. Similarly, we can have 891 (297 × 3) imposter attempts per user (99 × 3 = 297 images from 99 users) and hence 89100 (891 × 100) in the whole database.

4.1. Fingerprint Based Vault. Fingerprint is a good old biometric trait for the personal authentication and its minutiae features have also found a place in the fuzzy vault scheme [2–4]. However, the proposed vault is intended to pursue the textural features from the fingerprints obtained with the application of Gabor filterbank, as detailed in [31]. Here we take recourse to the publically available FVC 2004 DB1 database, having 100 users with three samples each. The core point is detected as in [31] and ROIs are cropped using the core point as the centre point. The detection of core point itself is a challenging task and many enrolled sample images get rejected due to the false core point. A sample image from the database and the corresponding ROI are shown in Figure 5.

The cropped ROI is of size 153 × 153 while the original fingerprint image is of size 640 × 480. We create multiple Gabor filters of the size 33 × 33 with mean $\mu = 0$, sigma $\sigma = 5.6569$, and orientations $(\text{ang} \times (\pi/8))^0$, where ang = 0, 1, 2 $\cdots$ 7. The Gabor filters at each orientation are convolved with ROIs and the real parts of this convolution are divided into nonoverlapping windows of size 15 × 15. A feature vector of size 832 (104 × 8) is generated. In order to test the performance of the extracted features, the database is divided into two training images and one test image. Next, genuine and imposter scores are generated using the Euclidean distance, shown in Figure 6(a). For use in fuzzy vault, the extracted features are transformed using K-L transform to the reduced feature vector of size 90. The other parameters of the fingerprint based fuzzy vault are given in Table 6. Table 1 shows the value of FAR and FRR for varying values of tolerance. The ROC curve for FAR versus GAR (100-FRR) is shown in Figure 6(b).

4.2. Palmprint Based Vault. Despite the current popularity of the palmprint as a biometric trait only a few palmprint based cryptosystems exist in the literature [18, 23]. However, there is no attempt on utilizing the palmprint features in the

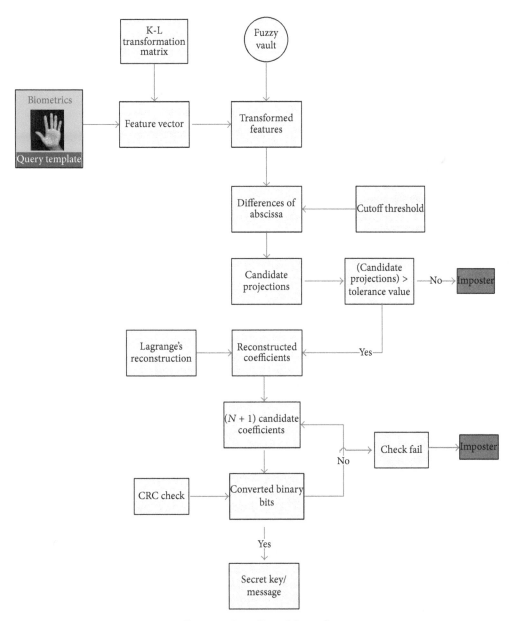

FIGURE 4: Decoding of the vault.

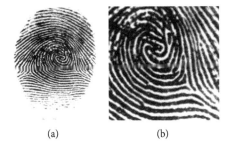

(a)   (b)

FIGURE 5: (a) Sample image from FVC 2004 DB1 database, (b) ROI cropped from core point.

polynomial based fuzzy vault approach. We therefore embark on the palmprint features to evaluate the polynomial based

fuzzy vault scheme. The database for the palmprint owes it allegiance to the publically available PolyU V2 [33]. The ROI and feature extraction method are the same as detailed in [27].

The palmprint image and the extracted ROI are shown in Figure 7. The palmprint images of size 384×384 are cut into ROIs of size 128×128. Multiple Gabor filters each of the size 35×35 with mean $\mu = 0.0916$, and sigma $\sigma = 5.6179$ with orientations $0°$, $45°$, $90°$, and $135°$ are convolved with ROIs and the resulting real Gabor images are down sampled to 91×91. The real Gabor images are ROIs are then divided into nonoverlapping windows of size 7×7 and the mean values of these windows are stored as a Gabor feature vector of size 676 (169×4). In order to test the performance of the Gabor features, the PolyU database of 150 users and 5 samples each is divided into 3 training and 2 test images for each user.

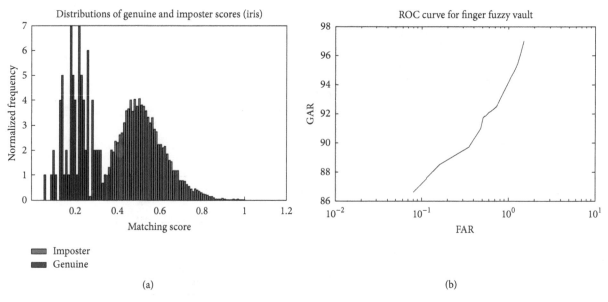

(a)

(b)

FIGURE 6: (a) Score distribution in FVC 04 database, (b) ROC of fingerprint based fuzzy vault.

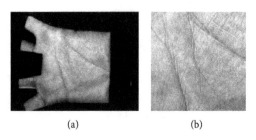

(a)

(b)

FIGURE 7: (a) Sample image from PolyU database V2, (b) corresponding ROI image.

TABLE 1: Performance of the fuzzy vault based on fingerprint FVC 2004 DB1 database (1 template 2 queries).

Tolerance	15	16	17	18	19	**20**	21	22	23	24
FAR (%)	1.5	1.26	1.12	0.95	0.72	**0.51**	0.48	0.35	0.16	0.08
FRR (%)	3.0	4.56	5.21	6.0	7.5	**8.3**	9.0	10.3	11.5	13.4

TABLE 2: Performance of the fuzzy vault based on the 150 users palmprint database (1 template 2 queries).

Tolerance	17	18	19	20	21	**22**	23	24	25	26
FAR (%)	7.48	4.58	2.72	1.56	0.86	**0.46**	0.22	0.10	0.04	0.02
FRR (%)	2.0	3.0	4.33	5.00	7.0	**7.33**	9.0	10.0	11.33	14.33

TABLE 3: Performance of the fuzzy vault based on 150 users palmprint database (1 template 4 queries).

Tolerance	19	20	21	22	23	**24**	25	26	27	28
FAR (%)	10	6.52	3.99	2.28	1.25	**0.65**	0.32	0.16	0.07	0.03
FRR (%)	4.83	5.66	6.66	7.16	7.83	**8.66**	10.33	11.83	13.83	14.66

The corresponding ROC is shown in Figure 8(c). It can be observed that, increase in the number of query templates has very less effect on the proposed vault as reflected in FAR of 0.65% for FRR of 8.66%.

The genuine and imposter scores are computed using the Euclidean distance based classifier, as shown in Figure 8(a).

For the palmprint based fuzzy vault, 90 significant features are selected out of 676 Gabor features for the polynomial projection using K-L transform. The parameters of the vault are given in Table 6. Two sets of experiments are conducted on PolyU database, with the first set involving 150 users with 3 samples per user. Out of the 3 enrolled images, one image is randomly selected for encoding the vault (template) and the rest 2 images are kept for testing (query). Table 2 shows the FAR and FRR values for this experiment with the varying values of tolerance. Its ROC is shown in Figure 8(b).

The next set of experiments makes use of samples per user. One sample is embarked for encoding the template and the rest 4 samples are for the query. The FAR and FRR obtained from this experiment are given in Table 3.

4.3. *Iris Based Vault.* Another set of experiments is carried out on the publically available CASIA I iris database [34] having 108 users with 3 samples per user which is the standard benchmark [35] for the evaluation of iris. The image normalization and Log Gabor based feature extraction are the same as in [30]. A sample iris image and the normalized enhanced iris strip are shown in Figures 9(a) and 9(b). The Log Gabor filter has a central frequency of 18 and radial bandwidth ratio of 0.55 [30].

The enhanced iris strip of size 50×512 is divided into windows of size 7×7 and mean of each window is taken as a feature leading to 522 features, which are reduced to 90 using K-L transform and the reduced features encode the vault. The genuine and imposter scores are generated by dividing the database into 2 training and 1 test images. The distribution of scores is shown in Figure 10(a). The parameters of the iris

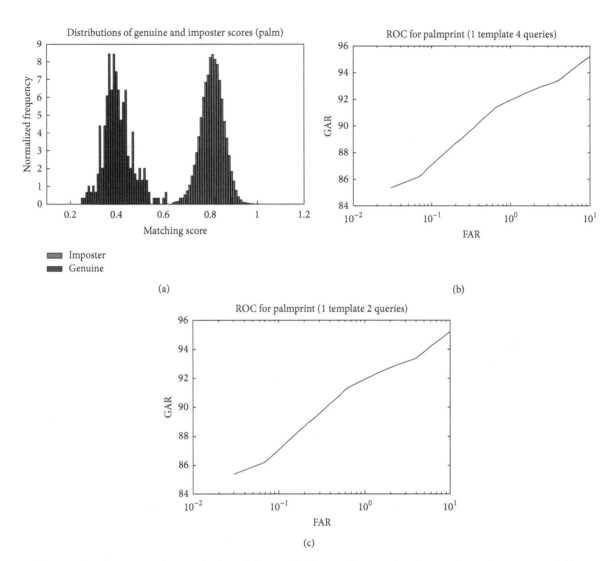

FIGURE 8: (a) Score distribution in PolyU V2 database, (b) ROC of palmprint fuzzy vault with 1 template and 4 queries, and (c) ROC of the same vault fuzzy vault with 1 template and 2 queries.

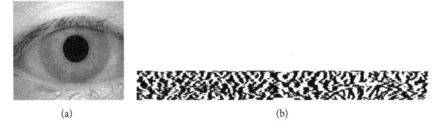

FIGURE 9: (a) Iris sample image, (b) iris normalized strip enhanced with Log Gabor filter.

based fuzzy vault are given in Table 6. Table 4 presents FARs and FRRs for the varying values of tolerance. Figure 10(b) shows the ROC generated from these error rates.

4.4. Hand Vein Based Vault. To test the performance of the proposed vault on a variety of biometric modalities, the use of the infrared thermal hand vein images is also made. Beneath the skin, vein patterns are too harder to intercept

for an intruder; hence is a safer biometric trait. Realizing the inherent potential of the infrared thermal hand vein patterns as a biometric trait, these are some works on its use for authentication [36–38].

Since there is no database of the infrared thermal hand veins patterns, a database has been created at Biometrics Research Laboratory, IIT, Delhi. This database consists of infrared thermal hand vein images of 100 users with three

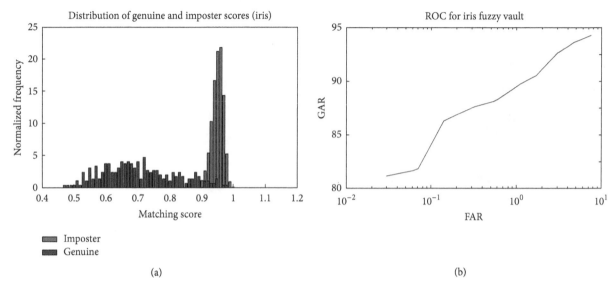

(a)   (b)

FIGURE 10: (a) Score distribution in CASIA I database, (b) ROC of iris based fuzzy vault.

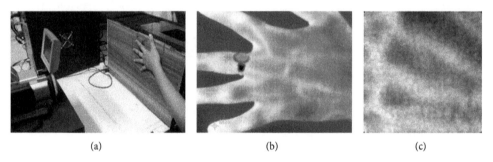

(a)   (b)   (c)

FIGURE 11: (a) Camera setup, (b) captured image, and (c) normalized image.

TABLE 4: Performance of the vault based on the 108 users iris database (1 template 3 queries).

Tolerance	18	19	20	21	22	23	**24**	25	26	27
FAR (%)	7.45	4.85	2.97	1.73	1.08	0.57	**0.31**	0.14	0.07	0.03
FRR (%)	5.75	6.37	7.45	9.45	10.30	11.85	**12.46**	13.70	18.24	18.86

images. The camera setup, image acquisition, and image normalization (ROI extraction) of the hand vein images are the same as in [36]. A sample image and the corresponding normalized image are shown in Figure 11. Here, the Gabor wavelet features [36] are employed for the vault implementation. The parameters used for the vein based fuzzy vault are given in Table 6.

The ROIs of size 104×104 extracted from the infrared hand vein images of size 320×240 are enhanced by Gabor wavelet filters with orientations $0°, 45°, 90°$, and $135°$. The real parts of the convolved images are called real-Gabor images. The real-Gabor images are divided into windows of size 8×8 and thus yielding a total of 676 (169×4) Gabor features. Using these features, genuine and imposter scores are generated by dividing the database into 2 training and 1 test, as shown in Figure 12(a).

These features are reduced to 90 features by the application of K-L transform. The parameters of vein fuzzy vault are given in Table 6. The values of FAR and FRR for different values of threshold are given in Table 5. The corresponding ROC is shown in Figure 12(b).

5. Discussion

The fuzzy vault of this paper has two main features. (1) it is carried out on the feature vector extracted using Gabor filters which are robust and easy to implement and have less time complexity. In comparison, minutiae features are computationally difficult to extract, suffer from the problem of false and spurious minutiae points, and pose problems in the alignment in the fuzzy vault [4]. (2) It leads to low error rates and hence is comparable to the previous fuzzy vaults [1–4]. The fingerprint based vault generates FAR of 0.51 at FRR of 8.3, palmprint based vault yields FAR of 0.46 at of FRR: 7.33, and iris based vault gives FAR of 0.31 at FRR of 12.6. The high error rates due to fingerprint and iris based vaults are on account of features from sliding windows (see Section 4.3). Incorporating the minutiae features of fingerprint [4] and Hamming distance from iris code may produce better results [30]. However, the proposed approach

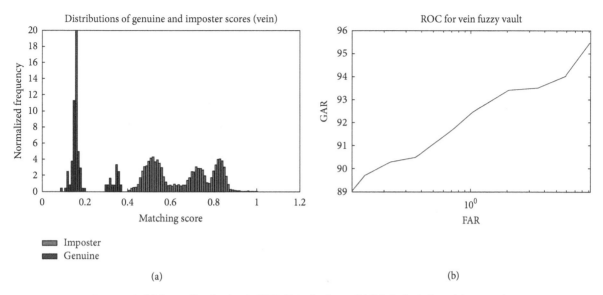

FIGURE 12: (a) Score distribution in IITD Vein database, (b) ROC of vein based fuzzy vault.

TABLE 5: Performance of the proposed fuzzy vault based on the hand vein database.

Tolerance	17	18	19	20	21	**22**	23	24	25	26
FAR (%)	9.27	5.8	3.5	2.07	1.07	**0.64**	0.36	0.23	0.14	0.11
FRR (%)	4.5	6.0	6.5	6.6	7.5	**8.5**	9.5	9.7	10.3	11

TABLE 6: Description of the parameter used in different vaults.

Parameter	Biometric database			
	Fingerprint	Palmprint	Iris	Hand veins
No of users	100	150	108	100
No of samples per user	3	5	4	3
Value of cutoff threshold (α)	21	0.2	21	35
Best value of tolerance (β)	20	24	24	22

is simpler. The results reported by hand vein based vault are as follows: FAR: 0.64 and FRR: 8.5. Infrared thermal hand veins are for the first time utilized for fuzzy vault in this work. The experimental results show that hand vein based vault is comparable to fingerprint, palmprint, and iris based vaults and can serve as a benchmark for the evaluation of fuzzy vault.

The vulnerability of fuzzy vault to different attacks is addressed in [29, 39]. The issues of security related to the fuzzy vault based cryptosystem are discussed in [1, 4]. Here, we discuss the security issues to circumvent the random attacks on the proposed fuzzy vault. The degree of the polynomial N is taken as 7 to hide a secret key of size 392 bits with feature vector of size 90. If 910 chaff points are added to the vault, the total number of possible combinations is $^{1000}_{8}C \approx 2.4 \times 10^{19}$ and out of these $^{90}_{8}C \approx 7.7 \times 10^9$ combinations can successfully decode the vault. The probability of decoding the

vault with one combination is $(7.7 \times 10^9/2.4 \times 10^{19}) \approx 3.2 \times 10^{-10}$ and the number of calculations needed is $(2.4 \times 10^{19}/ 7.7 \times 10^9) \approx 3.1 \times 10^9$. Thus, for the polynomial of degree 7, the probability of breaking this vault is 3.2×10^{-10}. However, if the degree is reduced to 6 this probability is increased to 3.8×10^{-8} and length of the secret key is changed to 343. The number of chaff points is chosen to be approximately 10 times greater than the genuine points.

6. Conclusions

The current popularity of the biometric modalities, like iris, palmprint, hand veins, and so forth, is behind the motivation to investigate the polynomial based fuzzy vault. This paper therefore presents a new scheme for the fuzzy vault based on the texture features of these traits. The prior work on the polynomial based fuzzy vault deals with the minutiae points as the biometric data. The fuzzy vault is a kind of biometric cryptosystems that spring forth from the integration of both the secret key and the biometric features, and, once this is locked in the vault, it is computationally very difficult to intrude the key or retrieve the stored features without the knowledge of any one of them.

In the proposed scheme, a new method of generating the polynomial coefficients, which can hide a secret key of 392 bits with the polynomial of degree 7, is developed. The original features from the biometric modalities are transformed using K-L transform for encoding the vault. The cutoff threshold is learned from the transformed features to separate out the chaff points from the original features. The transformation matrix and the cutoff threshold are saved and the original and the transformed features are discarded from the database for the security reasons. The proposed vault is implemented separately on a variety of biometric databases, including the publically available, fingerprint (FVC 2004), palmprint (PolyU V2), and iris (CASIAV1); and hand Veins. The performance of the proposed vault can be further improved by using multiple biometric traits like palmprint and fingerprint or palmprint of both the palms of a user.

Conflict of Interests

The authors declare that there is no conflict of interests regarding the publication of this paper.

References

[1] U. Uludag, S. Pankanti, S. Prabhakar, and A. K. Jain, "Biometric cryptosystems: issues and challenges," *Proceedings of the IEEE*, vol. 92, no. 6, pp. 948–959, 2004.

[2] U. Uludag, S. Pankanti, and A. K. Jain, "Fuzzy vault for fingerprints," in *Audio- and Video-Based Biometric Person Authentication*, vol. 3546 of *Lecture Notes in Computer Science*, pp. 310–319, Springer, 2005.

[3] U. Uludag and A. K. Jain, "Securing fingerprint template: fuzzy vault with helper data," in *Proceedings of the Conference on Computer Vision and Pattern Recognition Workshops*, p. 163, New York, NY, USA, June 2006.

[4] K. Nandakumar, A. K. Jain, and S. Pankanti, "Fingerprint-based fuzzy vault: Implementation and performance," *IEEE Transactions on Information Forensics and Security*, vol. 2, no. 4, pp. 744–757, 2007.

[5] F. Monrose, M. K. Reiter, and S. Wetzel, "Password hardening based on keystroke dynamics," in *Proceedings of the 6th ACM Conference on Computer and Communications Security (CCS '99)*, pp. 73–82, November 1999.

[6] F. Hao, R. Anderson, and J. Daugman, "Combining crypto with biometrics effectively," *IEEE Transactions on Computers*, vol. 55, no. 9, pp. 1081–1088, 2006.

[7] C. Sautar, D. Roberge, A. Stoianov, R. Gilroy, and B. V. K. Vijaya Kumar, "Biometric encryption," *Information Management and Computer Security*, vol. 9, no. 5, pp. 205–212, 2001.

[8] Y. Dodis, R. Ostrovsky, L. Reyzin, and A. Smith, "Fuzzy extractors: how to generate strong keys from biometrics and other noisy data," Cryptology Eprint Archive, Tech. Rep 235, 2006.

[9] A. Juels and M. Sudan, "A fuzzy vault scheme," in *Proceedings of the IEEE International Symposium on Information Theory*, p. 408, July 2002.

[10] K. Nandakumar and A. K. Jain, "Multibiometric template security using fuzzy vault," in *Proceedings of the IEEE 2nd International Conference on Biometrics: Theory, Applications and Systems (BTAS '08)*, pp. 1–6, Arlington, Va, USA, October 2008.

[11] A. Goh and D. C. L. Ngo, "Computation of cryptographic keys from face biometrics," in *Communications and Multimedia Security. Advanced Techniques for Network and Data Protection*, vol. 2828 of *Lecture Notes in Computer Science*, pp. 1–13, Springer, 2003.

[12] N. K. Ratha, J. H. Connell, and R. M. Bolle, "Enhancing security and privacy in biometrics-based authentication systems," *IBM Systems Journal*, vol. 40, no. 3, pp. 614–634, 2001.

[13] G. I. Davida, Y. Frankel, and B. J. Matt, "On enabling secure applications through off-line biometric identification," in *Proceedings of the IEEE Symposium on Security and Privacy*, pp. 148–157, Oakland, Calif, USA, May 1998.

[14] Y. J. Chang, W. Zhang, and T. Chen, "Biometrics-based cryptographic key generation," in *Proceedings of the IEEE International Conference on Multimedia and Expo*, pp. 2203–2206, 2004.

[15] T. Connie, A. Teoh, M. Goh, and D. Ngo, "PalmHashing: a novel approach for cancelable biometrics," *Information Processing Letters*, vol. 93, no. 1, pp. 1–5, 2005.

[16] A. Kong, K.-H. Cheung, D. Zhang, M. Kamel, and J. You, "An analysis of BioHashing and its variants," *Pattern Recognition*, vol. 39, no. 7, pp. 1359–1368, 2006.

[17] A. Kong, D. Zhang, and M. Kamel, "Three measures for secure palmprint identification," *Pattern Recognition*, vol. 41, no. 4, pp. 1329–1337, 2008.

[18] X. Wu, D. Zhang, and K. Wang, "A palmprint cryptosystem," in *Advances in Biometrics*, vol. 4642, pp. 1035–1042, Springer, 2007.

[19] X. Boyen, "Reusable cryptographic fuzzy extractors," in *Proceedings of the 11th ACM Conference on Computer and Communications Security (CCS '04)*, pp. 82–91, ACM Press, October 2004.

[20] A. Juel and M. Wttenberg, "A fuzzy vault commitment scheme," in *Proceedings of the 6th ACM conference on Computer and Communications Security*, G. Tsudik, Ed., pp. 408–412, 2002.

[21] E. R. Berlekamp, *Algebraic Coding Theory*, McGraw-Hill, New York, NY, USA, 1968.

[22] A. Nagar and S. Chaudhury, "Biometrics based asymmetric cryptosystem design using modified fuzzy vault scheme," in *Proceedings of the 18th International Conference on Pattern Recognition (ICPR '06)*, pp. 537–540, Hong Kong, China, August 2006.

[23] A. Kumar and A. Kumar, "Development of a new cryptographic construct using palmprint-based fuzzy vault," *Eurasip Journal on Advances in Signal Processing*, vol. 2009, Article ID 967046, 2009.

[24] Y. J. Lee, K. R. Park, S. J. Lee, K. Bae, and J. Kim, "A new method for generating an invariant iris private key based on the fuzzy vault system," *IEEE Transactions on Systems, Man, and Cybernetics, B: Cybernetics*, vol. 38, no. 5, pp. 1302–1313, 2008.

[25] X. Wu, D. Zhang, and K. Wang, "A palmprint cryptosystem," in *Advances in Biometrics*, vol. 4642 of *Lecture Notes in Computer Science*, pp. 1035–1042, 2007.

[26] M. Freire-Santos, J. Fierrez-Aguilar, and J. Ortega-Garcia, "Cryptographic key generation using handwritten signature," in *Biometric Technology for Human Identification III*, vol. 6202 of *Proceedings of SPIE*, pp. 225–231, April 2006.

[27] D. Zhang, W.-K. Kong, J. You, and M. Wong, "Online palmprint identification," *IEEE Transactions on Pattern Analysis and Machine Intelligence*, vol. 25, no. 9, pp. 1041–1050, 2003.

[28] S. Ribaric and I. Fratric, "A biometric identification system based on eigenpalm and eigenfinger features," *IEEE Transactions on Pattern Analysis and Machine Intelligence*, vol. 27, no. 11, pp. 1698–1709, 2005.

[29] W. J. Scheirer and T. E. Boult, "Cracking fuzzy vaults and biometric encryption," in *Proceedings of the Biometrics Symposium*, pp. 1–6, Baltimore, Md, USA, September 2007.

[30] A. Kumar and A. Passi, "Comparison and combination of iris matchers for reliable personal authentication," *Pattern Recognition*, vol. 43, no. 3, pp. 1016–1026, 2010.

[31] A. K. Jain, S. Prabhakar, L. Hong, and S. Pankanti, "Filterbank-based fingerprint matching," *IEEE Transactions on Image Processing*, vol. 9, no. 5, pp. 846–859, 2000.

[32] http://en.wikipedia.org/wiki/Uniform_distribution_%28continuous%29.

[33] "The PolyU Palmprint Database ver.2.0," http://www.comp.polyu.edu.hk/~biometrics.

[34] CASIA IRIS Database, 2008, http://www.cbsr.ia.ac.cn/english/IrisDatabase.asp.

[35] H. Proença and L. A. Alexandre, "Toward noncooperative iris recognition: a classification approach using multiple signatures," *IEEE Transactions on Pattern Analysis and Machine Intelligence*, vol. 29, no. 4, pp. 607–612, 2007.

[36] A. Kumar, M. Hanmandlu, and H. M. Gupta, "Online biometric authentication using hand vein patterns," in *Proceedings of the IEEE Symposium on Computational Intelligence for Security and Defense Applications (CISDA '09)*, Ottawa, Canada, July 2009.

[37] L. Wang, G. Leedham, and S.-Y. Cho, "Infrared imaging of hand vein patterns for biometric purposes," *IET Computer Vision*, vol. 1, no. 3-4, pp. 113–122, 2007.

[38] C.-L. Lin and K.-C. Fan, "Biometric verification using thermal images of palm-dorsa vein patterns," *IEEE Transactions on Circuits and Systems for Video Technology*, vol. 14, no. 2, pp. 199–213, 2004.

[39] A. Kholmatov and B. Yanikoglu, "Realization of correlation attack against the Fuzzy Vault scheme," in *Security, Forensics, Steganography, and Watermarking of Multimedia Contents X*, vol. 6819 of *Proceedings of SPIE*, January 2008.

2

Performance Evaluation of Noise Reduction Filters for Color Images through Normalized Color Difference (NCD) Decomposition

Fabrizio Russo

Department of Engineering and Architecture, University of Trieste, Via A. Valerio 10, 34127 Trieste, Italy

Correspondence should be addressed to Fabrizio Russo; rusfab@univ.trieste.it

Academic Editors: F. J. Cuevas-de-la-Rosa, A. Nikolaidis, S.-H. Ong, and N. A. Schmid

Removing noise without producing image distortion is the challenging goal for any image denoising filter. Thus, the different amounts of residual noise and unwanted blur should be evaluated to analyze the actual performance of a denoising process. In this paper a novel full-reference method for measuring such features in color images is presented. The proposed approach is based on the decomposition of the normalized color difference (NCD) into three components that separately take into account different classes of filtering errors such as the inaccuracy in filtering noise pulses, the inaccuracy in reducing Gaussian noise, and the amount of collateral distortion. Computer simulations show that the proposed method offers significant advantages over other measures of filtering performance in the literature, including the recently proposed vector techniques.

1. Introduction

It is known that removal of noise and preservation of color/structural information are very difficult and challenging issues in the design of image denoising filters [1]. Indeed, the quality of a filtered image is typically impaired by the superposition of two different effects: insufficient noise cancellation and unwanted collateral distortion produced by the filtering. Since the different amounts of these effects should *separately* be taken into account to analyze the behavior of any image denoising technique, the development of appropriate metrics is of paramount importance.

Until recently, the most common methods to evaluate the quality of denoised images were combinations of visual inspection and objective measurements based on the computation of pixelwise differences between the original and the processed image. Typically, the mean squared error (MSE) or the peak signal-to-noise ratio (PSNR) was adopted to measure the noise cancellation, whereas the mean absolute error (MAE) represented the most commonly used metrics to evaluate the edge preservation. All the aforementioned measures are typically evaluated in the RGB coordinate system, that is, the most popular color space for a variety of applications.

In order to deal with the human perception of colors (not adequately described by the RGB space), another kind of metrics, namely, the *normalized color difference* (NCD), was proposed [1–3]. Such measure is evaluated in the perceptually uniform CIE Luv (or CIE Lab) color spaces in order to appraise the perceptual closeness of a filtered picture to the uncorrupted original. The results of most filters in the literature have been evaluated by resorting to the aforementioned measures or combinations of them [4–19]. Such evaluation techniques, however, have a major drawback. They have limited accuracy in estimating the different filtering features. As already observed for grayscale [20] and color images [21], MSE and MAE cannot accurately measure noise removal and detail preservation, because they cannot separate these features. Although the MAE is more sensitive to distortion than the MSE, it also depends upon the residual noise. On the other hand, even if the MSE is more sensitive to the remaining noise than the MAE, it is affected by the amount of distortion produced by a filter too. Similarly, the NCD takes into account all the filtering errors in perceptually uniform color spaces without distinguishing error contributions caused by filtering distortion or by insufficient noise cancellation. The same limitation also affects metrics that try to estimate the *perceived*

Performance Evaluation of Noise Reduction Filters for Color Images through Normalized Color
Difference (NCD) Decomposition

15

quality of an image in the form of a single score [22, 23]. Again, they cannot distinguish between noise cancellation and detail preservation yielded by a filter because different combi nations of image blur and unfiltered noise can lead to the same score. Recently proposed measures such as the *vector root mean squared error* (VRMSE) are a more appropriate choice because they give a separate evaluation of the mentioned features. A limitation of such techniques, however, is the fact that they work in the RGB [24] and YUV [25] nonuniform color spaces and measure the noise removal and the detail blur in the luminance component of the image only. Furthermore, they cannot address the case of mixed (impulse and Gaussian) noise in color data.

In this paper a new method for measuring the objective quality of filtered images is presented. The proposed approach consists in the decomposition of the NCD into three different components that, respectively, measure how much a filter is good at removing noise pulses, reducing Gaussian noise, and preserving the image details. The method is more accurate than our previous vector techniques and can address the case of mixed noise.

The rest of the paper is organized as follows. Section 2 describes the proposed approach, Section 3 explains how the method works, Section 4 discusses the results of many computer simulations, and, finally, Section 5 reports the conclusion.

2. The Proposed Method

The proposed method is specifically designed to address the case of mixed noise. Thus, let us deal with images corrupted by impulse and Gaussian noise as well. Formally, let $\bar{\mathbf{r}}(\mathbf{c}) = [\bar{r}_L(\mathbf{c}), \bar{r}_u(\mathbf{c}), \bar{r}_v(\mathbf{c})]^T$ be the vector (in the Luv color space) representing the pixel at spatial position $\mathbf{c} = [c_1, c_2]$ in the original noise-free image and let $\bar{\mathbf{y}}(\mathbf{c}) = [\bar{y}_L(\mathbf{c}), \bar{y}_u(\mathbf{c}), \bar{y}_v(\mathbf{c})]^T$ be the corresponding pixel in the filtered picture. It is known that the NCD is defined by the following relationship [1]:

$$\text{NCD} = \sum_{\mathbf{c} \in D} \left(\left(\bar{y}_L(\mathbf{c}) - \bar{r}_L(\mathbf{c}) \right)^2 + \left(\bar{y}_u(\mathbf{c}) - \bar{r}_u(\mathbf{c}) \right)^2 \right.$$

$$\left. + \left(\bar{y}_v(\mathbf{c}) - \bar{r}_v(\mathbf{c}) \right)^2 \right)^{1/2} \tag{1}$$

$$\times \left(\sum_{\mathbf{c} \in C} \sqrt{\left(\bar{r}_L(\mathbf{c}) \right)^2 + \left(\bar{r}_u(\mathbf{c}) \right)^2 + \left(\bar{r}_v(\mathbf{c}) \right)^2} \right)^{-1},$$

where C denotes the overall set of coordinates of the processed pixels and $D \equiv C$. In our approach, we want to decompose the NCD into three components NCD_{imp}, NCD_{gau}, and NCD_{dis}, as follows:

$$\text{NCD} = \text{NCD}_{\text{imp}} + \text{NCD}_{\text{gau}} + \text{NCD}_{\text{dis}}, \tag{2}$$

where NCD_{imp} is the component that deals with partially removed noise pulses, NCD_{gau} takes into account the unfiltered Gaussian noise, and finally NCD_{dis} measures the unwanted distortion produced by the filtering. Since impulse noise generally affects only a subset of the image pixels, we

can easily define the NCD_{imp} component using relation (1), where D represents in this case the subset C_1 of coordinates where noise pulses occurred ($D \equiv C_1$).

The NCD_{gau} and NCD_{dis} must be evaluated in the subset C_2 of pixel coordinates where impulse noise has not been superimposed. Their definition is more difficult because it is expected that almost every pixel in C_2 is degraded by Gaussian noise. In this case, a possible choice for measuring the noise cancellation and the edge preservation could be to focus on the uniform and nonuniform areas, according to visual perception. A more effective solution for separating the evaluation of distortion from that of the residual noise consists, however, in determining the *distortion area*, that is, the pixel regions where the filter (adopting the same param eter settings) would blur the original noise-free image. In principle, a map of the differences between the original and the blurred picture would suffice for perfectly noiseless synthetic test images. In practice, most test pictures used in the literature contain small amounts of noise. Thus, a soft threshold approach is needed. For the computation of such distortion area, the RGB color space suffices. Let $\mathbf{r}(\mathbf{c}) = [r_R(\mathbf{c}), r_G(\mathbf{c}), r_B(\mathbf{c})]^T$ be the vector (in the RGB color coordinate system) representing the pixel at spatial position $\mathbf{c} = [c_1, c_2]$ in the original noise-free image and let $\mathbf{s}(\mathbf{c}) = [s_R(\mathbf{c}), s_G(\mathbf{c}), s_B(\mathbf{c})]^T$ be the corresponding pixel in the blurred picture that is produced when the original noise-free image is filtered (adopting the same parameter settings). Let $\delta(\mathbf{c})$ represent the dissimilarity (or distance) between $s(\mathbf{c})$ and $r(\mathbf{c})$:

$$\delta(\mathbf{c})$$
$$= \sqrt{\left(s_R(\mathbf{c}) - r_R(\mathbf{c}) \right)^2 + \left(s_G(\mathbf{c}) - r_G(\mathbf{c}) \right)^2 + \left(s_B(\mathbf{c}) - r_B(\mathbf{c}) \right)^2}. \tag{3}$$

Thus, we shall define the NCD_{gau} and NCD_{dis} as follows:

$$\text{NCD}_{\text{dis}} = \frac{\sum_{\mathbf{c} \in C_2} \beta(\mathbf{c}) \Delta E(\mathbf{c})}{\sum_{\mathbf{c} \in C} \sqrt{\left(\bar{r}_L(\mathbf{c}) \right)^2 + \left(\bar{r}_u(\mathbf{c}) \right)^2 + \left(\bar{r}_v(\mathbf{c}) \right)^2}},$$

$$\text{NCD}_{\text{gau}} = \frac{\sum_{\mathbf{c} \in C_2} [1 - \beta(\mathbf{c})] \Delta E(\mathbf{c})}{\sum_{\mathbf{c} \in C} \sqrt{\left(\bar{r}_L(\mathbf{c}) \right)^2 + \left(\bar{r}_u(\mathbf{c}) \right)^2 + \left(\bar{r}_v(\mathbf{c}) \right)^2}}, \tag{4}$$

where $\Delta E(\mathbf{c})$ is the color difference (or error) evaluated in the Luv perceptually uniform color space:

$$\Delta E(\mathbf{c}) = \left(\left(\bar{y}_L(\mathbf{c}) - \bar{r}_L(\mathbf{c}) \right)^2 + \left(\bar{y}_u(\mathbf{c}) - \bar{r}_u(\mathbf{c}) \right)^2 \right.$$

$$\left. + \left(\bar{y}_v(\mathbf{c}) - \bar{r}_v(\mathbf{c}) \right)^2 \right)^{1/2} \tag{5}$$

and $\beta(\mathbf{c})$ denotes the degree of blur at location $\mathbf{c} = [c_1, c_2]$. We evaluate this degree by means of the parameterized function depicted in Figure 1, where a and b are parameters.

Clearly, the NCD_{dis} mainly collects the color errors in the distortion area ($\beta = 1$), whereas the NCD_{gau} mainly deals with the errors that are located in the uniform regions ($\beta = 0$). For synthetic test images (including perfectly uniform regions), a crisp threshold is the natural choice ($a = b$,

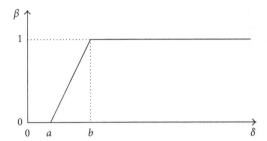

FIGURE 1: Graphical representation of the function β.

TABLE 1: List of NCD, NCD_{gau}, and NCD_{dis} evaluations for $(2N+1)\times$ $(2N + 1)$ vector mean filters.

N	NCD $(\times 10^2)$	NCD_{gau} $(\times 10^2)$	NCD_{dis} $(\times 10^2)$
2	10.92	2.72	8.21
3	13.15	1.96	11.19
4	14.73	1.55	13.18
5	16.05	1.29	14.75

$a \approx 0$). For test images represented by real pictures having nonzero noise variance in the background, a soft threshold $(a > 0, b > a)$ is a more suitable choice. Since the noise variance should be small (typically $\sigma^2 \leq 4$), small values for parameters a and b are appropriate; for example, $a = 4$ and $b = 20$. This choice is based on a heuristic approach (too small values could wrongly extend the distortion area and then yield an excess of NCD_{dis}, whereas too large values would produce the opposite effect). Notice that, in the proposed approach, once a and b have been chosen, the extension of the distortion area depends upon the kind of filter and the window size, as it will be shown in the next section. It should be observed that if impulse noise is the only kind of noise degrading the image, the NCD is decomposed into two components only: the residual noise component NCD_{imp} and a distortion component NCD_{dis} that, in this case, can be evaluated by the difference $\text{NCD} - \text{NCD}_{\text{imp}}$. Similarly, if the picture is corrupted by Gaussian noise only, the NCD is again decomposed into two components NCD_{gau} and NCD_{dis} only. As mentioned in Section 1, the NCD computes all the color errors in a perceptually uniform color space in order to evaluate the perceptual closeness of a filtered image to the uncorrupted original. Clearly, the NCD by itself could not distinguish between errors caused by filtering distortion or by insufficient noise cancellation. Splitting the NCD into appropriate components, such as the NCD_{imp}, NCD_{gau}, and NCD_{dis}, removes this limitation and retains the specific advantage of the NCD approach.

3. How the Method Works

In order to analyze the behavior of the proposed method, we generated the test image shown in Figure 2(a). In this picture, perfectly uniform regions and image edges are located into different areas. We produced a noisy picture by adding zero-mean Gaussian noise (with standard deviation $\sigma = 30$) into some uniform regions only (Figure 2(b)). In this experiment we resorted to the vector mean filter because its behavior is well known. We processed the noisy picture by adopting $(2N + 1) \times (2N + 1)$ filters with increasing window size ($N = 2, 3, 4, 5$). The results of the processing are depicted in Figure 3. From visual inspection, we can easily see that the noise is reduced at the price of an increasing detail blur (left to right). It is expected that measures of residual noise and unwanted blur should yield numerical evaluations that comply with these observations.

The distortion areas computed in our method are shown in Figure 4, where black and white, respectively, denote $\beta = 0$ and $\beta = 1$. To evaluate these areas we chose a crisp threshold $(a = b = 0)$, so that β became a two-valued quantity revealing distortion $(\delta > 0 \Rightarrow \beta = 1)$ or no distortion $(\delta = 0 \Rightarrow \beta = 0)$. The extension of such areas increases as the window size increases, as it should be. The results given by our method are listed in Table 1. We can observe that the proposed NCD decomposition is in perfect agreement with the filtering behavior. The values of the NCD_{gau} (third column) decrease as the noise cancellation becomes stronger. Similarly, larger values of the NCD_{dis} highlight the growing blur in the filtered images.

For real images used as test pictures, a soft threshold approach is required, as mentioned in the previous section. In this case, in order to improve the accuracy of the NCD_{gau} and NCD_{dis} evaluations, we also adopt a simple calibration procedure that subtracts from NCD_{gau} (and adds to NCD_{dis}) the possibly nonzero $\text{NCD}^*_{\text{gau}}$ component measured in the uncorrupted image.

4. Results of Computer Simulations

In order to evaluate the performance of the proposed technique, we report and discuss in this section the results of many computer simulations based on images of the well-known Kodak test set [26]. In the following experiments four pictures from this set are considered. They are depicted in Figure 5. All of these images are 24-bit color pictures whose size is 512-by-512 pixels.

In this first experiment we briefly highlight the advantages of our method over the classical MSE and MAE evaluations (an in-depth analysis of the inaccuracy of MAE and MSE is reported in [21]. We generated two images having very different combinations of residual noise and edge preservation, as in [21]. We adopted vector median filters having different window sizes to produce these results. Figure 6(a) shows the input noisy picture where each channel component is degraded by fixed valued impulse noise with probability $p \approx 40\%$. The filtered images are shown in Figure 6(b) (smaller window yielding more residual noise and less blur) and in Figure 6(c) (larger window giving less residual noise and more blur). The differences in terms of detail preservation and noise removal are apparent from visual inspection. However, they cannot be distinguished in terms of MSE and MAE (see Table 2).

Performance Evaluation of Noise Reduction Filters for Color Images through Normalized Color Difference (NCD) Decomposition

17

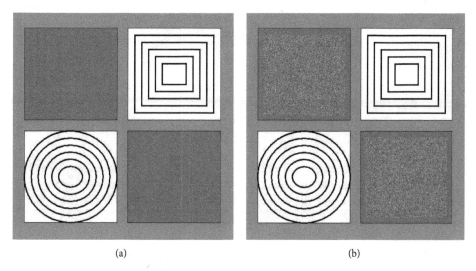

FIGURE 2: Test images: (a) noise-free and (b) corrupted by Gaussian noise.

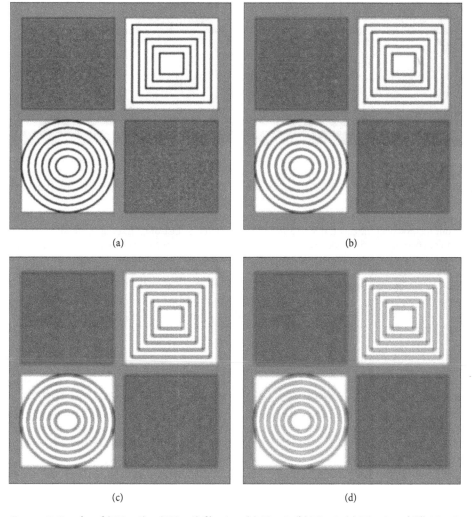

FIGURE 3: Results of $(2N + 1) \times (2N + 1)$ filtering: (a) $N = 2$, (b) $N = 3$, (c) $N = 4$, and (d) $N = 5$.

FIGURE 4: Distortion areas for $(2N + 1) \times (2N + 1)$ windows: (a) $N = 2$, (b) $N = 3$, (c) $N = 4$, and (d) $N = 5$.

TABLE 2: Advantages of our method over the classical MSE and MAE evaluations ("Parrots" image corrupted by fixed-value impulse noise and filtered by 5-point and 5×5 vector median operators).

Image	MSE	MAE	NCD_{imp} $(\times 10^2)$	NCD_{dis} $(\times 10^2)$
Figure 6(b)	77	3.6	3.37	1.42
Figure 6(c)	77	3.6	1.58	2.08

TABLE 3: List of CQI, NCD_{gau}, and NCD_{dis} evaluations ("Flowers" image corrupted by Gaussian noise and filtered by 3×3 and 5×5 vector mean operators).

Image	CQI	NCD_{gau} $(\times 10^2)$	NCD_{dis} $(\times 10^2)$
Figure 7(b)	0.744	11.04	4.90
Figure 7(c)	0.744	4.91	7.07

Conversely, our method correctly characterizes the mentioned filtering behavior. The NCD_{imp} can measure the different amounts of residual noise, whereas the MSE cannot (the filtered images have the same MSE). The NCD_{dis} can focus on the image distortion only, whereas the MAE cannot (the filtered images have the same MAE).

In the second experiment we considered an example of image quality index that follows human perception: the *color quality index* CQI [27]. As in the previous case, we generated two images with different combinations of unfiltered noise and collateral blur. The input picture, corrupted by Gaussian noise ($\sigma = 22$), is reported in Figure 7(a). We adopted vector mean filters having different window sizes to produce

the results in Figure 7(b) (more residual noise, less blur) and Figure 7(c) (less residual noise, more blur). The list of quantitative evaluations is reported in Table 3. The same score is obtained (CQI = 0.744) for both images, because different mixtures of residual noise and distortion yield the same loss of perceived image quality. Again, our method can easily separate (and measure) such effects.

In the third experiment we considered for a comparison our previous vector technique operating in the YIQ color space [25]. In this approach, the MSE evaluated in the luminance channel is split into two components MSE_A and MSE_B that, respectively, estimate the noise cancellation and the detail preservation. We chose the "House" picture as test

Performance Evaluation of Noise Reduction Filters for Color Images through Normalized Color Difference (NCD) Decomposition

19

FIGURE 5: Test images used in the experiments: (a) Parrots, (b) Flowers, (c) House, and (d) Boat.

FIGURE 6: (a) Noisy data, (b) result yielded by the 5-point vector median, and (c) result yielded by the 5 × 5 vector median.

FIGURE 7: (a) Noisy data, (b) result yielded by the 3×3 vector mean filter, and (c) result yielded by the 5×5 vector mean filter.

FIGURE 8: Results of $(2N + 1) \times (2N + 1)$ vector mean filtering: (a) $N = 2$, (b) $N = 3$, (c) $N = 4$, and (d) $N = 5$.

image and we generated a noisy version of it by adding zero-mean Gaussian noise with $\sigma = 20$.

As done in Section 3, we adopted the well-known vector mean filter and we processed the noisy data by adopting $(2N + 1) \times (2N + 1)$ operators with increasing window size ($N = 2, 3, 4, 5$). The results are reported in Table 4. Portions of the processed images are shown in Figure 8. It can be seen that the residual noise decreases as the window becomes larger. Hence, it is expected that the corresponding filtering errors decrease. However, this does not occur for the MSE_A: growing values of the MSE_A characterize images filtered with larger windows (second column in Table 4). The proposed NCD_{gau} is much more accurate (fourth column). Its values become smaller as the smoothing effect increases, as it should be.

TABLE 4: List of MSE_A, MSE_B, NCD_{gau}, and NCD_{dis} values ("House" image corrupted by Gaussian noise with $\sigma = 20$ and filtered by $(2N + 1) \times (2N + 1)$ vector mean operators).

N	MSE_A	MSE_B	NCD_{gau} $(\times 10^2)$	NCD_{dis} $(\times 10^2)$
2	23.94	30.74	3.42	8.19
3	30.19	37.49	1.88	9.25
4	34.93	41.82	1.17	10.20
5	38.97	45.07	0.79	11.04

The same behavior can be observed if we adopt different test pictures, such as the "Boat" picture (Table 5).

Performance Evaluation of Noise Reduction Filters for Color Images through Normalized Color
Difference (NCD) Decomposition

21

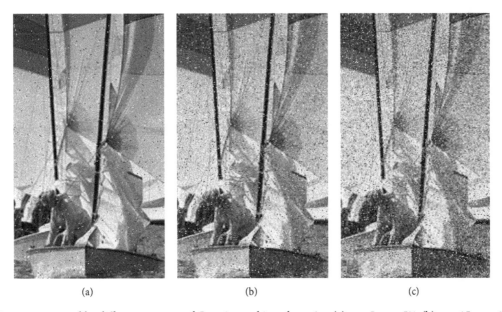

FIGURE 9: Test images corrupted by different amounts of Gaussian and impulse noise: (a) $\sigma = 5$, $p = 5\%$; (b) $\sigma = 15$, $p = 15\%$; (c) $\sigma = 25$, and $p = 25\%$.

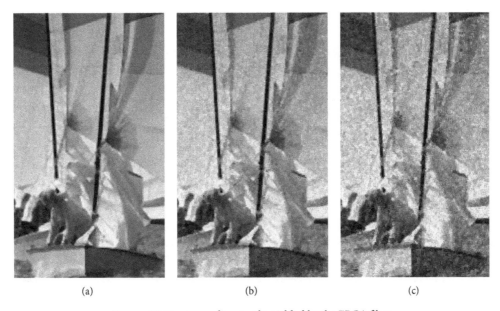

FIGURE 10: Corresponding results yielded by the FPGA filter.

TABLE 5: List of MSE_A, MSE_B, NCD_{gau}, and NCD_{dis} values ("Boat" image corrupted by Gaussian noise with $\sigma = 20$ and filtered by $(2N+1) \times (2N+1)$ vector mean operators).

N	MSE_A	MSE_B	NCD_{gau} $(\times 10^2)$	NCD_{dis} $(\times 10^2)$
2	21.59	32.31	3.83	6.44
3	32.16	45.20	2.24	7.37
4	41.79	54.94	1.44	8.20
5	50.34	62.14	1.00	8.94

The different performance of the previous and new method mainly resides in the different error decomposition schemes. The previous method focused on the uniform and nonuniform areas of a picture to distinguish between noise cancellation and detail preservation, according to visual perception. Here, the MSE_A and MSE_B components are simply obtained by resorting to an edge map given by the Sobel operator. However, since this map does not depend upon the actual filtering action, errors due to blur (possibly located in the exterior of this map) can wrongly be added to the MSE_A, thus increasing its value. The decomposition scheme adopted in the proposed method, on the contrary, is based on a distortion area that depends upon the actual filtering: it can increase when the smoothing is stronger and generates more blur.

(a)   (b)   (c)

FIGURE 11: Test images corrupted by different amounts of Gaussian and impulse noise: (a) $\sigma = 5$, $p = 5\%$; (b) $\sigma = 15$, $p = 15\%$; (c) $\sigma = 25$, and $p = 25\%$.

(a)   (b)   (c)

FIGURE 12: Corresponding results yielded by the FPGA filter.

Thus, even in the presence of large window filters, errors caused by blur are correctly included into the corresponding NCD_{dis} component. Consequently, the NCD_{gau} can correctly take into account the residual noise only.

In the fourth experiment we finally considered the case of mixed noise. We chose the "Boat" image and we generated three noisy pictures by adding growing amounts of Gaussian and impulse noise (Figure 9). We filtered the noisy pictures by using the FPGA filter [14] because it is known that this operator is very effective in removing mixed noise from color images. We set the filtering parameters according to

the values of the standard deviation σ (Gaussian noise) and probability p (impulse noise), as suggested in [14]. The filtered pictures are shown in Figure 10 for visual inspection. The corresponding evaluations given by the new technique and the previous one are listed in Table 6. The different amounts of residual impulse and Gaussian noise are, respectively, measured by the NCD_{imp} and NCD_{gau} components (proposed method). Clearly, the sole MSE_A cannot separate these features (second column), like all other existing metrics in the literature. Similar results can be obtained if we adopt different pictures, such as the "House" image (Figure 11).

Performance Evaluation of Noise Reduction Filters for Color Images through Normalized Color
Difference (NCD) Decomposition

23

TABLE 6: List of MSE_A, MSE_B, NCD_{imp}, NCD_{gau}, and NCD_{dis} values ("Boat" image corrupted by growing amounts of mixed noise and filtered by the FPGA operator).

Image	MSE_A	MSE_B	NCD_{imp} ($\times 10^2$)	NCD_{gau} ($\times 10^2$)	NCD_{dis} ($\times 10^2$)
Figure 10(a)	8.43	7.60	0.39	3.87	2.90
Figure 10(b)	18.18	12.48	2.79	11.64	3.73
Figure 10(c)	38.46	20.62	7.36	18.25	4.53

TABLE 7: List of MSE_A, MSE_B, NCD_{imp}, NCD_{gau}, and NCD_{dis} values ("House" image corrupted by growing amounts of mixed noise and filtered by the FPGA operator).

Image	MSE_A	MSE_B	NCD_{imp} ($\times 10^2$)	NCD_{gau} ($\times 10^2$)	NCD_{dis} ($\times 10^2$)
Figure 12(a)	12.03	10.74	0.45	3.67	4.38
Figure 12(b)	21.67	15.17	2.96	11.02	5.52
Figure 12(c)	41.43	22.39	7.66	17.35	6.68

The filtered data are shown in Figure 12 for visual inspection. The corresponding evaluations given by the new method and the previous one are listed in Table 7.

5. Conclusions

Performance evaluation of noise reduction techniques needs appropriate full-reference metrics able to measure the different amounts of residual noise and filtering distortion. In this paper we have presented a new method for evaluating such features in color images restored from impulse and Gaussian noise. The approach is based on the decomposition of the NCD into three components that, respectively, measure the ability of a filter to remove noise pulses (NCD_{imp}), to reduce Gaussian noise (NCD_{gau}), and to preserve the image details (NCD_{dis}). These new measures retain the specific advantage of the NCD, that is, the evaluation of color errors in a perceptually uniform color space. On the other hand, they overcome the limitation of the sole NCD that cannot distinguish between color errors due to filtering distortion and insufficient noise cancellation.

Results of computer simulations dealing with different pictures corrupted by impulse and Gaussian noise have shown that the proposed method outperforms classical and vector metrics in the literature in the evaluation of the different amounts of residual noise and distortion given by a denoising filter.

Conflict of Interests

The author declares that there is no conflict of interests regarding the publication of this paper.

References

[1] K. N. Plataniotis and A. N. Venetsanopoulos, *Color Image Processing and Application*, Springer, New York, NY, USA, 2000.

[2] R. Lukac, B. Smolka, K. Martin, K. N. Plataniotis, and A. N. Venetsanopoulos, "Vector filtering for color imaging," *IEEE Signal Processing Magazine*, vol. 22, no. 1, pp. 74–86, 2005.

[3] R. Lukac and K. N. Plataniotis, "A taxonomy of color image filtering and enhancement solutions," in *Advances in Imaging and Electron Physics*, W. Hawkes, Ed., vol. 140, pp. 187–264, Elsevier, New York, NY, USA, 2006.

[4] R. Lukac, B. Smolka, K. N. Plataniotis, and A. N. Venetsanopoulos, "Selection weighted vector directional filters," *Computer Vision and Image Understanding*, vol. 94, no. 1–3, pp. 140–167, 2004.

[5] R. Lukac, B. Smolka, K. N. Plataniotis, and A. N. Venetsanopoulos, "Vector sigma filters for noise detection and removal in color images," *Journal of Visual Communication and Image Representation*, vol. 17, no. 1, pp. 1–26, 2006.

[6] Y. Li, G. R. Arce, and J. Bacca, "Weighted median filters for multichannel signals," *IEEE Transactions on Signal Processing*, vol. 54, no. 11, pp. 4271–4281, 2006.

[7] S. Schulte, V. De Witte, M. Nachtegael, D. van der Weken, and E. E. Kerre, "Fuzzy two-step filter for impulse noise reduction from color images," *IEEE Transactions on Image Processing*, vol. 15, no. 11, pp. 3567–3578, 2006.

[8] S. Schulte, V. De Witte, and E. E. Kerre, "A fuzzy noise reduction method for color images," *IEEE Transactions on Image Processing*, vol. 16, no. 5, pp. 1425–1436, 2007.

[9] S. Schulte, S. Morillas, V. Gregori, and E. E. Kerre, "A new fuzzy color correlated impulse noise reduction method," *IEEE Transactions on Image Processing*, vol. 16, no. 10, pp. 2565–2575, 2007.

[10] P.-E. Ng and K.-K. Ma, "A switching median filter with boundary discriminative noise detection for extremely corrupted images," *IEEE Transactions on Image Processing*, vol. 15, no. 6, pp. 1506–1516, 2006.

[11] Y. Dong and S. Xu, "A new directional weighted median filter for removal of random-valued impulse noise," *IEEE Signal Processing Letters*, vol. 14, no. 3, pp. 193–196, 2007.

[12] Y. Li, F.-L. Chung, and S. Wang, "A robust neuro-fuzzy network approach to impulse noise filtering for color images," *Applied Soft Computing Journal*, vol. 8, no. 2, pp. 872–884, 2008.

[13] Z. Xu, H. R. Wu, B. Qiu, and X. Yu, "Geometric features-based filtering for suppression of impulse noise in color images," *IEEE Transactions on Image Processing*, vol. 18, no. 8, pp. 1742–1759, 2009.

[14] S. Morillas, V. Gregori, and A. Hervás, "Fuzzy peer groups for reducing mixed Gaussian-impulse noise from color images," *IEEE Transactions on Image Processing*, vol. 18, no. 7, pp. 1452–1466, 2009.

[15] C. Brito-Loeza and K. Chen, "On high-order denoising models and fast algorithms for vector-valued images," *IEEE Transactions on Image Processing*, vol. 19, no. 6, pp. 1518–1527, 2010.

[16] T. Howlader and Y. P. Chaubey, "Noise reduction of cDNA microarray images using complex wavelets," *IEEE Transactions on Image Processing*, vol. 19, no. 8, pp. 1953–1967, 2010.

[17] T. Mélange, M. Nachtegael, and E. E. Kerre, "Fuzzy random impulse noise removal from color image sequences," *IEEE Transactions on Image Processing*, vol. 20, no. 4, pp. 959–970, 2011.

[18] D. Zhai, M. Hao, and J. M. Mendel, "A non-singleton interval type-2 fuzzy logic system for universal image noise removal using quantum-behaved particle swarm optimization," in *Proceedings of the IEEE International Conference on Fuzzy Systems (FUZZ '11)*, pp. 957–964, Taipei, Taiwan, June 2011.

[19] M. E. Yuksel and A. Basturk, "Application of type-2 fuzzy logic filtering to reduce noise in color images," *IEEE Computational Intelligence MagazIne*, vol. 7, no. 3, pp. 25–35, 2012.

[20] F. Russo, "New method for performance evaluation of grayscale image denoising filters," *IEEE Signal Processing Letters*, vol. 17, no. 5, pp. 417–420, 2010.

[21] F. Russo, "Accurate tools for analyzing the behavior of impulse noise reduction filters in color images," *Journal of Signal and Information Processing, Scientific Research Publishing*, vol. 4, pp. 42–50, 2013.

[22] N. Ponomarenko, F. Battisti, K. Egiazarian, J. Astola, and V. Lukin, "Metrics performance comparison for color image database," in *Proceedings of the 4th International Workshop on Video Processing and Quality Metrics for Consumer Electronics*, Scottsdale, Ariz, USA, January 2009.

[23] D. M. Chandler, "Seven challenges in image quality assessment: past, present, and future research," *ISRN Signal Processing*, vol. 2013, Article ID 905685, 53 pages, 2013.

[24] F. Russo, A. De Angelis, and P. Carbone, "A vector approach to quality assessment of color images," in *Proceedings of the IEEE International Instrumentation and Measurement Technology Conference (I2MTC '08)*, pp. 814–818, Victoria, Canada, May 2008.

[25] A. De Angelis, A. Moschitta, F. Russo, and P. Carbone, "A vector approach for image quality assessment and some metrological considerations," *IEEE Transactions on Instrumentation and Measurement*, vol. 58, no. 1, pp. 14–25, 2009.

[26] "Kodak Lossless True Color Image Suite," http://r0k.us/graphics/kodak/.

[27] A. Medda and V. DeBrunner, "Color image quality index based on the UIQI," in *Proceedings of the 7th IEEE Southwest Symposium on Image Analysis and Interpretation*, pp. 213–217, March 2006.

3

Active Object Recognition with a Space-Variant Retina

Christopher Kanan

Jet Propulsion Laboratory, California Institute of Technology, Pasadena, CA 91109, USA

Correspondence should be addressed to Christopher Kanan; ckanan@caltech.edu

Academic Editors: H. Erdogan, O. Ghita, D. Hernandez, A. Nikolaidis, and J. P. Siebert

When independent component analysis (ICA) is applied to color natural images, the representation it learns has spatiochromatic properties similar to the responses of neurons in primary visual cortex. Existing models of ICA have only been applied to pixel patches. This does not take into account the space-variant nature of human vision. To address this, we use the space-variant log-polar transformation to acquire samples from color natural images, and then we apply ICA to the acquired samples. We analyze the spatiochromatic properties of the learned ICA filters. Qualitatively, the model matches the receptive field properties of neurons in primary visual cortex, including exhibiting the same opponent-color structure and a higher density of receptive fields in the foveal region compared to the periphery. We also adopt the "self-taught learning" paradigm from machine learning to assess the model's efficacy at active object and face classification, and the model is competitive with the best approaches in computer vision.

1. Introduction

In humans and other simian primates, central foveal vision has an exceedingly high spatial resolution (acuity) compared to the periphery. This space-variant scheme enables a large field of view, while allowing visual processing to be efficient. The human retina contains about six million cone photoreceptors but sends only about one million axons to the brain [1]. By employing a space variant representation, the retina is able to greatly reduce the dimensionality of the visual input, with eye movements allowing fine details to be resolved if necessary. The retina's space-variant representation is reflected in early visual cortex's retinotopic map About half of primary visual cortex (V1) is devoted solely to processing the central 15 degrees of visual angle [2, 3]. This enormous overrepresentation of the fovea in V1 is known as cortical magnification [4].

Neurons in V1 have localized an orientation sensitive receptive fields (RFs). V1-like RFs can be algorithmically learned using independent component analysis (ICA) [5–8]. ICA finds a linear transformation that makes the outputs as statistically independent as possible [5], and when ICA is applied to achromatic natural image patches, it produces basis functions that have properties similar to neurons in V1. Moreover, when ICA is applied to color image patches, it produces RFs with V1-like opponent-color characteristics, with the majority of the RFs exhibiting either dark-light opponency, blue-yellow opponency, or red-green opponency [6–8].

Filters learned from unlabeled natural images using ICA and other unsupervised learning algorithms can be used as a replacement for hand-engineered features in computer vision tasks such as object recognition. This is known as self-taught learning when the natural images that the filters are learned from are distinct from the dataset used for evaluating their efficacy [9]. Methods using self-taught learning have achieved state-of-the-art accuracy on many datasets (e.g., [9–12]).

Previous work has focused on applying ICA to square image patches of uniform resolution. Here, we use ICA to learn filters from space-variant image samples acquired using simulated fixations. We analyze the properties of the learned filters, and we adopt the self-taught learning paradigm to assess their efficacy when used for object recognition. We review related models in the discussion.

2. Space-Variant Model of Early Vision

Our model consists of a series of subcomponents, which are depicted in Figure 1. We first describe the space-variant

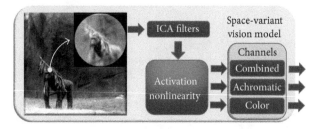

FIGURE 1: A cartoon schematic of our space-variant visual feature model. The model samples a region of the image in a space-variant manner, and this representation is fed into a bank of ICA filters. A learned activation nonlinearity modulates the activity of the filters. Finally the filters are subdivided into multiple channels, which project to an object recognition model.

representation we use, and then how we learn the space-variant ICA filters.

2.1. Cone-Like Representation. When our model of space-variant vision fixates a region of an image, it converts the image from standard RGB (sRGB) colorspace to LMS colorspace [13], which more closely resembles the responses of the long, medium, and short wavelength cone photoreceptors in the human retina. Subsequently, we apply a cone-like nonlinearity to the LMS pixels. This preprocessing helps the model cope with large-scale changes in brightness [6, 10, 14], and it is related to gamma correction [15]. The formulation we use is given by

$$F_{\text{cone}}(z) = \max\left(\frac{\log(\gamma + 1) - \log(F_{\text{LMS}}(z) + \gamma)}{(\log(\gamma + 1) - \log(\gamma))(\gamma - 1)} + 1, 0\right),$$
(1)

where γ controls the normalization strength. In our experiments $\gamma = 0.01$. The nonlinearity is shown in Figure 2.

2.2. A Space-Variant Representation. We use Bolduc and Levine's [16, 17] log-polar model of space-variant vision. Log-polar representations have been used to model both cortical magnification [18] and the retina [17]. Unlike other log-polar models (e.g., [18]), Bolduc and Levine's model does not have a foveal blind spot. Moreover, it incorporates overlapping RFs, which produces images of superior quality [19], and the RFs in the fovea are of uniform size. Each unit in this representation can be interpreted as a bipolar cell, which pools pixels in a cone-like space. The mammalian retina contains at least 10 distinct bipolar cell types [20], and most of them are diffuse; that is, they pool the responses of multiple cones.

We briefly describe Bolduc and Levine's [16, 17] model. The full derivation is given in [17]. A log-polar mapping is governed by equations for the eccentricity of each ring of RFs from the center of the visual field and the spacing between individual RFs, that is, the grid rays. Bolduc and Levine's model uses separate equations for the foveal region and the

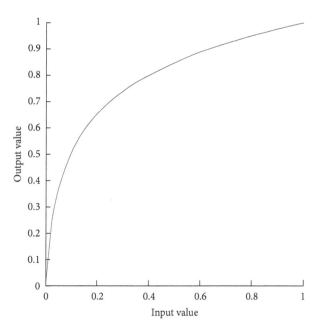

FIGURE 2: The cone nonlinearity plotted with $\gamma = 0.01$.

periphery. The ray spacing angle formula outside of the fovea is given by

$$\theta(\alpha, \omega) = 2\pi\left(\text{round}\left(2\pi(\arccos(z))^{-1}\right)\right)^{-1},$$
(2)

where α is the ratio of the RF size to eccentricity, $z = 1 - 0.5\alpha^2(1 - \omega)^2$, and ω is the amount of RF overlap. The use of the round function ensures an integer number of grid rays. The eccentricity ε of each peripheral ring $s \in \{0, 1, \ldots, L\}$ is given by

$$\varepsilon(\alpha, \omega, s, f) = \left(-\frac{\alpha(1 - 2\omega) + d}{\alpha - 2}\right)^s f,$$
(3)

where f is the radius of the fovea, $d = \sqrt{4 + \alpha^2((1 - 2\omega)^2 - 1)}$, and L is the total number of peripheral layers. The radius of peripheral RFs at eccentricity ε is given by

$$r(\alpha, \omega, s, f) = \frac{\alpha}{2}\varepsilon(\alpha, \omega, s, f).$$
(4)

Foveal RFs are all constrained to be the same size as the inner most ring of the periphery; that is,

$$r_{\text{fovea}}(\alpha, \omega, 0, f) = \frac{\alpha}{2}f.$$
(5)

Constraining foveal RFs to be the same size means that there are a decreasing number of RFs in each foveal ring as the center of the retina is approached, in contrast to peripheral rings, which each contains the same number of RFs. The eccentricity of foveal ring κ is given by

$$\varepsilon_{\text{fovea}}(\kappa) = (\varepsilon(\alpha, \omega, 1, f) - f)\kappa.$$
(6)

The ray spacing angle formula between RFs in foveal ring κ is given by $\theta_{\text{fovea}}(\kappa) = \theta(\alpha f / \varepsilon_{\text{fovea}}(\kappa), \omega)$.

We use normalized circular RFs for the retina, which act as linear filters. A retina RF j at location (x_j, y_j) with radius r_j is defined as follows:

$$H_j\left(x', y'\right) = \frac{h_j\left(x', y'\right)}{\displaystyle\int\int_{-\infty}^{\infty} h_j\left(x, y\right) dx\, dy}, \qquad (7)$$

where

$$h_j(x, y) = \sqrt{\max\left(r_j^2 - \left(x - x_j\right)^2 - \left(y - y_j\right)^2, 0\right)}. \qquad (8)$$

The retina we used in experiments is shown in Figure 3. We set $\alpha = 0.2$ and used a RF overlap of 50%, that is, $\omega = 0.5$, which are biologically plausible values [17]. We set the fovea's radius to 7 pixels and we used 15 peripheral layers. These settings yield a retina with a radius of 35 pixels that reduces the dimensionality from 3749 pixels to 1304 retina RFs (296 in the fovea, 1008 in the periphery).

Our images are resized, so that their shortest side is 160 pixels, with the other side rescaled to preserve the image's aspect ratio. If this canonical size is altered, then the fovea's radius should be changed as well. This change will not alter the total number of RFs.

To use our retina with color images, we sample each color channel independently. After sampling a region of an image with the retina, we subtract each color channel's mean and then divide the by the vector's Euclidean norm. Sampling the image with our retina yields $\mathbf{r}$, a 3912-dimensional unit length vector of retinal fixation features (1304 dimensions per color channel).

2.3. Learning a Space-Variant Model of V1. We learned ICA filters from 584 images from the McGill color image dataset [21]. Each image is randomly fixated 200 times, with each fixation location chosen with uniform probability. The images are not padded, and fixations are constrained to be within images.

Prior to ICA, we first reduce the dimensionality of the fixation data from 3912 dimensions to 1000 dimensions using principal component analysis (PCA), which preserves more than 99.4% of the variance. We then learn ICA filters using the Efficient Fast ICA algorithm [22]. We denote the learned ICA filters using the matrix $\mathbf{U} = [\mathbf{u}_1, \ldots, \mathbf{u}_n]^T$, with the rows of $\mathbf{U}$ containing the ICA filters. The learned ICA basis functions are shown in Figure 4.

2.4. ICA Filter Activation Function. For object recognition, the discriminative power of ICA filters can be increased by taking the absolute value of the responses and then applying the cumulative distribution function (CDF) of generalized Gaussian distributions to the ICA filter responses [10, 12]. We pursue a similar approach, but we use the CDF of the exponential distribution instead. The CDF of the exponential distribution is computationally more efficient to calculate, and it is easier to fit since it has only one parameter. For

each ICA filter $\mathbf{u}_i^T$ (the ith row of $\mathbf{U}$), we fit an exponential distribution's rate parameter λ_i to the absolute value of the filter responses to the fixations extracted from the McGill dataset [21]. Fitting was done using MATLAB's "fitdist" function. The final ICA activation nonlinearity is given for each ICA filter by

$$g_i = 1 - \exp\left(-\lambda_i \left|\mathbf{u}_i^T \mathbf{r}\right|\right), \qquad (9)$$

where g_i is the ith element of the vector $\mathbf{g}$.

3. Analysis of Learned Receptive Fields

We fit Gabor functions to the ICA filters to analyze their properties. Gabor functions are localized and oriented band-pass filters given by the product of a sinusoid and a Gaussian envelope [23], and they are a common model for V1 RFs. To do this, we represent the ICA filters in Cartesian space and convert them to grayscale using the Decolorize algorithm [24], which preserves chromatic contrast. In general, Gabor functions were a good fit to the learned filters, with a median R^2 value of 0.81; however, 70 of the 1000 fits were poor ($R^2 <$ 0.5) and we did not further analyze their spatial properties.

Figure 6 shows a scatter plot of the peak frequencies and orientations of the Gabor filter fits, revealing that they cover a wide spectrum of orientations and frequencies. While the orientations are relatively evenly covered irrespective of the filter's location, most of the filters sensitive to higher spatial frequencies are located in the foveal region. We also found that there was a greater number of ICA filters in the foveal region compared to the periphery (see Figure 5), with the RFs getting progressively larger outside of the fovea (see Figure 7).

4. Image Classification with Gnostic Fields

4.1. Gnostic Fields. A gnostic field is a brain-inspired object classification model [26], based on the ideas of the neuroscientist Jerzy Konorski [27]. An overview of the model is given in Figure 8. Gnostic fields have been shown to achieve state-of-the-art accuracy at image classification using color SIFT features. We use a gnostic field with our space-variant ICA features. We briefly provide the details necessary to implement gnostic fields here, but see [26] for additional information.

A gnostic field's input is segregated into one or more channels [26], which helps it cope with irrelevant features. We used three channels: (1) all 1000 ICA filters, (2) the 744 achromatic ICA filters, and (3) the 256 color ICA filters. We let $\mathbf{g}_c$ be a vector that denotes features from channel c, which is a subset of the dimensions of $\mathbf{g}$.

Whitened PCA (WPCA) [5] is applied to each channel independently to learn a decorrelating transformation that normalizes that channel's variance; that is,

$$\mathbf{W}_c = \left(\mathbf{D}_c + \xi \mathbf{I}\right)^{-1/2} \mathbf{E}_c^T, \qquad (10)$$

where $\mathbf{I}$ is the identity matrix, the columns of the matrix $\mathbf{E}_c$ contain the eigenvectors of the channel's covariance matrix calculated using the fixations from the McGill dataset, $\mathbf{D}_c$ is

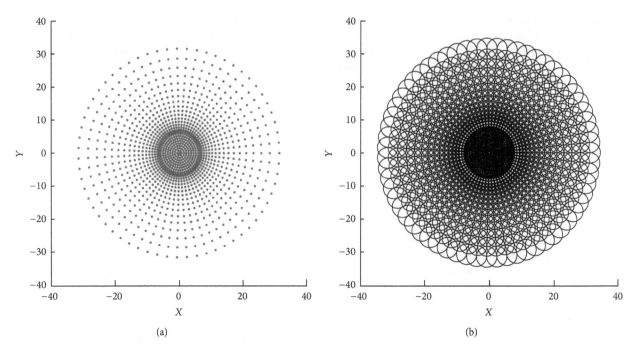

(a)

(b)

FIGURE 3: (a) The center of each retina RF, with a red circle drawn around the fovea. (b) A depiction of the retina's RF sizes. Each RF operated on between 1 (fovea) and 32 pixels.

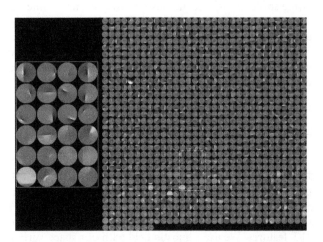

FIGURE 4: The 1000 V1-like basis functions learned using ICA. Two distinct populations of 256 chromatic and 744 achromatic filters were learned. The learned features are Gabor like, and they share the dark-light, red-green, and blue-yellow opponency characteristics of V1 neurons [6–8].

the diagonal matrix of eigenvalues, and ξ is a regularization parameter, with $\xi = 0.01$ in experiments. The output is then made unit length, which allows measurements of similarity using dot products [28]. At each time step t, this yields whitened and normalized vector $\mathbf{f}_{c,t}$, that is,

$$\mathbf{f}_{c,t} = \frac{\mathbf{W}_c \mathbf{g}_{c,t}}{\|\mathbf{W}_c \mathbf{g}_{c,t}\|}. \qquad (11)$$

Let $\mathbf{x}_t = [x_t \;\; y_t \;\; 1]^T$ denote the (x_t, y_t) location of the fixation, with the coordinates normalized by the image size to be

between -1 and 1. To incorporate this location information into the unit length features, we normalize $\mathbf{x}_t$ to unit length and weight it by δ; that is, $\widehat{\mathbf{x}}_t = \delta(\mathbf{x}_t/\|\mathbf{x}_t\|)$, with δ controlling the strength of the fixation location's influence. The $\widehat{\mathbf{x}}_t$ vector is concatenated to $\mathbf{f}_{c,t}$, which is then renormalized to unit length, yielding $\widehat{\mathbf{f}}_{c,t}$. In our experiments, $\delta = 0.01$.

A gnostic field is made up of multiple gnostic sets, with one set per category. Each gnostic set contains neurons that assess how similar the fixation features are to previous observations from the category. For each gnostic set, the activity of a neuron j for category k and from channel c is given by the dot product

$$a_{c,k,j}\left(\mathbf{f}_{c,t}\right) = \mathbf{v}_{c,k,j} \cdot \widehat{\mathbf{f}}_{c,t}, \qquad (12)$$

where $\mathbf{v}_{c,k,j}$ is the neuron's weight vector.

The output of the gnostic set for category k and channel c is given by the most active neuron:

$$\varphi_{c,k}\left(\mathbf{f}_{c,t}\right) = \max_j a_{c,k,j}\left(\mathbf{f}_{c,t}\right). \qquad (13)$$

Max pooling enables the gnostic set to vigorously respond to features matching the category's training data.

Spherical k-means [29] is an unsupervised clustering algorithm for unit length data that is used to learn the localized $\mathbf{v}_{c,k,j}$ units for each of the K gnostic sets and C channels [26]. The number of units in a gnostic set depends on the number of fixations from that category, albeit with fewer units being recruited as the number of fixations increases. To implement this, the number of $\mathbf{v}_{c,k,j}$ units learned for a category k from channel c is given by

$$m(k,c) = \min\left(\left\lceil b(\log(n_{k,c})+1)^2 \right\rceil, n_{k,c}\right), \qquad (14)$$

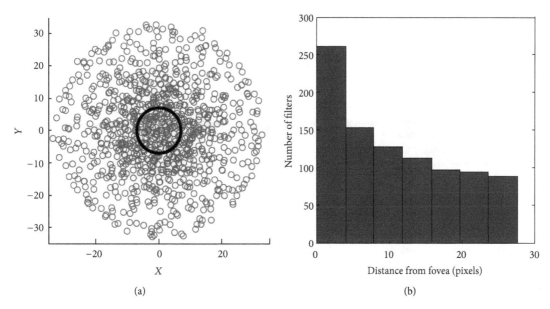

(a)   (b)

FIGURE 5: (a) The center location of the Gabor functions fit to the ICA filters. The fovea is contained within the black circle. (b) A histogram of the Gabor function centers as a function of the distance from the fovea, which reveals that the number of filters is decreasing farther from the fovea.

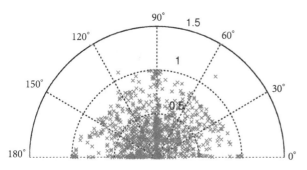

FIGURE 6: Scatter plot of the peak frequencies and orientations of Gabor functions fit to the ICA filters. The filters cover a wide spectrum of orientations and frequencies.

where $n_{k,c}$ is the total number of fixations from category k and b regulates the number of units learned ($b = 10$ in our experiments). This equation is plotted in Figure 9.

Inhibitive competition is used to suppress the least active gnostic sets. This is implemented for the K gnostic sets by attenuating their activity using

$$q_{c,k}\left(\mathbf{f}_{c,t}\right) = \max\left(\varphi_{c,k}\left(\mathbf{f}_{c,t}\right) - \theta_{c,t}, 0\right), \qquad (15)$$

with the threshold $\theta_{c,t} = (1/K)\sum_{k'}\varphi_{c,k'}(\mathbf{f}_{c,t})$. Subsequently, the nonzero responses are normalized using

$$\beta_{c,k}\left(\mathbf{f}_{c,t}\right) = \nu_{c,t}q_{c,k}\left(\mathbf{f}_{c,t}\right), \qquad (16)$$

with

$$\nu_{c,t} = \frac{\sum_{k'} q_{c,k'}\left(\mathbf{f}_{c,t}\right)}{\left(K^{-1} + \sum_{k'} q_{c,k'}\left(\mathbf{f}_{c,t}\right)^2\right)^{3/2}}, \qquad (17)$$

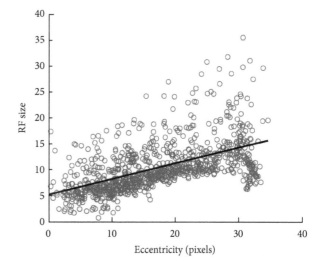

FIGURE 7: Plot of ICA filter/RF size as a function of eccentricity, along with a linear regression line. The size of the RFs was taken to be the area of the Gaussian envelope at full width at half maximum of the Gabor functions fit to the ICA filters. Like neurons in V1, RF size increases with eccentricity [25].

acting as a form of variance-modulated divisive normalization [26].

As fixations are acquired over time, the gnostic field accumulates categorical evidence from each channel

$$\psi_{c,k}\left(\mathbf{f}_{c,1}, \ldots, \mathbf{f}_{c,T}\right) = \sum_{t=1}^{T}\beta_{c,k}\left(\mathbf{f}_{c,t}\right). \qquad (18)$$

Subsequently, the responses from all of these evidence accumulation units are combined across all categories and

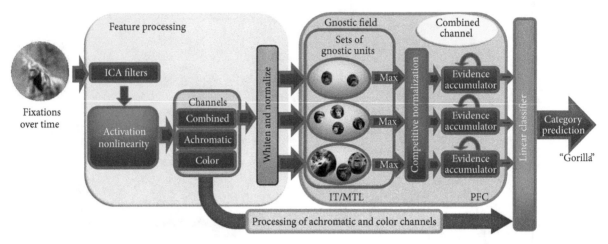

FIGURE 8: A high-level depiction of a gnostic field for classifying nonhuman apes using our space-variant ICA filters. The model splits the ICA filter output into chromatic, achromatic, and combined channels. This visual information projects to a gnostic set for each category, with units in the gorilla gnostic set responding strongest. The output of each gnostic set is given by the most active unit, and subsequent competitive normalization adjusts the activity to suppress the output of the chimpanzee and orangutan sets. Finally, evidence from the current fixation is added to the model's beliefs, and information from all categories and channels is combined using a linear classifier.

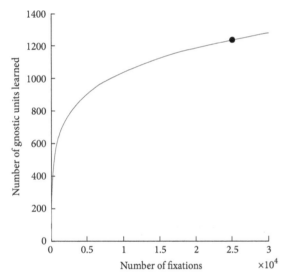

FIGURE 9: The total number of units learned for a gnostic set as a function of the number of fixations extracted from images labeled with the gnostic set's category. The black dot indicates the number of units learned for each Caltech-256 category with 50 training images per category and 500 fixations per image, so each gnostic set contained 1239 units learned from 25000 fixations.

channels into a single vector Ψ. This vector is then made mean zero and normalized to unit length.

A linear multicategory classifier decodes the activity of these pooling units. This allows less discriminative channels to be downweighted and it helps the model cope with confused categories. The model's predicted category is given by $\tilde{k} = \mathrm{argmax}_k \mathbf{w}_k \cdot \Psi$, where $\mathbf{w}_k$ is the weight vector for category k. The $\mathbf{w}_k$ weights were learned with the LIBLINEAR toolbox [30] using Crammer and Singer's multiclass linear support vector machine formulation [31], with a low cost parameter (0.0001).

4.2. Face and Object Recognition Experiments.

We assess performance of the space-variant ICA features using two computer vision datasets: the Aleix and Robert (AR) face dataset [32] and Caltech-256 [33]. Training and testing consisted of extracting 500 fixations per image from random locations without replacement. We did not attempt to tune the number of fixations.

AR contains 4,000 color face images under varying expression, dress (disguise), and lighting conditions. We use images from 120 people, with 26 images each. Example images are shown in Figure 10(a). Results are shown in Figure 11. Our model performs slightly better than the best algorithms.

Caltech-256 [33] consists of images found using Google image search from 256 object categories. Example Caltech-256 images are shown in Figure 10(b). It exhibits a large amount of interclass variability. We adopt the standard Caltech-256 evaluation scheme [36]. We train on a variable number of randomly chosen images per category and test on 25 other randomly chosen images per category. We report the mean per-class accuracy over five cross-validation runs in Figure 12.

We performed an additional experiment on Caltech-256 to assess the impact of omitting the location information in the fixation features. Omitting it caused performance to drop by 3.6% when using 50 training images per category.

To examine how well gnostic fields trained using each channel individually performed compared to our main results using the multichannel model, we performed another experiment with Caltech-256 using 50 training instances per category. The multichannel approach performed best, and the chromatic filters alone worked comparatively poorly. These results are shown in Table 1.

We conducted additional experiments to examine performance as a function of the number of fixations used during testing. These results are shown in Figure 13. For both

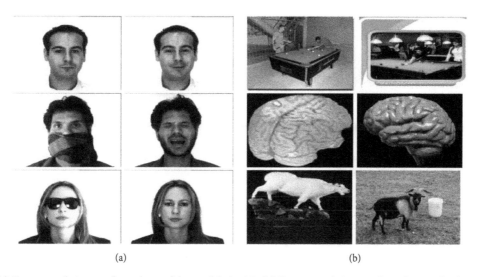

<table>
<tr><td>(a)</td><td>(b)</td></tr>
</table>

FIGURE 10: (a) Two example images from three of the models in AR. (b) Two example images from three Caltech-256 categories.

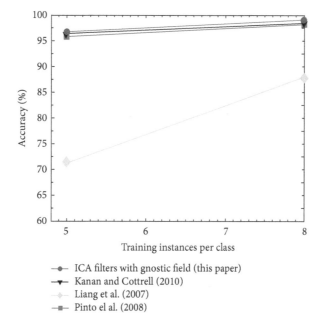

FIGURE 11: Mean per-class accuracy on the AR Face dataset of our approach compared with the methods of [10, 34, 35]. Chance performance is 1/120. Kanan and Cottrell [10] used a nonfoveated model of active vision (see discussion). Pinto et al. [35] used V1 + Gabor features with a linear SVM.

datasets, performance quickly rises; however, Caltech-256 appears to need more fixations to approach its maximum performance. In both cases, it is likely that choosing fixations in a more intelligent manner would greatly decrease the number of fixations needed (see Section 5).

5. Discussion

We applied ICA to spatially-variant samples of chromatic images. Our goal was to analyze the properties of the learned filters and to assess their efficacy at object recognition using the self-taught learning paradigm.

TABLE 1: Mean per-class accuracy on Caltech-256 using 50 training instances per class for each channel specific gnostic field, along with the multichannel approach that combines all three channels.

Achromatic	Chromatic	All	Multichannel
45.6 ± 0.5	31.4 ± 0.4	48.4 ± 0.5	50.8 ± 0.5

Our fixation-based approach to object recognition is similar to the NIMBLE model [10]. NIMBLE used a square retina, which pooled ICA filter responses learned from square patches. Instead of a Gnostic Field, NIMBLE used a Bayesian approach to update its beliefs as it acquired fixations. NIMBLE was unable to scale to large datasets because it compared

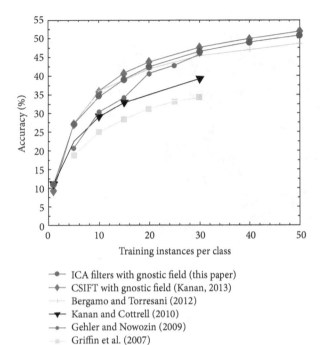

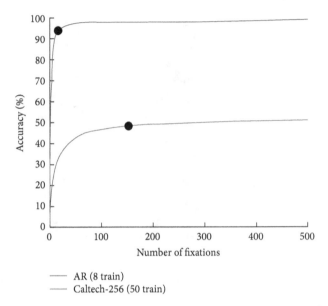

FIGURE 13: Our approach's mean per-class accuracy on AR and Caltech-256 as a function of the number of test fixations. For AR, 8 training instances per category were used, and for Caltech-256, 50 training instances per category were used. The results are averaged over five cross-validation runs. The black dots indicate the number of fixations needed to achieve 95% of the maximum accuracy (17 for AR and 152 for Caltech-256).

FIGURE 12: Mean per-class accuracy for our approach on Caltech-256 as a function of the number of training instances compared to the methods of [10, 26, 33, 36, 37]. Chance performance is 1/256. Kanan [26] used a gnostic field with color SIFT features, and our space-variant ICA filters achieve almost the same accuracy (slightly more for one training instance), despite being a self-taught approach. Bergamo and Torresani [37] combined five kinds of features (color GIST, oriented HOG, unoriented HOG, SSIM, and SIFT) into a metadescriptor using spatial-pyramid histograms. Gehler and Nowozin [36] used five types of engineered features (PHOG, SIFT, LBP, V1+ Gabors, and region covariance) and used multiple kernel learning to combine 39 different kernels. Kanan and Cottrell [10] used a nonfoveated model of active vision (see discussion). Griffin et al. [33] provides baseline results.

new fixations using nearest neighbor density estimation to all stored fixations for each category. For example, on Caltech-256 with 500 training fixations per image and 50 training instances per category, NIMBLE would store 25000 high dimensional fixation features per class, whereas a gnostic field would only learn 1239 gnostic units. This allows gnostic fields to be faster and more memory efficient, while also being more biologically plausible.

Like us, Vincent et al. [38] learned filters from a space-variant representation, but instead of ICA they used an unsupervised learning algorithm that penalized firing rate. Their algorithm also learned Gabor-like filters. They found that RF size increases away from the fovea, and that more filters are learned in the fovea compared to the periphery. While they were primarily interested in the RF properties, it would be interesting to examine how well their filters work for object recognition.

Log-polar representations can be made rotation and scale tolerant with respect to the center of a fixation [39], since changes in rotation and scale consist of "spinning" the retina or having it "zoom" in or out. Exploiting this could lead to

improved object recognition performance, although if used in all situations it is likely to cause a loss of discriminative power (see [40] for an extensive discussion of the discriminative power-invariance tradeoff).

We are currently exploring avenues for developing a better controller for choosing the location of fixations. In our experiments we randomly chose the locations of fixations, but it is likely that significant gains in performance could be obtained by using a smarter controller that chose the next fixation location based on evidence acquired during previous fixations. The controller could also manipulate the rotation and size of the retina, potentially allowing it to increase its tolerance to changes in scale and rotation. One approach to learning a controller is to use reinforcement learning [41], with the reward function being crafted to reduce uncertainty about the object being viewed as quickly as possible. An alternative to reinforcement learning for fixation control was proposed by Larochelle and Hinton [42]. They developed a special kind of restricted Boltzmann machine that accumulated evidence over time. Their model learned a controller that selected among fixation locations on a $m \times m$ grid ($m \leq 7$ in their experiments), with the controller trained to choose the grid location most likely to lead to the correct label prediction.

A better controller would allow us to compare the model's simulated eye movements to the eye movements of humans when engaged in various visual tasks. We could also explore how changes in the retinal input might impact the way the controller behaves. For example, we could induce an artificial scotoma into our retinal model. Scotomas are regions of diminished visual acuity, which are caused by diseases such as retinitis pigmentosa and age-related macular degeneration. Inducing an artificial scotoma would allow us to examine how the scotoma alters the acquired policy and if the changes are consistent with eye tracking studies in humans that have similar scotomas.

6. Conclusions

Here, for the first time, ICA was applied to a spatially-variant input, and we showed that this produces filters that share many spatiochromatic properties with V1 neurons, including eccentricity properties. Further, we showed that when these features are used with an object recognition system, they rival the best hand-engineered features in discriminative performance, despite being entirely self-taught.

Acknowledgments

The author would like to thank Akinyinka Omigbodun and Garrison Cottrell for feedback on earlier versions of this paper. This work was completed, while the author was affiliated with the University of California San Diego. This work was supported in part by NSF Science of Learning Center Grants SBE-0542013 and SMA-1041755 to the Temporal Dynamics of Learning Center.

References

[1] C. A. Curcio and K. A. Allen, "Topography of ganglion cells in human retina," *Journal of Comparative Neurology*, vol. 300, no. 1, pp. 5–25, 1990.

[2] R. F. Dougherty, V. M. Koch, A. A. Brewer, B. Fischer, J. Modersitzki, and B. A. Wandell, "Visual field representations and locations of visual areas v1/2/3 in human visual cortex," *Journal of Vision*, vol. 3, no. 10, pp. 586–598, 2003.

[3] S. A. Engel, G. H. Glover, and B. A. Wandell, "Retinotopic organization in human visual cortex and the spatial precision of functional MRI," *Cerebral Cortex*, vol. 7, no. 2, pp. 181–192, 1997.

[4] P. M. Daniel and D. Whitteridge, "The representation of the visual field on the cerebral cortex in monkeys," *The Journal of Physiology*, vol. 159, pp. 203–221, 1961.

[5] A. J. Bell and T. J. Sejnowski, "The "independent components" of natural scenes are edge filters," *Vision Research*, vol. 37, no. 23, pp. 3327–3338, 1997.

[6] M. S. Caywood, B. Willmore, and D. J. Tolhurst, "Independent components of color natural scenes resemble V1 neurons in their spatial and color tuning," *Journal of Neurophysiology*, vol. 91, no. 6, pp. 2859–2873, 2004.

[7] T. W. Lee, T. Wachtler, and T. J. Sejnowski, "Color opponency is an efficient representation of spectral properties in natural scenes," *Vision Research*, vol. 42, no. 17, pp. 2095–2103, 2002.

[8] T. Wachtler, E. Doi, T. W. Lee, and T. J. Sejnowski, "Cone selectivity derived from the responses of the retinal cone mosaic to natural scenes," *Journal of Vision*, vol. 7, no. 8, article 6, 2007.

[9] R. Raina, A. Battle, H. Lee, B. Packer, and A. Y. Ng, "Self-taught learning: transfer learning from unlabeled data," in *Proceedings of the 24th International Conference on Machine Learning (ICML '07)*, pp. 759–766, June 2007.

[10] C. Kanan and G. Cottrell, "Robust classification of objects, faces, and flowers using natural image statistics," in *Proceedings of the IEEE Computer Society Conference on Computer Vision and Pattern Recognition (CVPR '10)*, pp. 2472–2479, June 2010.

[11] Q. V. Le, M. A. Ranzato, R. Monga et al., "Building high-level features using large scale unsupervised learning," in *Proceedings of the International Conference on Machine Learning (ICML '12)*, pp. 81–88, 2012.

[12] H. Shan and G. W. Cottrell, "Looking around the backyard helps to recognize faces and digits," in *Proceedings of the 26th IEEE Conference on Computer Vision and Pattern Recognition (CVPR '08)*, June 2008.

[13] M. D. Fairchild, *Color Appearance Models*, Wiley Interscience, 2nd edition, 2005.

[14] C. Kanan, A. Flores, and G. W. Cottrell, "Color constancy algorithms for object and face recognition," in *Advances in Visual Computing*, vol. 6453 of *Lecture Notes in Computer Science*, no. 1, pp. 199–210, 2010.

[15] C. Kanan and G. W. Cottrell, "Color-to-grayscale: does the method matter in image recognition?" *PLoS ONE*, vol. 7, no. 1, Article ID e29740, 2012.

[16] M. Bolduc and M. D. Levine, "A real-time foveated sensor with overlapping receptive fields," *Real-Time Imaging*, vol. 3, no. 3, pp. 195–212, 1997.

[17] M. Bolduc and M. D. Levine, "A review of biologically motivated space-variant data reduction models for robotic vision," *Computer Vision and Image Understanding*, vol. 69, no. 2, pp. 170–184, 1998.

[18] E. L. Schwartz, "Spatial mapping in the primate sensory projection: analytic structure and relevance to perception," *Biological Cybernetics*, vol. 25, no. 4, pp. 181–194, 1977.

[19] M. Chessa, S. P. Sabatini, F. Solari, and F. Tatti, "A quantitative comparison of speed and reliability for log-polar mapping techniques," in *Computer Vision Systems*, vol. 6962 of *Lecture Notes in Computer Science*, pp. 41–50, 2011.

[20] R. H. Masland, "The fundamental plan of the retina," *Nature Neuroscience*, vol. 4, no. 9, pp. 877–886, 2001.

[21] A. Olmos and F. A. A. Kingdom, "A biologically inspired algorithm for the recovery of shading and reflectance images," *Perception*, vol. 33, no. 12, pp. 1463–1473, 2004.

[22] Z. Koldovský, P. Tichavský, and E. Oja, "Efficient variant of algorithm FastICA for independent component analysis attaining the Cramér-Rao lower bound," *IEEE Transactions on Neural Networks*, vol. 17, no. 5, pp. 1265–1277, 2006.

[23] J. P. Jones and L. A. Palmer, "An evaluation of the two-dimensional Gabor filter model of simple receptive fields in cat striate cortex," *Journal of Neurophysiology*, vol. 58, no. 6, pp. 1233–1258, 1987.

[24] M. Grundland and N. A. Dodgson, "Decolorize: fast, contrast enhancing, color to grayscale conversion," *Pattern Recognition*, vol. 40, no. 11, pp. 2891–2896, 2007.

[25] R. Gattass, C. G. Gross, and J. H. Sandell, "Visual topography of V2 in the Macaque," *Journal of Comparative Neurology*, vol. 201, no. 4, pp. 519–539, 1981.

[26] C. Kanan, "Recognizing sights, smells, and sounds with gnostic fields," *PLoS ONE*, vol. 8, no. 1, Article ID e54088, 2013.

[27] J. Konorski, *Integrative Activity of the Brain*, University of Chicago Press, Chicago, Ill, USA, 1967.

[28] M. Kouh and T. Poggio, "A canonical neural circuit for cortical nonlinear operations," *Neural Computation*, vol. 20, no. 6, pp. 1427–1451, 2008.

[29] I. S. Dhillon and D. S. Modha, "Concept decompositions for large sparse text data using clustering," *Machine Learning*, vol. 42, no. 1-2, pp. 143–175, 2001.

[30] R. E. Fan, K. W. Chang, C. J. Hsieh, X. R. Wang, and C. J. Lin, "LIBLINEAR: a library for large linear classification," *Journal of Machine Learning Research*, vol. 9, pp. 1871–1874, 2008.

[31] K. Crammer and Y. Singer, "On the algorithmic implementation of multiclass kernel-based vector machines," *Journal of Machine Learning Research*, vol. 2, pp. 265–292, 2001.

[32] A. M. Martinez and R. Benavente, "The AR face database," Tech. Rep. 24, CVC, 1998.

[33] G. Griffin, A. D. Holub, and P. Perona, "The Caltech-256 object category dataset," Tech. Rep. CNS-TR-2007-001, Caltech, Pasadena, Calif, USA, 2007.

[34] Y. Liang, C. Li, W. Gong, and Y. Pan, "Uncorrelated linear discriminant analysis based on weighted pairwise Fisher criterion," *Pattern Recognition*, vol. 40, no. 12, pp. 3606–3615, 2007.

[35] N. Pinto, D. D. Cox, and J. J. DiCarlo, "Why is real-world visual object recognition hard?" *PLoS Computational Biology*, vol. 4, no. 1, article e27, 2008.

[36] P. Gehler and S. Nowozin, "On feature combination for multiclass object classificationpages," in *Proceedings of the IEEE 12th International Conference on Computer Vision (ICCV '09)*, pp. 221–228, IEEE Computer Society, Los Alamitos, Calif, USA, 2009.

[37] A. Bergamo and L. Torresani, "Meta-class features for large-scale object categorization on a budget," in *Proceedings of the IEEE Computer Vision and Pattern Recognition (CVPR '12)*, 2012.

[38] B. T. Vincent, R. J. Baddeley, T. Troscianko, and I. D. Gilchrist, "Is the early visual system optimised to be energy efficient?" *Network: Computation in Neural Systems*, vol. 16, no. 2-3, pp. 175–190, 2005.

[39] V. Javier Traver and A. Bernardino, "A review of log-polar imaging for visual perception in robotics," *Robotics and Autonomous Systems*, vol. 58, no. 4, pp. 378–398, 2010.

[40] M. Varma and D. Ray, "Learning the discriminative power-invariance trade-off," in *Proceedings of the 2007 IEEE 11th International Conference on Computer Vision (ICCV '07)*, October 2007.

[41] R. S. Sutton and A. G. Barto, *Reinforcement Learning: An Introduction*, MIT Press, Cambridge, Mass, USA, 1998.

[42] H. Larochelle and G. Hinton, "Learning to combine foveal glimpses with a third-order Boltzmann machine," in *Proceedings of the 24th Annual Conference on Neural Information Processing Systems 2010 (NIPS '10)*, December 2010.

4

Affine-Invariant Feature Extraction for Activity Recognition

Samy Sadek,[1] **Ayoub Al-Hamadi,**[2] **Gerald Krell,**[2] **and Bernd Michaelis**[2]

[1] *Department of Mathematics and Computer Science, Faculty of Science, Sohag University, 82524 Sohag, Egypt*
[2] *Institute for Information Technology and Communications (IIKT), Otto von Guericke University Magdeburg, 39106 Magdeburg, Germany*

Correspondence should be addressed to Samy Sadek; samy.technik@gmail.com

Academic Editors: A. Gasteratos, D. P. Mukherjee, and A. Torsello

We propose an innovative approach for human activity recognition based on affine-invariant shape representation and SVM-based feature classification. In this approach, a compact computationally efficient affine-invariant representation of action shapes is developed by using affine moment invariants. Dynamic affine invariants are derived from the 3D spatiotemporal action volume and the average image created from the 3D volume and classified by an SVM classifier. On two standard benchmark action datasets (KTH and Weizmann datasets), the approach yields promising results that compare favorably with those previously reported in the literature, while maintaining real-time performance.

1. Introduction

Visual recognition and interpretation of human-induced actions and events are among the most active research areas in computer vision, pattern recognition, and image understanding communities [1]. Although a great deal of progress has been made in automatic recognition of human actions during the last two decades, the approaches proposed in the literature remain limited in their ability. This leads to a need for much research work to be conducted to address the ongoing challenges and develop more efficient approaches. It is clear that developing good algorithms for solving the problem of human action recognition would yield huge potential for a large number of potential applications, for example, the search and the structuring of large video archives, human-computer interaction, video surveillance, gesture recognition, and robot learning and control. In fact, the nonrigid nature of human body and clothes in video sequences, resulting from drastic illumination changes, changing in pose, and erratic motion patterns, presents the grand challenge to human detection and action recognition. In addition, while the real-time performance is a major concern in computer vision, especially for embedded computer vision systems, the majority of state-of-the-art human action recognition systems often employ sophisticated feature extraction and learning techniques, creating a barrier to

the real-time performance of these systems. This suggests a trade-off between accuracy and real-time performance. The remainder of this paper commences by briefly reviewing the most relevant literature in this area of human action recognition in Section 2. Then, in Section 3, we describe the details of the proposed method for action recognition. The experimental results corroborating the proposed method effectiveness are presented and analyzed in Section 4. Finally, in Section 5, we conclude and mention possible future work.

2. The Literature Overview

Recent few years have witnessed a resurgence of interest in more research on the analysis and interpretation of human motion motivated by the rise of security concerns and increased ubiquity and affordability of digital media production equipment. Human action can generally be recognized using various visual cues such as motion [2, 3] and shape [4, 5]. Scanning the literature, one notices that a significant body of work in human action recognition focuses on using spatial-temporal key points and local feature descriptors [6]. The local features are extracted from the region around each key point detected by the key point detection process. These features are then quantized to provide a discrete set of visual words before they are fed

FIGURE 1: GMM background subtraction: the first and third rows display two sequences of walking and running actions from KTH and Weizmann action datasets, respectively, while the second and fourth rows show the results of background subtraction where foreground objects are shown in cyan color.

into the classification module. Another thread of research is concerned with analyzing patterns of motion to recognize human actions. For instance, in [7], periodic motions are detected and classified to recognize actions. Alternatively, some researchers have opted to use both motion and shape cues. In [8], the authors detect the similarity between video segments using a space-time correlation model. In [9], Rodriguez et al. present a template-based approach using a Maximum Average Correlation Height (MACH) filter to capture intraclass variabilities. Likewise, a significant amount of work is targeted at modelling and understanding human motions by constructing elaborated temporal dynamic models [10]. There is also an attractive area of research which focuses on using generative topic models for visual recognition based on the so-called Bag-of-Words (BoW) model [11]. The underlying concept of a BoW is that each video sequence is represented by counting the number of occurrences of descriptor prototypes, so-called visual words. Topic models are built and then applied to the BoW representation. Three examples of commonly used topic models include Correlated Topic Models (CTMs) [11], Latent Dirichlet Allocation (LDA) [12], and probabilistic Latent Semantic Analysis (pLSA) [13].

3. Proposed Methodology

In this section, the proposed method for action recognition is described. The main steps of the framework are explained in detail along the following subsections.

3.1. Background Subtraction. In this paper, we use Gaussian Mixture Model (GMM) as a basis to model background distribution. Formally speaking, let X_t be a pixel in the current frame I_t, where t is the frame index. Then, each pixel can be modeled separately by a mixture of K Gaussians:

$$P(X_t) = \sum_{i=1}^{K} \omega_{i,t} \eta (X_t; \mu_{i,t}, \Sigma_{i,t}), \qquad (1)$$

Where η is a Gaussian probability density function. $\mu_{i,t}$, $\Sigma_{i,t}$, and $\omega_{i,t}$ are the mean, covariance, and an estimate of the weight of the ith Gaussian in the mixture at time t, respectively. K is the number of distributions, which is set to 5 in experiments. Before the foreground is detected, the background is updated (see [14] for details about the updating procedure). After the updates are done, the weights $\omega_{i,t}$ are normalized. By applying a threshold T (set to 0.6 in our experiments), the background distribution remains on top with the lowest variance, where

$$B = \arg\min_{b} \left(\frac{\sum_{i=1}^{b} \omega_{i,t}}{\sum_{i=1}^{K} \omega_{i,t}} > T \right). \qquad (2)$$

Finally, all pixels X_t that match none of the components are good candidates to be marked as foreground. An example of GMM background subtraction can be seen in Figure 1.

3.2. Average Images from 3D Action Volumes. The 3D volume in the spatio-temporal (XYT) domain is formed by piling

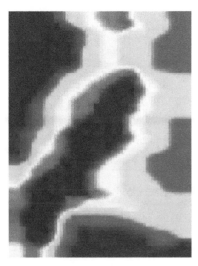

FIGURE 2: 2D average image created from the 3D spatio-temporal volume of a walking sequence.

up the target region in the image sequences of one action cycle, which is used to partition the sequences for the spatiotemporal volume. An action cycle is a fundamental unit to describe the action. In this work, we assume that the spatio-temporal volume consists of a number of small voxels. The average image $I_{av}(x, y)$ is defined as

$$I_{av}(x, y) = \frac{1}{\tau} \sum_{t=0}^{\tau-1} I(x, y, t), \qquad (3)$$

where τ is the number of frames in action cycle (we use $\tau = 25$ in our experiments). $I(x, y, t)$ represents the density of the voxels at time t. An example of average image created from the 3D spatio-temporal volume of the running sequence is shown in Figure 2. For characterizing these 2D average images, the 2D affine moment invariants are considered as features [26].

3.3. Feature Extraction. As is well known, the moments describe shape properties of an object as it appears. Affine moment invariants are moment-based descriptors, which are invariant under a general affine transform. Six affine moment invariants can be conventionally derived from the central moments [27] as follows:

$$I_1 = \frac{1}{\eta_{00}^4} \left[\eta_{20}\eta_{02} - \eta_{11}^2 \right],$$

$$I_2 = \frac{1}{\eta_{00}^{10}} \left[\eta_{03}^2\eta_{30}^2 - 6\eta_{30}\eta_{21}\eta_{12}\eta_{03} + 4\eta_{30}\eta_{12}^3 \right.$$
$$\left. + 4\eta_{03}\eta_{21}^3 - 3\eta_{21}^2\eta_{12}^2 \right],$$

$$I_3 = \frac{1}{\eta_{00}^7} \left[\eta_{20} \left(\eta_{21}\eta_{03} - \eta_{12}^2 \right) - \eta_{11} \left(\eta_{30}\eta_{03} - \eta_{21}\eta_{12} \right) \right.$$
$$\left. + \eta_{02} \left(\eta_{03}\eta_{12} - \eta_{21}^2 \right) \right],$$

$$I_4 = \frac{1}{\eta_{00}^{11}} \left[\eta_{20}^3\eta_{03}^2 - 6\eta_{20}^2\eta_{11}\eta_{12}\eta_{03} - 6\eta_{20}^2\eta_{02}\eta_{21}\eta_{03} \right.$$
$$+ 9\eta_{20}^2\eta_{02}\eta_{12}^2 + 12\eta_{20}\eta_{11}^2\eta_{21}\eta_{03}$$
$$+ 6\eta_{20}\eta_{11}\eta_{02}\eta_{30}\eta_{03} + 18\eta_{20}\eta_{11}\eta_{02}\eta_{30}\eta_{12}$$
$$- 8\eta_{11}^3\eta_{30}\eta_{03} - 6\eta_{20}\eta_{02}^2\eta_{30}\eta_{12} + 9\eta_{20}\eta_{02}^2\eta_{21}^2$$
$$\left. + 12\eta_{11}^2\eta_{02}\eta_{30}\eta_{12} - 6\eta_{11}\eta_{02}^2\eta_{30}\eta_{12} + \eta_{02}^3\eta_{30}^3 \right],$$

$$I_5 = \frac{1}{\eta_{00}^6} \left[\eta_{40}\eta_{04} - 4\eta_{31}\eta_{13} + 3\eta_{22}^2 \right],$$

$$I_6 = \frac{1}{\eta_{00}^9} \left[\eta_{40}\eta_{04}\eta_{22} + 2\eta_{31}\eta_{13}\eta_{22} - \eta_{40}\eta_{13}^2 \right.$$
$$\left. - \eta_{04}\eta_{13}^2 - \eta_{22}^3 \right],$$

$$(4)$$

where η_{pq} is the central moment of order $p + q$.

For a spatio-temporal (XYT) space, the 3D moment of order ($p + q + r$) of 3D object $\mathcal{O}$ is derived using the same procedure of the 2D centralized moment:

$$\eta_{pqr} = \sum_{(x,y,t) \in \mathcal{O}} \left(x - x_g \right)^p \left(y - y_g \right)^q \left(t - t_g \right)^r I(x, y, t),$$

$$(5)$$

Where (x_g, y_g, t_g) is the centroid of object in the spatio-temporal space. Based on the definition of the 3D moment in (5), six 3D affine moment invariants can be defined. The first two of these moment invariants are given by

$$J_1 = \frac{1}{\eta_{000}^5} \left[\eta_{200}\eta_{020}\eta_{002} + 2\eta_{110}\eta_{101}\eta_{011} - \eta_{200}\eta_{011}^2 \right.$$
$$\left. - \eta_{020}\eta_{101}^2 - \eta_{002}\eta_{110}^2 \right],$$

$$J_2 = \frac{1}{\eta_{000}^7} \left[\eta_{400} \left(\eta_{040}\eta_{004} + 3\eta_{022}^2 - 4\eta_{013}\eta_{031} \right) \right.$$
$$+ 3\eta_{202} \left(\eta_{040}\eta_{202} - 4\eta_{112}\eta_{130} + 4\eta_{121}^2 \right)$$
$$+ 12\eta_{211} \left(\eta_{022}\eta_{211} + \eta_{103}\eta_{130} - \eta_{031}\eta_{202} \right.$$
$$\left. - \eta_{121}\eta_{112} \right)$$
$$+ 4\eta_{310} \left(\eta_{031}\eta_{103} - \eta_{004}\eta_{220} \right.$$
$$\left. + 3\eta_{013}\eta_{121} - 3\eta_{022}\eta_{112} \right)$$
$$+ 3\eta_{220} \left(\eta_{004}\eta_{220} + 2\eta_{022}\eta_{202} \right.$$
$$\left. + 4\eta_{112} - 4\eta_{013}\eta_{311} - 4\eta_{121}\eta_{103} \right)$$
$$+ 4\eta_{301} \left(\eta_{013}\eta_{130} - \eta_{040}\eta_{103} + 3\eta_{031}\eta_{112} \right.$$
$$\left. - 3\eta_{022}\eta_{121} \right) \right].$$

$$(6)$$

Due to their long formulae, the remaining four moment invariants are not displayed here (refer to [28]). Figure 3

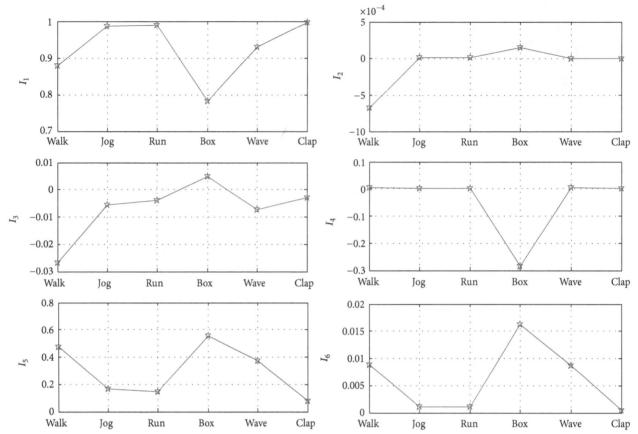

FIGURE 3: Plots of 2D affine moment invariants (I_i, $i = 1, \ldots, 6$) computed on the average images of walking, jogging, running, boxing, waving, and clapping sequences.

shows a series of plots of 2D dynamic affine invariants with different action classes computed on the average images of action sequences.

3.4. Action Classification Using SVM.

In this section, we formulate the action recognition task as a multiclass learning problem, where there is one class for each action, and the goal is to assign an action to an individual in each video sequence [1, 29]. There are various supervised learning algorithms by which action recognizer can be trained. Support Vector Machines (SVMs) are used in this work due to their outstanding generalization capability and reputation of a highly accurate paradigm [30]. SVMs that provide a best solution to data overfitting in neural networks are based on the structural risk minimization principle from computational theory. Originally, SVMs were designed to handle dichotomic classes in a higher dimensional space where a maximal separating hyperplane is created. On each side of this hyperplane, two parallel hyperplanes are conducted. Then, SVM attempts to find the separating hyperplane that maximizes the distance between the two parallel hyperplanes (see Figure 4). Intuitively, a good separation is achieved by the hyperplane having the largest distance. Hence, the larger the margin, the lower the generalization error of the classifier. Formally, let $\mathscr{D} = \{(\mathbf{x}_i, y_i) \mid \mathbf{x}_i \in \mathbb{R}^d, y_i \in \{-1, +1\}\}$ be a training dataset; Vapnik [30] shows that the problem is best

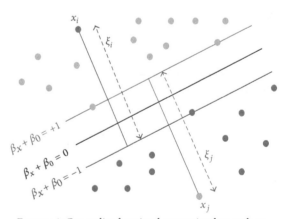

FIGURE 4: Generalized optimal separating hyperplane.

addressed by allowing some examples to violate the margin constraints. These potential violations are formulated with some positive slack variables ξ_i and a penalty parameter $C \geq 0$ that penalize the margin violations. Thus, the generalized optimal separating hyperplane is determined by solving the following quadratic programming problem:

$$\min_{\boldsymbol{\beta}, \beta_0} \frac{1}{2} \|\boldsymbol{\beta}\|^2 + C \sum_i \xi_i \tag{7}$$

subject to $(y_i(\langle \mathbf{x}_i, \boldsymbol{\beta} \rangle + \beta_0) \geq 1 - \xi_i \; \forall i) \wedge (\xi_i \geq 0 \; \forall i)$.

Geometrically, $\boldsymbol{\beta} \in \mathbb{R}^d$ is a vector going through the center and perpendicular to the separating hyperplane. The offset parameter β_0 is added to allow the margin to increase and not to force the hyperplane to pass through the origin that restricts the solution. For computational purposes, it is more convenient to solve SVM in its dual formulation. This can be accomplished by forming the Lagrangian and then optimizing over the Lagrange multiplier $\boldsymbol{\alpha}$. The resulting decision function has weight vector $\boldsymbol{\beta} = \sum_i \alpha_i \mathbf{x}_i y_i, 0 \le \alpha_i \le C$. The instances $\mathbf{x}_i$ with $\alpha_i > 0$ are called *support vectors*, as they uniquely define the maximum margin hyperplane.

In the current approach, several classes of actions are created. Several one-versus-all SVM classifiers are trained using affine moment features extracted from action sequences in the training dataset. For each action sequence, a set of six 2D affine moment invariants is extracted from the average image. Also, another set of six 3D affine moment invariants is extracted from the spatio-temporal silhouette sequence. Then, SVM classifiers are trained on these features to learn various categories of actions.

4. Experiments and Results

To evaluate the proposed approach, two main experiments were carried out, and the results we achieved were compared with those reported by other state-of-the-art methods.

4.1. Experiment 1. We conducted this experiment using KTH action dataset [31]. To illustrate the effectiveness of the method, the obtained results are compared with those of other similar state-of-the-art methods. The KTH dataset contains action sequences, comprised of six types of human actions (i.e., walking, jogging, running, boxing, hand waving, and hand clapping). These actions are performed by a total of 25 individuals in four different settings (i.e., outdoors, outdoors with scale variation, outdoors with different clothes, and indoors). All sequences were acquired by a static camera at 25 fps and a spatial resolution of 160×120 pixels over homogeneous backgrounds. To the best of our knowledge, there is no other similar dataset already available in the literature of sequences acquired on different environments. In order to prepare the experiments and to provide an unbiased estimation of the generalization abilities of the classification process, a set of sequences (75% of all sequences) performed by 18 subjects was used for training, and other sequences (the remaining 25%) performed by the other 7 subjects were set aside as a test set. SVMs with Gaussian radial basis function (RBF) kernel are trained on the training set, while the evaluation of the recognition performance is performed on the test set.

The confusion matrix that shows the recognition results achieved on the KTH action dataset is given in Table 1, while the comparison of the obtained results with those obtained by other methods available in the literature is shown in Table 3. As follows from the figures tabulated in Table 1, most actions are correctly classified. Furthermore, there is a high distinction between arm actions and leg actions. Most of the mistakes where confusions occur are between "jogging" and "running" actions and between "boxing" and

TABLE 1: Confusion matrix for the KTH dataset.

Action	Walking	Running	Jogging	Boxing	Waving	Clapping
Walking	0.94	0.01	0.05	0.00	0.00	0.00
Running	0.00	0.96	0.04	0.00	0.00	0.00
Jogging	0.04	0.08	0.88	0.00	0.00	0.00
Boxing	0.00	0.00	0.00	0.94	0.02	0.04
Waving	0.00	0.00	0.00	0.02	0.93	0.05
Clapping	0.00	0.00	0.00	0.01	0.03	0.96

"clapping" actions. This is intuitively plausible due to the fact of high similarity between each pair of these actions. From the comparison given by Table 3, it turns out that our method performs competitively with other state-of-the-art methods. It is pertinent to mention here that the state-of-the-art methods with which we compare our method have used the same dataset and the same experimental conditions; therefore, the comparison seems to be quite fair.

4.2. Experiment 2. This second experiment was conducted using the Weizmann action dataset provided by Blank et al. [32] in 2005, which contains a total of 90 video clips (i.e., 5098 frames) performed by 9 individuals. Each video clip contains one person performing an action. There are 10 categories of action involved in the dataset, namely, *walking, running, jumping, jumping in place, bending, jacking, skipping, galloping sideways, one-hand waving,* and *two-hand waving.* Typically, all the clips in the dataset are sampled at 25 Hz and last about 2 seconds with image frame size of 180×144. In order to provide an unbiased estimate of the generalization abilities of the proposed method, we have used the leave-one-out cross-validation (LOOCV) technique in the validation process. As the name suggests, this involves using a group of sequences from a single subject in the original dataset as the testing data and the remaining sequences as the training data. This is repeated such that each group of sequences in the dataset is used once as the validation. Again, as with the first experiment, SVMs with Gaussian RBF kernel are trained on the training set, while the evaluation of the recognition performance is performed on the test set.

The confusion matrix in Table 2 provides the recognition results obtained by the proposed method, where correct responses define the main diagonal. From the figures in the matrix, a number of points can be drawn. The majority of actions are correctly classified. An average recognition rate of 97.8% is achieved with our proposed method. What is more, there is a clear distinction between arm actions and leg actions. The mistakes where confusions occur are only between *skip* and *jump* actions and between *jump* and *run* actions. This intuitively seems to be reasonable due to the fact of high closeness or similarity among the actions in each pair of these actions. In order to quantify the effectiveness of the method, the obtained results are compared qualitatively with those obtained previously by other investigators. The outcome of this comparison is presented in Table 3. In the light of this comparison, one can see that the proposed method is competitive with the state-of-the-art methods.

TABLE 2: Confusion matrix for the Weizmann dataset.

Action	Bend	Jump	Pjump	Walk	Run	Side	Jack	Skip	Wave 1	Wave 2
Bend	1.00	0.00	0.00	0.00	0.00	0.00	0.00	0.00	0.00	0.00
Jump	0.00	1.00	0.00	0.00	0.00	0.00	0.00	0.00	0.00	0.00
Pjump	0.00	0.00	1.00	0.00	0.00	0.00	0.00	0.00	0.00	0.00
Walk	0.00	0.00	0.00	1.00	0.00	0.00	0.00	0.00	0.00	0.00
Run	0.00	0.00	0.00	0.00	0.90	0.00	0.00	0.10	0.00	0.00
Side	0.00	0.00	0.00	0.00	0.00	1.00	0.00	0.00	0.00	0.00
Jack	0.00	0.00	0.00	0.00	0.00	0.00	1.00	0.00	0.00	0.00
Skip	0.00	0.00	0.00	0.00	0.10	0.00	0.00	0.90	0.00	0.00
Wave 1	0.00	0.00	0.00	0.00	0.00	0.00	0.00	0.00	1.00	0.00
Wave 2	0.00	0.00	0.00	0.00	0.00	0.00	0.00	0.00	0.00	1.00

TABLE 3: Comparison with the state of the art on the KTH and Weizmann datasets.

Method	KTH	Weizmann
Our method	93.5%	98.0%
Liu and Shah [15]	92.8%	—
Wang and Mori [16]	92.5%	—
Jhuang et al. [17]	91.7%	—
Rodriguez et al. [9]	88.6%	—
Rapantzikos et al. [18]	88.3%	—
Dollár et al. [19]	81.2%	—
Ke et al. [20]	63.0%	—
Fathi and Mori [21]	—	100%
Bregonzio et al. [22]	—	96.6%
Zhang et al. [23]	—	92.8%
Niebles et al. [24]	—	90.0%
Dollár et al. [19]	—	85.2%
Kläser et al. [25]	—	84.3%

It is worthwhile to mention that all the methods that we compared our method with, except the method proposed in [21], have used similar experimental setups; thus, the comparison seems to be meaningful and fair. A final remark concerns the real-time performance of our approach. The proposed action recognizer runs at 18fps on average (using a 2.8 GHz Intel dual core machine with 4 GB of RAM, running 32-bit Windows 7 Professional).

5. Conclusion and Future Work

In this paper, we have introduced an approach for activity recognition based on affine moment invariants for activity representation and SVMs for feature classification. On two benchmark action datasets, the results obtained by the proposed approach were compared favorably with those published in the literature. The primary focus of our future work will be to investigate the empirical validation of the approach on more realistic datasets presenting many technical challenges in data handling, such as object articulation, occlusion, and significant background clutter.

References

[1] S. Sadek, A. Al-Hamadi, B. Michaelis, and U. Sayed, "Recognizing human actions: a fuzzy approach via chord-length shape features," *ISRN Machine Vision*, vol. 1, pp. 1–9, 2012.

[2] A. A. Efros, A. C. Berg, G. Mori, and J. Malik, "Recognizing action at a distance," in *Proceedings of the 9th IEEE International Conference on Computer Vision (ICCV '03)*, vol. 2, pp. 726–733, October 2003.

[3] S. Sadek, A. Al-Hamadi, B. Michaelis, and U. Sayed, "Towards robust human action retrieval in video," in *Proceedings of the British Machine Vision Conference (BMVC '10)*, Aberystwyth, UK, September 2010.

[4] S. Sadek, A. Al-Hamadi, B. Michaelis, and U. Sayed, "Human activity recognition: a scheme using multiple cues," in *Proceedings of the International Symposium on Visual Computing (ISVC '10)*, vol. 1, pp. 574–583, Las Vegas, Nev, USA, November 2010.

[5] S. Sadek, A. Al-Hamadi, M. Elmezain, B. Michaelis, and U. Sayed, "Human activity recognition via temporal moment invariants," in *Proceedings of the 10th IEEE International Symposium on Signal Processing and Information Technology (ISSPIT '10)*, pp. 79–84, Luxor, Egypt, December 2010.

[6] S. Sadek, A. Al-Hamadi, B. Michaelis, and U. Sayed, "An action recognition scheme using fuzzy log-polar histogram and temporal self-similarity," *EURASIP Journal on Advances in Signal Processing*, vol. 2011, Article ID 540375, 2011.

[7] R. Cutler and L. S. Davis, "Robust real-time periodic motion detection, analysis, and applications," *IEEE Transactions on*

Pattern Analysis and Machine Intelligence, vol. 22, no. 8, pp. 781–796, 2000.

[8] E. Shechtman and M. Irani, "Space-time behavior based correlation," in *Proceedings of the IEEE Computer Society Conference on Computer Vision and Pattern Recognition (CVPR '05)*, vol. 1, pp. 405–412, June 2005.

[9] M. D. Rodriguez, J. Ahmed, and M. Shah, "Action MACH: a spatio-temporal maximum average correlation height filter for action recognition," in *Proceedings of the 26th IEEE Conference on Computer Vision and Pattern Recognition (CVPR '08)*, June 2008.

[10] N. Ikizler and D. Forsyth, "Searching video for complex activities with finite state models," in *Proceedings of the IEEE Computer Society Conference on Computer Vision and Pattern Recognition (CVPR '07)*, June 2007.

[11] D. M. Blei and J. D. Lafferty, "Correlated topic models," in *Advances in Neural Information Processing Systems (NIPS)*, vol. 18, pp. 147–154, 2006.

[12] D. M. Blei, A. Y. Ng, and M. I. Jordan, "Latent Dirichlet allocation," *Journal of Machine Learning Research*, vol. 3, no. 4-5, pp. 993–1022, 2003.

[13] T. Hofmann, "Probabilistic latent semantic indexing," in *Proceedings of the 22nd Annual International ACM SIGIR Conference on Research and Development in Information Retrieval (SIGIR '99)*, pp. 50–57, 1999.

[14] S. J. McKenna, Y. Raja, and S. Gong, "Tracking colour objects using adaptive mixture models," *Image and Vision Computing*, vol. 17, no. 3-4, pp. 225–231, 1999.

[15] J. Liu and M. Shah, "Learning human actions via information maximization," in *Proceedings of the 26th IEEE Conference on Computer Vision and Pattern Recognition (CVPR '08)*, June 2008.

[16] Y. Wang and G. Mori, "Max-Margin hidden conditional random fields for human action recognition," in *Proceedings of the IEEE Computer Society Conference on Computer Vision and Pattern Recognition Workshops (CVPR '09)*, pp. 872–879, June 2009.

[17] H. Jhuang, T. Serre, L. Wolf, and T. Poggio, "A biologically inspired system for action recognition," in *Proceedings of the 11th IEEE International Conference on Computer Vision (ICCV '07)*, pp. 257–267, October 2007.

[18] K. Rapantzikos, Y. Avrithis, and S. Kollias, "Dense saliency-based spatiotemporal feature points for action recognition," in *Proceedings of the IEEE Computer Society Conference on Computer Vision and Pattern Recognition Workshops (CVPR '09)*, pp. 1454–1461, June 2009.

[19] P. Dollár, V. Rabaud, G. Cottrell, and S. Belongie, "Behavior recognition via sparse spatio-temporal features," in *Proceedings of the 2nd Joint IEEE International Workshop on Visual Surveillance and Performance Evaluation of Tracking and Surveillance (VS-PETS '05)*, pp. 65–72, October 2005.

[20] Y. Ke, R. Sukthankar, and M. Hebert, "Efficient visual event detection using volumetric features," in *Proceedings of the 10th IEEE International Conference on Computer Vision (ICCV '05)*, pp. 166–173, October 2005.

[21] A. Fathi and G. Mori, "Action recognition by learning mid-level motion features," in *Proceedings of the 26th IEEE Conference on Computer Vision and Pattern Recognition (CVPR '08)*, June 2008.

[22] M. Bregonzio, S. Gong, and T. Xiang, "Recognising action as clouds of space-time interest points," in *Proceedings of the IEEE Computer Society Conference on Computer Vision and Pattern Recognition Workshops (CVPR '09)*, pp. 1948–1955, June 2009.

[23] Z. Zhang, Y. Hu, S. Chan, and L.-T. Chia, "Motion context: a new representation for human action recognition," in *Proceeding of the European Conference on Computer Vision (ECCV '08)*, vol. 4, pp. 817–829, 2008.

[24] J. C. Niebles, H. Wang, and L. Fei-Fei, "Unsupervised learning of human action categories using spatial-temporal words," *International Journal of Computer Vision*, vol. 79, no. 3, pp. 299–318, 2008.

[25] A. Kläser, M. Marszaek, and C. Schmid, "A spatiotemporal descriptor based on 3D-gradients," in *Proceedings of the British Machine Vision Conference (BMVC '08)*, 2008.

[26] S. Sadek, A. Al-Hamadi, B. Michaelis, and U. Sayed, "Human action recognition via affine moment invariants," in *Proceedings of the 21st International Conference on Pattern Recognition (ICPR '12)*, pp. 218–221, Tsukuba Science City, Japan, November 2012.

[27] J. Flusser and T. Suk, "Pattern recognition by affine moment invariants," *Pattern Recognition*, vol. 26, no. 1, pp. 167–174, 1993.

[28] D. Xu and H. Li, "3-D affine moment invariants generated by geometric primitives," in *Proceedings of the 18th International Conference on Pattern Recognition (ICPR '06)*, pp. 544–547, August 2006.

[29] S. Sadek, A. Al-Hamadi, B. Michaelis, and U. Sayed, "An SVM approach for activity recognition based on chord-length-function shape features," in *Proceedings of the IEEE International Conference on Image Processing (ICIP '12)*, pp. 767–770, Orlando, Fla, USA, October 2012.

[30] V. N. Vapnik, *The Nature of Statistical Learning Theory*, Springer, New York, NY, USA, 1995.

[31] C. Schüldt, I. Laptev, and B. Caputo, "Recognizing human actions: a local SVM approach," in *Proceedings of the 17th International Conference on Pattern Recognition (ICPR '04)*, pp. 32–36, 2004.

[32] M. Blank, L. Gorelick, E. Shechtman, M. Irani, and R. Basri, "Actions as space-time shapes," in *Proceedings of the 10th IEEE International Conference on Computer Vision (ICCV '05)*, vol. 2, pp. 1395–1402, October 2005.

5

LoCoBoard: Low-Cost Interactive Whiteboard Using Computer Vision Algorithms

Christophe Soares,[1,2] **Rui S. Moreira,**[1,2] **José M. Torres,**[1] **and Pedro Sobral**[1]

[1] *ISUS Group, FCT, University Fernando Pessoa, Porto, Portugal*
[2] *INESC TEC, FEUP, University of Porto, Porto, Portugal*

Correspondence should be addressed to Christophe Soares; csoares@ufp.edu.pt

Academic Editors: M. A. Rahman and T. Zhang

In the current digital age, the adoption of natural interfaces between humans and machines is increasingly important. This trend is particularly significant in the education sector where interactive tools and applications can ease the presentation and comprehension of complex concepts, stimulate collaborative work, and improve teaching practices. An important step towards this vision, interactive whiteboards are gaining widespread adoption in various levels of education. Nevertheless, these solutions are usually expensive, making their acceptance slow, especially in countries with more fragile economies. In this context, we present the low-cost interactive whiteboard (LoCoBoard) project, an open-source interactive whiteboard with low-cost hardware requirements, usually accessible in our daily lives, for an easy installation: a webcam-equipped computer, a video projector, and an infrared pointing device. The detection software framework offers five different Pointer Location algorithms with support for the Tangible User Interface Object protocol and also adapts to support multiple operating systems. We discuss the detailed physical and logical structure of LoCoBoard and compare its performance with that of similar systems. We believe that the proposed solution may represent a valuable contribution to ease the access to interactive whiteboards and increase widespread use with obvious benefits.

1. Introduction

Over the past decades, the computing power evolution has been remarkable, but human computer interaction (HCI) is still being realized, in most cases, through the traditional keyboard and mouse. The future of HCI should rely more on the use of natural interfaces, such as haptic, speech, and gestures. In particular, the use of natural interfaces through Interactive Whiteboards (IWs) in education environments can ease the presentation and comprehension of complex concepts, allow collaborative work between teachers and students and improve pedagogical practices. Although there are wide ranges of commercial IW solutions, they are generally expensive and difficult to afford and implement by a large number of education institutions.

The main goal of this project consists in developing an open source software-based IW solution, based on usually accessible hardware in our daily lives, that is, a video projector, a laptop with a webcam, and an Infra-Red (IR)

pointing device. The LoCoBoard [1] prototype uses computer vision algorithms for processing captured images through the webcam and interpret the user interactions. Each developed algorithm tries to isolate sets of pixels with common characteristics (cf. binary large objects-blob) from each image and is tested in its performance, accuracy, and CPU load. The application is proactive, adapting itself to the environment light conditions (cf. Background Subtraction techniques [2]). Coordinates of detected user interaction points are then used to control the cursor/interaction on the computer or distributed to other applications, through Tangible User Interface Objects (TUIO) protocol [3]. The developed prototype reveals that with this software running on a common computer, it is possible to obtain a generic, low-cost, easy to install, and useful IW system for any classroom.

The rest of the paper is organized as follows. In Section 2, we briefly discuss the current state, mostly open-source, for interactive surfaces in general and interactive whiteboards in particular. In Section 3, we present the physical and logical structure of the LoCoBoard system. Section 4 is devoted to presenting the quantitative and qualitative evaluation carried out. We introduce a comparative evaluation between the five Pointer Location (PL) detection algorithms implemented within the LoCoBoard system and also a comparison with other available systems. We conclude the paper in Section 5.

2. State of the Art

In the last years, there has been quite active research in developing solutions for interactive surfaces, in general, ranging from small sized displays to large interactive whiteboards [4]. The LoCoBoard system, described in this paper, has been conceived, in first hand, for working as an interactive whiteboard system, targeted to be used with existing whiteboard surfaces, universally present in class and meeting rooms, although it can easily be adapted to setup an interactive table using multitouch gestures (cf. Algorithm A5, see Algorithm 6).

Interactive whiteboards can be a valuable aid in the process of teaching although some problems may arise when teachers fail to appreciate that interactivity requires a new approach to pedagogy [5]. Also, the use of pen and touch, in interactive whiteboards, for tasks such as data exploration or others, constitutes a challenge for rethinking conventional application solutions [6]. Nevertheless, one of the major problems of typical commercially available whiteboards solutions continues to be their excessive prices, avoiding the proliferation of this valuable educative tool as a way to enhance educative practices.

As mentioned in [7], there are five main techniques, being refined by the open community research efforts that allow for the creation of a stable multitouch hardware systems: frustrated total internal reflection (FTIR); rear diffused illumination (Rear DI); laser light plane (LLP); diffused surface illumination (DSI); and LED light plane (LED-LP). All these five key techniques work in conjunction with image sensing devices (e.g., cameras) and presume the use of computer vision techniques to process the image signal produced. Besides those techniques, there are other sensing hardware devices frequently used, based on sensors such as the resistive, capacitive, motion, and others, or a combination of more than one of the listed. Several solutions are presented in literature, demonstrating the application of these types of technology [8]. In general, multitouch technologies, using more or less complex hardware setups, have been in use for some time, triggering a challenge for user interfaces designers [9].

Two significant requirements that guide the development of the LoCoBoard system were: (i) the system should be simple to setup and (ii) it should be low cost. This leaded to the decision of using a hardware setup based solely in a camera and an infrared pen, besides the computer and projector.

Other touch systems based on overhead cameras are also presented in the literature. The PlayAnywhere system [10] considers the camera and projector sitting off to the side of the active surface. The solution proposed in [11] uses a pair of cameras mounted above the surface.

Some other popular interactive whiteboard systems based on the Nintendo Wii remote command, the wiimote, are the ones presented by Lee [12] and Schmidt [13]. Both systems provide software libraries to implement the interactive whiteboard. The wiimote also has inspired several works in the interaction area using diverse types of sensing technology, such as accelerometers [14].

All the presented systems based on image sensing (i.e., video cameras), with or without extra sensor devices, need software libraries to process the video input signal and transform it into pointing devices locations and/or commands to be passed to a client application. Among the most used software libraries are Touchlib [15] and Community Core Vision (CCV aka tbeta) [16] from the NUI Group and the reacTIVision framework [17].

Those pointing device commands can be sent by the tracker application to the client application using appropriate protocols. The protocol TUIO [3], based on Open Sound Control (OSC) interface [18], is a popular open framework that defines a common protocol and APL for tangible multitouch surfaces. Using the TUIO, the client application, for instance, an application written in ActionScript 3 language and Adobe Flash, can reside in the same computer or a different computer of the tracker application, for instance, the LoCoBoard system.

3. LoCoBoard System

3.1. Overview. The LoCoBoard system overview is presented in Figure 1. We can see a computer running the LoCoBoard software, a camera which allows us to sense/capture the interactions on the projected image, an infra-red (IR) pointing device to generate the interaction, and a video projector to output the computer application image over the whiteboard. The pointing device, presented in Figure 2, was built using an IR led installed on top of a traditional whiteboard pen. Switching on and off the IR led in the pen, allows the user to interact directly with the computer through the whiteboard surface. The supported kinds of interactions are click and drag, single and double mouse click. The camera is equipped, with an IR band-pass filter, to discard unwanted light wavelengths from the captured images, easing the real-time detection of the IR pointing device. A photographic film can be used as a straightforward IR band-pass filter. Since all the hardware is widely available and is much cheaper than traditional interactive whiteboards, this project could be easily replicated in many education institutions.

Figure 3 presents the software architecture of the LoCoBoard system. On top of the already described hardware layer, we have the computer operating system. The LoCoBoard system was designed to support the most widely used operating systems, that is, Microsoft Windows, Linux, and Mac OS X. Regarding the libraries, OpenCV computer vision framework [19] is used to manage image acquisition and to preprocess those images. Although in the current version OpenCV offers some blob detection capabilities, they are not used in this system. We have developed, implemented, and tested our own blob detection algorithms in

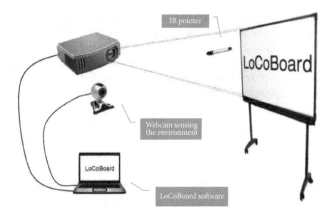

FIGURE 1: Overview of the LoCoBoard system.

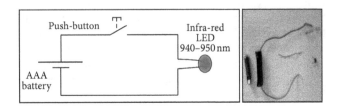

FIGURE 2: Components of the Infrared Pointer device.

LoCoBoard. The Oscpack framework [20] provides interoperability between LoCoBoard and any TUIO [3] compliant client application. The TUIO protocol is also used in applications like the Touchlib or CCV [16]. A detailed description of the four LoCoBoard building blocks is presented in Section 3.2.

The system operation starts with a calibration process to map the projected image area in the whiteboard as seen by the video camera (cf. geometrical transformation), back into the original computer coordinate space (cf. monitor resolution). This task is essential to enable a real-time and robust process of Pointer Location detection using the computer coordinates. After the calibration phase, the LoCoBoard system starts interpreting the camera output identifying the mouse interaction through the displacement of the IR Pointer over the projected image. We also report in real-time the coordinates of the detected IR dots (one or two PL) using the TUIO protocol [3] and enabling the support for existing multitouch applications based on this protocol.

3.2. Implementing LoCoBoard. The LoCoBoard's block diagram, presented in Figure 3, reveals the core of the application. The image acquisition and preprocessing phase is responsible to grab and filter the images captured by the camera. Using OpenCV, we improve image quality and ease the IR Blob recognition. In the Pointer Location (PL) detection phase, we apply our developed algorithms to detect and track IR Blobs. Finally, the last component reports the interaction coordinates using TUIO protocol and updates the cursor position.

3.2.1. Image Acquisition and Preprocessing. The image acquisition block maps the computer resolution on the projection image captured through the camera using the OpenCV framework transformation matrix. We apply filters, in each image, to remove eventual interferences and noises induced by other light sources. There are often other IR emitters in the environment, which may interfere with the IR pointing device (e.g., lamps, sunlight, etc.). Hence, to improve system accuracy, we use a physical (e.g., photo film) and logical IR band-pass filter (e.g., proactive background subtraction model). We use a foreground and background extraction model to identify and remove unwanted IR interferences from the image. The background filtering algorithm dynamically adapts its model to the variations on the environment light conditions.

3.2.2. Pointer Location Detection Algorithms. The image received from the previous block is then handled by the PL detection algorithms. An image is represented by a matrix where each pixel is coded by three values corresponding to the RGB color model. This image is then converted to gray scale in order to reduce the pixel state space. This transformation is useful in real time systems, where the color is not relevant since image processing can be more efficient and decrease the amount of time to process PL detection algorithm. PL coordinates are then searched on a gray scale image. For each PL found by the system, we return its pixel position using Cartesian coordinates. The Cartesian coordinates are reported setting the upper left corner pixel as (0, 0) and the lower right corner pixel as (width and height of the image). The system handles different image sizes depending on the camera resolution. The better the camera resolution the higher the system accuracy. However, large camera resolutions and high frame-rates substantially increase the CPU load. Image resolution and frame rate can be adjusted to allow better support on legacy computers.

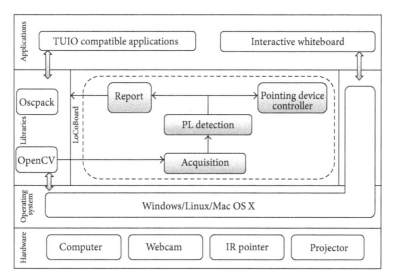

FIGURE 3: Logical architecture of LoCoBoard.

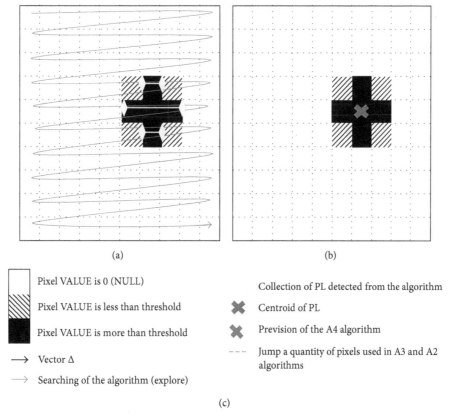

FIGURE 4: Algorithm A1 process. The first step: analyzing and collecting Pointers Location over the threshold (a), the second step: identifying the centroid (b), and terminology used in the algorithms representation (c).

In the following two subsections, we describe the PL detection algorithms. Figure 4(c) shows the common visual symbology used in the algorithms descriptions.

Single Pointer Location (Algorithms A1, A2, A3, and A4). (See Algorithms 1, 2, 3, and 5).

(1) A1: this algorithm performs a scan on the image pixel by pixel as illustrated in Figure 4 and Algorithm 1, to find a pixel with a luminance value exceeding a threshold set by the program during the calibration phase. This algorithm collects the coordinates of all points that have a value above the threshold and returns the average of the values in a row and column axis.

(2) A2: the traditional linear search algorithm (cf. A1) is modified using a step value S to speed up the search phase and returns when a pixel value grater than the threshold is found.

```
function ALGORITHM (image_height, image_width, image, threshold) return coordinates of the PL
centroid
inputs:        image_height, height of the image
               image_width, width of the image
               image, captured grayscale image
               threshold, lower limit of brightness to identify pixels belonging to PL blob
size ← 0
colValue ← 0
rowValue ← 0
row ← 0
    while row < image_height do
       column ← 0
       while column < image_width do
          if image[row][column] ≥ threshold then
             colValue ← colValue + column
             rowValue ← rowValue + row
             size ← size + 1
          column ← column + 1
       row ← row + 1
colValue ← colValue/size
rowValue ← rowValue/size
return (rowValue, colValue)
```

ALGORITHM 1: Pseudo code Algorithm A1.

```
function ALGORITHM (image_height, image_width, image, threshold, step) return coordinates of the PL centroid
inputs:        image_height, height of the image
               image_width, width of the image
               image, captured grayscale image
               threshold, lower limit of brightness to identify pixels belonging to PL blob
               step, interval between consecutive processed pixels per row during search
size ← 0
colValue ← 0
rowValue ← 0
index ← 0
    while index < image_height * image_width do
       row ← index/image_width
       column ← index % image_width
       if image[row][column] ≥ threshold then
          colValue ← colValue + column
          rowValue ← rowValue + row
          size ← size + 1
       index ← index + step
colValue ← colValue/size
rowValue ← rowValue/size
return (rowValue, colValue)
```

ALGORITHM 2: Pseudo code Algorithm A2.

The best results are obtained when S is lower than half the size of the PL. With S greater than the PL size (overfitting), we may never find the PL on the image.

Thus, between two pixels readings, the algorithm ignores $S-1$ pixels (see Figure 5 and Algorithm 2). The process to calculate the coordinates of PL is the same as in the previous algorithm (cf. A1). This algorithm provides accurate results on the centroid PL estimation, when S is small. However, the larger the S value the faster will be the image processing.

(3) A3: this algorithm focuses on reducing processing costs per image when a PL is present, but it is not in the right lower corner of the image. We use a linear search as described for Algorithm A2 (see Figure 6 and Algorithm 3). Unlike the previous algorithm (cf. A2), A3 stops the linear search as soon as it finds the first suitable pixel. After identifying this pixel in the image, another algorithm is applied, in this area, to determine the center coordinates of the PL (see Figure 6(b)). This algorithm searches in four directions

```
function ALGORITHM (image_height, image_width, image, threshold, step) return coordinates of PL centroid, or
failure
inputs:        image_height, height of the image
               image_width, width of the image
               image, captured grayscale image
               threshold, lower limit of brightness to identify pixels belonging to PL blob
               step, interval between consecutive processed pixels per row during search
size ← 0
index ← 0
   while index < image_height ⋆ image_width do
      row ← index/image_width
      column ← index % image_width
      if image [row ][column ] ≥ threshold  then
         (centroid.row, centroid.col ← FINDCENTER(image_height, image_width, image, threshold, row, column)
         return (centroid.row, centroid.col)
      index ← index + step
   return failure/⋆ didn't found any center ⋆/
```

ALGORITHM 3: Pseudo code Algorithm A3.

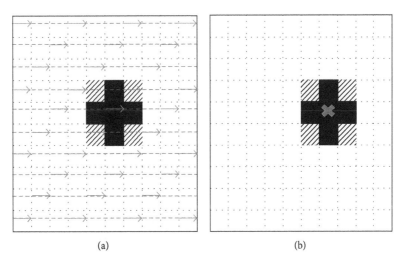

(a)   (b)

FIGURE 5: Algorithm A2 process. The first step: analyzing and collecting Points Location over the threshold (a) and the second step: identifying the centroid (b).

starting from the over the threshold pixel previous found. We search horizontally (west and east) to detect the maximum and minimum values on the row-axis and vertically (north and south) to detect the maximum and minimum values on the column-axis. These two sets of values ({min row-axis, max row-axis}; {min column-axis, max column-axis}) correspond to the prediction center for the PL (see Figure 6(b)).

(4) A4: A4 Algorithm uses a different approach since its focus is on tracking PL over consecutive images. Hence, it should present better results, that is, less processing cost and time elapsed to detect PL, when a previous detected PL moves on consecutive images (e.g., dragging the pointing device). The algorithm uses a vector to store information about the PL displacement, that is, the difference of PL positions between two consecutive images. Consider three consecutive images: F_1, F_2, and F_3. All respectively contain a PL in movement/displacement, which has the respective coordinates, $P_1 = (x_1, y_1)$, $P_2 = (x_2, y_2)$, and $P_3 = (x_3, y_3)$.

The value of the PL displacement vector, between F_1 and F_2, Δs is calculated as follows:

$$\Delta s = (\Delta x, \Delta y) = (x_2 - x_1, y_2 - y_1). \tag{1}$$

The algorithm uses Δs to predict the future position of P_3 and then execute from this prediction a spiral search to find the real coordinates of PL in F_3 (see Figure 7(a)). This approach assumes that the displacement is similar between consecutive images unless the IR pen stops abruptly. The estimation of P_3 coordinates in F_3 is calculated through the formula:

$$\widehat{P}_3 = P_2 + \Delta s = (x_2 + \Delta x, y_2 + \Delta y). \tag{2}$$

The algorithm uses the estimation of P_3 as a starting point to initiate the spiral search. On average, this algorithm provides better results when compared with searching PL from the origin. A traditional spiral search can be time consuming due to nonlinear memory accesses. Hence, we use a lookup

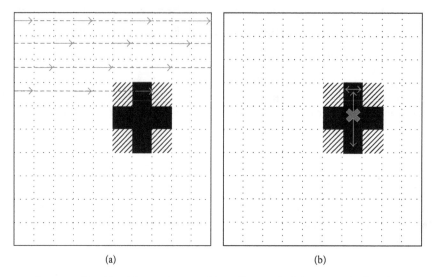

FIGURE 6: The Algorithm A3 Process (a) and how to find the centroid of PL (b).

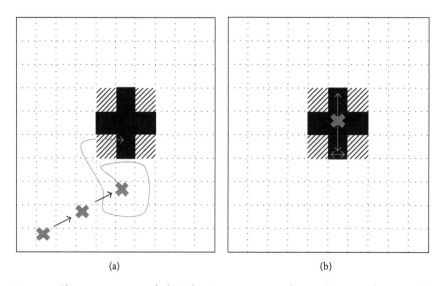

FIGURE 7: The representation of Algorithm A4 process—prediction (a) centroid process (b).

table with the distance related to row-axis and column-axis, which by addition would apply the movement of a spiral as can be seen in Figure 7(a). Spiral search algorithm can be inefficient, when compared to linear search methods, when a PL suddenly moves to an unpredicted position or disappears from the image. The spiral search repeatedly performs jumps between different memory areas while the linear search processes consecutive storage positions. Therefore, when the algorithm reaches the maximum spiral size N and fails, a linear search strategy is applied. After the search phase, the coordinates for the PL centroid are obtained as previously described (see Figure 7(b)).

Multiple Pointers Location (Algorithm A5). The multipoint algorithm uses an ordinary linear search and recursively collects and labels the foreground pixels information for all existing PLs in the image (see in Figure 8(a)). For each of those groups, the centroid coordinates are determined as illustrated in Figure 8(b). Although this algorithm can detect

a large number of PLs, we only track up to two simultaneous PLs in the LoCoBoard system.

3.3. LoCoBoard Output. After PL detection algorithm, we need to report the centroid coordinates using the TUIO protocol to enable user interaction or directly control the mouse/cursor on the computer. For TUIO report, the kind of action triggered depends on the client TUIO application; optionally, we could also include in the TUIO reports the intensity value and the size of the detected PL per image. For the computer, LoCoBoard [1] system handles these actions and emulates on the same equipment: click (single or double) and move/drag. We interpret that the user wants to do a double click when the IR emitter (cf. Pointer Location) remains active on the same region in consecutive images during one second (time is setup as a property and could be overwrite). In other cases, we will consider that the user emulates a single click. The drag movement is a particular

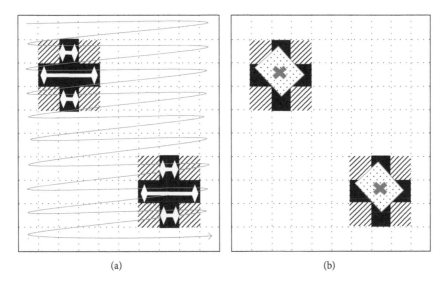

FIGURE 8: The representation of Algorithm A5 process (a), find groups and their centroid (b).

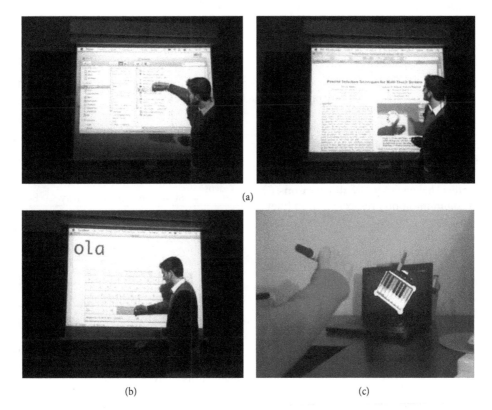

FIGURE 9: LoCoBoard project interaction with other application.

case of a single click, where we detect a click followed by a movement of the PL in consecutive images, source and destination correspond, respectively, to the coordinate first appearance and the disappearance for this PL movement.

We also need to execute a calibration between the projection and the native computer resolution. This will allow the determination of the correspondence between the PL detected coordinate on the projection and the computer's mouse.

3.3.1. Interactive Whiteboard. We tested the interaction accuracy performing the following functions operations: (i) opening files in finder/explorer, (ii) navigating to a URL using the Firefox WEB browser and a virtual keyboard to insert the characters, (iii) drawing in Paint and (iv) interacting with Google Earth. We select applications that require an intensive use of the mouse and that are better suited to use with an interactive whiteboard (e.g., Google Earth)—see Figure 9.

function FINDCENTER (*image_height, image_width, image, threshold, row, column*) **return** identifies the centroid coordinates of a PL region

inputs: *image_height*, height of the image
         image_width, width of the image
         image, captured grayscale image
         threshold, lower limit of brightness to identify pixels belonging to PL blob
         row, row coordinate of known pixel belonging to PL blob
         column, column coordinate of known pixel belonging to PL blob

minCol ← column
maxCol ← column
While *maxCol < image_width* AND image[row][*maxCol*] ≥ *threshold* **do**
      maxCol ← maxCol + 1
while *minCol ≥ 0* AND image[row][*minCol*] ≥ *threshold* **do**
      minCol ← minCol − 1
distanceCol ← maxCol − minCol
centerCol ← minCol + distanceCol/2
minRow ← row
maxRow ← row
while maxRow < *image_height* AND image[*maxRow*][*centerCol*] ≥ *threshold* **do**
      maxRow ← maxRow + 1
while minRow ≥ 0 AND image[*minRow*][*centerCol*] ≥ *threshold* **do**
      minRow ← minRow − 1
distanceRow ← maxCol − minCol
centerRow ← minCol + distanceRow/2
return (*centerRow, centerCol*)

ALGORITHM 4: Find center function.

3.3.2. TUIO Applications. These applications interact with the LoCoBoard using the TUIO protocol. The LoCoBoard system is able to report the PL locations using the same protocol. That the protocol has been used for three reasons: (i) establish a common communication protocol between interactive applications and sensing frameworks like CCV/Tbeta or Touchlib; (ii) separate the PL tracking framework development from any interactive application, and (iii) reuse a large number of already developed TUIO compatible, interactive applications. TUIO compliant applications are generally developed in flash in order to allow multiple PL interaction since current operating systems only handle one single pointing device interaction at a time. We use a demo application to manipulate some pictures and other applications, that is, Piano Player on Figure 9(c) or TUIO Pictures Gallery, use two PL allowing users to: (i) zoom, (ii) move/drag, and (iii) rotate pictures. The interpretation of the perceived coordinates depends on the TUIO compliant application (Algorithm 4).

4. Evaluation

To illustrate the PL detection approach, we first have applied it to a set of prerecorded videos which depicts a classic use case interaction scenario and we assess the performance of each PL detection algorithm. Later, we present a comparison between the LoCoBoard approach and other related systems, namely, CCV aka Tbeta. All the experiments have been conducted on the same machine: an Apple MacBook (Model

TABLE 1: Subset of videos with a description of their characteristics used for the evaluation.

Videos	Conditions	
	Simulation kind of activity	Environment condition
Video 1	Interaction clicks	Without noise
Video 2	Drag/movement	Without noise
Video 3	Mixture	Without noise
Video 4	Interaction clicks	With noise
Video 5	Drag/movement	With noise
Video 6	Mixture	With noise

4.1), 2.4 Ghz and 4 GB ram. Connectivity on the equipment has been limited to guarantee the same situation for different algorithms analysis.

4.1. Benchmark Analysis. We evaluate the different PL detection algorithms presented in Section 3.2.2 regarding its computational performance under different test conditions. Six videos were created with several interaction scenarios, and the algorithms (A1 to A5) were used for PL tracking on each of them (see Table 1). The videos include various types of interactions with the IR pointer: clicks, drags, and a mixture of both. Some videos had the presence of sources of interference in the background image (e.g., natural lamp lights, sun light, etc.). During the simulation, IR interaction clicks appear at random places in the image and drags happened through the image using random movements.

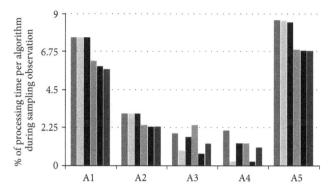

FIGURE 10: Duration of each processing run-time per algorithm per video.

TABLE 2: Error estimation of PL per algorithm.

Ground truth	Algorithms				
	A1	A2	A3	A4	A5
First PL	1	0	3	4.12	0
Second PL	1.41	1	3.16	3.16	1
Third PL	1.41	1.41	3.61	3.16	1
Fourth PL	1.41	1.41	3.61	3.16	1
Fifth PL	1.41	1.41	3.61	3.16	1

Light variations (noise) were created in the environment allowing the test of PL detection accuracy in the presence of light interference. Videos with noise are preprocessed with a background subtraction algorithm, using a proactive learning method, to remove background and identify any noise.

4.1.1. Performance. In order to measure the performance of each algorithm, we compare time profiles from each of them during execution. The figures represent that the amount of time each algorithm was executing during sampling. The parameters values used were: for A2 and A3, $S = 3$ (step value); and for the A4, $N = 5$ (maximum spiral size). We can see in Figure 10 that the most efficient algorithms were A3 and A4 (due to prediction mechanism in videos 2 and 5), followed by A2, A1, and A5, the latter being the least efficient (due to the exhaustive linear search on all the image and an estimation on possible multiple PL).

4.1.2. Accuracy. The accuracy in the detection of PL is essential. We use five images (500 × 500 pixels), each with a unique PL, where we previously known the real coordinates (i.e., ground truth). We then used the algorithms to estimate the coordinates and compare the results with the real PL coordinates. This procedure was repeated with the five algorithms, in each of the images. The results presented in Table 2 correspond to the Euclidean distance between the estimated and the actual positions of the PL. Lower Euclidean distances correspond to better algorithm accuracy. In Table 2, we can see that A2 and A5 have the best result in this test.

We also analyzed the behavior of the PL detection algorithms using six different geometric forms for the PL (see Figure 11). To quantify the accuracy, we reused Euclidean distance as previously stated. Algorithm A4 reuses a detection

FIGURE 11: Different geometric representations used to depict PL.

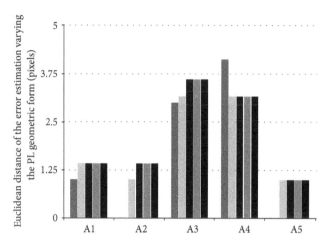

FIGURE 12: Evaluation of the accuracy of each of the algorithms in terms of the geometric forms of PL.

TABLE 3: CPU consumption comparison between the LocoBoard and the CCV (Tbeta).

CPU %	Applications system for PL detection	
	CCV (Tbeta)	LoCoBoard
Minimum	64.1%	14.0%
Maximum	73.3%	52.8%
Mean	68.3%	32.1%

algorithms (A1, A2, or A3) if the search in the predicted area of interest/region was not successful and as such was not relevant to be tested here. From our results (see Figure 12), it is clear that the geometric shape of PL affects the precision of some algorithms. In particular, the A3 offers the worst accuracy while A1 and A5 show the highest precision levels. However, all algorithms performed worse when the PL shape approximates a lozenge. Algorithm A2 maintains an almost constant error rate regardless of the PL shape.

From this experiment, we realized that certain PL shapes can provide more accurate results than others. This may be relevant in the choice for the IR light source used in the pointing device. We found that the best results were achieved when the PL shape is close to a square or circle. Also, as we were expecting, we observed that algorithms using a total linear search in the image (A1 and A5) present better results.

4.1.3. Processing/Profiling. This experiment compares the CPU load of the LoCoBoard and CCV applications for the same tasks. This comparison was made by collecting twenty samples of the CPU load per application using a profiling tool. Results for this test are presented in Table 3 where we can see that LoCoBoard induces a lower CPU load than CCV. This

TABLE 4: Qualitative comparison LocoBoard with related systems.

App./criteria	Cost	Equipment	Compatibility	Support	TUIO	Usability
LoCoBoard [1]	Low	Camera, IR-Pointer, Pass-IR filter	Windows, Mac OS X, Linux	Single*	Yes	Simple
Johnny Lee Whiteboard [12]	Moderate	Wiimote, Bluetooth adapter, IR-Pointer	Windows	Single	No	Moderate
Uweschmidt [13]	Moderate	Wiimote, Bluetooth adapter, IR-Pointer	Windows, Mac OS X, Linux	Single	Yes	Moderate
CCV/Tbeta [16]	Low	Camera, IR-Pointer, Pass-IR filter	Windows, Mac OS X, Linux	Multi	Yes	Moderate
Touchlib [15]	Low	Camera, IR-Pointer, Pass-IR filter, IDE compiler	Win	Multi	Yes	Complex

*note: multipoint is supported but was not the main focus, since operating systems are not prepared off the shelf to handle multiple source of input.

```
function ALGORITHM (image_height, image_width, image, threshold, lookup_table, est_row, est_col) return centroid
    coordinates of a PL, or failure
inputs:     image_height, height of the image
            image_width, width of the image
            image, captured grayscale image
            threshold, lower limit of brightness to identify pixels belonging to PL blob
            lookup_table, predefined spiral search path relative to estimation of PL centroid in current image
            est_row, estimated row location for PL centroid in current image
            est_col, estimated column location for PL centroid in current image

for index ← 0 to SIZE(lookup_table) do
    column ← est_col + lookup_table[index].x
    row ← est_row + lookup_table[index].y
    if image[row][column] ≥ threshold then
        (centroid.row, centroid.col) ← FINDCENTER(image_height, image_width, image, threshold, row, column)
        return (centroid.row, centroid.col )
return failure/*didn't found any center—will use another search algorithm for the rest of the image*/
```

ALGORITHM 5: Pseudo code Algorithm A4.

is perhaps due to the fine tuned PL detection algorithms we use while the CCV uses generic functions implemented in the OpenCV library.

4.2. Comparison with Other Systems. This section presents a qualitative evaluation of LoCoBoard [1] prototype with related systems, using the following criteria.

(1) Cost: this is defined through a three levels scale: Low (contemplating systems that cost less than thirty euro), Average (for costs less than fifty euro), and High (corresponding to all others). The cost does not include computer and projector values.

(2) Equipment: this serves to list the material required to mount an interactive whiteboard, again, without considering the computer and projector.

(3) Compatibility: this property relates to the supported platforms (e.g., Mac, Linux, or Windows).

(4) Multiple PL support: states if the system is able or unable to support multiple pointers location.

(5) TUIO [20]: defines if the application provides support for the TUIO protocol.

(6) Ease of setup: here we access the complexity to deploy the system. We use a three level scale: Simple (reproduce the deployment is less than four steps), Moderate (less than six steps) and Complex (all the others).

The qualitative evaluation results are summarized in Table 4 [1]. Besides the fact that LoCoBoard is a low-cost and multiplatform system, one can observe that an important additional attribute is the fact that it represents a turnkey system for someone searching a ready to use interactive whiteboard solution to implement.

5. Conclusions and Future Work

The work described in this paper consisted in the designing of a simple, economic, easy to setup, user friendly and effective solution for an interactive whiteboard. LoCoBoard is an open-source project shared with the community and offers an alternative to the already existing platforms of PL detection (cf. Touchlib and CCV).

```
function ALGORITHM (image_height, image_width, image, threshold) return centroids' coordinates of each
identified PL
inputs:    image_height, height of the image
           image_width, width of the image
           image, captured grayscale image
           threshold, lower limit of brightness to identify pixels belonging to PL blob
/* recursive function to compute the connected components of a binary image */
LB ← (−1)*threshold(image, threshold)
label ← 0
for L ← 0 to image_height
    for P ← 0 to image_width
        if LB[L,P] = −1 then
            label ← label + 1
            SEARCH(LB, label, L, P)
            /* FINDCENTROID function returns centroid of just labeled region */
            (centroids.row[label], centroids.col[label]) ← FINDCENTROID(LB, L, P, label)
return (centroids.row, centroids.col)

function SEARCH(LB, label, L, P)
    LB[L,P] ← label
    Nset ← NEIGHBORS(L,P)
    for each [L', P'] in Nset
        if LB [L', P'] = −1 then
            SEARCH(LB, label, L', P')
```

ALGORITHM 6: Pseudo code Algorithm A5 adapted from [21, page 57].

We have conducted several experiments to assess the functionality and efficiency of the LoCoBoard system and to benchmark it with some popular alternative open-source options. Using different experiment scenarios (cf. six videos, see Section 4), we observed that background noise (e.g., extreme environment illumination conditions) could disturb the functioning and affect the efficiency of the presented algorithms. Also, based on these experiments we could conclude that Algorithm A4 attained better results, using less time than all the others for processing the data set used.

As a future work directions, we pretend to continue the improvement of the platform and also the test and deployment of applications, to interact with the LoCoBoard, to be used in the classroom. We pretend to test and evaluate the entire setting in, larger scale, real environments. We also initiate working on multiple PL algorithms (cf. A5), since a full multitouch aware system is becoming increasingly prominent. Additionally, we plan to develop a complete test scenario to identify the most promising algorithmic approaches for the several software modules of the LoCoBoard system (e.g., increasing the number of videos used as a sample).

Finally, we intent to improve the adopted background subtraction model to filter any noise from the captured images. This is fundamental since all estimation algorithms are dramatically affected by the noise presence in the natural environment.

Acknowledgment

C. Soares thanks the FCT—Foundation for Science and Technology, Portugal, for Ph.D. Grant SFRH/BD/64210/2009.

References

[1] C. Soares, LoCoBoard: Quadro Interactivo de Baixo Custo recorrendo a Algoritmos de Visão por Computador [M.S. thesis], Universidade Fernando Pessoa, Porto, Portugal, 2009.

[2] Y. Benezeth, P. M. Jodoin, B. Emile, H. Laurent, and C. Rosenberger, "Comparative study of background subtraction algorithms," Journal of Electronic Imaging, vol. 19, no. 3, 2010.

[3] T. Bovermann, R. Bencina, E. Costanza, and M. Kaltenbrunner, "TUIO: a protocol for table-top tangible user interfaces," in Proceedings of the 6th International Workshop on Gesture in Human-Computer Interaction and Simulation (GW '05), 2005.

[4] R. Chang, F. Wang, and P. You, "A survey on the development of multi-touch technology," in Proceedings of the 2010 Asia-Pacific Conference on Wearable Computing Systems (APWCS '10), pp. 363–366, IEEE Computer Society, Washington, DC, USA, April 2010.

[5] D. Glover and D. Miller, "Running with technology: the pedagogic impact of the large-scale introduction of interactive whiteboards in one secondary school," Journal of InFormation Technology For Teacher Education, vol. 10, no. 3, pp. 257–278, 2001.

[6] J. Walny, B. Lee, P. Johns, N. H. Riche, and S. Carpendale, "Understanding pen and touch interaction for data exploration on interactive whiteboards," IEEE Transactions on Visualization and Computer Graphics, vol. 18, no. 12, pp. 2779–2788, 2012.

[7] N. Group, Multi-Touch Technologies, NUI Group, 1st edition, 2009.

[8] J. Teichert, M. Herrlich, B. Walther-Franks et al., "Advancing large interactive surfaces for use in the real world," Advances in Human-Computer Interaction, vol. 2010, Article ID 657937, 10 pages, 2010.

[9] P. I. S. Lei and A. K. Y. Wong, "The multiple-touch user interface revolution," IT Professional, vol. 11, no. 1, pp. 42–49, 2009.

[10] A. D. Wilson, "Playanywhere: a compact interactive tabletop projection-vision system," in *Proceedings of the 18th annual ACM symposium on User interface software and technology (UIST '05)*, pp. 83–92, ACM, New York, NY, USA, 2005.

[11] A. Agarwal, S. Izadi, M. Chandraker, and A. Blake, "High precision multi-touch sensing on surfaces using overhead cameras," in *Proceedings of the 2nd Annual IEEE International Workshop on Horizontal Interactive Human-Computer Systems (Tabletop '07)*, pp. 197–200, IEEE Computer Society, Washington, DC, USA, October 2007.

[12] J. C. Lee, "Hacking the nintendo wii remote," *IEEE Pervasive Computing*, vol. 7, no. 3, pp. 39–45, 2008.

[13] U. Schmidt, Wiimote whiteboard, 2008, http://www.uweschmidt.org/wiimote-whiteboard.

[14] T. Vajk, P. Coulton, W. Bamford, and R. Edwards, "Using a mobile phone as a "wii-like" controller for playing games on a large public display," *International Journal of Computer Games Technology*, vol. 2008, Article ID 539078, 6 pages, 2008.

[15] N. Group, Touchlib: A multi-touch development kit, 2008 http://nuigroup.com/touchlib/.

[16] N. Group, Community core vision—ccv, http://ccv.nuigroup .com/, 2010.

[17] M. Kaltenbrunner and R. Bencina, "Reactivision: a computer-vision framework for table-based tangible interaction," in *Proceedings of the 1st international conference on Tangible and embedded interaction (TEI '07)*, pp. 69–74, ACM, New York, NY, USA, February 2007.

[18] M. Wright, A. Freed, and A. Momeni, "Opensound control: state of the art 2003," in in *Proceedings of the 2003 conference on New interfaces for musical expression (NIME '03)*, pp. 153–160, National University of Singapore, Singapore, 2003.

[19] G. Bradski and A. Kaehler, *Learning OpenCV: Computer Vision with the OpenCV Library*, O'Reilly Media, 1st edition, 2008.

[20] R. Bencima, "oscpack—a simple c++ OSC packet manipulation library," 2006, http://www.rossbencina.com/code/oscpack.

[21] R. Haralick and L. Shapiro, *Computer and Robot Vision*, vol. 1, Addison Wesley, 1992.

6

Resection-Intersection Bundle Adjustment Revisited

Ruan Lakemond, Clinton Fookes, and Sridha Sridharan

Image and Video Research Laboratory, Queensland University of Technology, GPO Box 2434, 2 George Street, Brisbane, QLD 4001, Australia

Correspondence should be addressed to Ruan Lakemond; ruan.lakemond@gmail.com

Academic Editors: A. Gasteratos and M. Pardàs

Bundle adjustment is one of the essential components of the computer vision toolbox. This paper revisits the resection-intersection approach, which has previously been shown to have inferior convergence properties. Modifications are proposed that greatly improve the performance of this method, resulting in a fast and accurate approach. Firstly, a linear triangulation step is added to the intersection stage, yielding higher accuracy and improved convergence rate. Secondly, the effect of parameter updates is tracked in order to reduce wasteful computation; only variables coupled to significantly changing variables are updated. This leads to significant improvements in computation time, at the cost of a small, controllable increase in error. Loop closures are handled effectively without the need for additional network modelling. The proposed approach is shown experimentally to yield comparable accuracy to a full sparse bundle adjustment (20% error increase) while computation time scales much better with the number of variables. Experiments on a progressive reconstruction system show the proposed method to be more efficient by a factor of 65 to 177, and 4.5 times more accurate (increasing over time) than a localised sparse bundle adjustment approach.

1. Introduction

The nonlinear error minimisation step commonly referred to as bundle adjustment is a key step in many systems that recover projective geometry from image correspondences. While linear solutions are available in most cases, their accuracy is generally below requirements. Linear methods usually only serve as good initialisation for bundle adjustment [1]. Bundle adjustment remains a relatively computationally expensive part of the reconstruction process, despite a number of attempts to make it more efficient [2–4].

Resection-intersection is an implementation of bundle adjustment that interleaves the steps of refining camera parameters (resection) and 3D points (intersection). In this configuration each camera is treated as being independent of other cameras and each point is treated as being independent of others. While this has a number of advantages leading to reducing time spent on each iteration, the convergence rate is slow, primarily because interactions between variables are not accounted for, and because of redundancies between the two steps.

This paper proposes modifications to the classic resection-intersection algorithm that improve its accuracy and convergence rate and efficiently manages the propagation of parameter updates through a large, weakly overlapping network of cameras. The proposed algorithm is highly scalable, robust to high initial error, converges rapidly, and attains an error level comparable to a full bundle adjustment. It is a good choice for systems with many variables. Where high accuracy is paramount, the proposed approach can be inserted between attaining an initial solution and a full bundle adjustment to greatly reduce the amount of work that the full BA stage needs to perform. The update propagation control system makes the algorithm inherently well-suited to progressive reconstruction problems, where reconstructed data is added in batches (e.g., a Structure from Motion (SFM) system). Refinement effort is localised to the new data, while significant parameter updates are propagated to the existing data. Events such as loop closures are handled effectively, without the need for any additional network modelling or event detection.

2. Background

In general terms, bundle adjustment is the process of refining the parameters of a set of cameras and structure points to optimally fit a set of image observations. The problem has been studied in great depth [1].

Where the reconstruction involves one or more moving cameras, the number of observations and parameters to optimise overgrows rapidly as the video length increases. The resulting computational complexity can be a hindrance to achieving large scale or real time reconstruction. The primary approach to improving the efficiency of bundle adjustment is to take advantage of the inherent sparsity of the problem. Sparsity arises from the fact that not all world points are visible in all cameras and due to the independence of the model variables. Each point is independent of every other point and each camera is independent of every other camera, and the solution is only coupled through commonly visible points. An example implementation that uses sparse data structures and solvers to perform a Newton iteration is [2]. This implementation uses a matrix data structure that only stores nonzero values and it does not include zero elements in the matrix computations. Despite using sparse representations, the Jacobian and Hessian matrices require large amounts of memory, and operations on these matrices can be time consuming. Implementations for multiple processors and graphics processor type hardware have recently been made available [5] to apply more processing power to this demanding problem.

Many reconstruction problems are approached in a sequential manner. Data is added one camera at a time or one batch of cameras at a time. The nonlinear minimisation step is also performed progressively, since the accuracy of the solution at any time influences the subsequent reconstruction process. In these cases it is common that data that has already been refined does not need to be refined much more in subsequent steps. Using bundle adjustment directly in this case results in exponentially increasing processing time as the data grows. Most of the processing effort results in little improvement in the model, as previous refinement has dealt with most of the error.

A number of approaches have been proposed to attempt to localise the refinement effort to the data that requires refinement. Hierarchical bundle adjustment [6] (HBA) breaks the reconstruction up into small sections of cameras and recursively combines the data again in a hierarchical scheme. A typical scheme is to refine triplets of cameras and to recursively combine pairs of neighbouring groups using a 3D registration algorithm [3]. The registration step is required because a global datum (reference coordinate system) can not be defined for all groups. Local bundle adjustment [4] (LBA) only refines the most recent n frames while including the most recent $N > n$ frames in the cost function in order to constrain the datum. This approach removes the need for registering subsections of the structure but does result in progressive error accumulation and datum drift over long sequences.

The above localised methods make use of a camera-wise localisation and do not provide a good approach to point-wise localisation. A side effect is that in many cases only a subset of the observations of a given world point are included in the minimisation at a time. This increases error drift and accumulation and introduces inconsistencies in datum control. In situations where the camera path intersects or nearly intersects itself (a scenario commonly referred to as loop closure) this problem becomes most pronounced, since the error between spatially close cameras can become very large relative to the error between temporally adjacent cameras.

Relative bundle adjustment [7, 8] (RBA) models the camera network using relative pose transformations between cameras within a network graph. This is said to eliminate the need for a global datum. Loop closures are dealt with by adding additional edges and relative pose parameters to the graph where cameras meet, though it is not clear how camera pairs defining a loop closure are identified. Processing localisation is achieved by searching the graph, starting at the latest camera, for cameras where the reprojection error changes by more than a set threshold. All points visible to these cameras are included in the optimisation. Additional cameras that view any of these points are included in the optimisation, but their parameters are fixed. The drawbacks of this method are the need to maintain a camera connectivity graph and the need to detect loop closures in some manner. Retrieving camera's parameters requires computing a chain of cameras between the reference and target camera, due to the relative camera representation.

Resection-intersection (RI) treats each camera and point as being independent and refines each of these individually, instead of jointly. The RI technique has several characteristics that could be beneficial to reducing computation time as follows.

(i) The sparsity of the overall problem is exploited to the full; refining a single point or camera is a dense problem.

(ii) The datum is very well defined during each refinement step; all observed world points define the coordinate frame for the camera being refined and all the observing cameras define the coordinate frame for the point being refined.

(iii) Reregistration is not required, as in hierarchical bundle adjustment [3], for example, and the algorithm is much less susceptible to relative datum drift.

(iv) Processing is focussed on smaller amounts of data for longer, since the refinement process is applied to a relatively small set of parameters and observations at a time. Depending on the hardware architecture used, this can eliminate the transfer of data between larger, slower memory resources and the processor's fast caches for the duration of the inner refinement loop, thereby greatly reducing delays.

(v) Parallel implementation of the algorithm is made simple. All cameras can be refined in parallel and all points can be refined in parallel, as long as there is good separation between the camera step and point step.

```
(1.1)  begin
(1.2)      while Significant total change recorded do
(1.3)          foreach Camera with significant change do
(1.4)              Reset camera's change to zero.
(1.5)              Apply LM refinement to camera parameters.
(1.6)              Distribute error change resulting from refinement to points visible in current camera.
(1.7)          end
(1.8)          foreach Point with significant change do
(1.9)              Reset point's change to zero.
(1.10)             Triangulate using linear method.
(1.11)             Apply LM refinement to point.
(1.12)             Distribute change due to refinement to observing cameras.
(1.13)         end
(1.14)     end
(1.15) end
```

ALGORITHM 1: Resection-intersection with linear triangulation and update tracking.

(vi) Processing can easily be localised by omitting to refine points or cameras that do not need refinement.

Unfortunately, algorithms based on resection-intersection converge slowly because they do not model the interactions between variables. The size of the Newton step is consistently underestimated and parameter updates are propagated slowly through the network. The effects of slow convergence outweigh the reduction in individual iteration times, leading to poor performance [1].

3. Improved Resection-Intersection

Algorithm 1 gives a brief overview of the proposed resection-intersection (RI) algorithm. Let a model element be defined as a set of parameters associated with either one camera or one point. The RI algorithm essentially refines one element at a time. Each iteration consists of refining cameras (resection stage) then refining points (intersection stage). The Levenberg Marquardt (LM) algorithm is used to perform refinement, since the refinement of individual elements is a dense problem. The proposed algorithm includes two modifications over existing algorithms: an additional linear triangulation step and a change tracking system. To help ensure stability, an update is only applied if it results in reduced error.

3.1. Repeated Linear Triangulation. Resection and intersection are two subproblems with significantly different properties. Cameras are more complex entities than points. The linear or quasilinear methods used to initialize cameras [9, 10] can be unstable and imprecise, that is why bundle adjustment is so important. The linear multiview triangulation algorithm used to find points is, in contrast, simple and highly stable (given sufficient camera baseline) [3]. The poor accuracy of initial camera estimates is the most significant source of error in estimating point locations.

A linear triangulation step is added into the intersection stage, so that each point is retriangulated before applying LM refinement. This step takes advantage of the stable, inexpensive triangulation method to apply the camera updates to

the point, before continuing on to nonlinear refinement. The effect is that a large update is applied to the point with a small amount of computation effort.

3.2. Change Tracking. The second major addition to the RI algorithm is an update tracking system. A scalar change accumulator is associated with each model element, where a model element is defined as either a single camera or a single point. For every parameter update, the resulting change in reprojection error is recorded against each model element affected by the updated parameters. For example, when a camera is refined, the change in error is computed as $e_\Delta = 1 - (e_1/e_0)$, where e is the reprojection error averaged over all observations made by that camera. e_0 is computed before refinement and e_1 is the error after refinement. The change, e_Δ, is then added to all the world points visible in the current camera, while the change value of the camera that was refined is set to zero. The total change affecting each point is accumulated from all observing cameras and normalised according to

$$e_p = n^{-1} \sum_{i=1}^{m} e_{\Delta i}, \tag{1}$$

where n is the number of cameras viewing point p and m is the number of refinement operations applied to these cameras (more than one refinement pass may be applied before e_p is reset to zero). An equivalent approach is applied while refining points to distribute the change in error to observing cameras.

A model element is only refined if its normalised change value is above a threshold. The result is that each model element is only refined if it is directly associated with significant updates made elsewhere in the model. The change value is computed such that the local change value is of comparable scale as the global change in reprojection error. The change threshold can therefore be set equal to the overall convergence threshold. Modifications made outside the refinement algorithm system must also be recorded in the change tracking system. All new elements and elements with new observations are given a high change value so that they are refined at least once. Deletions (such as deleting outlier observations) result in a unit change which is added to any associated world points and observing cameras.

The change tracking system reduces computational effort by only propagating parameter updates related to significant change. It is also a very effective method for localising computational effort in progressive reconstruction systems, where data is added to the solution in sections. All new data is refined at least once and older data is only refined if needed. This method handles loop closures intrinsically, without the need to model the network topology.

4. Experimental Validation

Experiments were carried out using real and simulated data to assess the performance of the modified resection-intersection algorithm. This paper considers the case where a large volume of structure and observation data must be processed and where accuracy is of high priority. Both simulated and real data are processed progressively; cameras and points are added in chronologically ordered batches and refinement is applied at key frames.

The sparse bundle adjustment (SBA) implementation from [2] was used as reference implementation. A localised version of SBA (Local SBA) was produced by providing the SBA algorithm with a subsection of the data, similar to what is done in [4]. A sequence of cameras spanning four key frames is refined, with additional cameras spanning a further eight key frames included but held fixed. The fixed sequence is included in the cost function computation, but the camera parameters are not altered. This provides a method for constraining the datum for the subsection that is refined. The lengths of these sections were manually tuned to balance accuracy against processing times. Shorter sequences result in lower computational cost but increased error drift.

Three versions of the Resection-intersection algorithm were tested as follows:

(1) RI with LM: the original RI algorithm using LM refinement for both cameras and points,

(2) RI with triangulation: uses LM for cameras but linear triangulation for points,

(3) RI with triangulation + LM: uses LM for cameras; points are refined by first using linear triangulation, then LM, as outlined in Algorithm 1.

All RI-based algorithms use the change tracking system detailed in Section 3.2.

All experiments were implemented in C/C++ and executed in a single thread on an 8-core desktop computer with 16 Gb of local memory.

4.1. Simulation Experiments. Simulated data was produced by randomly generating a cloud of 3D points and a set of cameras with fixed calibration, outside the convex hull of the points. Image observations were produced by projecting the points using the cameras. Random noise with a Gaussian distribution and mean amplitude of 5% of the point cloud width was added independently to all points, camera pose

parameters and observations. The point data was generated to simulate points that are becoming visible and eventually occluded as the sequence continues. The sequence begins with an initial set of points. After each batch of cameras has been added and projections have been taken, some new points are added and some old points are removed before producing the next set of cameras and projections.

Two sets of data were produced: a small set to accommodate evaluation of the time consuming SBA algorithm and a large set to test the faster algorithms on more data. The small set consists of 400 initial points, with 50 points added and removed after every set of 10 cameras is added. A total of 400 cameras are generated. The large set consists of 10000 initial points, with 1000 points added and removed after every set of 10 cameras is added. A total of 1000 cameras are generated.

Two experiments were performed: a convergence experiment and a progressive data addition experiment.

4.1.1. Convergence. The entire small data set is used for this experiment. Each refinement algorithm is applied once to the data and the results of each iteration of the algorithm are recorded to study its convergence path. Convergence thresholds were set very low (10^{-12}) in order to have the algorithms run for many iterations, up to a maximum of 100 iterations. The results are shown in Figure 1, where the solution reprojection error is plotted against the time at which an iteration is completed.

The original RI algorithm completes each iteration in relatively short time but converges very slowly, as previously observed [1]. The proposed method using both linear triangulation and LM to refine points is much more effective, while individual iterations take only a fraction more time. Compared to SBA, the proposed method yields a final error only 0.2% higher in much shorter time. Using only triangulation to refine points results in the shortest iteration time, while the end result is almost exactly equal to the method that also uses LM refinement. This method converges in only 6 iterations. The rapid convergence can be attributed to the fact that the linear triangulation method is optimal under Gaussian noise. Under real image conditions, its performance may be significantly different.

4.1.2. Progressive Reconstruction. This experiment treats the data as a progressive reconstruction that requires refinement after each key frame. Data is added to the solution in batches of 10 cameras at a time, as described above. A refinement algorithm is applied after each batch of data is added and its performance measured. Results are presented by plotting reprojection error and refinement processing time against the camera index at which refinement was performed. The reprojection error at index j is computed as the error for cameras 0 to j.

Results for the small data set are presented in Figure 2, and Figure 3 shows the results for the large data set.

All methods initially yield a low error due to overfitting to the initially small amount of data. The time taken to complete each full SBA pass increases rapidly as data is added. The SBA method achieves a model error only 6% lower than

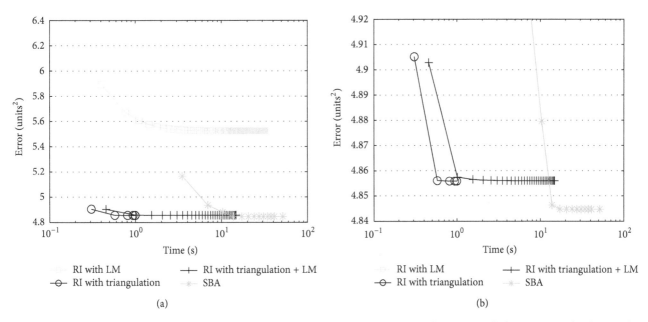

FIGURE 1: Progress of iterative refinement processes plot against process time. Each marker indicates the end of an iteration of each algorithm. Both plots show the same data at different error scales.

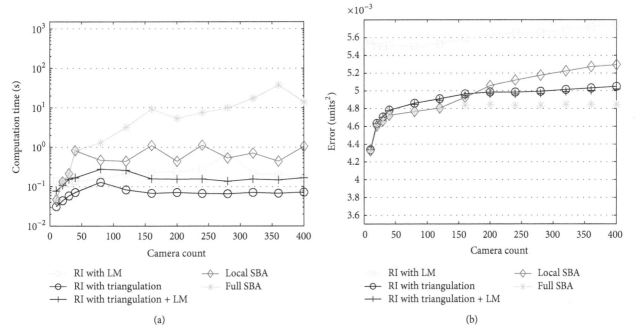

FIGURE 2: Small simulated data set results. Data is added to the reconstruction progressively and nonlinear refinement is applied at key frames. The refinement time (a) and resulting error (b) are plotted against key frame indices.

the other methods in the small data experiment. Both LSBA and the proposed methods show approximately constant time performance as the data set grows. LSBA initially produces the same error as SBA. Once the processing window comes into effect, its processing time stops increasing and its error starts increasing. For the large data test, the proposed RI method with both triangulation and LM refinement requires on average 6.3 times less computation time than LSBA. The method using only triangulation is 13.7 times faster than

LSBA but shows greater error drift as the sequence length grows. The original RI algorithm again shows significantly higher error and even becomes unstable during the large data test.

4.2. Real Data Experiment. The real data experiment was produced using an SFM system designed for high accuracy tracking. For each image in the sequence, the camera pose

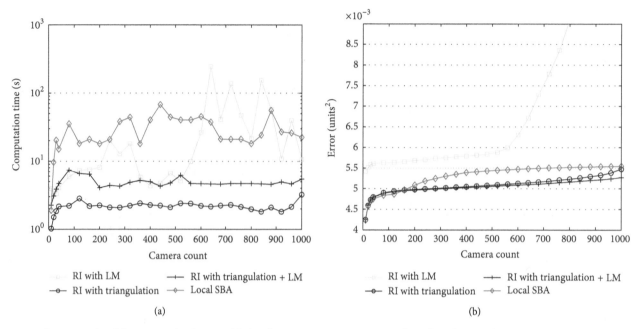

(a)   (b)

FIGURE 3: Large simulated data set results. Data is added to the reconstruction progressively and nonlinear refinement is applied at key frames. The refinement time (a) and resulting error (b) are plotted against key frame indices.

is recovered using the ePnP algorithm [9], followed by LM minimisation applied to the new camera pose parameters only. Outlier rejection is used at this stage to remove gross tracking errors. Key frames are selected at frames where the baseline between key frames surpasses a threshold. At each key frame, new world points are triangulated and the refinement process is applied, with all cameras in-between key frames included in the minimisation.

The data used in this experiment consists of video captured in an office environment. A camera was carried by hand down the three isles of the office multiple times with different orientations. The camera path includes several loops and overlapping sections. Figure 4 shows example images from the data set and Figure 5 shows two views of the final reconstruction. The model contains 7×10^4 points viewed from 6813 cameras, to produce 1.7×10^7 observations.

Figures 6 and 7 show the results for the real data experiment. The full SBA algorithm increases in processing time nearly exponentially. The SBA algorithm was terminated when its run time became excessive, since this is no longer reasonable for practical use. Local SBA requires approximately constant processing time (variations are mostly due to local data conditions) but suffers from large accumulating error over the course of the reconstruction. Large error spikes are also observed, but the algorithm tends to recover from these to maintain a reasonable error profile. The error produced by Local SBA can be reduced by extending the length of the local processing region, at the expense of increased processing time.

Resection-intersection using only LM to refine points is the fastest on average but yields poor accuracy. The accuracy can be improved by tightening the convergence threshold,

FIGURE 4: Example frames from the real video data set.

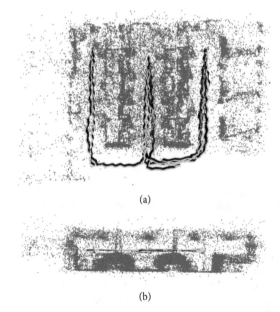

(a)

(b)

FIGURE 5: Real video data set reconstruction. Small blue (dark) dots indicate world points; larger green (light) dots indicate camera centres, with black lines indicating camera viewing direction. The large number of cameras results in the camera path appearing as a line. (a) top view and (b) front view.

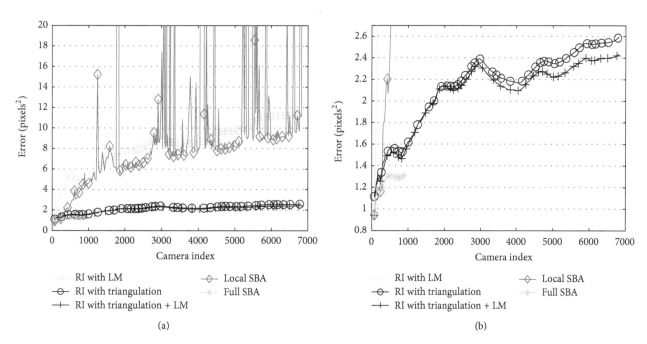

FIGURE 6: Real video SFM reconstruction results. Data is added to the reconstruction progressively and nonlinear refinement is applied at key frames. The error after refinement is plotted against key frame indices at two different error scales.

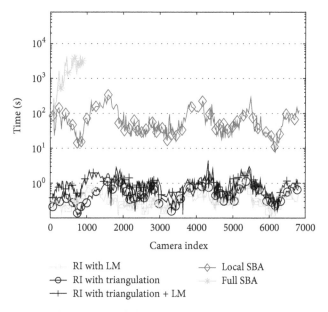

FIGURE 7: Real video SFM reconstruction results. Data is added to the reconstruction progressively and nonlinear refinement is applied at key frames. The refinement time is plotted against key frame indices.

but only a small improvement can be achieved at the cost of processing time increasing by orders of magnitude.

The proposed linear triangulation addition to the RI algorithm results in a significant improvement in accuracy over the original RI algorithm, while maintaining a low computation time. RI with triangulation and LM yields an error 88% lower than Local SBA at the conclusion of the sequence and exhibits a slower overall increase in error, while reducing the processing time by a factor of 65 on average. Disabling the LM step after triangulation results in a slight increase in the error growth over time (6% higher error over the entire sequence) but reduces computation time further by 45%. The proposed methods yield a reconstruction error approximately 20% higher than full SBA.

5. Conclusions and Future Work

This paper proposes modifications to the resection-intersection method for bundle adjustment that makes the method much more effective and efficient. The proposed methods are suitable for large scale reconstructions and for use in Structure from Motion systems.

Two modifications to the RI algorithm are proposed. Firstly, adding a linear triangulation step into the intersection stage greatly improves accuracy and convergence speed. This approach is so effective that the nonlinear refinement of world points can be omitted, resulting in further reduction in computation time of 45%, with a very small increase in error. Secondly, a change tracking system is proposed to localise the computational effort so that stable parameters are not subject to redundant processing. Change tracking is particularly effective for progressive reconstructions, where the addition of new data has a limited effect on existing data. Loop closures are handled intrinsically without the need for additional camera network modelling or closure detection.

Simulation experiments show that the proposed method converges much more quickly than the original RI algorithm and a full Newton method, while the final error is only a few percent higher than the full Newton method. Experiments on a real SFM system show that the proposed methods can maintain approximately constant processing time independent of image sequence length, while maintaining good accuracy. Compared to a localised sparse bundle adjustment (SBA) algorithm, the proposed RI with triangulation and nonlinear refinement of points requires 65 times less computation time, while maintaining 4 times lower error, slower error growth over time, and much more stable results. Omitting the nonlinear refinement step in the intersection phase results in processing time 177 times faster than Local SBA, while the error increases only slightly faster than the method using nonlinear refinement (6% increase over 7000 frames). These results show that the nonlinear refinement of world point parameters is of limited value, given accurate camera estimates.

Conflict of Interests

The authors declare that there is no conflict of interests regarding the publication of this paper.

Acknowledgment

This project was supported by the Australian Research Council Grant no. LP0990135.

References

[1] B. Triggs, P. F. McLauchlan, R. I. Hartley, and A. W. Fitzgibbon, "Bundle adjustment: a modern synthesis," in *Vision Algorithms: Theory and Practice*, vol. 1883 of *Lecture Notes in Compute Science*, pp. 298–372, Springer, 2000.

[2] M. I. A. Lourakis and A. A. Argyros, "SBA: a software package for generic sparse bundle adjustment," *ACM Transactions on Mathematical Software*, vol. 36, no. 1, article 2, 2009.

[3] R. Hartley and A. Zisserman, *Multiple View Geometry in Computer Vision*, Cambridge University Press, New York, NY, USA, 2nd edition, 2003.

[4] E. Mouragnon, M. Lhuillier, M. Dhome, F. Dekeyser, and P. Sayd, "Generic and real-time structure from motion using local bundle adjustment," *Image and Vision Computing*, vol. 27, no. 8, pp. 1178–1193, 2009.

[5] C. Wu, S. Agarwal, B. Curless, and S. M. Seitz, "Multicore bundle adjustment," in *Proceedings of the IEEE Conference on Computer Vision and Pattern Recognition (CVPR '11)*, pp. 3057–3064, June 2011.

[6] H.-Y. Shum, Q. Ke, and Z. Zhang, "Efficient bundle adjustment with virtual key frames: a hierarchical approach to multi-frame structure from motion," in *Proceedings of the IEEE Computer Society Conference on Computer Vision and Pattern Recognition (CVPR '99)*, vol. 2, pp. 2538–2543, Fort Collins, Colo, USA, June 1999.

[7] G. Sibley, "Relative bundle adjustment," Technical Report 2307/09, University of Oxford, 2009.

[8] G. Sibley, C. Mei, I. Reid, and P. Newman, "Adaptive relative bundle," in *Proceedings of the Robotics: Science and Systems*, pp. 1–8, University of Washington , Seattle, Wash, USA, June 2009.

[9] V. Lepetit, F. Moreno-Noguer, and P. Fua, "Epnp: an accurate o(n) solution to the pnp problem," *International Journal of Computer Vision*, vol. 81, no. 2, pp. 155–166, 2009.

[10] V. Pradeep and J. Lim, "Egomotion estimation using assorted features," *International Journal of Computer Vision*, vol. 98, no. 2, pp. 202–216, 2012.

7

Fast Exact Nearest Neighbour Matching in High Dimensions Using d-D Sort

Ruan Lakemond, Clinton Fookes, and Sridha Sridharan

Image and Video Research Laboratory, Queensland University of Technology, GPO Box 2434, 2 George Street, Brisbane, QLD 4001, Australia

Correspondence should be addressed to Ruan Lakemond; r.lakemond@qut.edu.au

Academic Editors: O. Ghita and S. Mattoccia

Data structures such as k-D trees and hierarchical k-means trees perform very well in approximate k nearest neighbour matching, but are only marginally more effective than linear search when performing exact matching in high-dimensional image descriptor data. This paper presents several improvements to linear search that allows it to outperform existing methods and recommends two approaches to exact matching. The first method reduces the number of operations by evaluating the distance measure in order of significance of the query dimensions and terminating when the partial distance exceeds the search threshold. This method does not require preprocessing and significantly outperforms existing methods. The second method improves query speed further by presorting the data using a data structure called d-D sort. The order information is used as a priority queue to reduce the time taken to find the exact match and to restrict the range of data searched. Construction of the d-D sort structure is very simple to implement, does not require any parameter tuning, and requires significantly less time than the best-performing tree structure, and data can be added to the structure relatively efficiently.

1. Introduction

The k nearest neighbour matching (kNN) problem is encountered in many applications of computer science. It is the problem of finding the k points in a database nearest to a given query point. The complexity of a simple linear search is proportional to dn, where n is the number of database entries and d is the number of data dimensions. Many attempts have been made to reduce the search time by implementing data storage and indexing structures so that the minimum number of data points has to be compared to the query point. Unfortunately, these methods are only effective in low dimensions or when using approximate nearest neighbour matching [1, 2]. Where an exact solution is required in dimensions greater than 20, linear search is only a fraction slower than the best existing search structure.

This paper proposes methods for improving the performance of linear search for the purpose of exact nearest neighbour matching using typical visual descriptors, such as the scale invariant feature transform (SIFT) [3, 4]. Many modern visual descriptors, such as gradient location and orientation histogram (GLOH) [5], are based on SIFT and have very similar characteristics from a search perspective. First, it is shown that simple modifications to the linear algorithm can allow it to outperform all existing search structures, without the need for any data preprocessing. Secondly, by presorting the data it is possible to reduce search time further. A multidimensional sorting data structure called d-D Sort is introduced that is trivially simple to construct, does not require any parameter tuning, and supports an efficient data addition operation. Thirdly, intersecting the search sphere with the data unit sphere is used to reduce the search space.

The proposed methods are compared to leading methods based on k-D trees and k-means trees [1, 2]. A set of SIFT descriptors were extracted from the MIRFLICKR-1 M image collection [6] for this purpose. Two approaches are recommended based on the results. The first requires no preprocessing and significantly outperforms leading tree structures that require a large amount of preprocessing. The second improves results further at the cost of additional memory and preprocessing. Which method is best depends on the application.

2. Related Work

The most popular indexing and search methods are based on k-D trees [7] and hierarchical k-means trees [8, 9]. Due to the so-called curse of dimensionality [10], these methods become less effective as the data dimensionality increases. In the exact matching case, linear search is the best method for data with more than 20 dimensions. In many applications, such as where feature vocabularies are used instead of original features [11], an exact match is not essential. Many methods have been proposed to reduce computation time by finding approximate matches.

A probabilistic best-bin-first search algorithm for k-D trees was proposed in [12], where the total number of data points evaluated is fixed to limit computation time. This method does not enforce explicit bounds on the accuracy of the result. In [1] a method is proposed which ensures that, given tolerance ϵ, the distance between a query and a selected nearest neighbour is within a factor $(1 + \epsilon)$ of the distance between the query and the true nearest neighbour. The construction process does not depend on ϵ. A priority queue search is used, where the priority is determined by the distance of cells in the tree from the query point. Cells further than $\text{dist}(q, p)/(1 + \epsilon)$ are not evaluated, where q is the query and p is the current kth neighbour. These best-bin-first and approximate matching methods can also be applied to k-means trees in a very similar fashion.

While k-D trees and hierarchical k-means trees on average yield similar results, their relative performance depends on the data and type of search query. A procedure for selecting between these algorithms and automatically tuning their parameters is presented in [2]. This procedure constructs a set of sample structures with various parameters from a subset of the data. The parameters of the best performing structure are then used to build the complete data structure. The construction time can be significantly increased by the parameter selection process.

More recently, locality sensitive hashing (LSH) has become a very popular approach to approximate matching. Hashing functions are used to map high-dimensional vectors to buckets. The hashing functions are designed to maximise the likelihood that similar descriptors are mapped to the same bucket. The query point is also hashed multiple times to select target buckets. The descriptors in the target buckets are then compared to the query using the original descriptors in a post-verification stage. The choice of hashing functions needs to be made with the aid of training data that is very similar to the final application data. This method is highly effective for approximate matching, but a large number of buckets need to be selected to ensure that the exact match is found, leading to unremarkable performance in exact matching [13, 14].

This paper focuses on the exact matching case, where the true nearest neighbour is required. Systems based on k-D trees and k-means trees support guaranteed exact search, but at best outperform linear search by only a fraction. Instead of modifying these structures, this paper investigates methods

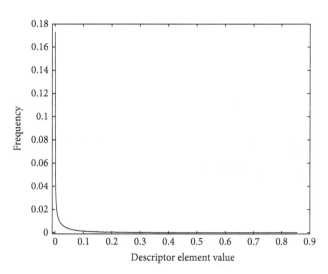

FIGURE 1: Distribution of descriptor element values for a 128-dimensional SIFT descriptor computed from a large set of MSER features.

for improving linear search and shows that it can outperform the above methods.

3. Improved Linear Search

The objective of visual descriptor extraction is usually to capture some structure. Consequently, the elements of the resulting descriptor vector are not uniformly distributed, but exhibit some structure as well. Additionally, these feature vectors are frequently normalised to have unit length and only have positive values. Figure 1 shows the distribution of descriptor element values for a 128-dimensional SIFT descriptor computed from a large set of maximally stable extremal region (MSER) features [15], extracted from a natural scene. It can be seen that this distribution is approximately exponential. For an evenly distributed unit vector descriptor, one would expect the median value to be near $d^{-1/2}$; however, only 15% of the elements of the SIFT descriptor are above this value. It can therefore be said that most descriptors consist of a small set of relatively large values and a majority of small values (and often many zeros). Since the larger values of any descriptor are both rare and responsible for the majority of the distance between unit vector descriptors, it is possible to evaluate a large component of the distance by considering only a small number of dimensions.

3.1. Partial Distance Evaluation. While the exact distance between a query descriptor and the nearest k descriptors is usually of interest, the distance to other descriptors is not, except to determine that all other descriptors are more distant than the kth descriptor. Evaluation of the distance measure can therefore be aborted once it exceeds the distance to the current best candidate for descriptor k (used as a threshold). In the case of normalised vectors, the number of evaluated dimensions can be further reduced by evaluating the distance measure in order of the significance of the query dimensions. This does not generalise to unnormalised, uniformly distributed data. While partial distances have been used before [16], the computation in order of significance is novel. All that is required for ordered partial distance computation is to find the order of significance of the query dimensions. This can be done using a sorting operation in $O(d \log(d))$ time.

The effectiveness of this method depends on how long it takes the search algorithm to encounter the nearest neighbour. At the start of the search, a relatively large search threshold is used (tight search thresholds have been shown to be ineffective [4]), resulting in complete distance computation for at least the first descriptor. As descriptors closer to the query are encountered, the search threshold is decreased and the partial evaluation becomes more effective.

Implementing the above improvements is trivial and requires only the following three modifications.

(1) Sort the query dimensions according to significance.

(2) Modify the distance function so that the distance measure is computed in order of query dimension significance.

(3) The distance function should terminate as soon as the partially computed distance exceeds a threshold.

3.2. Searching on Sorted Arrays. Presorting the data according to one of the dimensions can be used to improve performance in two ways. Firstly, the sorted dimension can be used as a search priority queue. Bilinear search can be used to find a starting point that is close to the query point in at least one dimension, from where the search progresses outwards. If the sorted dimension is one of the more significant query dimensions, then the linear search is more likely to encounter the nearest neighbour early in the search, thereby improving the effectiveness of partial distance evaluation. The inverse is true if selecting a dimension that is one of the least significant query dimensions (this is demonstrated experimentally in Section 5). The best results are achieved by sorting the data on every dimension and by selecting the order associated with the query's dominant dimension.

Secondly, the sorted dimension can be used to restrict the search range. A naive approach to defining the search limits would be to simply search in the range $[q_j - r, q_j + r]$, where $\mathbf{q}$ is the query, r is the current search threshold (distance to kth nearest neighbour), and j is the query's dominant dimension. This is equivalent to stopping the search when the ordered partial distance exceeds the threshold on the first dimension. Because the data is normalised to unit vectors, much tighter constraints are possible. The search limits on q_j are set to the minimum and maximum values that satisfy the intersection of the data unit hypersphere and the search radius hypersphere.

The data space can be defined as

$$\mathbf{x} \in \mathbb{R}^d,$$

$$x_i = \mathbf{x}\{i\} \in [0, 1], \tag{1}$$

$$\mathbf{x}^\top \mathbf{x} = 1.$$

The boundary, $\mathbf{b} \in \mathbf{x}$, of the search space around query point $\mathbf{q} \in \mathbf{x}$ additionally satisfies the constraint:

$$(\mathbf{b} - \mathbf{q})^\top (\mathbf{b} - \mathbf{q}) = r^2,$$

$$\therefore \mathbf{b}^\top \mathbf{q} = 1 - \frac{r^2}{2}. \tag{2}$$

Let $\mathbf{b} = \mathbf{p} + \mathbf{s}$, where $\mathbf{p} = \mathbf{q}\sqrt{1 - r^2/2}$ is the component of $\mathbf{b}$ parallel to $\mathbf{q}$ and $\mathbf{s}$ is the orthogonal component such that $\mathbf{s}^\top \mathbf{q} = \mathbf{s}^\top \mathbf{p} = 0$. The length of $\mathbf{s}$ is found as

$$\mathbf{b}^\top \mathbf{b} = 1$$

$$(\mathbf{s} + \mathbf{p})^\top (\mathbf{s} + \mathbf{p}) = 1,$$

$$\mathbf{s}^\top \mathbf{s} + 2\mathbf{s}^\top \mathbf{p} + \mathbf{p}^\top \mathbf{p} = 1, \tag{3}$$

$$\mathbf{s}^\top \mathbf{s} = \frac{r^2}{2}.$$

In order to maximise b_j, choose $\mathbf{s}$ so that $|b_i|$ is minimised for all $i \neq j$, that is, $s_i \propto -q_i$. Add scale factor a to correct the length and select s_j to satisfy the orthogonality constraint:

$$s_i = -aq_i, \quad \forall i \neq j,$$

$$\mathbf{s}^\top \mathbf{q} = s_j q_j - a \sum_{\forall i \neq j} q_i^2 = 0, \tag{4}$$

$$\therefore s_j = a\frac{\sum_{\forall i \neq j} q_i^2}{q_j}.$$

Let $c = \sum_{\forall i \neq j} q_i^2$ and solve for a using the known length of $\mathbf{s}$:

$$s_j = a\frac{c}{q_j},$$

$$\mathbf{s}^\top \mathbf{s} = s_j^2 + \sum_{\forall i \neq j} s_i^2,$$

$$\frac{r^2}{2} = a^2\frac{c^2}{q_j^2} + a^2 c, \tag{5}$$

$$a^2 = \frac{r^2}{2\left(c^2/q_j^2 + c\right)},$$

$$\therefore s_j = \frac{rc}{q_j\sqrt{2\left(c^2/q_j^2 + c\right)}} = rg.$$

Similarly, b_j can be minimised, resulting in $s_j = -rg$. Note that g depends only on q and can be computed once per query.

The above equations only find $\mathbf{b}$ with minimum or maximum value of b_j if the search area is not bounded by one of the coordinate axes. If the j-axis intersects the search area, then the maximum value of b_j is 1, and if any other axis intersects the search area, then the minimum value of b_j is 0. Let r_u be the distance between $\mathbf{q}$ and the unit vector along dimension j, and let r_l be the distance between $\mathbf{q}$ and the unit vector along the minimum dimension of $\mathbf{q}$. The upper and lower search limits along dimension j are then,

$$t_u = \begin{cases} q_j \sqrt{1 - \dfrac{r^2}{2}} + rg, & r < r_u, \\ 1, & r \geq r_u, \end{cases}$$

$$t_l = \begin{cases} q_j \sqrt{1 - \dfrac{r^2}{2}} - rg, & r < r_l, \\ 0, & r \geq r_l. \end{cases} \tag{6}$$

4. The d-D Sort System

A search structure named d-D sort is used to implement the sorted linear search improvements presented in the previous section.

4.1. Construction. The d-D Sort structure consist of d index arrays, $o = \{o_1, o_2, \ldots, o_d\}$, with each $o_i = \{o_{i1}, o_{i2}, \ldots, o_{in}\}$ indexing the descriptor data, $\mathbf{x}$, in order of dimension i. It requires nd memory in addition to the data. Construction is extremely simple; sort the descriptor data according to each dimension and write the result in o (instead of actually reordering the data), requiring $O(dn \log(n))$ time.

4.2. Adding Data. Adding additional data to the d-D Sort structure is relatively simple as well. The new data, $\mathbf{x}'$, is appended to the existing data, $\mathbf{x}'' = \{\mathbf{x}, \mathbf{x}'\}$. The ordering arrays are updated by finding the position of the new data. This can be achieved efficiently using binary search in $O(d \log(n))$ time and array insertion operations in linear time. For a large batch of new descriptors, a more efficient solution is to sort the new data first ($O(dn' \log n')$ time) and then merge the result with the existing order arrays ($O(d(n+n'))$ time), rather than performing multiple separate insertions. This addition operation is faster than a complete reconstruction where the new data contains fewer descriptors than the existing data.

4.3. Queries. All matching queries are variants of a k nearest neighbours (kNNs) query with a maximum distance threshold. The algorithm is listed in Algorithm 1.

Other types of queries are essentially specialisations of the above algorithm. KNN without a threshold is achieved by setting r to a very large initial value. Nearest neighbour ratio matching [4] is equivalent to 1NN matching with the additional requirement that no second match is found in the radius $(1 + \delta)e_r\{1\}$. In this case r is updated as $r \leftarrow (1 + \delta)e$ in line (1.16), and the final match is invalidated if any second nearest neighbour is found to be within r.

Two possible methods can be applied to further speed up the query process while sacrificing exact results. Firstly, the number of descriptors visited can be limited. It is possible to compute the worst case accuracy of this approach for each individual query, but it is not possible to enforce a lower accuracy bound on all queries. Alternatively, the distance threshold can be reduced according to an accuracy

requirement, to reduce the number of descriptors visited. The convention used in [1] for describing approximation tolerance is used: given tolerance ϵ, the distance between a query and a selected nearest neighbour must be within a factor $(1 + \epsilon)$ of the distance between the query and the true nearest neighbour. This is implemented in the d-D Sort query algorithm in line (1.16). As is shown in the experimental evaluation, this method can reduce search time, but the search accuracy degrades more rapidly than with other search structures.

The computation time of the query operation is highly dependant on the data distribution. Sorting the query requires $O(d \log(d))$ operations and the initial binary search requires $O(\log(n))$ operations. Searching for k exact matches requires at best $\Omega(kd)$ operations and at worst $O(nd)$ operations (requiring an invalid query $\mathbf{q} = \mathbf{0}$ or data spherically symmetric around $\mathbf{q}$). In practice, the total number of data points visited is much smaller than n, and much fewer than d dimensions are evaluated for most visited points.

5. Experimental Evaluation

The following eight search methods were compared experimentally:

(1) linear search,

(2) linear search using partial distance computation,

(3) linear search using significance ordered partial distance computation,

(4) d-D Sort structured search,

(5) 1-D Sort search,

(6) the k-D tree from the approximate nearest neighbor (ANN) library [1],

(7) the b-D tree from the approximate nearest neighbor (ANN) library [1],

(8) the fast library for approximate nearest neighbors (FLANN) [2].

Publicly available C/C++ implementations by the original authors were used for ANN and FLANN. The FLANN method was set to use 1000 points in its an automatic parameter selection process. The 1-D Sort method sorts the data on the first dimension only. This method is added to the evaluation to demonstrate the importance of using the order of the most significant query dimension as search priority queue.

A set of data was generated using a characteristic scale determinant of Hessian feature detector [17, 18] and SIFT descriptor [3, 4] to extract 1 million descriptors from a subset of the MIRFLICKR-1 M image collection [6]. These descriptors are normalised to have an L_2 norm of 1 and consists of strictly positive values.

Figure 2 plots construction times and average query time results for a set of queries produced by extracting features for an image not included in the dataset. This is the most difficult test case, since the queries are rarely very close to any points in the dataset. Query time results are expressed

Input: $\mathbf{x}, o, \mathbf{q}, k, r, \epsilon$
Output: n_r, i_r, e_r

(1.1) **begin**

(1.2)   Sort query, $\mathbf{q}$ in ascending order, yielding order array o_q.

(1.3)   Select prime dimension, $j \leftarrow o_q\{d\}$.

(1.4)   Select data order vector $o_j = o\{j\}$ as the search order.

(1.5)   Compute r_u and r_l.

(1.6)   Compute g according to (5).

(1.7)   Compute initial search range, $[t_u, t_l]$, according to (6).

(1.8)   Use binary search to find $i_0 \leftarrow \arg\min_i \left| \mathbf{x}\{o_j\{i\}\}\{j\} - q_j \right|$.

(1.9)   **foreach** $i \in [1, n]$ in order of increasing distance from i_0 **do**

(1.10)   If $\mathbf{x}\{o_j\{i\}\}\{j\}$ is out of search range $[t_u, t_l]$, terminate.

(1.11)   Compute distance $e = \mathrm{dist}\left(\mathbf{x}\{o_j\{i\}\}, \mathbf{q}\right)$ using the ordered partial distance method.

(1.12)   **if** $e < r$ **then**

(1.13)   Insert i, e in results list, i_r, e_r.

(1.14)   Increment n_r (up to k).

(1.15)   **if** $n_r = k$ **then**

(1.16)   Reduce the search range, $r \leftarrow e_k/(1 + \epsilon)$.

(1.17)   Recompute $[t_u, t_l]$ according to (6).

(1.18)   **end**

(1.19)   **end**

(1.20)   **end**

(1.21) **end**

ALGORITHM 1: kNN Query Algorithm for the d-D Sort Structure.

TABLE 1: 1NN query performance using a 128000-point dataset. Each column shows results for query descriptors extracted from an image related to the data in a different way. Results are presented as the ratio between linear search time and the given method's search time.

Method	Not in database	Rotated copy	Exact copy
ANN b-D tree	0.297	0.292	0.2872
ANN k-D tree	0.503	0.498	0.4909
FLANN	1.450	2.483	23.13
Linear	1.000	1.000	1.000
Linear partial	1.392	2.124	12.62
Linear ordered partial	2.588	4.397	12.62
d-D sort	3.404	7.032	2246.0

in terms of a relative increase in speed over the time taken to do a simple linear search ($t_{\mathrm{linear}}/t_{\mathrm{test}}$). Table 1 lists 1NN performance for queries from an image that is not in the database (same as Figure 2(b)), a rotated version of an image that is in the database, and an exact copy of an image in the database.

Data structure construction times are plotted in Figure 2(a) for those methods that require preprocessing. The d-D Sort structure construction time is comparable to that of the b-D tree on average, while the construction time increases more slowly than the k-D Tree. FLANN takes the longest to construct due to the simulation process it uses to select parameters. Figure 3 shows the time taken to append 100 descriptors to a d-D Sort structure of increasing size. It can be seen that the addition method is more efficient when

adding a relatively small number of points to the database, compared to rebuilding the structure completely.

Figure 2(b) plots the relative exact 1NN query performance against the size of the database. A matching threshold of 2.0 was used. It can be seen that using only partial distance computation is sufficient to bring the speed of linear search up to that of the best tree structure method (FLANN). Ordered partial distance adds a further improvement, all without any data preprocessing. The d-D Sort structure achieves the best performance by a significant margin, demonstrating the benefits of presorting the data. In contrast, 1-D Sort performs worse than the ordered partial distance method. This shows that sorting on an arbitrary dimension is not beneficial for all queries and that it is necessary to sort on the query's most significant dimension.

The effect of matching threshold on query performance is examined in Figure 2(c). Smaller thresholds reduce the search space and improve matching speed in general. Of the linear methods, the d-D Sort structure is best able to take advantage of smaller thresholds. The k-D Tree and b-D Tree structures benefit the most from smaller thresholds, with k-D Tree surpassing d-D Sort at a relatively small threshold of 0.2.

The number of nearest neighbours selected impacts the partial distance computation, since the greater distance to the kth match leads to a greater search threshold. Figure 2(d) plots the query performance against k. A decrease in performance can be seen for d-D Sort and modified linear methods, while the ANN and FLANN methods are unaffected. The linear methods remain the most efficient.

The d-D Sort structure supports approximate matching by reducing the search threshold below what is needed to

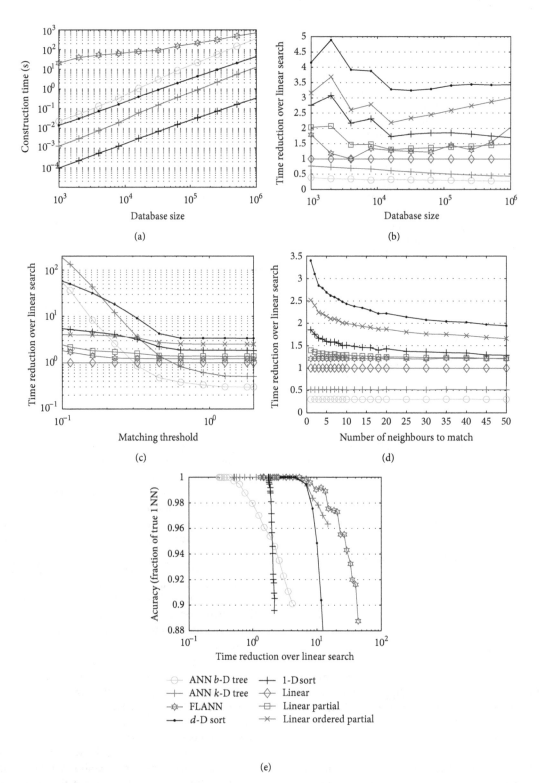

(a)

(b)

(c)

(d)

(e)

FIGURE 2: Results for SIFT descriptor data experiment using euclidean distance. (a) Search structure construction time plots against database size. (b) Exact 1NN query time, normalised according to linear search time, plots against database size. A threshold of 2.0 was used. (c) Exact 1NN query time, normalised according to linear search time, plots against threshold for 100 k descriptor database. (d) Exact query time, normalised according to linear search time, plots against the number of neighbours to find. A 100 k descriptor database and threshold of 2.0 was used. (e) Accuracy of approximate 1NN query plots against query time, normalised according to linear search time. A 100 k descriptor database and threshold of 2.0 were used.

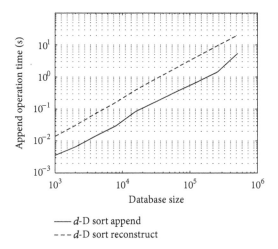

FIGURE 3: The time required to append 100 SIFT descriptors to a d-D sort structure plot against the number of descriptors already in the structure. The time taken to construct the database anew is included for reference.

prove an exact match. Figure 2(b) plots the match accuracy against the relative query performance for approximate nearest neighbour matching. Match accuracy is measured as the proportion of matches returned that are the true matches. It can be seen that approximate matching leads to more than an order of magnitude improvement in performance at the cost of a slight reduction in accuracy. The accuracy of the d-D Sort structure drops more quickly than that of ANN k-D tree or FLANN. While d-D Sort consistently outperforms the other methods in guaranteed exact matching, it is not the best choice for approximate matching.

The effect of the similarity between queries and the data is demonstrated by Table 1. The first column shows results from an image not in the database, which is the same as one of the points in Figure 2(b). The second column lists results of matching a rotated version of an image in the database and the third column is for an exact copy of a database image. The absolute time performance of linear search is the same for all three cases. The ANN methods perform the same for all three cases as well, which is unexpected. FLANN shows a significant increase in performance. This is the expected behaviour, since the closer true match allows for reduced search space. Both modified linear methods show an improvement in performance, though the improvement is less pronounced than with FLANN. In the exact copy case the modified linear methods practically become equivalent, since any nonzero dimension of the query is sufficient to exclude a potential match after the true nearest neighbour has been found. The d-D Sort method shows the best improvement in performance, with performance more than doubling between the outlier case and the rotated image case. In the exact case, the initial bilinear search always delivers the exact match, resulting in $\log(n)$ search time and extremely fast performance. Unfortunately the exact match case does not have many applications. This last result really shows not only that exact matching is possible using a one dimensional feature,

but also that d-D Sort is able to take advantage of close similarity.

6. Conclusion

Data structures such as k-D trees and hierarchical k-means trees are only marginally more effective than linear search when performing exact k nearest neighbour matching in high-dimensional local image descriptor data. Of these, the best-performing method is the FLANN approach [2], which improves performance by a factor of 2.5 at best, but typically yields an improvement of less than 1.5-fold. At the same time, this data structure requires more than a minute to construct for even small datasets.

This paper presents several performance improvements to the linear search method for exact k nearest neighbour matching. It is shown that evaluating the distance measure in order of the significance of query dimensions and terminating when the search threshold is reached can improve linear search time by 1.7–4.4-fold (usually at least 2.6 fold). These modifications are simple to implement and do not require any data preprocessing. Secondly, the d-D sort structure is introduced. This structure essentially presorts the data according to every dimension. No parameter tuning is required and data can be added efficiently. Using the sort order associated with the query's most significant dimension as a priority queue and to limit the search range improves results further. The d-D Sort-based search showed an improvement over linear search of 2–7-fold (usually at least 3.2-fold), while the preprocessing time can be several orders of magnitude less than that of FLANN. While it is possible to implement approximate nearest neighbour search using the d-D Sort structure, results show that the accuracy of this method decreases more rapidly than that of ANN and FLANN and does not yield the same performance-accuracy ratio.

In summary, this paper proposes two approaches for exact nearest neighbour search in normalised high-dimensional descriptor data. The first is the use of partial distance computation in order of significance of the query dimensions. This does not require any data preprocessing and yields best results when preprocessing time would be a significant factor, for example, when matching between a small set of images. The second approach is to use the d-D sort structure and proposed query mechanism, which yield the best query time performance without the need for any parameter tuning. This yields the best performance where the preprocessing time is small compared to the number of queries that will be performed. The d-D Sort structure also supports data addition for problems where the matching database grows progressively.

Acknowledgment

This project was supported by Australian Research Council Grant no. LP0990135.

References

[1] S. Arya, D. M. Mount, N. S. Netanyahu, R. Silverman, and A. Y. Wu, "An optimal algorithm for approximate nearest neighbor searching in fixed dimensions," *Journal of the ACM*, vol. 45, no. 6, pp. 891–923, 1998.

[2] M. Muja and D. G. Lowe, "Fast approximate nearest neighbors with automatic algorithm configuration," in *Proceedings of the International Conference on Computer Vision Theory and Applications (VISAPP'09)*, pp. 331–340, February 2009.

[3] D. G. Lowe, "Object recognition from local scale-invariant features," in *Proceedings of the 7th IEEE International Conference on Computer Vision (ICCV'99)*, vol. 2, pp. 1150–1157, Kerkyra, Greece, September 1999.

[4] D. G. Lowe, "Distinctive image features from scale-invariant keypoints," *International Journal of Computer Vision*, vol. 60, no. 2, pp. 91–110, 2004.

[5] K. Mikolajczyk and C. Schmid, "A performance evaluation of local descriptors," *IEEE Transactions on Pattern Analysis and Machine Intelligence*, vol. 27, no. 10, pp. 1615–1630, 2005.

[6] M. J. Huiskes and M. S. Lew, "The MIR Flickr retrieval evaluation," in *Proceedings of the 1st ACM International Conference on Multimedia Information Retrieval (MIR'08)*, pp. 39–43, August 2008.

[7] J. H. Friedman, J. L. Bentley, and R. A. Finkel, "An algorithm for finding best matches in logarithmic expected time," *ACM Transactions on Mathematical Software*, vol. 3, no. 3, pp. 209–226, 1977.

[8] K. Fukunaga and P. M. Narendra, "A branch and bound algorithm for computing k-nearest neighbors," *IEEE Transactions on Computers*, vol. 24, no. 7, pp. 750–753, 1975.

[9] S. Brin, "Near neighbor search in large metric spaces.," in *Proceedings of the 21th International Conference on Very Large Data Bases (VLDB'95)*, pp. 574–584, 1995.

[10] M. Houle, H. Kriegel, P. Kröger, E. Schubert, and A. Zimek, *Can Shared-Neighbor Distances Defeat the Curse of Dimensionality?* vol. 6187 of *Lecture Notes in Computer Science*, Springer, Berlin, Germany, 2010.

[11] D. Nistér and H. Stewénius, "Scalable recognition with a vocabulary tree," in *Proceedings of the IEEE Computer Society Conference on Computer Vision and Pattern Recognition (CVPR'06)*, vol. 2, pp. 2161–2168, June 2006.

[12] J. S. Beis and D. G. Lowe, "Shape indexing using approximate nearest-neighbour search in high-dimensional spaces," in *Proceedings of the IEEE Computer Society Conference on Computer Vision and Pattern Recognition*, pp. 1000–1006, June 1997.

[13] M. Aly, P. Welinder, M. Munich, and P. Perona, "Scaling object recognition: benchmark of current state of the art techniques," in *Proceedings of the 12th IEEE International Conference on Computer Vision Workshops (ICCV Workshops'09)*, pp. 2117–2124, Kyoto, Japan, October 2009.

[14] L. Paulevé, H. Jégou, and L. Amsaleg, "Locality sensitive hashing: a comparison of hash function types and querying mechanisms," *Pattern Recognition Letters*, vol. 31, no. 11, pp. 1348–1358, 2010.

[15] J. Matas, O. Chum, M. Urban, and T. Pajdla, "Robust wide baseline stereo from maximally stable extremal regions," in *Proceedings of the British Machine Vision Conference*, vol. 1, pp. 384–393, 2002.

[16] C. D. Bei and R. M. Gray, "An improvement of the minimum distortion encoding algorithm for vector quantization," *IEEE Transactions on Communications*, vol. 33, no. 10, pp. 1132–1133, 1985.

[17] R. Lakemond, C. Fookes, and S. Sridharan, "Negative determinant of hessian features," in *Proceedings of the International Conference on Digital Image Computing: Techniques and Applications*, pp. 530–535, Queensland, Australia, December 2011.

[18] R. Lakemond, D. N. R. McKinnon, C. Fookes, and S. Sridharan, "A feature clustering algorithm for scale-space analysis of image structures," in *Proceedings of the International Conference on Signal Processing and Communication Systems*, pp. 186–192, Gold Coast, Australia, December 2007.

8

Multimodal Markov Random Field for Image Reranking Based on Relevance Feedback

Ricardo Omar Chávez, Hugo Jair Escalante, Manuel Montes-y-Gómez, and Luis Enrique Sucar

Department of Computer Sciences, Instituto Nacional de Astrofíssica, Óptica y Electrónica, Luis Enrique Erro No. 1, 72840 Tonantzintla, PUE, Mexico

Correspondence should be addressed to Hugo Jair Escalante; hugo.jair@gmail.com

Academic Editors: H. Erdogan, N. Grammalidis, N. D. A. Mascarenhas, and W. L. Woo

This paper introduces a multimodal approach for reranking of image retrieval results based on relevance feedback. We consider the problem of reordering the ranked list of images returned by an image retrieval system, in such a way that relevant images to a query are moved to the first positions of the list. We propose a Markov random field (MRF) model that aims at classifying the images in the initial retrieval-result list as relevant or irrelevant; the output of the MRF is used to generate a new list of ranked images. The MRF takes into account (1) the rank information provided by the initial retrieval system, (2) similarities among images in the list, and (3) relevance feedback information. Hence, the problem of image reranking is reduced to that of minimizing an energy function that represents a trade-off between image relevance and interimage similarity. The proposed MRF is a multimodal as it can take advantage of both visual and textual information by which images are described with. We report experimental results in the IAPR TC12 collection using visual and textual features to represent images. Experimental results show that our method is able to improve the ranking provided by the base retrieval system. Also, the multimodal MRF outperforms unimodal (i.e., either text-based or image-based) MRFs that we have developed in previous work. Furthermore, the proposed MRF outperforms baseline multimodal methods that combine information from unimodal MRFs.

1. Introduction

Images are the main source of information available after text; this fact is due to the availability of inexpensive image registration (e.g., photographic cameras and cell phones) and data storage devices (large volume hard drives), which have given rise to the existence of millions of digital images stored in many databases around the world. However, stored information is useless if we cannot access the specific data we are interested in. Thus, the development of effective methods for the organization and exploration of image collections is a crucial task [1–3].

In a standard image retrieval scenario one has available a collection of images and users want to access images stored in that collection, where images can be annotated (i.e., associated to a textual description). Images are represented by features extracted from them. Users formulate queries (which are associated to their information needs) by using either sample images, a textual description, or a combination of both. Queries are represented by features extracted from them and the retrieval process reduces to comparing the representations of documents in the collection to that of the queries. Images in the collection are sorted in descending order of similarity and are shown to users in response to their queries.

Image retrieval has been an active research area since more than two decades ago [1–6]. During that time, a wide variety of content-based (i.e., that use visual features derived from the image) [1], text-based (i.e., that use text associated to the image) [2], and multimodal [3, 7] (i.e., that combine visual and textual features) retrieval techniques have been proposed, which have proved to be effective in varied scenarios. Nevertheless, current retrieval methods still have problems for retrieving most of relevant images to a given query in the first positions. The latter is due to the fact that modeling user intention from queries is, in general, a highly subjective and difficult task, hence, postprocessing and refinement strategies have been adopted [3, 4, 8–21].

Postretrieval techniques aim at refining retrieval results by feature reweighting, query modification, document reranking, and relevance feedback. The common idea is to interact with the user in order to learn or to improve a model of the underlying user's information need. Acceptable results have been obtained with such methods, however, they still have several limitations, including

(i) the need of extensive user interaction (One should note that, when available, user interaction should be included in postretrieval techniques as it is evident that information provided by the user is by far more reliable than that we would obtain with fully automatic approaches. Hence, we think that in general the goal of postprocessing methods should be the minimization of user interaction, instead of the development of fully automatic techniques.)

(ii) the multiple execution of retrieval models

(iii) the on-line construction of classification methods

(iv) the lack of contextual information in the postretrieval processing, which may be helpful for better modeling users' information needs

(v) the computational cost that involves processing the entire collection of documents for each feedback iteration and

(vi) the incapacity of methods to work with multimodal information.

This paper introduces an alternative postretrieval technique that aims at improving the results provided by an image retrieval system and that overcomes some of the limitations of current postretrieval methods. In particular, we face the problem of reranking the list of images as returned by an image retrieval system. This problem is motivated by the availability of retrieval systems that present high-recall and low-precision performance [7, 22], which evidences that the corresponding retrieval model is able to retrieve many relevant images but they are not placed in the right positions. Hence, given a list of ranked images, the problem we approach consists of moving relevant images to the first positions and displacing irrelevant ones to the final positions in the list.

We propose a solution to the reranking problem based on a multimodal Markov random field (MRF) that aims at classifying the ranked images as relevant or irrelevant. Each image in the list is associated to a binary random variable in the MRF (i.e., a node), and the value of each random variable indicates whether an image is considered relevant (when it takes the value 1) or not (when it takes the value 0). The MRF takes into account (1) the rank information provided by the base retrieval system, (2) similarities among images in the list, and (3) relevance feedback information. In this way, we reduce the problem of image reranking to that of minimizing an energy function that represents a trade-off between image relevance and interimage similarity.

Rank information provided by the retrieval system is the base of our method, which is further enriched with contextual (i.e., multimodal similarities among images) and relevance feedback information. The motivation for taking context into account is that relevant images to a query will be similar to each other and to the query, to some extent; whereas irrelevant images will be different among them. (One should note that irrelevant images will be somewhat similar to the query inevitably as that is why they were retrieved in the first place.) We consider relevance feedback as a seed generation mechanism for propagating the relevancy/irrelevancy status of nodes in the MRF. Our MRF is a multimodal as it can take advantage of both visual and textual information by which images are described. The proposed MRF does not require multiple executions of retrieval models nor training classification methods and it could work without user intervention. In consequence, our multimodal MRF overcomes the main limitations of current post-processing techniques, see Section 2.

We report experimental results in the IAPR TC12 collection [23] that show the validity of our formulation. This collection comprises 20, 000 images with manual annotations in three languages, and it is accompanied with sample queries and relevance judgements; this benchmark has been widely used for the evaluation of multimodal image retrieval systems [7, 22, 24, 25]. Experimental results show that our method is able to improve the ranking provided by a given retrieval system. Our multimodal MRF also outperforms unimodal (i.e., either text-based or image-based) MRFs that we have developed in previous work [26, 27]. Further, the proposed MRF outperforms baseline multimodal methods that combine information from unimodal MRFs. Our results motivate further research on the development of multimodal MRFs for related tasks, for example, for retrieval-result diversification [12, 25].

The contributions of this paper are as follows.

(i) We introduce a novel MRF model that incorporates multimodal information for image reranking. The proposed model is able to improve the ranking of the base retrieval system. The MRF relies on manual relevance feedback, thus it is a user adaptive technique, although it could work with automatic relevance feedback as well. Also, since our MRF works with a list of ranked images, it is not tied with a specific retrieval system nor with a particular architecture, image collection, or information modalities.

(ii) We propose an energy function for the MRF that incorporates information provided by the base retrieval system, relevance feedback, and interimage similarity. The energy function allows us to model the relationships among these sources of information. Also, the structure of the proposed MRF naturally allows us to take contextual information into account, which is often disregarded in usual post-retrieval techniques, although it proved very useful for our model.

(iii) We introduce baseline methods for multimodal image reranking based on ideas from late fusion and inter-media relevance feedback. The proposed formulations combine information from unimodal MRFs for image reranking and are able to improve the performance of the base retrieval system.

The rest of this paper is organized as follows. The next section reviews related work on image retrieval with emphasis on post-retrieval methods that incorporate relevance feedback. Section 3 presents background information that will be helpful for understanding the rest of the paper. Section 4 introduces the multimodal Markov random field for image reranking. Section 5 describes baseline techniques to which we compare our multimodal method. Section 6 describes the experimental setting we adopted and presents results on the IAPR TC12 collection. Section 7 presents the conclusions derived from this work and outlines future work directions.

2. Related Work

Given a database of images and a query formulated by a user, the goal of image retrieval systems is to return images in the database that are relevant to the query [1, 3]. The core of retrieval systems is the retrieval model which specifies how images/queries are represented, how they are compared, and how results are shown to users. However, because of the difficulty of the task and of the subjectivity of user intention modeling, retrieval models are often equipped with automatic or manual post-retrieval mechanisms that aim at refining and improving the outputs of retrieval systems [4, 10, 11].

2.1. Relevance Feedback. By far, the main post-retrieval technique used in image retrieval is relevance feedback (RF) and its variants thereof [3, 4, 7, 10, 11, 28–37]. RF aims to refine the retrieval results of an image retrieval system by taking advantage of information provided by the user. In each iteration of RF, the user indicates what images are relevant (or irrelevant) to her/his information need, then a specific criterion is adopted for modifying/adapting the original query with the goal of improving the preceding retrieval result.

RF was first introduced into image retrieval by Rui et al. [10] more than one decade ago, and nowadays it is a fundamental component of successful retrieval systems [3, 4, 7, 11, 24, 25, 37]. Usually, feedback information is used to modify the weights assigned to different features when computing similarity between queries and images in the database [10, 38, 39]. Alternatively, the distance between each document and the nearest relevant/irrelevant feedback image has been used to rerank the set of images in the collection [40–42]. Adapting the similarity function according to feedback images and then running again the retrieval model is another common approach in RF [32].

Other researchers have adopted an active learning scenario for RF. The system asks the user to indicate whether *informative* images are relevant/irrelevant to her/his information need [30, 31, 43], where the *informativeness* of images depends on the active learning criterion. For example, Tong and Chang [31] ask the user to provide feedback on images lying at the margin of a support vector machine classifier that attempts to classify images as relevant/irrelevant to a query. Zhou et al. [30] rely on a cotraining mechanism for modifying the distance function for image retrieval.

Other variants are those based on supervised learning and information fusion. The former RF information is used for building a classifier, where relevant images are considered the positive examples and irrelevant images are considered the negative examples of a binary classification task [32, 44] or of a one-class classification problem [45]. For example, Yan et al. build a support vector classifier using as positive examples the query examples and as negative ones the most dissimilar video shots for content-based video retrieval [33, 34]. Conversely, late fusion techniques and dynamic list fusion methods have been used to combine information from multiple retrieval models with the goal of improving the performance of a single retrieval technique [8, 13, 14].

Most of the above-described strategies have been defined for content-based image retrieval, although they can be easily adapted for textual and multimodal systems. Recently, a multimodal version of RF has been proposed for image retrieval [15]. The so-called intermedia RF technique consists of performing two RF iterations in which the modalities used in the first and second iterations are different [15, 37]. For each RF iteration it can be adopted by any of the above-described variants of RF.

Whereas most of the above-cited works have reported acceptable performance, they present several limitations. Most of them require the multiple execution of a retrieval model or of the on-line construction of classification methods, and the latter formulation can be computationally expensive. Efficiency is a crucial factor in image retrieval because real time response is required [3, 20]. Techniques based on active learning require a large amount of user interaction in order to obtain acceptable performance; however, some users may not be willing to spend much time interacting with a system; thus, user interaction must be minimized or interactive systems must give support to *lazy* users. Additionally, most of the described methods do not take into account all of the available information (e.g., initial ranking and contextual information) for refining the retrieval results of the base system, which can be helpful for improving the effectiveness of post-retrieval techniques.

In this paper we propose a variant of RF that aims at alleviating some of the limitations of current methods. We propose a reranking technique for refining the output of an image retrieval system. Our approach does not require the multiple execution of a retrieval model (other than the included for the base retrieval method) nor the construction of a classifier. In fact, our method does not process the entire collection of documents in each iteration of feedback, but it focuses on the top-k retrieved documents. Whereas some documents can be out of reach for a particular query or user, this restriction makes the post-retrieval process very fast. Opposed to active-learning-based approaches, our method only requires minimal user interaction and it could even work without the need of a user at all (i.e., under a blind RF formulation). Additionally, the proposed model takes advantage of all of the information available during a retrieval session, namely, initial ranking as provided by the base retrieval system, multimodal similarity among the retrieved images (e.g., context), and RF information. A notable benefit of our approach is that it is not restricted to a particular retrieval system nor to a specific information modality or system architecture. Thus, our method offers advantages in terms of generality as it can be used with any retrieval system, efficiency and effectiveness.

2.2. Reranking Methods. Similar document reranking approaches have been proposed elsewhere [16–21, 40–42]. Giacinto and Roli have developed reranking methods that rely on the distance of each document in the collection to the nearest relevant and irrelevant image as marked by the user [40–42]. The intuition behind that method is that a relevant image will present a small distance to relevant images marked by the user and large distance to irrelevant images identified by the user. Our MRF is based on a generalization of that idea: relevant images will show a small distance to relevant images marked by the user and at the same time they will be similar to each other; irrelevant images will lie at a considerable distance from relevant images identified by the user and they can have low similarity among them. Thus, differently from the work of Giacinto and Roli, we consider contextual information for reranking the list of images (besides we do not process the entire collection at each feedback iteration).

Cui et al. describe a reranking approach based on visual features for Web image retrieval systems [20]. Under their approach, query images are categorized into one of five intention categories; then, depending on the category of the query, different feature weights (computed off-line) are used to compute a new ranking for images according to the RankBoost framework [46]. Whereas this approach is very efficient, it is limited to five intention categories; further, they rely on pretrained models for detecting user intention in query images, which are expensive to train and subject to uncertainty. The method does not consider multimodal information nor supports relevance feedback. The experimental evaluation presented in [20] is performed over a large number of images but restricted to a small vocabulary.

Lin et al. [21] and Marakakis et al. [16] introduce image reranking approaches. Lin et al. use the relevance model from Lavrenko and Croft [47] to rerank Web images using global information (i.e., textual information obtained from the HTML page that contains the image) [21]. The proposed model takes into account information from the base system, although it disregards context and relevance feedback information. Also, limited performance is reported in a small scale experimental setting. Marakakis et al. propose an alternative probabilistic reranking technique that attempts to model relevancy from relevance feedback [16]. As most of the reported work, this method requires to process the entire collection of documents in each feedback iteration;

additionally, if the feedback images change drastically the model must be trained again.

Tian et al. describe a Bayesian formulation for reranking the list of videos obtained with textual queries [17]. Their goal is to infer the final list of ranking scores from the initial list of scores and similarities among videos, under the premise that visually similar videos must be assigned similar ranking scores. Jing and Baluja propose a formulation similar to that of Google's page rank for image reranking in the task of product image retrieval [18]. Important (*authority*) images are identified based on their similarity with other images under consideration. The latter model was evaluated on a large scale product data set. The above approaches are closely related to our proposal, although they focus on image reranking based exclusively on visual similarities; also they do not give support to multimodal queries. Further, these methods do not incorporate other information available such as query-document similarity and RF information.

Yao et al. introduce a multimodal co-reranking approach [19], where visual and textual similarities are used to rerank the list of images provided by a textual image retrieval technique. The proposed technique is based on random walks over visual and textual similarity graphs. As with other techniques, neither multimodal query similarities nor RF information is considered by this method.

In previous work [26, 27] we have explored a similar approach where a (unimodal) MRF model has been used with either textual or visual features for image reranking. We explored the combination of internal and external similarity for improving the ranking of images. The best results obtained from that work improved the retrieval performance of the initial list up to 66% in the textual case, and 51% in the visual case when 10 relevance feedback images were considered, and up to 20% and 8%, respectively, when a single image was taken as feedback. Results from [26, 27] showed that in most of the cases both methods identified complementary sets of relevant images, motivating the development of the multimodal technique introduced in this paper.

3. Markov Random Fields

Markov random fields (MRFs) are a type of undirected probabilistic graphical models that aim at modeling dependencies among variables of the problem in turn [48]. MRFs have a long history within image processing and computer vision [49, 50]. They were first proposed for denoising digital images [48] and since then a large number of applications and extensions have been proposed. Classical applications include image segmentation [51] and image filtering [52]; although, recently they have been successfully applied for image annotation [53], region labeling [54, 55], and information retrieval [56–58] with great success.

MRF modeling has appealing features for problems that involve the optimization of configurations of variables that present interdependencies among them. They rely on a strict probabilistic modeling, yet they allow the incorporation of prior knowledge by means of potential functions. For these reasons, we adopted an MRF model for reranking images

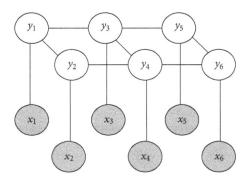

FIGURE 1: Graphical representation of a first-order MRF. Observed variables (X) are shaded.

listed by an image retrieval system. The rest of this section summarizes the formalism of MRFs.

An MRF is a set of random variables $F = \{f_1, \ldots, f_N\}$ indexed by nodes of a graph where the following conditions hold:

$$P(f_i) \geq 0, \quad \forall f_i \in F, \tag{1}$$

$$P(f_i \mid f_{s-\{i\}}) = P(f_i \mid \mathcal{N}(f_i)), \tag{2}$$

where $\mathcal{N}(f_i)$ is the set of neighbors of f_i according to the neighboring system $\mathcal{N}$. Formula (1) is the so-called positivity condition and avoids negative probability values, whereas expression (2) states that the value of a random variable depends only on the set of neighbors of that variable, that is, the Markovian condition.

It has been shown that an MRF follows a Gibbs distribution [52], where a Gibbs distribution of the possible configurations of F with respect to $\mathcal{N}$ has the following form:

$$P(f) = Z^{-1} \times e^{-(1/T)E(f)}, \tag{3}$$

where Z is a normalization constant, and T is the so-called temperature parameter (a common choice is $T = 1$) and $E(F)$ is an energy function of the following form:

$$E(F) = \sum_{c \in C} V_c(f) = \sum_{\{i\} \in C_1} V_1(f_i) + \sum_{\{i,j\} \in C_2} V_2(f_i, f_j) + \cdots, \tag{4}$$

where "$\cdots$" denotes possible potentials V_c defined over higher order neighborhoods $C_3, C_4, \ldots, C_K$; each C_i defines a neighborhood system of order i between the nodes of the MRF. For example, Figure 1 shows an MRF with a neighborhood system of order 2. Often the set F is considered as the union of two subsets of random variables $X \cup Y$; where X is the set of observed variables and Y is the set of output variables, which state we would like to predict. Potentials V_c are problem dependent and commonly they are learned from data.

One of the main problems in MRFs is that of selecting the most probable configuration of F (i.e., an assignment of values to each variable f_i of the field). This configuration is obtained by minimizing Formula (4). For this purpose, a variety of optimization techniques have been used, including iterated conditioned modes (ICMs) [59], simulated annealing [60], and graph cuts [61]. ICM is one of the most used inference methods [48]; it is an iterative optimization procedure that performs local moves on the values of the nodes of the MRF. ICM fixes the value of all but one node in the MRF and determines the value of the remaining node by looking for the value minimizing Formula (4), and this process is repeated for all nodes and iterated several times. ICM does not guarantee finding the global optimum of Formula (4). However, it allows us to obtain acceptable locally optimal solutions; besides, it is a highly efficient method. Since efficiency is a crucial aspect in the considered reranking problem, we used ICM for inference in the multimodal MRF for image reranking.

4. Multimodal Markov Random Field for Image Reranking

The multimodal MRF we propose takes as input a list of N-ranked images, provided by an image retrieval system, and attempts to rerank the images in the list in such a way that relevant images are put before irrelevant ones. The proposed method can be added as a postprocessing stage for any image retrieval system, as it does not rely on information from a particular system. Figure 2 shows a schematic diagram of the proposed multimodal MRF. Besides the position of images in the list, the model incorporates interimage and query-image similarities as well as relevance feedback information. The rest of this section describes the multimodal MRF we propose.

We consider a MRF in which each node $F = \{f_1, \ldots, f_N\}$ corresponds to a document (image + text caption) in the list returned by a given retrieval system; each f_i is binary random variable such that when $f_i = 1$ the ith-image is considered to be relevant to the search intention and when $f_i = 0$ the corresponding image is considered to be irrelevant. Figure 3 shows a diagram of the MRF for image reranking. The task of the multimodal MRF is to divide images in the list into relevant and irrelevant ones by varying the values of $F = \{f_1, \ldots, f_N\}$. Based on the final configuration of the MRF, we generate a new list of images by placing in the first positions those images i for which $f_i = 1$, followed by the rest of images (i.e., images with $f_j = 0$); where we keep the relative position of images in the original list (i.e., images with $f_i = 1$ are put first in the order they appeared in the original list, followed by images for which $f_j = 0$ in the respective order).

We define an energy function for the multimodal MRF that attempts to model the relevancy status of images in terms of: (1) the information provided by the base retrieval system augmented with image-query similarity; (2) similarities among images in the list; and (3) relevance feedback information. Our hypothesis is, on the one hand, that relevant images must be very similar to the query (as they are supposedly relevant) and they must be similar to each other, as all relevant images are related to a common topic. On the other hand, irrelevant images must be less similar to the query than relevant ones and irrelevant images must be less similar

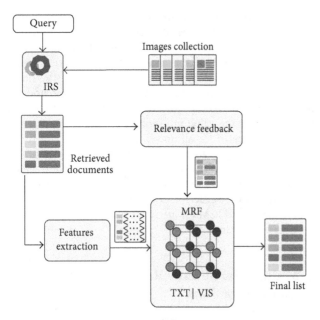

FIGURE 2: Schematic diagram for the proposed multimodal MRF. The MRF takes as input the list of images retrieved by an image retrieval system (IRS), relevance feedback information, and multimodal (textual and visual) features extracted from the images in the list. The structure of the MRF is depicted in Figure 3. The output of the model is a list of reranked images.

to each other, as they are not related to a common topic. The configuration of the MRF that minimizes the energy function is used to generate the new ranking.

4.1. Energy Function.

The energy function of the multimodal MRF specifies how likely is that a configuration of the MRF (i.e., an assignment of values to each node f_i) is the best ranking for the images in the list. We define an energy function that incorporates interimage similarity, query-image similarity, rank information provided by the retrieval system, and relevance feedback information provided by the user. The underlying idea is that a combination of these information sources is beneficial for characterizing *good ranks*. Further, since the proposed model is multimodal, we take into account both textual and visual similarity. More specifically we propose an energy function of the following form:

$$U(F) = \sigma E_T(F) + (1 - \sigma) E_V(F), \quad (5)$$

where $E_T(F)$ and $E_V(F)$ are individual energy functions defined for the textual and visual modalities, respectively, while the scalar σ is introduced for weighting the influence of each modality. Since both $E_T(F)$ and $E_V(F)$ only differ in the way that similarity is estimated, we provide a general description of the form of the individual energy functions. In Section 4.2 we provide details on how we estimate the similarity for textual and visual features.

One should note that Formula (5) can be extended easily to incorporate information from more than two modalities. In that case, we would have an individual energy function per modality, which implies having means to compute similarity

for each modality. While it is rather easy to extend the multimodal MRF to consider more modalities, we think that the inference process will become more difficult. This is because we will be optimizing an energy function with as many objectives as modalities. In that scenario the selection of σ weights will be crucial. We would like to explore this research direction as future work.

Each individual energy function (i.e., $E_T(F)$ and $E_V(F)$) has the following form:

$$E(F) = \lambda \left(\sum_{f_i \in F} V_c(f_i, N_i) \right) + (1 - \lambda) \left(\sum_{f_i \in F} V_a(f_i) \right), \quad (6)$$

where N_i is the set of neighbors for node f_i, V_c accounts for information of the association between neighboring images, whereas V_a is the observation potential and it accounts for information that is associated to a single image, see Figure 3. λ is a scalar that weights the importance of both V_a and V_c.

We assume that each node in the multimodal MRF is connected to each other, that is, a fully connected graph. Since the number of images in the list is relatively small, considering a complete graph is not a computational issue and it allows us to consider the relations among all documents in the list. However, it is worth noting that both elements of the energy function in formula (6) are quadratic; that is, $O(V_c) = O(n^2)$ and $O(V_a) = O(n^2)$ being n the number of documents contained in the retrieved list. Thus, $O(E) = O(n^2) + O(n^2) = O(\max(n^2, n^2)) = O(n^2)$ and since λ is a constant, it is a depreciable element from the complexity calculation.

4.1.1. Interaction Potential.

The interaction potential V_c is defined as follows:

$$V_c(f_i, N_i) = \begin{cases} S(f_i, N_i^R) + (1 - S(f_i, N_i^I)), & \text{if } f_i = 0, \\ S(f_i, N_i^I) + (1 - S(f_i, N_i^R)), & \text{if } f_i = 1, \end{cases} \quad (7)$$

where $S(f_i, N_i^R)$ is the average similarity between image f_i and its neighbors with relevant value N_i^R. Conversely, $S(f_i, N_i^I)$ represents the average similarity between the image associated with node f_i and its neighbors with irrelevant value N_i^I. Thus, we divide the neighbors of node f_i into two subsets: the neighbors with relevant value, N_i^R, and the neighbors with irrelevant value N_i^I (i.e., $N_i = N_i^R \cup N_i^I$ and $N_i^R \cap N_i^I = \emptyset$).

Under the proposed MRF the minimization of formula (6) leads to improved rankings; hence, we seek configurations of the MRF with low values of $V_c(f_i, N_i)$. Accordingly, if an image is being considered relevant (i.e., $f_i = 1$), low values of $V_c(f_i, N_i)$ are obtained when the hypothetically relevant image is not too similar to irrelevant images and highly similar to relevant images. On the other hand, when a node is being considered irrelevant (i.e., $f_i = 0$), low values of $V_c(f_i, N_i)$ are obtained when the hypothetically irrelevant image is not too similar to relevant images and highly similar

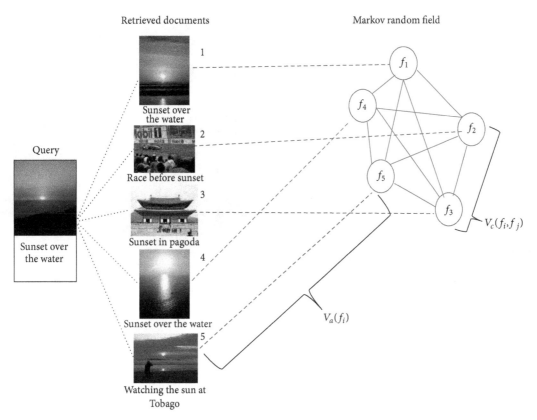

FIGURE 3: Diagram of the proposed MRF for image reranking. Each image in the original list is associated to a node in the MRF. We incorporate in the model the position of the document in the original list, the similarity of images to the query and the similarity among images. Single node information is incorporated through the $V_a(f_i)$ potential (dashed lines), while contextual information is introduced via the $V_c(f_i, f_j)$ potential (solid lines).

to irrelevant ones. Intuitively, V_c assesses how much support we give same-valued images to keep the current value, and how much support we give oppose-valued images to change to the contrary value.

We compute the similarity $S(f_i, f_j)$ between a pair of images I_i and I_j, associated to nodes f_i and f_j, respectively, by comparing their visual or textual features. The particular similarity functions we consider are defined in such a way that they always return a normalized quantity (i.e., $S(f_i, f_j) \in [0, 1]$), see Section 4.2.

4.1.2. Observation Potential. The observation potential V_a is defined as follows:

$$V_a(f_i) = \begin{cases} S_q(f_i, q) \times \delta\left(r(f_i)^{-1}\right), & \text{if } f_i = 0 \\ \left(1 - S_q(f_i, q)\right) \times \delta\left(r(f_i)\right), & \text{if } f_i = 1. \end{cases} \quad (8)$$

V_a captures the affinity between the image associated to node f_i and the query q, measured by a similarity term and by using information in the original list. On the one hand, $S_q(f_i, q)$, indicates how similar is the image associated to node f_i to the query q. On the other hand, δ is a function that transforms the positions, $r(f_i)$ (resp., inverse of the position, $r(f_i)^{-1}$) of image f_i in the original list into a real value.

The transformation δ is described as follows:

$$\delta(x) = \frac{\exp(x/20)}{\exp(5)} \quad (9)$$

when $f_i = 1$, $\delta(x)$ takes values proportional to the position of the image in the list and when $f_i = 0$, $\delta(x)$ takes values proportional to the inverse of the position in the list. The position (inverse of the position) of images is weighted exponentially because we want the position (resp., inverse of the position) to have more influence for the top-ranked (resp., bottom-ranked) images. The values 20 and 5 in expression (9) were fixed by trial and error on preliminary experimentation.

The observation potential incorporates information from the initial retrieval system; however, one should note that we only use the position of images in the list, which is independent of the retrieval system that was used to obtain the initial list. V_a is based on the assumption that relevant images are very similar to the query and at the same time it is very likely that they appear in the top positions; on the other hand, irrelevant images are less similar to the query and it is very likely that they appear in the bottom positions of the list.

4.1.3. Relevance Feedback. We use relevance feedback information as a seed for building the initial configuration of the MRF; that is, we set $f_i = 1$ for relevance feedback images and we set $f_j = 0$ for the rest. In this way, the multimodal MRF starts the energy minimization process knowing what images are potentially relevant to the query. Thus, the inference process consists of identifying further relevant images in the list by propagating through the MRF the relevance feedback information. Since we assume that relevance feedback images are indeed relevant to the query, they are considered to be relevant during the whole energy minimization process (i.e., the corresponding nodes are never set to 0).

Relevance feedback can be performed either automatically or manually. In previous work we have studied the use of manual and automatic relevance feedback for unimodal MRFs [26, 27]. We found that under both forms of feedback the unimodal MRFs can improve the retrieval performance of the initial list. However, as expected, improvements were larger when using manual relevance feedback. Therefore, in this work we limit ourselves to explore the performance of the multimodal MRF using manual relevance feedback and we postpone to future work experiments with pseudo-relevance feedback.

4.1.4. Inference in the Multimodal MRF. As stated before, the configuration that minimizes expression (5) is used for generating the new image ranking. In this work, such configuration is obtained via heuristic optimization using the iterated conditioned modes (ICMs) algorithm [59]. We also performed experiments with simulated annealing (SA). However, SA increases significantly the computational burden of the optimization process and the quality of solutions is comparable to that obtained with ICM. Hence we preferred ICM over SA. Graph cuts are another option to explore for future work, although it is also a time-consuming method.

4.2. Similarity Estimation. In Section 4.1 we described the form of the unimodal energy functions we consider. In this section we describe how similarity is estimated for textual and visual features. The proposed similarity measures are basically the normalized number of common words or SIFT features in the images that are compared. Before describing the similarity measures we describe the textual and visual features we extract from annotated images.

4.2.1. Visual and Textual Features. We consider images that are annotated with textual descriptions; specifically, we consider images from the IAPR TC12 collection [23], which was used extensively in the context of ImageCLEF [22]. Figure 4 shows a sample image from the IAPR TC12 collection. For representing images we consider visual features, extracted from the image itself, and textual features, extracted from its corresponding caption. Regarding Web-based collections, we can use a preprocessing step to extract the text from HTML files containing the analyzed image.

As textual features we use a binary bag of words representation, where each image is represented by a binary vector that indicates the presence (1) or absence (0) of words from the collection vocabulary in the document.

As visual features we consider the set of SIFT (Scale-Invariant Feature Transform) features extracted from the image [62]. In preliminary experiments we have explored

⟨TITLE⟩ The Plaza de Armas ⟨/TITLE⟩
⟨DESCRIPTION⟩ a yellow building with white columns in the background; two palm trees in front of the house; cars parked in front of the house; a woman and a child are walking over the square; ⟨/DESCRIPTION⟩

FIGURE 4: Example of an image from the IAPR TC-12 collection and its set of descriptive fields: *title* and *description*.

other types of textual (e.g., *n*-grams and the *tf-idf* weighting scheme) and visual (e.g., color, texture, and shape) features; however, the best results with our multimodal MRF were obtained by using the binary bag of words together with the SIFT features. Images in the retrieved list and the corresponding queries are represented using the above multimodal features.

4.2.2. Similarity for Textual Features. For the estimation of similarity in terms of textual features we propose the following functions.

(i) The similarity between two images I_i and I_j associated to nodes f_i and f_j in terms of their textual representation is defined as follows:

$$S\left(f_i, f_j\right) = \frac{\left|I_i \cap I_j\right|}{\left|I_i \cup I_j\right|}, \tag{10}$$

where $|I_i \cap I_j|$ and $|I_i \cup I_j|$ are the number of words that occur in the intersection and union, respectively, of the textual representations of I_i and I_j. This similarity function is the ratio between the number of words that are common for both documents and the number of different words that occur in either document.

(ii) The similarity between an image I_i associated to node f_i and query q using textual information is defined as follows:

$$S_q\left(f_i, q\right) = \frac{\left|I_i \cap q\right|}{\left|q\right|}. \tag{11}$$

The difference between $S_q(f_i, q)$ and $S(f_i, f_j)$ is the denominator $|q|$, which represents the number of words in the query. This difference is justified because we want $S_q(f_i, q)$ to be independent of the length of the documents.

4.2.3. Similarity for Visual Features. For the estimation of similarity in terms of SIFT features we propose the following functions.

(i) The similarity between two images I_i and I_j associated to nodes f_i and f_j in terms of their visual representation is defined as follows:

$$S(f_i, f_j) = \frac{2 \times \text{match}(f_i, f_j)}{\text{count}(f_i) + \text{count}(f_j)}, \qquad (12)$$

where match (f_i, f_j) is the number of similar descriptors between images I_i and I_j as described by Lowe [62] and count (f_i) is the number of SIFT features found in image I_i.

(ii) The similarity between an image I_i associated to node f_i and the sample images $q_1, \ldots, q_H$ that compose the query q is defined as follows (One should note that queries in the IAPR TC12 collection are composed of 3 sample images, i.e., $H = 3$, see Section 6.1.)

$$S_q(f_i, q) = \max_h \left(\frac{\text{match}(I_i, q_{1,\ldots,H})}{\text{count}(q_{1,\ldots,H})} \right), \qquad (13)$$

where H is the number of available query images. Thus we take the maximum similarity of the image I_i to any query image q_h, as with the textual features, we want the similarity function to be independent of the number of SIFT features in image I_i.

5. Baseline Multimodal Methods

The multimodal MRF introduced in Section 4 is a way of combining the information from the unimodal energy functions E_T and E_V, which take into account either textual or visual information, respectively. While in previous work we have studied the benefits of E_T and E_V for image reranking separately [26], it is clear that there are other alternatives for combining information from E_T and E_V. The rest of this section describes two of such alternative methods based on MRFs that incorporate multimodal information, these techniques are considered baselines to which we compare our multimodal MRF.

The first strategy is a late fusion approach in which we run two unimodal MRFs, one using E_V and the other using E_T, for reranking the list provided by the image retrieval system. The two reranked lists generated with the unimodal methods are combined to obtain a new list of images. The new list is generated by applying the CombMNZ technique, which combines the lists of results through redundancy and position information to reallocate the elements in a new order [63]. We call this strategy late fusion.

Figure 5 shows a diagram of this strategy. The intuitive idea of the late fusion approach is that since each unimodal MRF is based on information from different modalities, the resultant lists may contain complimentary ranking information, thus the combination of both lists may result in an even better ranking than those obtained through the unimodal MRFs.

We developed another alternative technique that is inspired by the so-called intermedia relevance feedback approach widely used in multimodal image retrieval [37]. The proposed technique consists of the serial application of unimodal MRFs, where a different energy function (E_V or E_T) is used each time. The initial list is reranked with a unimodal MRF method using either E_T or E_V, next the resultant reranked list is used as input for a second unimodal MRF, this time using a different energy function than that used in the first stage. The resultant list is the output of the method. We call this strategy intermedia relevance feedback.

Figure 6 shows the scheme of the intermedia relevance feedback strategy and its two possible configurations (i.e., using first E_V then E_T and vice versa). Intuitively, we assume that the list reranked by an initial (unimodal) MRF can be further improved by reranking it using another MRF, but this time using different information.

6. Experiments and Results

We conducted several experiments for evaluating the performance of the multimodal MRF described in Section 4 and that of the two alternative strategies introduced in Section 5. The goals of our experiments were (i) to evaluate the performance of the multimodal MRF under different parameter settings, (ii) to compare the performance of the multimodal MRF to the base retrieval system and to unimodal MRFs, and (iii) to compare the performance of the proposed multimodal MRF to that of the alternative multimodal methods for image reranking. The rest of this section describes the experimental results and highlights our main findings.

6.1. Experimental Setup. For our experiments we used the IAPR TC12 collection with topics and ground-truth data as used in ImageCLEF2008 [23], see Figure 4 for a sample image. This collection has been widely used by the image retrieval community, see for example [7, 13, 14, 22–27, 37, 54, 64]. The benchmark comprises $20,000$ images with manual annotations in three languages; it is accompanied with sample queries and relevance judgements. Complexity of queries ranges from very simple (e.g., *destinations in Venezuela*) to extremely difficult (e.g., *creative group pictures in Uyuni* or *church with more than two towers*) and most queries require the combination of visual and textual information in order to obtain relevant documents. The considered ground-truth data contains 39 queries, where each query is composed of 3 sample images and a textual description. Figure 7 shows a sample query as considered in our experiments.

As base image retrieval system we considered the system that our group developed for the photographic retrieval task at ImageCLEF2008 and selected a particular list of images

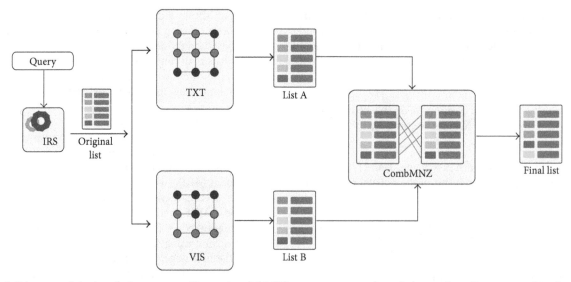

FIGURE 5: Diagram of the late fusion strategy. Two unimodal MRFs are run separately and the resultant lists are combined using the CombMNZ technique.

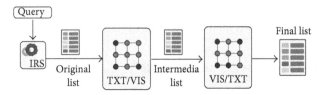

FIGURE 6: Diagram of the intermedia relevance feedback strategy. One unimodal MRF is applied after the other using different information (i.e., textual or visual).

⟨title⟩ animal swimmimg ⟨/title⟩
⟨narr⟩ Relevant images will show one or more animals
(fish, birds, reptiles, etc.) swimming in a body of water.
Images of people swimming in water are note relevant.
Images of animals that are not swimming are not not
relevant. ⟨/narr⟩

FIGURE 7: Query example for the photo retrieval track from the ImageCLEF2008 forum. Each query includes, among other fields, a field *title* summarizing the query objective, and a field *narrative* specifying textually which images are relevant to the query. Three sample images are associated to each query.

that was evaluated in that forum. The specific list of images we considered (referred to as SRI TIA-TXTIMG) was ranked third in terms of recall in ImageCLEF2008 [64], which means that most of the relevant documents were retrieved. However, documents in that list were not placed in the right positions as it was ranked 77th in terms of mean average precision (MAP). Hence, there is a considerable potential of improvement for our reranking techniques. As input data for the proposed method we considered the top 100 images retrieved by the image retrieval system for each of the 39 queries. For evaluation we used the average over the 39 topics of the MAP as leading measure [65], although we also report precision (P) at different numbers of retrieved documents.

Each trial of our experiments proceeds as follows. We provide the original list as input to the technique under evaluation. Next, using ground truth information, we simulate a manual relevance feedback session by identifying k relevance feedback images in the list (i.e., we randomly select k-relevant images, as indicated in the ground-truth information, that are contained in the list), for different values for k. These k-images are used as initial configuration for the method under evaluation. The ICM algorithm is run for 50 iterations (as maximum) trying to minimize the corresponding energy function, although in average it took only 7 iterations to converge. The final configuration of the method is used to generate a new list of ranked images. Finally, the retrieval performance of the reranked list is evaluated.

In the following, when mentioning a statistically significant difference between results we will refer to a paired *t*-Student test using a $\alpha = 0.05\%$ confidence level [66, 67]. We consider this test because it is one of the mostly used for evaluating information retrieval systems.

6.2. *Multimodal MRFs versus Unimodal MRFs.* In the first experiment we compared the performance of the multimodal MRF to that obtained by the base image retrieval system and that reported with unimodal MRFs. The goal of this experiment was to (a) quantify the improvement offered by the multimodal MRF for image reranking over the initial list and (b) to evaluate the difference in performance when using multimodal or unimodal information for the MRF.

Figure 8 compares the average MAP obtained with the multimodal MRF to that obtained by the base image retrieval

TABLE 1: MAP, precision at 5 (P5), 10 (P10), and 20 (P20) documents obtained by different parameter settings of the proposed multimodal MRF (columns 6–9), compared to the performance one would obtain with relevance feedback alone (columns 2–5). Column 1 indicates the parameter settings for the corresponding row as follows: the first value is $k \in \{1, 3, 5, 8, 10\}$, the number of relevance feedback images, λ_V is the value of λ for the visual energy function (i.e., E_V), and λ_T is the value of λ for the textual energy function (i.e., E_T).

Base IRS	P5	P10	P20	MAP			
SRI TIA-TXTIMG	0.4769	0.4538	0.3910	0.2359			

$\sigma = 1$		Only relevance feedback				Multimodal MRF	
Configuration	P5	P10	P20	MAP	P5	P10	P20	MAP
$k = 1; \lambda_V = 0.5; \lambda_T = 1.0$	0.5641	0.4897	0.4038	0.2486	0.6051	0.5436	0.4756	0.2852
$k = 3; \lambda_V = 0.5; \lambda_T = 1.0$	0.7846	0.5872	0.4359	0.2742	0.7897	0.6282	0.5141	0.3123
$k = 5; \lambda_V = 0.5; \lambda_T = 1.0$	1.0000	0.6795	0.4782	0.2984	1.0000	0.7256	0.5551	0.3344
$k = 8; \lambda_V = 0.5; \lambda_T = 1.0$	1.0000	0.8692	0.5577	0.3352	1.0000	0.8846	0.6359	0.3752
$k = 10; \lambda_V = 0.5; \lambda_T = 1.0$	1.0000	0.9744	0.6128	0.3560	1.0000	0.9744	0.6628	0.3919

$\sigma = 0.7$		Only relevance feedback				Multimodal MRF	
Configuration	P5	P10	P20	MAP	P5	P10	P20	MAP
$k = 1; \lambda_V = 0.5; \lambda_T = 1.0$	0.5641	0.4897	0.4038	0.2486	0.6462	0.5744	0.5038	0.2960
$k = 3; \lambda_V = 1.0; \lambda_T = 1.0$	0.7846	0.5872	0.4359	0.2742	0.8000	0.6282	0.5205	0.3153
$k = 5; \lambda_V = 0.7; \lambda_T = 1.0$	1.0000	0.6795	0.4782	0.2984	1.0000	0.7256	0.5615	0.3375
$k = 8; \lambda_V = 0.0; \lambda_T = 0.5$	1.0000	0.8692	0.5577	0.3352	1.0000	0.8718	0.5897	0.3470
$k = 10; \lambda_V = 0.7; \lambda_T = 1.0$	1.0000	0.9744	0.6128	0.3560	1.0000	0.9744	0.6731	0.3936

$\sigma = 0.5$		Only relevance feedback				Multimodal MRF	
Configuration	P5	P10	P20	MAP	P5	P10	P20	MAP
$k = 1; \lambda_V = 0.7; \lambda_T = 1.0$	0.5641	0.4897	0.4038	0.2486	0.6513	0.5821	0.5077	0.2956
$k = 3; \lambda_V = 0.7; \lambda_T = 1.0$	0.7846	0.5872	0.4359	0.2742	0.8103	0.6487	0.5282	0.3154
$k = 5; \lambda_V = 1.0; \lambda_T = 1.0$	1.0000	0.6795	0.4782	0.2984	1.0000	0.7256	0.5718	0.3358
$k = 8; \lambda_V = 1.0; \lambda_T = 1.0$	1.0000	0.8692	0.5577	0.3352	1.0000	0.8923	0.6500	0.3801
$k = 10; \lambda_V = 1.0; \lambda_T = 1.0$	1.0000	0.9744	0.6128	0.3560	1.0000	0.9744	0.6885	0.3966

$\sigma = 0.3$		Only relevance feedback				Multimodal MRF	
Configuration	P5	P10	P20	MAP	P5	P10	P20	MAP
$k = 1; \lambda_V = 1.0, \lambda_T = 0.7$	0.5641	0.4897	0.4038	0.2486	0.6718	0.5923	0.5167	0.3004
$k = 3; \lambda_V = 1.0, \lambda_T = 1.0$	0.7846	0.5872	0.4359	0.2742	0.8051	0.6436	0.5359	0.3142
$k = 5; \lambda_V = 1.0, \lambda_T = 1.0$	1.0000	0.6795	0.4782	0.2984	1.0000	0.7462	0.5987	0.3432
$k = 8; \lambda_V = 1.0, \lambda_T = 1.0$	1.0000	0.8692	0.5577	0.3352	1.0000	0.9000	0.6833	0.3851
$k = 10; \lambda_V = 1.0, \lambda_T = 1.0$	1.0000	0.9744	0.6128	0.3560	1.0000	0.9744	0.7218	0.4031

$\sigma = 0$		Only relevance feedback				Multimodal MRF	
Configuration	P5	P10	P20	MAP	P5	P10	P20	MAP
$k = 1; \lambda_V = 0.3, \lambda_T = 1.0$	0.5641	0.4897	0.4038	0.2486	0.6513	0.5282	0.4128	0.2569
$k = 3; \lambda_V = 0.7, \lambda_T = 1.0$	0.7846	0.5872	0.4359	0.2742	0.8410	0.6205	0.4423	0.2795
$k = 5; \lambda_V = 0.0, \lambda_T = 1.0$	1.0000	0.6795	0.4782	0.2984	1.0000	0.7000	0.4846	0.3016
$k = 8; \lambda_V = 0.5, \lambda_T = 1.0$	1.0000	0.8692	0.5577	0.3352	1.0000	0.8821	0.5654	0.3374
$k = 10; \lambda_V = 0.7, \lambda_T = 1.0$	1.0000	0.9744	0.6128	0.3560	1.0000	0.9744	0.6205	0.3580

TABLE 2: Relative improvements (%) in terms of MAP of relevance feedback alone (RF), textual MRF (t-MRF), visual MRF (v-MRF), multimodal MRF (MM-MRF), the two intermedia relevance feedback variants (IRF ($T > V$) and IRF ($V > T$)), and the late fusion (LF) method over the base image retrieval system.

k	RF	t-MRF	v-MRF	MM-MRF	IRF $T > V$	IRF $V > T$	LF
1	5.38	20.90	8.90	**27.34**	24.16	23.31	16.53
3	16.24	32.39	18.48	33.70	34.29	**34.17**	27.64
5	26.49	41.75	27.85	**45.49**	42.81	42.48	36.12
8	42.09	59.05	43.03	**63.25**	59.60	59.52	52.40
10	50.91	66.13	51.76	**70.88**	66.77	66.47	59.81

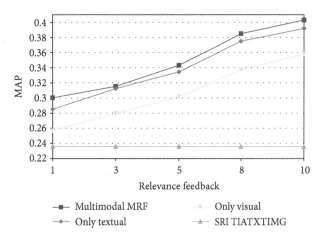

FIGURE 8: Comparison of the multimodal MRF (blue squares) with the base image retrieval system (green upwards-triangles), the textual MRF (red rhombus), and the visual MRF (yellow downwards-triangles). The plot shows the average MAP of each method (y-axis) against the number of relevant feedback images considered (x-axis).

system [64], the textual and the visual unimodal MRFs [26, 27]. We performed experiments with the following numbers of relevance feedback images: $k \in \{1, 3, 5, 8, 10\}$, which are used as seed for the reranking methods, see Section 4. The parameters of all of the methods were set empirically, in Section 6.3 we compare the performance of the multimodal MRF for different values of σ, λ, and k. The results for unimodal methods were taken from previous work [26, 27].

From this figure we can see that the three reranking techniques outperformed the base retrieval system, thus confirming that postprocessing techniques based on MRFs are beneficial for image reranking. As expected, improvements are larger for higher values of k, although there are important improvements even when $k = 1$, which is a very positive result as providing a single relevance feedback image is an easy task for the user.

The unimodal MRF based on textual features outperformed the corresponding MRF based on visual features. This result can be due to the fact that textual methods have traditionally reported much better performance than visual techniques in the IAPR TC12 collection [22, 64]. Another possibility is that we have not used the right visual features for effectively representing images. We performed preliminary experiments using color and texture features used in previous work [68], in addition to SIFT features, nevertheless our best results in image reranking were obtained with SIFT features. We will explore other types of visual features for representing images in future work.

The multimodal MRF consistently outperformed the results obtained by unimodal MRFs for all values of k, giving evidence that the combination of textual and visual features results in better reranking performance than using such modalities separately. The improvement was more important for the visual MRF, although the multimodal MRF outperforms the textual one by a significant margin, with exception of $k = 3$. We are not sure of what causes this result, but it

could be related to the fact that we have 3 query images that are considered for estimating similarity in individual energy functions, see Section 4.2. Anyways, one should note that small improvements in MAP are very difficult to obtain in this collection [22]. The differences between the unimodal MRFs and the multimodal MRF were statistically significant, see Section 6.1.

It is important to mention that (although results are not directly comparable (Results are not directly comparable as the entries evaluated in ImageCLEF2008 included the top 1000 ranked documents, whereas the results in this paper were computed with the top 100 documents only. Please note that using the top 1000 ranked documents would increase the performance of the multimodal MRF. For example, the initial list (i.e., SRI) achieved an MAP of almost 0.24 considering the top-100 images, while we obtained a MAP of 0.3066 when the top 1000 images were considered [64].)) the results in terms of MAP, obtained with the multimodal MRF as shown in Figure 8 would be ranked in positions 5th, 8th, 22nd, 29th, and 32th of the results (1042 entries) evaluated in ImageCLEF2008 [25], when using 10, 8, 5, 3, and 1 relevance feedback images, respectively. Recall the list of the retrieval system we considered was ranked 77th in terms of MAP. This result gives us an idea on the effectiveness of the proposed approach when compared to state-of-the-art systems.

One should note that since relevance feedback images are always considered relevant, regardless of the values of the energy function, they will be always relevant to the query in turn (as relevance feedback images are obtained via simulated relevance feedback [32]). Therefore, it is necessary to make a comparison of the results obtained by using relevance feedback alone (i.e., putting relevant images in the first positions and leaving the rest of the list unchanged) versus results from the multimodal MRF method. Accordingly, in the rest of the paper we also compare the performance of our reranking methods to that one we would obtain by using relevance feedback alone.

6.3. Parameter Settings for the Multimodal MRF. In a second experiment we evaluated the performance of our multimodal MRF under different parameter settings. The goal of the experiment is to get insights about the importance of each information modality and the information provided by the observation and interaction potentials.

The parameters that have a direct impact in the performance of the reranking methods based on MRFs are the following: λ, the scalar weighting the contribution of contextual and individual information into the energy functions (see Formula (6)); σ, the scalar weighting the contribution of textual and visual information into the multimodal MRF (see Formula (5)); and k, the number of relevance feedback images that are used as seed for the MRFs. Table 1 shows the performance of our multimodal MRF for different configurations of the just-mentioned parameters. The values of σ, λ_V, and λ_T were varied in the range $[0, 1]$; eleven equally spaced values in such interval were tried for each parameter. We show the best results obtained by each configuration of values for k, λ_V, and λ_T for the following fixed values of $\sigma = \{1, 0.7, 0.5, 0.3, 0\}$.

From Table 1 we can see that the multimodal MRF outperformed relevance feedback in all of the reported cases in terms of the MAP; all of the differences between columns 5 and 9 were statistically significant. When $\sigma = 0$ (i.e., no textual information was considered) we obtained worse results than those obtained with other values, confirming that visual features alone are not very useful for image reranking. Results with $\sigma = 1$ (i.e., no visual information was considered) were acceptable, although they were worse than those obtained with $\sigma = 0.3$, $\sigma = 0.5$, and $\sigma = 0.7$. The best results were obtained with $\sigma = 0.3$, thus giving evidence that multimodal information, under the considered features, is indeed helpful for image reranking and reflecting the fact that a higher weight (penalty) to the visual potential results in larger improvements.

From Table 1 we can also see that low values of λ_V were used for obtaining better retrieval results, which means that for the visual energy function (E_V) single node information was more helpful than contextual information (recall that each configuration of parameters, a row in Table 1, is the best configuration of values for λ_T and λ_V that was obtained for a fixed value of k and σ). The latter can be due to the fact that relevant images are not very similar to each other, giving evidence that relevant images may be *visually diverse* among them for ImageCLEF2008 topics. On the other hand, the values of λ_T were very close to 1 in general, which means that for the textual energy function (E_T) the contextual information was highly informative, while similarity between queries and images was not very helpful. The latter result indicates that relevant images have similar annotations. Hence, an interesting finding of our work is that it seems that relevant images are related to a common semantic topic (as they have similar high-level annotations) and at the same time, images are not visually similar (as there is a broad visual diversity among relevant images). Thus, a promising direction for jointly optimizing relevance and diversity may be the combination of both contextual textual information and individual visual information, we will explore this research direction as future work.

Regarding the number of relevance feedback images, we found that the larger the number of selected images the better the performance of the method. However, we would like to emphasize that even when a single image is provided by the (simulated) user, the multimodal MRF was able to significantly outperform the results obtained with relevance feedback alone. In fact, the differences in performance between relevance feedback and our multimodal MRF are larger when $k = 1$.

6.4. Comparison of Multimodal MRFs to Multimodal Alternatives.

In our third experiment we compared the performance of the multimodal MRF to that obtained by the baseline reranking methods described in Section 5. The goal of this experiment is to determine whether the multimodal MRF is able to improve the performance of alternative multimodal image reranking techniques. Figure 9 shows the average MAP obtained by all of the developed methods. Note that for the intermedia relevance feedback approach we performed

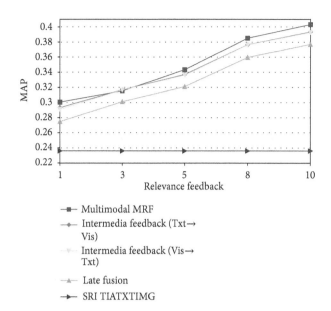

FIGURE 9: Comparison of the multimodal MRF (blue squares) and baseline methods described in Section 5 for different numbers of relevant documents. We show the performance of the base retrieval system (dark-red rightwards-triangles), the late fusion technique (green upwards-triangles), and intermedia relevance feedback in its two variants TXT > VIS (red rhombus) and VIS > TXT (yellow downwards-triangles). The plot shows the average MAP of each method (y-axis) against the number of relevant feedback images considered (x-axis).

experiments with both variants: using the textual MRF and then the visual MRF (TXT > VIS) and vice versa (VIS > TXT).

The plot shows that the multimodal MRF outperformed the other two techniques, and the differences were statistically significant for all but for the intermedia relevance feedback approach with $k = 3$ relevant documents. The late fusion approach achieved the smallest improvement over the base retrieval system, which can be due to the fact that we are weighting equally the contribution of visual and textual modalities for generating a new list of images. Hence, the influence of the list obtained with the visual MRF may affect the performance of the fusion.

The results obtained with both variants of the intermedia relevance feedback technique were very close to each other. Actually, it is very difficult to distinguish these results in Figure 9. This can be due to the fact that no matter how the ranking starts, there is a dominant MRF that generates the final ranking regardless of the stage in which it is applied; we assume that the textual MRF is the dominant technique for this experiment. Our assumption is based on the fact that the performance of intermedia relevance feedback is very close to that obtained by the textual MRF, see Figure 8.

With exception of $k = 3$, the multimodal MRF consistently outperformed the other baseline methods, hence proving that the specific form of the multimodal energy function is a better way to combine textual and visual information for image reranking with MRFs. Thus, it is beneficial to combine information in the interaction process (i.e., similar to early fusion technique [69]).

In average, the multimodal MRF took about 30 milliseconds to rerank a list of images. Hence, the efficiency of the proposed method is adequate for the standard image retrieval scenario that requires subsecond response times. One should note that the multimodal MRF is implemented in Matlab, therefore, lower response times would be expected when using programming languages as Java or C++, which are known to be more efficient than Matlab. Regarding the baseline methods, the late fusion approach obtained a similar average processing time to the multimodal MRF (i.e., ≈20 ms), whereas the intermedia relevance feedback method took an average of ≈50 ms to rerank a list of images.

Finally, Table 2 shows the relative improvements obtained by each method over the base image retrieval system. While these results are consistent with those reported in Figure 9, in this table we can appreciate the differences in terms of percentage of MAP improvement. The multimodal MRF obtained improvements over the base retrieval method that were superior to those achieved by the other methods. All of the differences reported in Table 2 were statistical significant. The multimodal MRF outperformed relevance feedback by 19.91% in average and the most competitive baseline (IRF $(T > V)$) by 2.6%.

7. Conclusions and Future Work

We have introduced a multimodal Markov random field for improving the order of a list of images as provided by an image retrieval system. The model incorporates similarity between images in the list, similarity between images and query, information obtained from the original order, and relevance feedback information. The reranking problem is faced as one of separating relevant from irrelevant images in the list. Our work included the development of potentials and energy functions based on textual and visual features that allowed us to differentiate relevant from irrelevant images. Additionally, we developed alternative multimodal strategies for image reranking based on MRFs.

Experimental results obtained in a benchmark collection composed of 20,000 annotated images showed the effectiveness of our method. In particular, results showed that the proposed method outperformed the base image retrieval system and a simple relevance feedback strategy. The proposed baselines achieved very competitive results, although the best results overall were obtained with our multimodal MRF. We studied the performance of the proposed model under different parameter settings and found that the combination of visual and textual information is more helpful than using unimodal MRFs separately. We also found that in the multimodal MRF the contextual potential was very important for the textual information, while image-query similarity was more helpful for the visual information. Thus, a future work direction is to study hybrid energy functions.

The contributions of this work are as follows. We proposed a novel image reranking technique that incorporates visual and textual information. To the best of our knowledge there are no similar works on (a) using MRFs for image result reranking nor on (b) image reranking methods that face the problem as one of combinatoric optimization. The proposed model was able to improve the ranking of the base retrieval system and the performance of the base list modified with relevance feedback information. Our approach incorporates contextual information, which is often disregarded in usual postretrieval techniques. The MRF relies on manual relevance feedback, hence it is a user adaptive mechanism. Moreover, since our MRF works with a list of ranked images, it is not tied with a specific retrieval system nor with a particular architecture, image collection or information modality.

As future work we would like to modify the multimodal MRF so that the reranking of images can be guided by the maximization of retrieval performance and result diversification. Another direct research direction would be extending the proposed MRF to take into account more than two modalities. Also, we would like to extend the multimodal MRF to incorporate levels of relevance instead of a binary relevance formulation. We think that a promising future work direction is the development of dynamic multimodal MRFs that can be used through retrieval sessions instead of reranking a single queries. Other research directions are exploring other types of visual features for representing images, performing experiments with other image retrieval systems, and testing the proposed method with other images collections, for example, unstructured collections like results from a Web search engine.

Acknowledgments

The authors are grateful to the reviewers, whose comments have helped them to improve significantly this paper. This work was supported by CONACyT under project Grant 61335 and scholarships 205834 and 205834.

References

[1] A. W. M. Smeulders, M. Worring, S. Santini, A. Gupta, and R. Jain, "Content-based image retrieval at the end of the early years," *IEEE Transactions on Pattern Analysis and Machine Intelligence*, vol. 22, no. 12, pp. 1349–1380, 2000.

[2] A. Goodrum, "Image information retrieval: an overview of current research," *Journal of Informing Science*, vol. 3, no. 2, pp. 63–66, 2000.

[3] R. Datta, D. Joshi, J. Li, and J. Z. Wang, "Image retrieval: ideas, influences, and trends of the new age," *ACM Computing Surveys*, vol. 40, no. 2, article 5, 2008.

[4] Y. Liu, D. Zhang, G. Lu, and W. Ma, "A survey of content-based image retrieval with high-level semantics," *Pattern Recognition*, vol. 40, no. 1, pp. 262–282, 2007.

[5] M. S. Lew, N. Sebe, C. Djeraba, and R. Jain, "Content-based multimedia information retrieval: state of the art and challenges," *ACM Transactions on Multimedia Computing, Communications and Applications*, vol. 2, no. 1, pp. 1–19, 2006.

[6] Y. Rui, T. Huang, and S. Chang, "Image retrieval: current techniques, promising directions and open issues," *Journal of Visual Communication and Image Representation*, vol. 10, no. 4, pp. 39–62, 1999.

[7] P. Clough, M. Grubinger, T. Deselaers, A. Hanbury, and H. Müller, "Overview of ImageCLEF 2006 Photographic retrieval

and object annotation tasks," in *Proceedings of the 7th Workshop of the Cross-Language Evaluation Forum (CLEF '07)*, vol. 4730 of *Lecture Notes in Computer Science*, pp. 579–594, Springer, 2007.

[8] P. K. Atry, M. A. Hossain, A. E. Saddik, and M. S. Kankanhalli, "Multimodal fusion for multimedia analysis," *Multimedia Systems*, vol. 16, no. 6, pp. 345–379, 2010.

[9] M. Broilo and F. G. B. De Natale, "A stochastic approach to image retrieval using relevance feedback and particle swarm optimization," *IEEE Transactions on Multimedia*, vol. 12, no. 4, pp. 267–277, 2010.

[10] Y. Rui, T. Huang, M. Ortega, and S. Mehrotra, "Relevance feedback: a power tool for interactive content-based image retrieval," *IEEE Transactions on Circuits and Systems For Video Technology*, vol. 8, no. 5, pp. 644–655, 1998.

[11] X. Zhou and T. Huang, "Relevance feedback in image retrieval: a comprehensive review," *Multimedia Systems*, vol. 8, pp. 536–544, 2003.

[12] T. Deselaers, T. Gass, P. Dreuw, and H. Ney, "Jointly optimising relevance and diversity in image retrieval," in *Proceedings of the ACM International Conference on Image and Video Retrieval (CIVR '09)*, pp. 296–303, ACM Press, July 2009, paper 39.

[13] H. J. Escalante, C. Hernandez, E. Sucar, and M. Montes, "Late fusion of heterogeneous methods for multimedia image retrieval," in *Proceedings of the ACM Multimedia Information Retrieval Conference*, pp. 172–179, ACM Press, Vancouver, Canada, 2008.

[14] A. Juàrez, M. Montes, L. Villaseñor, D. Pinto, and M. Pérez, "Selecting the N-top retrieval result lists for an effective data fusion," in *Proceedings of the 11th International Conference on Intelligent Text Processing and Computational Linguistics*, vol. 6008 of *Lecture Notes in Computer Science*, pp. 580–589, Springer, 2010.

[15] Y. Chang, W. Lin, and H.-H. Chen, "Combining text and image queries at ImageCLEF 2005," in *Working Notes of the CLEF Workshop*, Vienna, Austria, 2005.

[16] A. Marakakis, N. Galatsanos, A. Likas, and A. Stafylopatis, "Application of relevance feedback in content based image retrieval using gaussian mixture models," in *Proceedings of the 20th IEEE International Conference on Tools with Artificial Intelligence (ICTAI '08)*, pp. 141–148, November 2008.

[17] X. Tian, L. Yang, J. Wang, Y. Yang, X. Wu, and X. S. Hua, "Bayesian video search reranking," in *Proceedings of the 16th ACM International Conference on Multimedia*, pp. 131–140, ACM Press, Vancouver, Canada, 2008.

[18] Y. Jing and S. Baluja, "PageRank for product image search," in *Proceedings of the International World Wide Web Conference Committee*, pp. 307–315, ACM Press, Beijing, China, 2008.

[19] T. Yao, T. Mei, and C. W. Ngo, "Co-reranking by mutual reinforcement for image search," in *Proceedings of the ACM International Conference on Image and Video Retrieval*, pp. 34–41, ACM Press, Xian, China, 2010.

[20] J. Cui, F. Wen, and X. Tang, "Real time google and live image search re-ranking," in *Proceedings of the ACM Multimedia Information Retrieval Conference*, pp. 729–732, ACM Press, Vancouver, Canada, 2008.

[21] W. Lin, R. Jin, and A. Hauptmann, "A web image retrieval re-ranking with relevance model," in *Proceedings of the IEEE International Conference on Web Intelligence*, p. 242, 2003.

[22] H. Müller, P. Clough, T. Deselaers, and B. Caputo, *Image-CLEF: Experimental Evaluation in Visual Information Retrieval*, Springer Series on Information Retrieval, 2010.

[23] M. Grubinger, *Analysis and evaluation of visual information systems performance [Ph.D. thesis]*, School of Computer Science and Mathematics, Faculty of Health, Engineering and Science, Victoria University, Melbourne, Australia, 2007.

[24] P. Clough, M. Grubinger, T. Deselaers, A. Hanbury, and H. Müller, "Overview of the ImageCLEF 2007 photographic retrieval task," in *Proceedings of the 8th Workshop of the Cross-Language Evaluation Forum (CLEF '08)*, vol. 5152 of *Lecture Notes in Computer Science*, pp. 433–444, Springer, 2008.

[25] T. Arni, M. Sanderson, P. Clough, and M. Grubinger, "Overview of the ImageCLEF 2007 photographic retrieval task," in *Evaluating Systems for Multilingual and Multimodal Information Access*, vol. 5706 of *Lecture Notes in Computer Science*, pp. 500–511, Springer, 2009.

[26] R. O. Chàvez, M. Montes, and E. Sucar, "Using a markov random field for image re-ranking based on visual and textual features," *Computación y Sistemas*, vol. 14, no. 4, pp. 393–404, 2011.

[27] R. O. Chàvez, M. Montes, and E. Sucar, "Image Re-ranking based on relevance feedback combining internal and external similarities," in *Proceedings of the 23rd International FLAIRS Conference*, pp. 140–141, Daytona Beach, Fla, USA, 2010.

[28] I. J. Cox, M. L. Miller, T. P. Minka, T. V. Papathomas, and P. N. Yianilos, "The Bayesian image retrieval system, PicHunter: theory, implementation, and psychophysical experiments," *IEEE Transactions on Image Processing*, vol. 9, no. 1, pp. 20–37, 2000.

[29] C. Zhang, J. Y. Chai, and R. Jin, "User term feedback in interactive text-based image retrieval," in *Proceedings of the 28th Annual International ACM SIGIR Conference on Research and Development in Information Retrieval*, pp. 51–58, ACM Press, Salvador, Brazil, 2005.

[30] Z. H. Zhou, K. E. J. Chen, and H. B. Dai, "Enhancing relevance feedback in image retrieval using unlabeled data," *ACM Transactions on Information Systems*, vol. 24, no. 2, pp. 219–244, 2006.

[31] S. Tong and E. Chang, "Support vector machine active learning for image retrieval," in *Proceedings of the ninth ACM international conference on Multimedia*, pp. 107–118, ACM Press, Ottawa, Canada, 2001.

[32] T. Deselaers, R. Paredes, E. Vidal, and H. Ney, "Learning weighted distances for relevance feedback in image retrieval," in *Proceedings of the 19th International Conference on Pattern Recognition (ICPR '08)*, pp. 1–4, Tampa, Fla, USA, December 2008.

[33] R. Yan, A. G. Hauptmann, and R. Jin, "Negative pseudo-relevance feedback in content-based video retrieval," in *Proceedings of the 11th ACM International Conference on Multimedia*, pp. 343–346, ACM Press, Berkeley, Calif, USA, 2003.

[34] R. Yan, A. G. Hauptmann, and R. Jin, "Multimedia search with pseudo-relevance feedback," in *Proceedings of the International Conference on Image and Video Retrieval*, ACM Press, Urbana, Ill, USA, 2003.

[35] H. Ma, J. Zhu, M. R. Lyu, and I. King, "Bridging the semantic gap between image contents and tags," *IEEE Transactions on Multimedia*, vol. 12, no. 5, pp. 462–473, 2010.

[36] H. Tong, J. He, M. Li, W. Y. Ma, H. J. Zhang, and C. Zhang, "Manifoldranking-based keyword propagation for image retrieval," *EURASIP Journal on Applied Signal Processing*, vol. 2006, Article ID 079412, 2006.

[37] J. Ah-Pine, M. Bressan, S. Clinchant, G. Csurka, Y. Hoppenot, and J. M. Renders, "Crossing textual and visual content in different application scenarios," *Multimedia Tools and Applications*, vol. 42, no. 1, pp. 31–56, 2009.

[38] K. Porkaew and K. Chakrabarti, "Query refinement for multimedia similarity retrieval in MARS," in *Proceedings of the 7th ACM International Conference on Multimedia*, pp. 235–238, ACM Press, 1999.

[39] K. Porkaew, M. Ortega, and S. Mehrotra, "Query reformulation for content based multimedia retrieval in MARS," in *Proceedings of the 6th International Conference on Multimedia Computing and Systems (IEEE ICMCS '99)*, pp. 747–751, June 1999.

[40] G. Giacinto and F. Roli, "Nearest-prototype relevance feedback for content-based image retrieval," in *Proceedings of the 17th International Conference on Patternt Recognition*, vol. 2, pp. 989–992, Washington, DC, USA, 2004.

[41] G. Giacinto and F. Roli, "Instance-based relevance feedback for image retrieval," in *Advances in Neural Information Processing Systems*, vol. 17, pp. 489–496, MIT Press, 2005.

[42] G. Giacinto and F. Roli, "Instance-based relevance feedback in image retrieval using dissimilarity spaces," in *Case-Based Reason-Ing for Signals and Images*, pp. 419–430, Springer, 2007.

[43] P. H. Gosselin and M. Cord, "Active learing techniques for user interactive systems: application to image retrieval," in *Proceedings of the Workshop Machine Learning Techniques for Processing Multimedia Content*, Bonn, Germany, 2005.

[44] L. Setia, J. Ick, and H. Burkhardt, "SVM-based relevance feedback in image retrieval using invariant feature histograms," in *Proceedings of the IAPR Workshop on Machine Vision Applications*, Tsukuba Science City, Japan, 2005.

[45] Y. Chen, X. Zhou, and T. Huang, "One-class SVM for learning in image retrieval," in *Proceedings of the International Conference on Image Processing*, pp. 34–37, Thessaloniki, Greece, 2001.

[46] Y. Freund, R. Iyer, R. E. Schapire, and Y. Singer, "An efficient boosting algorithm for combining preferences," *Journal of Machine Learning Research*, vol. 4, no. 6, pp. 933–969, 2004.

[47] V. Lavrenko and W. B. Croft, "Relevance-based language models," in *Proceedings of the 24th Annual International ACM SIGIR Conference on Research and Development in Information Retrieval*, pp. 120–127, ACM Press, 2001.

[48] G. Winkler, *Image Analysis, Random Fields and Markov Chain Monte Carlo Methods*, Springer Series on Applications of Mathematics, Springer, 2006.

[49] S. Z. Li, *Markov Random Field Modeling in Image Analysis*, Springer, 2nd edition, 2001.

[50] S. Z. Li, "Markov random field models in computer vision," in *Proceedings of the European Conference on Computer Vision*, vol. 801 of *Lecture Notes in Computer Science*, pp. 361–370, Springer, Stockholm, Sweden, 1994.

[51] K. Held, E. Kops, B. Krause, W. Wells III, R. Kikinis, and H. Mueller, "Markov random field segmentation of brain MR images," *IEEE Transactions on Medical Imaging*, vol. 16, no. 6, pp. 878–886, 1997.

[52] S. Geman and D. Geman, "Stochastic relaxation, gibbs distributions, and the bayesian restoration of images," in *Readings in Computer Vision: Issues, Problems, Principles, and Paradigms*, pp. 564–584, 1987.

[53] P. Carbonetto, N. de Freitas, and K. Barnard, "A statistical model for general context object recognition," in *Proceedings of the 8th European Conference on Computer Vision*, vol. 3021 of *Lecture Notes in Computer Science*, pp. 350–362, Springer, Prague, Czech Republic, 2004.

[54] C. Hernandez and L. E. Sucar, "Markov random fields and spatial information to improve automatic image annotation," in *Proceedings of the Pacic-Rim Symposium on Image and Video Technology*, vol. 4872 of *Lecture Notes in Computer Science*, pp. 879–892, Springer, Santiago, Chile, 2007.

[55] H. J. Escalante, M. Montes, and L. E. Sucar, "Word Co-occurrence and markov random fields for improving automatic image annotation," in *Proceedings of the 18th British Machine Vision Conference*, vol. 2, pp. 600–609, Warwick, UK, 2007.

[56] D. Metzler and B. Croft, "A markov random field model for term dependencies," in *Proceedings of the 28th Annual International ACM SIGIR Conference on Research and Development in Information Retrieval*, pp. 472–479, ACM Press, 2005.

[57] D. Metzler and W. B. Croft, "Latent concept expansion using Markov random fields," in *Proceedings of the 30th Annual International ACM SIGIR Conference on Research and Development in Information Retrieval (SIGIR '07)*, pp. 311–318, ACM Press, July 2007.

[58] M. Lease, "An improved markov random field model for supporting verbose queries," in *Proceedings of the 32nd Annual International ACM SIGIR Conference on Research and Development in Information Retrieval (SIGIR '09)*, pp. 476–483, ACM Press, July 2009.

[59] J. Besag, "On the statistical analysis of dirty pictures," *Jounal of the Royal Statistical Society B*, vol. 48, pp. 259–302, 1986.

[60] S. Kirkpatrick, C. Gelatt, and M. Vecchi, "Optimization by simulated annealing," *Science*, vol. 220, no. 4598, pp. 671–680, 1983.

[61] Y. Boykov, O. Veksler, and R. Zabih, "Fast approximate energy minimization via graph cuts," *IEEE Transactions on Pattern Analysis and Machine Intelligence*, vol. 23, no. 11, pp. 1222–1239, 2001.

[62] D. G. Lowe, "Distinctive image features from scale-invariant keypoints," *International Journal of Computer Vision*, vol. 60, no. 2, pp. 91–110, 2004.

[63] E. A. Fox and J. A. Shaw, "Combination of multiple searches," in *Proceedings of The 3rd Text REtrieval Conference (TREC '04)*, NIST Publication, 1994.

[64] H. J. Escalante, J. A. Gonzalez, C. Hernandez et al., "Annotation-based expansion and late fusion of mixed methods for multimedia image retrieval," in *Evaluating Systems for Multilingual and Multimodal Information Access*, vol. 5706 of *Lecture Notes in Computer Science*, pp. 669–676, Springer, 2009.

[65] I. Mani, *Automatic Summarization (Natural Language Processing)*, John Benjamins Publishing Co, 2001.

[66] M. D. Smucker, J. Allan, and B. Carterette, "Agreement among statistical significance tests for information retrieval evaluation at varying sample sizes," in *Proceedings of the 32nd Annual International ACM SIGIR Conference on Research and Development in Information Retrieval (SIGIR '09)*, pp. 630–631, ACM Press, July 2009.

[67] K. G. Kanji, *100 Statistical Tests / Gopal K. Kanji*, Sage, London, UK, 1993.

[68] H. J. Escalante, C. A. Hernández, J. A. Gonzalez et al., "The segmented and annotated IAPR TC-12 benchmark," *Computer Vision and Image Understanding*, vol. 114, no. 4, pp. 419–428, 2010.

[69] C. Snoek, M. Worring, A. Smeulders, and W. M. Arnold, "Early versus late fusion in semantic video analysis," in *Proceedings of the 13th Annual ACM International Conference on Multimedia (MULTIMEDIA '05)*, pp. 399–402, ACM Press, New York, NY, USA, 2005.

9

Towards Understanding the Formation of Uniform Local Binary Patterns

Olli Lahdenoja, Jonne Poikonen, and Mika Laiho

Business and Innovation Development BID Technology, University of Turku, 20014 Turku, Finland

Correspondence should be addressed to Olli Lahdenoja; olanla@utu.fi

Academic Editors: O. Ghita and N. A. Schmid

The research reported in this paper focuses on the modeling of Local Binary Patterns (LBPs) and presents an a priori model where LBPs are considered as combinations of permutations. The aim is to increase the understanding of the mechanisms related to the formation of uniform LBPs. Uniform patterns are known to exhibit high discriminative capability; however, so far the reasons for this have not been fully explored. We report an observation that although the overall a priori probability of uniform LBPs is high, it is mostly due to the high probability of only certain classes of patterns, while the a priori probability of other patterns is very low. In order to examine this behavior, the relationship between the runs up and down test for randomness of permutations and the uniform LBPs was studied. Quantitative experiments were then carried out to show that the relative effect of uniform patterns to the LBP histogram is strengthened with deterministic data, in comparison with the i.i.d. model. This was verified by using an a priori model as well as through experiments with natural image data. It was further illustrated that specific uniform LBP codes can also provide responses to salient shapes, that is, to monotonically changing intensity functions and edges within the image microstructure.

1. Introduction

The Local Binary Pattern (LBP) methodology [1] was first proposed as a texture descriptor, but it has later been applied to various other fields of computer vision: for example, face recognition, facial expression recognition, modeling motion and actions, as well as medical image analysis. Numerous modifications and improvements have been suggested to the original LBP methodology for various applications, while the LBPs have also been proposed for signal processing tasks beyond image processing (e.g., [2]). A detailed list of various applications and papers related to the LBP methodology is available in CMV Oulu pages [3].

Before the introduction of Local Binary Patterns, co-occurrence statistics descriptors based on binary features and n-tuples [4], as well as the texture unit and texture spectrum (TUTS) method [5], have been studied. N-tuples have been studied in, for example, [4, 6] for texture retrieval. It was discovered that the distribution of individual n-tuples could not reach the classification accuracy of quantized binary features such as BTCS [4].

The possibility of using only uniform and rotation invariant binary patterns distinguishes the Local Binary Pattern methodology from its predecessors, because it enables a more compact image representation. It has been widely accepted that uniform LBPs, which contain at most two circular 0-1 or 1-0 transitions, are highly applicable and thus have been frequently used in various applications—not only in texture analysis. While many modifications to the original LBP have been proposed, most image analysis applications still take advantage of a combination of LBP and uniform patterns, despite other modifications in sampling, such as applying Gabor filtering as a preprocessing step [7]. However, it has been unclear how these particular uniform patterns contribute to increasing the discriminative capabilities of the LBPs. It was shown in [8] that uniform patterns are a priori very frequent even with random data. The observations from the existing research raise naturally the question "Why are uniform patterns so discriminative?". It was also shown in [8] that the percentage of uniform patterns further increases with natural image data compared to a priori model. In this paper, some of the mechanisms related to this increase in occurrence probability will be addressed.

LBPs are represented in this paper as compositions of individual n-tuples, that is, permutations. We denote the set of all possible permutations as the "permutation space." The permutation model represents a middle ground in terms of the complexity between the image intensity representation and the binary pattern feature representation. The total number of permutations in the permutation space is smaller than the number of instances in the intensity space but higher than the amount of instances in the binary pattern space. The permutation based approach is applied here both through an a priori model and through experiments with natural images to examine the particularly discriminative quality of uniform LBPs. The aim of this study is also to better understand the relationship between uniform LBPs and the properties of deterministic nonrandom image data.

This paper is composed of eight sections. Section 2 contains an introduction to LBP methodology as well as background and related work. Section 3 defines the permutation space used and a priori probability model for the uniform patterns. In Section 4, a modification to the original permutation space is defined for modeling purposes, while in Section 5 the previously defined concepts are used to analyze the uniformity of Local Binary Patterns. In Section 6 qualitative and quantitative experiments with a priori model and natural image data are performed. Sections 7 and 8 provide further discussion and conclusions.

2. Background and Related Work

2.1. Derivation of Local Binary Patterns. A Local Binary Pattern is derived for a specific pixel neighborhood radius r by comparing the intensities of M discrete circular sample points to the intensity of the center pixel (clockwise or counterclockwise), starting from a certain angle. The comparison determines whether the corresponding location in the Local Binary Pattern of length M is 1 or 0. A value 1 is assigned if the center pixel intensity is smaller than the sample pixel intensity and 0 otherwise. Sample number $M = 8$ is the most commonly used, with circle radius $r = 1$; however, also other values for the radius and sample numbers can be used. If a sample point is located between pixels, the intensity value used for the comparison can be determined by *bilinear interpolation* (see Figure 1). Using this sampling procedure, sweeping over the whole image is denoted by LBP(M, r) [9, 10].

After the LBP extraction, each pixel in an image is replaced by a binary pattern, except at the borders of the image where all of the neighbour values do not exist. The *feature vector* of an image then consists of a histogram of the pixel LBPs. The initial length of the histogram is 2^M since each possible LBP is assigned a separate bin. If there are N regions in an image (e.g., a normalized face image could be divided into 7×7 blocks for enhancing the spatial accuracy of the histograms [9]), the histograms can be combined into a single histogram with a length of $N \cdot 2^M$.

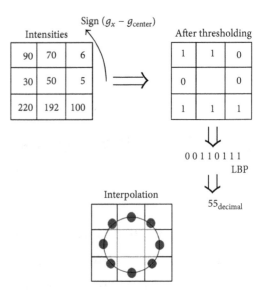

FIGURE 1: Derivation of Local Binary Patterns.

2.2. Uniform LBPs. Uniform Local Binary Patterns are patterns with at most two circular 0-1 and 1-0 transitions. For example, patterns 00111000, 11111111, 00000000, and 11011111 are uniform, and patterns 01010000, 01001110, or 10101100 are not uniform. Selecting only uniform patterns contributes to both reducing the length of the feature vector (LBP histogram) and improving the performance of classifiers using the LBP features (see [1, 9–11]). Uniform LBPs can also be applied to obtain rotation invariance [10]. In [12–14] global rotation invariance for the LBPs was achieved by applying a Discrete Fourier Transform to the uniform bins of the LBP histograms. In [13], the rotation invariance of LBP variants was also analyzed.

There are several methods for performing LBP histogram comparison. These include histogram intersection, log-likelihood statistics, and Chi-square statistics [9]. It is also possible to use multiple LBPs simultaneously, also with different radiuses, to describe a certain image location. The natural disadvantage of this is the further increase in the length of the feature vector.

2.3. Related Research. The use of uniform Local Binary Patterns was proposed in [15] as a way to reduce the high dimension of the original LBP feature vector. The use of uniform patterns can be seen as a *filter type* feature selection method [16], since it is related directly to the image data. Also, a *beam search* method was proposed in [15] using feedback from a classifier (for texture images), extending to a *wrapper type* feature selection [16]. Later, numerous other filter and wrapper type methods have been proposed for LBP feature selection, including Fisher separation criterion (FSC) based learning, Boosting (AdaBoost), LDA, and PCA; see [1] for a complete description. Face recognition has typically been used as a benchmark application. In [11] a machine learning approach was chosen to study which individual LBP bins were most discriminative in facial expression recognition. A boosting classifier was used, and 91.9% of the most discriminative patterns turned out to be uniform. However, it has been unclear how these particular uniform patterns contribute to increasing the discriminative capabilities of the LBP methodology.

In this paper, the space of all $n!$ possible n-tuples is constructed, and its relation to individual uniform and nonuniform LBP codes and to the class of all uniform LBP codes is modeled. Hence, we propose forming the LBPs as a result of an intermediate nonlinear rank ordering operation in order to facilitate the understanding of the Local Binary Patterns. Rank ordering and the census transform were introduced in [17] as nonparametric descriptors. Since then, many variants of descriptors based on ordinal intensity representation have been proposed. Recently, the local intensity order pattern (LIOP) descriptor showed excellent performance [18] in keypoint matching. It was further developed in [19]. In LIOP the numbers of occurrences of n-tuples among local patches are selected as histogram bins in a rotation invariant manner. The methods proposed in this paper can also support the design of new descriptors and promote understanding of the existing descriptors based on n-tuple processing, for example, [18, 19].

LBPs have also been described as vector quantized responses to linear filters [20]. This allows the analysis of the properties of the LBP operator and the modeling of its relationship to other filter bank based descriptors. The focus of this paper is also to provide an alternative approach to the filter bank based LBP decomposition [20] and to suggest an alternative approach to the previous work in [8] for analyzing the formation of uniform patterns.

In [8] a priori distribution of uniform LBPs was studied, and it was observed that their a priori probability is rather high also with independent identically distributed (i.i.d) data. This indicates that these patterns do not necessarily relate only to image structures such as small edges, corners, and line-ends, as was previously thought, but also to the LBP sampling process itself. The percentage of uniform patterns has been also shown to further increase from the estimated a priori probability [8] in applications using natural image data. The exact distribution of LBPs was studied by calculating the volume of multidimensional polytopes in [8]. It has also been shown that the minimum between the total number of zeros and ones in a LBP can be used to uniquely characterize the occurrence probability of the LBPs with i.i.d data [21]. However, in [21] the a priori probabilities were not linked to the occurrence frequencies of uniform patterns. In both studies [8, 21], a link between information theory and a priori occurrence probabilities of the LBPs was speculated.

In [8] the LBPs were modeled using a space partitioning approach, where the pixel intensities (see Definition 1) were mapped into LBP binary pattern space. In practice this means that, for example, for the LBP(8, 1) operator the dimension of the intensity space is 256^9, for 8-bit pixels, and a certain location of an image (consisting of a set of intensities) would represent an individual point in this space. This particular intensity set could then be further mapped into the LBP space.

Definition 1. The intensity space **I** used in derivation of Local Binary Patterns consists of sets of instances in space $\{I_1, I_2, I_3, \ldots, I_M\}$ ordered circularly around the center in addition to the center point $\{I_c\}$. Its dimension is $I_{\text{RANGE}}^{(M+1)}$, where I_{RANGE} represents the range of the intensities.

The a priori probabilities of LBPs in the case of continuously distributed i.i.d variables (as intensities) were considered already in [21]. The a priori probability of individual LBPs (for i.i.d data distribution without interpolation) is completely determined by its descriptor k (see Definition 2) according to (1), following the binomial distribution [8, 21].

Definition 2. The descriptor k [8, 21, 22] for a Local Binary Pattern is calculated as the minimum between the cardinalities of the sets consisting of 1 bits and 0 bits.

For example, the descriptor k for pattern 00110011 is four, for pattern 00000000 zero, and for pattern 01010100 three.

Theorem 3. *The probability of an LBP with M contour samples ($M \geq 3$) to occur with continuously distributed i.i.d. data [8, 21], without considering interpolation, given descriptor k is*

$$P_{LBP}(M, k) = \frac{k! \, (M - k)!}{(M + 1)!}. \tag{1}$$

3. Constructing the Permutation Space

3.1. Definition of the Permutation Space. We propose adding a "mid-space" between the intensity space and the LBP space, the permutation space illustrated in Figure 2. The concepts of root permutations and child LBPs in Figure 2 will be explained in the later sections. This provides an alternative approach to [8] in modeling the uniform patterns and allows modeling some of the fundamental differences between n-tuple and LBP based approaches for low level image representation [1, 18, 19]. An LBP is here modeled to consist of multiple instances of *unit permutations* located among the permutation space. The a priori probability of each unit permutation is equal with i.i.d data, which is readily well known within nonparametric statistics [23].

Definition 4. Let the intensity space **I** be defined as sets consisting of intensities $\{I_1, I_2, I_3, \ldots, I_M\}$ around the center in addition to the center point $\{I_c\}$ within a local LBP neighborhood. A unit permutation is defined as an individual permutation $\{R_1, R_2, R_3, \ldots, R_M\}$ around the center in addition to the center point rank $\{R_c\}$ formed by rank ordering the intensity samples I_n as R_n so that the smallest intensity is assigned a rank of 1. In the case of tied intensities, the ranks of the tied intensities are taken from an i.i.d distribution. The length of the unit permutation is then $(M + 1)$, where the number of contour samples in the corresponding LBP is equal to M.

The permutation space **P** contains all possible unit permutations for the circular neighborhood. It can be derived from the intensity space so that the number of instances is reduced (since, in practice $M \ll I_{\text{RANGE}}$). The number of

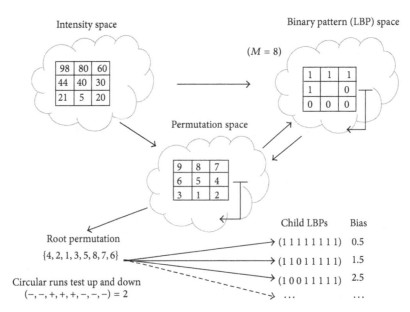

FIGURE 2: The concept of intensity space, permutation space, and binary pattern space.

instances in the permutation space is $(M + 1)!$. The binary pattern space $\mathbf{b}$ consists of instances of sets composed of bits $\{b_1, b_2, b_3, \ldots b_M\}$ excluding the center, for M being the number of contour samples among the LBP, respectively. The dimension of the binary pattern space is 2^M. The binary pattern space $\mathbf{b}$ can be produced directly from the high-dimensional intensity space as in [8]. It can also be derived indirectly through the permutation space consisting of reduced number of instances. Each individual LBP can also be projected back to the permutation space from the binary pattern space into a collection of unit permutations (see Figure 2).

In this paper, when considering the a priori probabilities, interpolation is not used. However, its effect to the final LBP distribution is evaluated in the experimental section using natural image data. Interpolation in the context of studying the uniform patterns has been considered more in depth in [8]. In general, the number of uniform patterns has shown to grow with interpolation [8], due to increased dependency and correlation between the neighboring sample points as they are averaged using bilinear weighting from their four neighbors.

3.2. Local Binary Pattern Operator for Permutations and Reverse Mapping. The mapping operator ϕ_{MAP} between the intensity space and the LBP space and between the permutation space and the LBP space is defined in the following. The mapping operator ϕ_{MAP} can be used for both permutation space and intensity space to derive an LBP. In the case of the permutation space, instead of intensities, the magnitudes of the ranks are considered. The mapping from an instance of the LBP space (a particular LBP code) into the permutation space $(\phi_{\mathrm{MAP}}^{-1})$ is defined indirectly as forming the set of all unit permutations which result in this particular LBP according to the ϕ_{MAP} operator.

Definition 5. (a) The LBP mapping operator ϕ_{MAP} is defined between the instances of spaces $\mathbf{I_n} \Rightarrow \mathbf{b_n}$, or $\mathbf{P_n} \Rightarrow \mathbf{b_n}$ as 1 for instances which have a magnitude greater or equal than the center and 0 for instances which have magnitude smaller than the center. In the case of mapping $\mathbf{P_n} \Rightarrow \mathbf{b_n}$ and ties between the center intensity $\{I_c\}$ and contour intensities $\mathbf{I_n}$, the rank of the center $\{R_c\}$ is assigned minimum within the combined set of the tied ranks $\{R_c, R_n\}$. This preserves the uniformity of the LBP also when the intermediate permutation space is used. The resulting LBP code is a concatenation $\{b_1, b_2, b_3, \ldots b_M\}$ of the individual bits.

(b) A mapping from intensity space to binary pattern space is defined by applying the LBP mapping operator ϕ_{MAP} for intensity set $\mathbf{I_n}$ resulting in binary pattern $\mathbf{b_n}$.

(c) A mapping from an instance of intensity space $\mathbf{I_n}$ to an instance of permutation space $\mathbf{P_n}$ is defined as $\mathbf{R}(\mathbf{I_n})$, where an operator $\mathbf{R}$ extracts the rank ordering of intensity samples among the intensity set $\mathbf{I_n}$ so that the smallest element will be assigned to value 1.

(d) A mapping from the permutation space into the binary pattern space is defined by applying the LBP mapping operator ϕ_{MAP} to the set of ranks $\mathbf{P_n}$ resulting in a binary pattern $\mathbf{b_n}$ among the binary pattern space.

(e) A reverse mapping ϕ_{MAP}^{-1} from an instance of binary pattern space $\mathbf{b_n}$ into permutation space $\mathbf{P_n}$ is defined indirectly as forming all the $\mathbf{P_n}$ elements according to the criteria ϕ_{MAP} results in a match (from all elements of $\mathbf{P_n} \Rightarrow \mathbf{b_n}$).

As an example, consider an arbitrary Local Binary Pattern, for example, $M = 8$ pattern 00110011. It is a result of applying the ϕ_{MAP} operator to a unit permutation, where the rank of the center pixel (ordinal value) is always 5 (rank of smallest being 1). An example of a permutation which could produce this particular LBP could be $\{5\}$ for center pixel and $\{1, 2, 9, 8, 3, 4, 6, 7\}$ for the other pixels.

This is not the only possible unit permutation for this particular LBP. The degree of freedom related to the unit permutations for a given LBP is determined by the following elements: the rank of the center pixel, the number of bits above the center pixel, that is, number of 1s in LBP code, and number of bits below the center, that is, number of 0's. The a priori probability of occurrence for an individual unit permutation is then constant $1/(M+1)!$, with i.i.d. data, where $M + 1$ is the length of the unit permutation and M is the number of contour samples in an LBP. Hence, the intensity space is divided into larger fractions of equal unit probability, still allowing the derivation of Local Binary Patterns.

In the case of LBP 00110011, the number of unit permutations invoked by the restriction "four locations above the center" is 4!, and the number of unit permutations invoked by the restriction "four locations below the center" is also 4!. As a consequence, the total occurrence probability of the LBP under consideration becomes $4! * 4!/[(8 + 1)!]$, from which $1/[8 + 1]!$ is assigned for each of the unit permutations. As another example, consider the LBP with $M = 5$, 01000, containing, for example, the unit permutation $\{5\}$ center (since four zeros are below it), $\{1, 6, 2, 3, 4\}$ contour, which results in a total cumulative probability of $1! * 4!/[(5 + 1)!]$ for all the unit permutations.

3.3. Modeling a Priori Distribution of Uniform Patterns Only with i.i.d. Data.

3.3. Modeling a Priori Distribution of Uniform Patterns Only with i.i.d. Data. Next we consider the total occurrence probability of all uniform patterns with i.i.d. data with respect to all LBPs. The number of uniform patterns with respect to descriptor k is described completely in (2) and (3) with respect to M and descriptor k. For (2) (even M) k varies between 0 and $M/2$, and for (3) (odd M) k varies between 0 and $(M - 1)/2$.

$$\#\text{uniform, even } M = \begin{cases} 2 & k = 0, \\ 2 * M & 0 < k < M/2, \\ M & k = M/2. \end{cases} \quad (2)$$

$$\#\text{uniform, odd } M = \begin{cases} 2 & k = 0, \\ 2 * M & 0 < k <= (M - 1)/2 \end{cases} \quad (3)$$

For example, consider an arbitrary LBP with $M = 4$. The case of $k = 0$ consists of uniform patterns 0000 and 1111. When $k = 1$, the uniform patterns are 0001, 0010, 0100, 1000, and the inversions of these patterns. In these cases all patterns are uniform. Descriptor value $k = 2$ (i.e. $M/2$) leads to the uniform patterns of 1100, 0110, 0011, and 1001. The other nonuniform patterns for the highest possible k value for $M = 4$ are 0101 and 1010.

With LBPs having $M \geq 4$ the total occurrence probability of the set of all uniform patterns, for i.i.d. data distribution and even M is,

$$P_{u2}^{\text{All}}(M) = \frac{2}{(M + 1)} + \frac{2M}{(M + 1)!} \sum_{k=1}^{M/2-1} k!\,(M - k)! \\ + \frac{M}{(M + 1)!}\left[\left(\frac{M}{2}\right)!\right]^2. \quad (4)$$

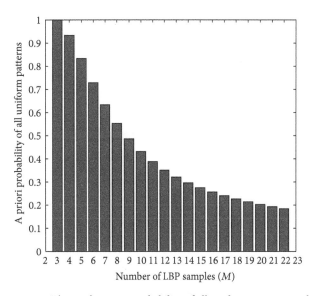

FIGURE 3: The total a priori probability of all uniform patterns with LBP sample number M according to (4) (for odd M the summation in (4) was adjusted according to (3)).

The first term of (4) includes the a priori probability of all-zero and all-one uniform LBPs, the second term is the sum of probabilities of patterns where k varies between 1 and $M/2-1$ for even M, and the third term includes the highest descriptor k uniform patterns.

According to the permutation concept proposed here, the number of all unit permutations for uniform patterns becomes then $(M + 1)! * P_{u2}^{\text{All}}$, while the total number of all permutations for modeling LBPs with sample number M becomes $(M+1)!$. In Figure 3 the total occurrence probability of uniform patterns is plotted with respect to the LBP sample number M using the (4) (for odd M the summation in (4) was adjusted according to (3)).

4. Modified Permutation Space

To analyze the formation of LBPs and uniform patterns in particular, we propose a modification to the permutation space by removing the center rank of a unit permutation. This requires the definitions of *an intermediate unit permutation*, *a root permutation*, and *an intermediate root permutation*.

A certain LBP can be composed of multiple unit permutations, but if an instance of the intensity space set is mapped to the LBP binary pattern space, a single unique intermediate unit permutation can be assigned to the permutation space and it can be uniquely used for determining the resulting LBP (neglecting ties).

Definition 6. An intermediate unit permutation is defined as a unit permutation $I_n \Rightarrow P_n \Rightarrow b_n$ as the permutation P_n. The directions of the arrows describe the order in which the rank ordering (R) and mapping (ϕ_{MAP}) are performed.

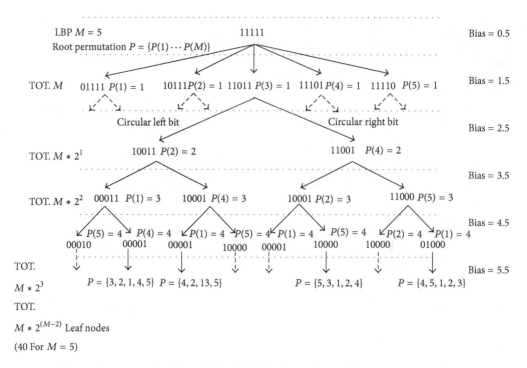

FIGURE 4: An example of forming the LBP $M = 5$ complete uniform root permutations.

TABLE 1: Root permutations.

Case	(A)	(B)	(C)
Permutations			
Center	9	4	9
Contour	3, 8, 2, 5, 4, 7, 1, 6	5, 8, 6, 9, 1, 2, 3, 7	2, 3, 4, 5, 6, 7, 8, 1
Root permutations			
Contour	3, 8, 2, 5, 4, 7, 1, 6	4, 7, 5, 8, 1, 2, 3, 6	2, 3, 4, 5, 6, 7, 8, 1
Child LBPs (Bias)			
0.5	11111111	11111111	11111111
1.5	11111101	11110111	11111110
2.5	11011101	11110011	01111110
3.5	01011101	11110001	00111110
4.5	01010101	01110001	00011110
5.5	01000101	01010001	00001110
6.5	01000100	01010000	00000110
7.5	01000000	00010000	00000010
8.5	00000000	00000000	00000000
Total uniform	4	6	9

Depending on the context, a root permutation may be derived from an intermediate unit permutation, which is simply extracted by rank ordering the intensity set without the center, or in more abstract case it may refer to a normal unit permutation from which the rank of the center pixel is removed (see Definition 7 and Table 1).

Definition 7. A root permutation is a unit permutation produced by removing the rank of the center. The rank of the center pixel is first removed from the unit permutation, and the rank ordering ($\mathbf{R(P_n)}$) is applied again for the magnitudes of the remaining ranks. An intermediate root permutation refers simply to an n-tuple formed by rank ordering the LBP contour sample intensities (without considering the center). The total length of the root permutation or the intermediate root permutation is then $\text{Card}(P_n) - 1$, that is, equal to M.

Two different LBPs or unit permutations can produce the same root permutation. For example, LBPs with $M = 4$, 0000 and 1111 could be composed of instances of permutations {5} center, {1, 2, 3, 4} contour, and 1 center, {2, 3, 4, 5} contour, respectively, the root permutation for both being {1, 2, 3, 4}. Given an arbitrary LBP, only if the full intensity set or the intermediate unit permutation is known, a certain root permutation can be used to describe that particular LBP. However, it will not be unique, since the information from the center intensity value or rank is missing.

Given a root permutation or an intermediate root permutation, multiple *child* LBPs can be generated if a new center pixel (called *bias*) is assigned. A root permutation is allowed to generate child LBPs by setting up a new bias level (instead of the center pixel). In practice, any bias value between or above the magnitudes of the ranks could be used, but for clarity we use threshold values in the middle of the integer ranks (0.5, 1.5, 2.5, 3.5, etc.). In Table 1, three root permutations are shown, and the child LBPs which can be generated by these root permutations are described by changing the center bias. One of the child LBPs will always represent the original LBP.

Definition 8. A child LBP is an LBP generated from the root permutation or from the intermediate root permutation by comparing successively the bias level to the magnitude of the root permutation ranks (one by one) and assigning bit 1 if the magnitude of the bias level is below the magnitude of the rank permutation and 0 otherwise (in the corresponding location). That is, the LBP mapping operator ϕ_{MAP} is applied to the root permutation by using the set bias as a center.

In Section 6, when performing the experiments, we will use an approach where all possible $M!$ root permutations (corresponding to contour samples of the LBPs) are pre-generated and the bias is then adjusted to each of its $M + 1$ possible locations for each root permutation.

4.1. Monotonicity of the Root Permutation. Consider fully ordered (with respect to some circular shift) root permutations of length M containing only one long increasing or decreasing run, in addition to the transitions from the smallest to the largest or from largest to the smallest. We describe next that for these root permutations, all of the child LBPs (generated by changing the center pixel bias) are uniform (See Table 1).

For the lowest and the highest bias value, the resulting child LBPs derived from the root permutation are all uniform since they consist of only all-zero and all-one LBPs. For the second lowest bias and the second highest bias, the resulting patterns are uniform since they include only one instance of one or zero (the descriptor k being one). The remaining bias values (between 2.5 to $M - 1.5$) for $M \geq 4$ are considered next.

The first observation is that each fully ordered permutation can be circularly shifted left or right H times in order to make it a monotonically increasing (or decreasing) permutation starting with the lowest (highest) element. It can also be shifted back so that the generated child LBP is not altered. Let us focus only on the length M (longest) up (or down) run while also omitting the circularity. Let {B} be the set of the root permutation instances below the bias value and {A} the set of the root permutation instances above the bias value. It is evident that for the set {B}, if the ordering of the permutations is monotonically increasing, then they are fully ordered in increasing order also in {A}. The same applies for the decreasing permutations.

When changing the bias by one (increasing or decreasing), the instance where the bit transition occurs, generated by the bias, also shifts by one to the right or to the left. While acknowledging the initial conditions which hold for descriptor k values 0 and 1 (as described before), it is evident that only one bit right next to the transition point can change and it will change to the direction which preserves the uniformity. See, for example, Table 1 Case C. The ordered root permutations are likely to be common with natural image data as pointed out in [4]. Also, statistically their likeliness to occur with random data should be lower than with deterministic data, which will be considered in the next section.

5. On the Relation between Runs Test for Permutations and Uniform Patterns

The simplest tests of randomness for two-valued data (e.g., coin-toss data) are based on estimating the total number of instances of each value or to count the number of successive instances of each [23]. For example, the sequence (T T T T T T T T) is not likely to be generated randomly, while the sequence (T F T T F F T T) would be more likely to result from a random process. If there are too many or too few instances of each value, the generating process is not likely to be random (i.i.d.).

The runs up and down test can be applied for numeric data, such as intensities or ranks, to examine the number of monotonically increasing (decreasing) sequences (runs). According to the runs test, monotonicity is the strongest indication of nonrandomness. If the length of the runs is high (few runs within the data), the data is not likely to be generated by a random process. In other words, the hypothesis of randomness is rejected.

Given a root permutation, if the changes from the smallest towards the largest element, or vice versa, occur always next to the set of elements which have previously been changed, all of the child LBPs will be uniform. We denote these root permutations as complete uniform root permutations (see Table 1 case C as an example). Fully ordered root permutations described in the previous section form a subset of complete uniform root permutations. For instance, permutations {6, 4, 1, 2, 3, 5}, {1, 2, 3, 4}, and {1, 2, 3, 4, 8, 7, 6, 5} are complete uniform root permutations (see also Figure 4).

Definition 9. Complete uniform root permutations are root permutations for which all of the child LBPs are uniform. The number of complete uniform root permutations is given by $M * 2^{M-2}$, $(M \geq 3)$, where M is the number of contour samples in LBP and the length of a root permutation.

The total number of complete uniform root permutations can be examined through the following example: consider the bias changing from its lowest level towards the highest (Figure 4). For the lowest level, only one uniform LBP can be found (of all ones, e.g., 11111 in the case of $M = 5$). For the second lowest bias level, all the child LBPs are also uniform, since only one bit is changed in comparison with the previous bias, and the other bits are 1s. For the following bias levels, uniform patterns will be generated if and only if the successive change among the child LBPs is always next to previous changed bits (either circularly to the left or to the right). For example, for an LBP of 11000111 (indexes 1, ..., 8) the next change to zero could occur only on index location 2 (to the left) or location 6 (to the right) in a circular manner.

The changing bit will also indicate the successive value of the root permutation formed among the path of the permutation tree (see Figure 4). The number of leaf nodes for this tree is then equal to the total number of complete uniform root permutations, which is $M * 2^{M-2}$, $(M \geq 3)$. It consists of M patterns for the second lowest bias and for each of these patterns, a perfect binary tree of height $M - 2$.

Definition 10. Runs up and down test result for the root permutations is defined as the total number of successive increasing or decreasing circular runs within a certain root permutation.

It was observed that all of the complete uniform root permutations with $M \leq 10$ matched to category two patterns (*n*-tuples) according to the circular runs test. However, in this paper the proof of the equivalence of the runs level 2 patterns and the complete uniform root permutations is omitted for $M > 10$. We emphasize that the number of runs according to the runs up and down test for permutations is not the same as the uniformity level of the pattern. The runs test for permutations is a more flexible and general test of randomness, and it can only be applied if the rank order statistics of the successive samples in a pattern are known, since a fixed threshold (bias) is not used as in LBP. The derivation of the rank order statistics is not necessary for extracting the LBPs, since the thresholding according to the center pixel's intensity value determines the pattern uniquely. However, the LBP can still be uniquely determined from the rank permutations. Hence, changing the bias level for generating the child LBPs from root permutations can be seen as a unifying approach between the LBPs and permutation space, where the contribution of the center pixel is adjusted by using the bias.

6. Experiments

6.1. Qualitative Tests on n-Tuples and LBPs. In this subsection, the distribution of the *n*-tuples (intermediate root permutations) is studied with natural image data. The objective is to characterize which individual *n*-tuples are most common with natural image data and to make implications on their role in the formation of uniform patterns. Also, the spatial response of the *n*-tuples to different image structures is studied with different kind of images. The runs level 2 intermediate root permutations described in the previous section will be shown to be among the most common *n*-tuples with natural image data. This observation can promote the understanding of the uniform patterns and their high occurrence probability with natural images in particular.

In Figures 6, 7, 8, and 9 the most common intermediate root permutations are shown for different test images of Figure 5. The total number of occurrences of each permutation is also shown. For each instance of a certain permutation in the corresponding test image, a neighborhood of 35 × 35 pixels was extracted and all of the local intensity blocks for the given permutation were combined, that is, added together. The intensity scale was then normalized based on the minimum and maximum values within the sum of the permutation blocks. In order to better distinguish between the true monotonic runs level 2 *n*-tuples in nonflat image areas, only patterns which did not contain ties were extracted.

When comparing the responses in Figures 6 and 9, it can be observed that with small neighborhood radius ($M = 6$ with $r = 2$) the *n*-tuples appear to correspond to edges in various orientations. It can also be observed

Test image 1: 2448 × 3264   Test image 2: 1728 × 2304

Test image 3: 2448 × 3264   Test image 4: 1728 × 2304

FIGURE 5: Test images used in the experiments. Test image 1 was chosen due to its fine texture within the leafs and the flowers in order to compare it with the Test images 2 and 3, which contain areas of monotonic changing intensity (representing the sky and the water). Test image 4 was chosen in order to study the effect of edge gradients to the *n*-tuples and LBPs.

that the most common intermediate root permutations are typically of runs level 2. Hence, the theoretical analysis in the previous sections is also supported by occurrence statistics of the natural images. It should be noted that the property described in the previous sections, stating that the runs level 2 root permutations will always produce a uniform pattern independently of the bias chosen, holds for the intermediate root permutations as well. Independently of the center chosen, these intermediate root permutations will always produce a uniform LBP (to the direction $I_n \Rightarrow P_n \Rightarrow b_n$). The orientations of the detected edges follow the direction of the most common gradients among the test images (see e.g., Figure 9 and the corresponding test image 4). In Figure 7, the local neighborhood is extended to M of 8 and radius of 8 using test image 2. It can be observed that now the monotonically changing image structures specific to the sky and to the water dominate the average intensity blocks. In Figure 8, M of 6 and radius of 6 are used. It can be observed that the intensity structures corresponding to the *n*-tuples become smoother compared to the lower radius. In this case the *n*-tuples capture larger scale changes.

Tests with repeated textures were also performed. The images shown in Figure 10, from the Outex [24] dataset, were used. In Figure 11, the response of the most common *n*-tuples within (8, 2) neighborhood with interpolation is shown using the Outex images. The most common permutations in Figure 11 correspond to the structures present in wood_012 texture sample. It consists of a gradually changing monotonic texture pattern. According to this experiment it would seem that especially monotonic changes contribute to the formation of runs level 2 patterns.

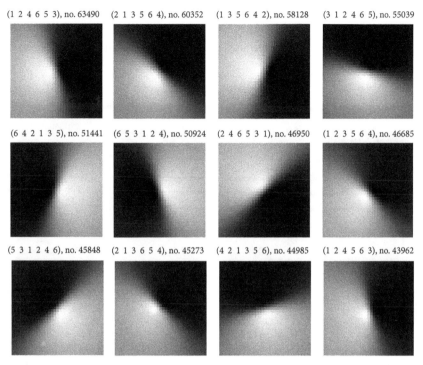

FIGURE 6: Average intensity patch of the 12 most common intermediate root permutations in (6, 2) neighborhood (with interpolation) using test image 1 of Figure 5. The first rank from the left corresponds to the Eastern direction, and the following ranks are formed to the counterclockwise direction (North-East, North, etc.).

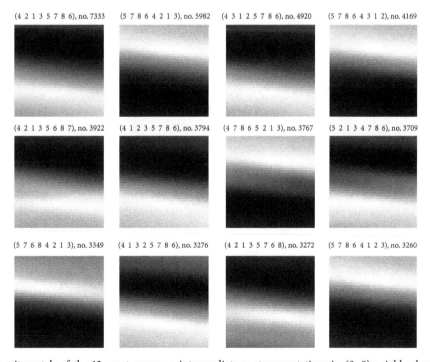

FIGURE 7: Average intensity patch of the 12 most common intermediate root permutations in (8, 8) neighborhood (with interpolation) using test image 2 of Figure 5. The first rank from the left corresponds to the Eastern direction, and the following ranks are formed to the counterclockwise direction (North-East, North, etc.) It can be observed that the most common intermediate root permutations with this radius correspond to monotonically changing edge functions characterizing the horizontal gradients of the input image.

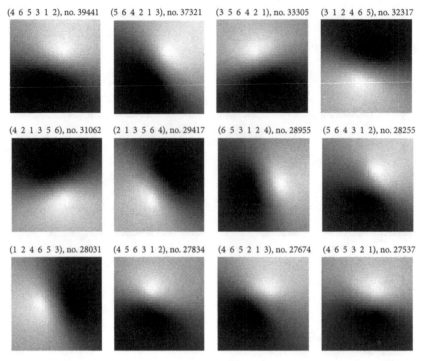

FIGURE 8: Average intensity patch of the 12 most common intermediate root permutations in (6, 6) neighborhood (with interpolation) using test image 3 of Figure 5. The first rank from the left corresponds to the Eastern direction, and the following ranks are formed to the counterclockwise direction (North-East, North, etc.).

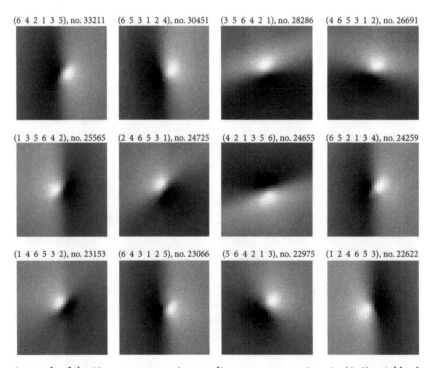

FIGURE 9: Average intensity patch of the 12 most common intermediate root permutations in (6, 2) neighborhood (with interpolation) using test image 4 of Figure 5. The first rank from the left corresponds to the Eastern direction, and the following ranks are formed to the counterclockwise direction (North-East, North, etc.) It can be observed that the most common intermediate root permutations correspond now to the main edge directions specific to the test image.

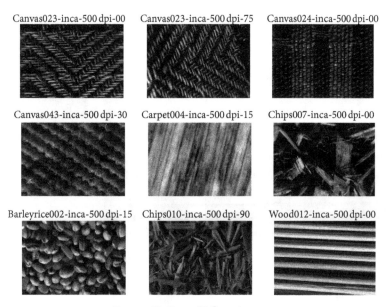

FIGURE 10: Outex [24] test images.

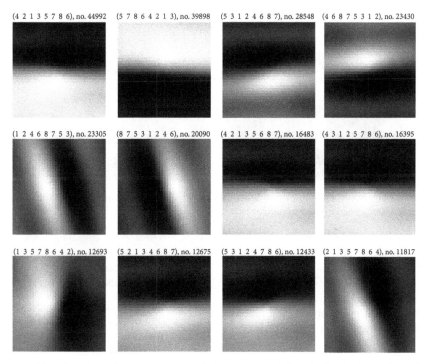

FIGURE 11: Average intensity patch of the 12 most common intermediate root permutations in (8, 2) neighborhood (with interpolation) using all of the selected Outex test images. The first rank from the left corresponds to the Eastern direction, and the following ranks are formed to the counterclockwise direction (North-East, North, etc.) It can be observed that the most common intermediate root permutations (n-tuples) seem to capture intensity patches corresponding to wood_012. The selected (M, r) combination might be too sensitive to noise. See, for example, similar intensity patches related to permutations (4 2 1 3 5 7 8 6) and (4 2 1 3 5 6 8 7).

Figure 12 shows the average intensity blocks of the LBPs in (6, 2) neighborhood related to the most common intermediate root permutation of test image 4, that is, permutation {6, 4, 2, 1, 3, 5}. The shown LBPs correspond to situation where the bias is changed gradually from its minimum value to the maximum value. It can be noted that as the descriptor k of the LBPs grows, the spatial support for the edges becomes stronger. With small k, the detected structure becomes limited to the proximity of the center pixel. If the permutation tree representation of Figure 4 is used (in this

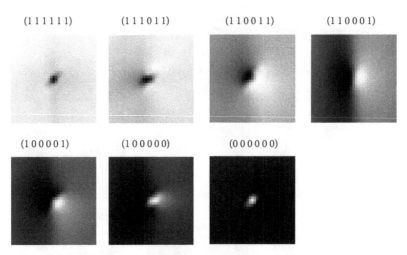

(1 1 1 1 1 1)   (1 1 1 0 1 1)   (1 1 0 0 1 1)   (1 1 0 0 0 1)

(1 0 0 0 0 1)   (1 0 0 0 0 0)   (0 0 0 0 0 0)

FIGURE 12: Average intensity patches of uniform LBPs in (6, 2) neighborhood corresponding to the most common intermediate root permutation in Figure 9, that is, permutation (6 4 2 1 3 5). Test image 4 was used. The first bit from the left corresponds to the Eastern direction, and the following bits are formed to the counterclockwise direction.

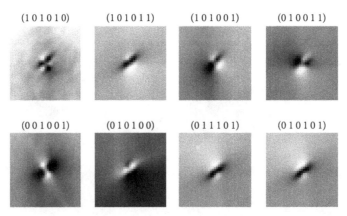

(1 0 1 0 1 0)   (1 0 1 0 1 1)   (1 0 1 0 0 1)   (0 1 0 0 1 1)

(0 0 1 0 0 1)   (0 1 0 1 0 0)   (0 1 1 1 0 1)   (0 1 0 1 0 1)

FIGURE 13: Average intensity patches of certain nonuniform LBPs. Test image 4 is used. The first bit from the left corresponds to the Eastern direction, and the following bits are formed to the counterclockwise direction.

case $M = 6$), the corresponding path for this runs level 2 permutation is {*LEFT, RIGHT, LEFT, RIGHT*} in a circular manner. With similar tests using nonuniform patterns, the response becomes partly limited to the area of the pattern itself, without significant edge support (see Figure 13).

6.2. Tests with a Priori Model. In this subsection, the a priori distribution of LBPs is further studied. The objective is to better understand which factors contribute to the formation of uniform patterns in particular. The proposed approach can also give new perspectives on the previous studies in [8, 21]. Based on the examples in Section 4 (e.g., Table 1), we hypothesize that root permutations which include monotonically ordered subsets would produce more uniform patterns than permutations of arbitrary order. This is analyzed first.

The total number of unit permutations (and final LBPs) was $(M+1)!$, corresponding to the number of instances in the constructed permutation space. The following experimental procedure was then applied.

(1) A table containing all possible $M!$ intermediate root permutations was constructed.

(2) Using these permutations as root permutations, the center bias was changed for each permutation $M + 1$ times in order to generate all the child LBPs for the permutation space corresponding to all unit permutations in given LBP neighborhood M.

In Figure 14, the length of the longest monotonic run among the root permutations is plotted, along with the total share of permutations resulting in uniform child LBPs. For example, in the case of $M = 10$, if the length of the longest monotonic run among the root permutations is 3, roughly 40% of the resulting LBPs are uniform, and if the length of the longest monotonic run is 7, roughly 70% of the resulting LBPs are uniform. These results would seem to support the given hypothesis.

Next, we studied the correspondence between the runs test and the relative share of uniform Local Binary Patterns.

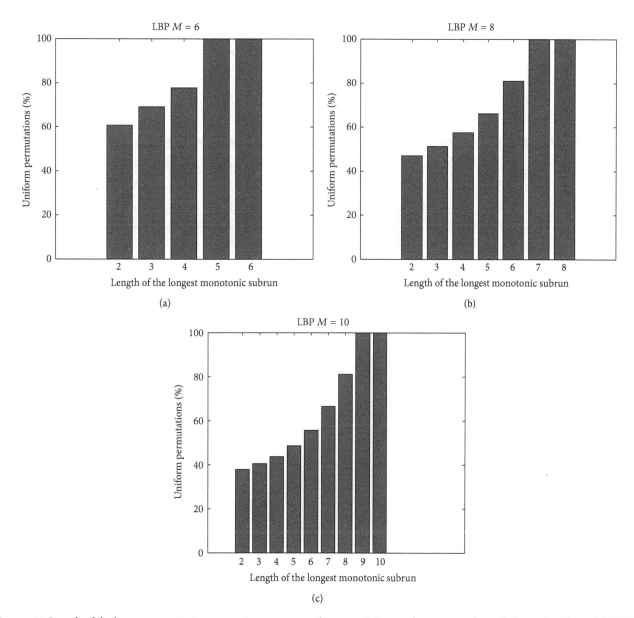

FIGURE 14: Length of the longest monotonic consecutive run among the permutations with respect to the total share of uniform child LBPs while going through all unit permutations.

In Figure 15, the setup was the same as previously used. The percentage of permutations resulting in a uniform child LBP is plotted, with respect to the total number of LBPs within the current category. The result of the circular up and down runs test for randomness is indexed on the x-axis. It can be observed that as the result of the runs up and down test for permutations decreases, the share of uniform patterns increases. It can also be observed that for the runs test result 2, all the LBPs are uniform.

In Figure 16 the data corresponding to the previous experimental setup is plotted with $M = 10$ and also with respect to descriptor k. It can be observed that, as k decreases, the share of permutations resulting in uniform LBP increases. Also, as the result of the circular up and down runs test for randomness decreases, the relative share of uniform permutations (frequency of permutations resulting in uniform patterns) increases. This implies that uniform patterns become more frequent with a stronger hypothesis of nonrandomness according to the runs test. According to Figure 16, for the descriptor k values 0 and 1, all of the root permutations result in uniform patterns, since all patterns (of all-zero LBP, all-one LBP, all-zero LBP including a single 1, and all-one LBP including a single 0) are then uniform. When the result of runs up and down test is 2, the patterns remain uniform despite the increase in k.

We also examined the relationship between the runs test and individual LBPs by considering their root permutations. It is clear that, for example, LBP 01010101 must contain at least 8 runs. However, LBP 10000 could contain various numbers of runs according to runs up and down test for randomness,

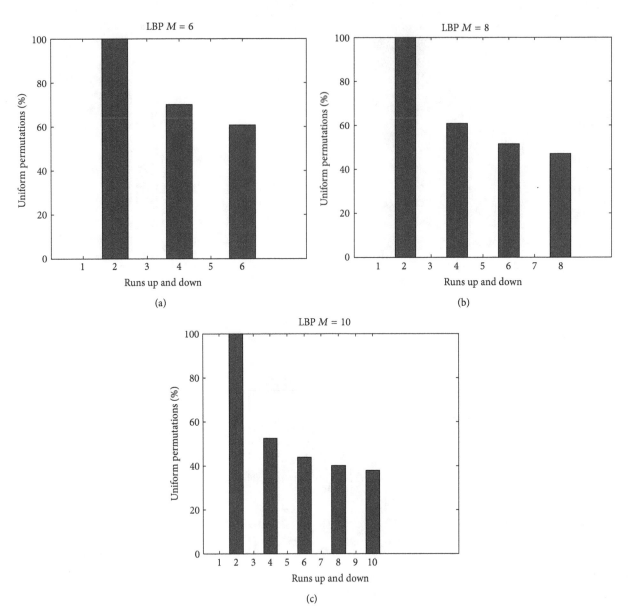

FIGURE 15: Number of root permutations resulting in uniform child LBPs with respect to total amount of permutations. The runs up and down test result for the randomness of the permutation is plotted on the x-axis.

since now the leftmost LBP bit (or the bit change next to it) alone restricts the degree of freedom of the underlying root permutations. The remaining long sequence of all zeros allow a large number of combinations considered as possible root permutations.

In the following, a reverse mapping ϕ_{MAP}^{-1} of Definition 5(e) is used. For LBPs with $M = 6$, 000101, 101110 the number of all circular runs among the root permutations varied between 4 and 6, with a mean of 4.667 and variance 0.908. For uniform $M = 6$ patterns 011100 and 111000 the runs test result varied between 2 and 6 with a mean of 3.33 and variance 1.829. The rotation of the patterns did not seem to affect the result, as was expected. For uniform pattern 00000000 the number of runs varied between 2 and 8 with a mean of 5.333 and variance 1.4223 (in this case,

the total number of root permutations was 8!). For uniform $M = 8$ pattern 01100000 the result of the runs test varied between 2 and 6 with a mean of 4.667 and variance 1.245. The results from the ϕ_{MAP}^{-1} test indicate that nonuniform patterns, in average, contain more runs than the uniform patterns, as can be expected.

In Figure 17, the number of uniform patterns (permutations resulting into uniform patterns) is shown, with respect to the length of the longest monotonic run and descriptor k, while using the same approach as in the previous figures of this subsection. It can be observed that maximum run lengths around 3, 4, and 5 provide most of the contribution to uniform Local Binary Patterns with LBP neighborhood of $M = 8$ in the case of the a priori model. As expected, as the descriptor k grows, the number of permutations resulting

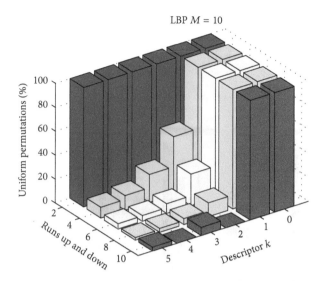

FIGURE 16: Number of runs among the root permutations, plotted with respect to descriptor k. Z-axis represents the probability of permutations resulting in uniform child LBP.

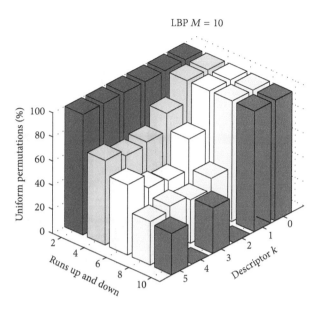

FIGURE 18: Percentage of uniform patterns with respect to the runs up and down test result and descriptor k. Natural images in LBP(10, 2) neighborhood with interpolation are used.

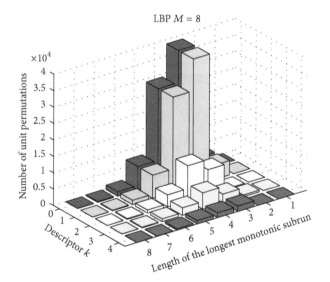

FIGURE 17: The longest monotonic run among root permutations, plotted with respect to descriptor k and only considering permutations resulting in uniform child LBPs.

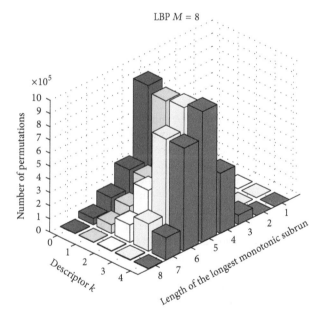

FIGURE 19: Number of intermediate root permutations resulting in uniform patterns with respect to the longest monotonic subrun and descriptor k. Natural images in LBP(8, 2) neighborhood with interpolation are used.

in uniform LBPs also decreases due to reduced number of binomial combinations. In general, the number of particular unit permutations related to high descriptor k LBPs is smaller (see (1)), emphasizing the relative effect of these particular unit permutations on the final LBP histogram.

6.3. Experiments with Natural Image Data. The experiments of the previous subsection with the a priori model are next considered in the case of natural image data, by using the test images of Figure 5. In the following, the effect of ties and the effect of runs level 2 permutations are considered separately. This allows studying the role of these two in the

formation of uniform patterns in particular. The grayscale range of all test images is 8 bits. Figures 18 and 19 correspond to the experiments with the a priori model shown in Figures 16 and 17, respectively. In Figure 18, the percentage of uniform patterns with respect to runs up and down test and descriptor k is shown. An increased percentage of uniform patterns with larger k values, in comparison with the a priori model, can be observed. These patterns correspond to monotonic edge

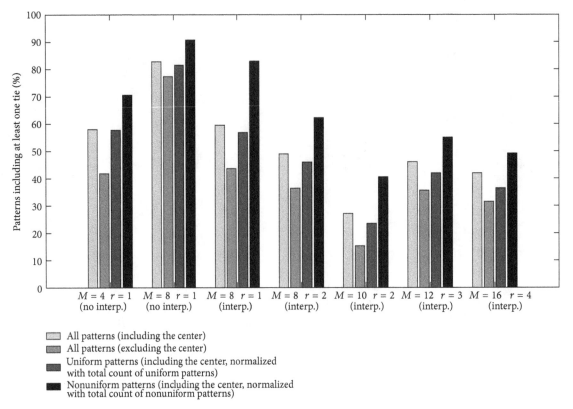

FIGURE 20: The effect of ties (neighboring pixels being of equal magnitude) to the formation of uniform patterns. It can be observed that on average, uniform patterns tend to contain less ties than nonuniform patterns.

structures in the images. In Figure 19 the number of uniform patterns is increased, especially for larger descriptor k values and longer run lengths. While being a priori is extremely rare, the high k patterns are actually among the most common ones with natural image data when only uniform patterns are considered. The results of Figures 17 and 19 also indicate that natural image data increases the monotonicity of the root permutations for the uniform patterns. As a consequence, the number of uniform patterns is increased.

The effect of ties is considered next. In Figure 20, the percentages of local neighborhoods containing at least one tie are shown with respect to neighborhood radius and the possible usage of interpolation using all of the test images of Figure 5. For uniform patterns, the percentage share of patterns containing at least one tie is also shown. It can be observed that ties are not, on average, more common among uniform patterns than with the other patterns. Similar results were obtained with the Outex textures of Figure 10. This implies that although ties could cause some minor increase in certain LBP bins (e.g., all-one bin or all-zero bin) within flat image areas, as could be predicted from the a priori model used in [8], it seems that they cannot explain most of the increase related to the occurrence frequency of uniform patterns, when using natural images. A possible explanation to this could be that ties tend to occur within flat image areas where the relative amount of i.i.d. noise is more significant.

In Figure 21, the percentage share of runs level 2 patterns is shown for each of the test images of Figure 5. A minor

increase in the number of these patterns can be observed for test images 2 and 3. This could be related to the large monotonic areas of the sky and the water present in these images. The a priori estimate of the number of runs level 2 permutations (corresponding to $M * 2^{M-2}/(M!)$, see Definition 9) is also shown in Figure 21. Natural images seem to increase the share of the runs level 2 permutations significantly, compared to the a priori estimate. The percentage share of runs level 2 permutations among uniform patterns is further shown for all of the test images in Figure 21 (as an overall average for test images 1–4). It can be observed that also with natural image data, the occurrence frequency of these permutations increases further among uniform patterns.

When studying Figure 21, it can be observed in the case of $M = 8$ that interpolation increases the share of runs level 2 permutations in each of the test images. The share of uniform patterns naturally increases also when using interpolation. It can be observed that while the number of runs level 2 patterns is significantly larger with the test images than with the a priori model, increasing the neighborhood radius decreases the number of runs level 2 patterns (see e.g., the results in (8, 1) and (8, 2) neighborhoods with interpolation). This could be explained by reduced correlation among the pixel intensities within the local neighborhood, as the radius increases.

6.4. Quantitative Tests. We also performed initial experiments with the FERET facial recognition database [25] (FAFB, FAFC, DUP1, and DUP2) sets and Outex TC 0012 [24]

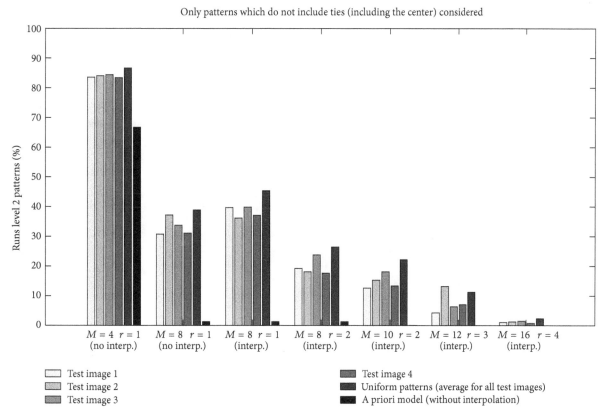

FIGURE 21: Percentage share of runs level 2 permutations among images 1–4 in various permutation neighborhoods. The bar corresponding to uniform patterns indicates the occurrence frequency of runs level 2 patterns among uniform patterns only. It can be observed that the average frequency of runs level 2 permutations increases compared to the a priori model in all neighborhoods and even further when the uniform patterns are considered.

rotation invariant texture categorization set to test whether the intermediate root permutations of runs level 2 would perform better in classification than traditional LBP with uniform patterns. In all of the following tests, if not explicitly noted, ties were coded in an increasing order of the rank magnitudes among the n-tuples, so that a neighborhood containing only tied intensities was assigned to the increasing permutation $\{1, 2, 3, \ldots, M\}$.

In Figure 22, the recognition rates for the FERET sets are shown. The length of the feature vector in $M = 6$ was 720 (i.e., factorial of 6). It can be observed, that using only runs level 2 n-tuples (total of 96 out of 720), the recognition rate was not significantly lower than with the full permutation histogram. Increasing the permutation neighborhood to (8, 2) with interpolation and using runs level 2 patterns only (total of 512 patterns out of 40320) an average recognition accuracy close to the reported LBP(8, 2) accuracy [9] was obtained. However, it appears that for larger M (say 8 or more) and small radiuses the number of runs level 2 permutations drops even with natural image data. This can be related to the effect of noise, the high dimension of the permutation histogram, and the substantially low a priori probability of the runs level 2 patterns. The a priori probability of runs level 2 patterns in $M = 8$ neighborhood (without considering interpolation) is as low as 1.27%, emphasizing the significant role of these

TABLE 2: Outex TC 0012 rotation invariant texture classification experiment.

Outex TC 0012	Recognition rate (%)	FV length
N-tuples (6, 2) ROT-INV interp. (runs 2 only)	47.6	16 bins
N-tuples (6, 2) ROT-INV interp. (all)	55.5	120 bins
N-tuples (8, 2) ROT-INV interp. (runs 2 only)	**58.8**	64 bins
LBP (8, 1) ROT-INV interp.	**64.6**	10 bins

permutation bins in the overall permutation histogram. To increase the number of runs level 2 patterns, we used a 4×4 averaging filter as a preprocessing step with M of 8.

The effect of ties to the performance of n-tuples can also be estimated from the results of Figure 22 with $M = 6$. It can be observed that neglecting ties reduces the recognition performance for radius of 2, but with larger radiuses the recognition accuracy is not significantly altered. The length of the individual block histogram in [9] for the LBPs was 59, which is smaller than for the permutations.

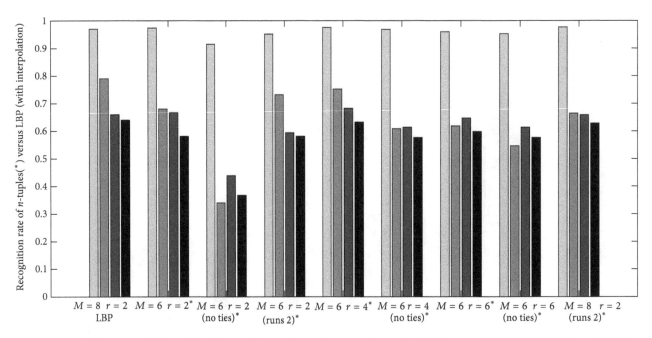

FIGURE 22: FERET face recognition results with n-tuples are shown in comparison with LBP. Test sets FAFB, FAFC, DUP1, and DUP2 are considered (from the left to the right). It can be observed that LBP outperforms n-tuples. Also for LBP the length of the feature vector is smaller.

In tests on rotation invariant texture classification (see the results of Table 2) with the Outex TC 0012 set [24], a rotation invariant mapping of intermediate root permutations (n-tuples) was used. For each available permutation pattern, M possible rotations were assigned, and these were then combined in a rotation invariant manner [10]. In the case of runs level 2 patterns only, a similar procedure was also performed. Using (6, 2) neighborhood the total number of runs level 2 patterns was 96, and for each rotation invariant bin, 6 rotated bins were assigned. The final length of the feature vector was then 16 bins. All rotation invariant n-tuples (i.e., not only runs level 2) in the (6, 2) neighborhood resulted in a feature vector length of 120 bins. In the (8, 2) neighborhood with interpolation using only runs level 2 patterns, by always assigning 8 patterns into the same rotation invariant category the final length of the feature vector became 64 bins for the n-tuples. The highest recognition rate for the n-tuples was obtained with these parameters using the runs level 2 patterns only. Also the feature vector length in the (8, 2) neighborhood was shorter than with the (6, 2), which would seem to indicate that the runs 2 n-tuples are among the most salient ones, if the n-tuples alone are considered. However, traditional rotation invariant LBP in a (8, 1) neighborhood with interpolation resulted in a better recognition rate (64.6% accuracy) in [14] with the same test set. Also, the length of the feature vector for the LBPs was shorter (10 bins). Log-likelihood distance metric with 1-nearest neighbor classification was used in these experiments.

The previous results raise naturally the question, why are LBPs more discriminative than n-tuples, despite the usage of a similar feature vector length reduction method (i.e. the usage of runs level 2 patterns) than the uniform patterns. According

to the previous qualitative and quantitative analysis (see also Figure 22), it appears that the performance of the n-tuples is decreased in comparison with LBPs for two reasons. First, their performance is decreased due to large number of ties among small local radiuses. However, this is changed if a larger radius is used. Second, a small change in the intensity order (i.e., on the permutation) for larger M (e.g., more than 6) changes the bin placement of the histograms and increases susceptibility to noise, which is not the case in LBP. Above-mentioned issues should be considered carefully when designing descriptors based on n-tuple processing. As a rule of thumb for selecting the number of samples in an n-tuple, the radius of the local neighborhood should be at least equal to the number of circular sample points M (see Figure 22). In the recently proposed LOCP descriptor [26] a binary representation of successive circular pairs in a local neighborhood was used. This approach avoids the negative effect of ties by changing the following circular bit only if the intensity is changed, that is, the bin placement of the permutation histogram does not change due to possible minor intensity order differences. As a consequence, robustness to noise could be achieved in [26] by only considering the neighboring circular pairs when deriving the binary pattern.

7. Discussion

In this work, the observation that Local Binary Patterns can be modeled as compositions of rank permutations was used to study some of the mechanisms related to the formation of uniform patterns. As previously observed, uniform patterns are a priori very frequent (with i.i.d. data), but this seems to be mostly explained by how they are located according to the descriptor k (see (1)–(4)). For most k values there are exactly $2 * M$ instances of uniform LBP rotations and inversions, while the number of all LBPs increases rapidly with descriptor k. As a consequence the relative contribution of uniform LBPs is larger at low k values. Therefore, according to a priori model, uniform LBPs contain a larger share of unit permutations compared to other LBPs and are very frequent.

According to our investigation, the contribution of uniform patterns seems to get even stronger with a stronger evidence of nonrandomness among the underlying data. This issue was quantitatively analyzed in this paper using the runs up and down test for permutations. Monotonicity among the root permutations would be a strong indicator of nonrandomness. In tests with natural images, the majority of the most common circular permutations belonged to category 2 according to the runs test, corresponding to monotonically changing intensity structures. Using natural image data also increased the length of monotonic runs among the permutations, compared to the a priori model.

With real-world images occurrence percentages of uniform patterns of 70–90% and beyond are typical [10]. For example, with $M = 16$ the percentage of uniform patterns in textures was in the range of 57.6–79.6% in [10], while the a priori probability that we estimated in this paper was less than 30% (see Figure 3) for i.i.d. data without interpolation. A considerable portion of this increase can be explained by the bilinear subsampling (interpolation when deriving the LBP code) as described in [8], but we also propose that a portion of this increase could be explained by the capability of the uniform patterns to respond to deterministic properties within the image microstructure.

The relatively high occurrence probability of uniform patterns a priori, and even higher occurrence probability with natural images, could be compared also with the relative occurrence probabilities of individual n-tuples [4], since we showed that LBPs could be seen as compositions of n-tuples. Monotonic n-tuples dominate the occurrence statistics of natural images [4], which tends to increase the share of uniform patterns. This behavior was modeled quantitatively in this paper (see Figure 14).

Permutations with runs test result 2 can be used to capture monotonic edges and monotonic spatial image features, as was shown in Section 6. By increasing the radius of the local neighborhood, also the extent of the detected change could be increased. The formation of these patterns was examined in Figure 4. The understanding of this behavior could facilitate the development of new image descriptors inspired by the uniformity principle of Local Binary Patterns. Initial tests on the performance of runs level 2 permutation histograms were performed in Section 6, and it appeared that their performance did not exceed the original LBP. However, since the formation of the runs level 2 permutations can also be modeled as a tree structure, a graph based matching approach for the permutations could also be possible.

The use of only certain permutations inspired by the uniform pattern principle would seem to enhance the properties of n-tuples (see the quantitative experiments in Section 6). However, for larger M the feature extraction cost is higher for the n-tuples and the required feature vector becomes longer. Therefore, in these cases the traditional LBP with uniformity is preferable. Future work includes examining the possibilities to enhance the performance of n-tuple based descriptors, for example, [18, 19] based on the principles proposed. We showed that the uniform pattern principle can be at least partly extended to n-tuples as well. This could provide a variety of alternatives for increasing the performance of n-tuple based descriptors. For example, the pooling scheme in [18, 19] could be adjusted, not only to take into account rotation but also to select n-tuples according to their runs test score. This could also allow increasing the number of neighborhood samples among pooled n-tuples without increasing the descriptor length significantly.

8. Conclusions

We proposed the modeling of LBPs through nonlinear intermediate mapping into permutations. The permutation set was further modified in order to gain a more flexible LBP model by removing the effect of the center pixel on the actual permutations and by modulating the effect of the center pixel by introducing an adjustable bias term. The approach proposed in this paper was intended to provide further understanding of the LBPs and of the uniform LBPs in particular. The notion of root permutations was introduced in order to model the formation process of uniform patterns. Monotonicity among the root permutations was shown to be in an important role in the increased share of uniform patterns with natural images. The possible relationship between the runs up and down test for randomness for permutations and the selection of uniform patterns for LBP histograms was also considered. According to our investigation, the response of uniform patterns is enhanced when the result of the runs test is low, that is, indicating nonrandomness and correlation.

The a priori occurrence probability of uniform LBPs is high. This has been previously observed to be a result from the sampling process itself as well as from the use of bilinear interpolation. In addition to this, we provided quantitative analysis on how the Local Binary Pattern methodology, together with selecting only the uniform patterns, can be seen as a process which further enhances the response of such deterministic underlying image intensity structures, which are not likely to be formed by statistically random distribution or phenomena. Being also shape primitives, the uniform Local Binary Patterns naturally embody response to various microshapes.

Acknowledgment

The research was funded by the Academy of Finland Project no. 254430.

References

[1] M. Pietikainen, A. Hadid, G. Zhao, and T. Ahonen, *Computer Vision Using Local Binary Patterns*, Springer, Berlin, Germany, 2011.

[2] N. Chatlani and J. J. Soraghan, "Local Binary patterns for 1D signal processing," in *Proceedings of the 18th European Signal Processing Conference*, pp. 95–99, Aalborg, Denmark, 2010.

[3] http://www.cse.oulu.fi/CMV/LBP_Bibliography/.

[4] L. Hepplewhite and T. J. Stonham, "Texture classification using N-tuple pattern recognition," in *Proceedings of International Conference on Pattern Recognition (ICPR '96)*, vol. 4, pp. 159–163, Vienna, Austria, 1996.

[5] L. Wang and D.-C. He, "Texture classification using texture spectrum," *Pattern Recognition*, vol. 23, no. 8, pp. 905–910, 1990.

[6] L. Hepplewhite and T. J. Stonham, "N-tuple texture recognition and the zero crossing sketch," *Electronics Letters*, vol. 33, no. 1, pp. 45–46, 1997.

[7] W. Zhang, S. Shan, W. Gao, X. Chen, and H. Zhang, "Local Gabor Binary Pattern Histogram Sequence (LGBPHS): a novel non-statistical model for face representation and recognition," in *Proceedings of the 10th IEEE International Conference on Computer Vision (ICCV '05)*, vol. 1, pp. 786–791, October 2005.

[8] F. Bianconi and A. Fernández, "On the occurrence probability of local binary patterns: a theoretical study," *Journal of Mathematical Imaging and Vision*, vol. 40, no. 3, pp. 259–268, 2011.

[9] T. Ahonen, A. Hadid, and M. Pietikäinen, "Face description with local binary patterns: application to face recognition," *IEEE Transactions on Pattern Analysis and Machine Intelligence*, vol. 28, no. 12, pp. 2037–2041, 2006.

[10] T. Ojala, M. Pietikäinen, and T. Mäenpää, "Multiresolution gray-scale and rotation invariant texture classification with local binary patterns," *IEEE Transactions on Pattern Analysis and Machine Intelligence*, vol. 24, no. 7, pp. 971–987, 2002.

[11] C. Shan and T. Gritti, "Learning discriminative LBP-histogram bins for facial expression recognition," in *Proceedings of British Machine Vision Conference (BMVC '08)*, Leeds, UK, 2008.

[12] T. Ahonen, J. Matas, C. He, and M. Pietikäinen, "Rotation invariant image description with local binary pattern histogram fourier features," in *Proceedings of Scandinavian Conference on Image Analysis (SCIA '09)*, vol. 5575 of *Lecture Notes in Computer Science*, pp. 61–70, 2009.

[13] A. Fernández, O. Ghita, E. González, F. Bianconi, and P. F. Whelan, "Evaluation of robustness against rotation of LBP, CCR and ILBP features in granite texture classification," *Machine Vision and Applications*, vol. 22, no. 6, pp. 913–926, 2011.

[14] G. Zhao, T. Ahonen, J. Matas, and M. Pietikäinen, "Rotation-invariant image and video description with local binary pattern features," *IEEE Transactions on Image Processing*, vol. 21, no. 4, pp. 1465–1477, 2012.

[15] T. Maenpaa, T. Ojala, and M. Pietikainen, "Robust texture classification by subsets of Local Binary Patterns," in *Proceedings of the 15th International Conference on Pattern Recognition*, vol. 3, pp. 947–950, Barcelona, Spain, 2000.

[16] I. Guyon and A. Elisseeff, "An introduction to variable and feature selection," *Journal of Machine Learning Research*, vol. 3, pp. 1157–1182, 2003.

[17] R. Zabih and J. Woodfill, "Non-parametric local transforms for computing visual correspondence," in *Proceedings of European Conference on Computer Vision*, pp. 151–158, Stockholm, Sweden, 1994.

[18] Z. Wang, B. Fan, and F. Wu, "Local intensity order pattern for feature description," in *Proceedings of IEEE International Conference on Computer Vision (ICCV '11)*, pp. 603–610, November 2011.

[19] B. Fan, F. Wu, and Z. Hu, "Rotationally invariant descriptors using intensity order pooling," *IEEE Transactions on Pattern Analysis and Machine Intelligence*, vol. 34, no. 10, pp. 2031–2045, 2012.

[20] T. Ahonen and M. Pietikäinen, "Image description using joint distribution of filter bank responses," *Pattern Recognition Letters*, vol. 30, no. 4, pp. 368–376, 2009.

[21] O. Lahdenoja, "A statistical approach for characterizing local binary patterns," TUCS Technical Report 795, 2006.

[22] O. Lahdenoja, M. Laiho, and A. Paasio, "Reducing the feature vector length in local binary pattern based face recognition," in *Proceedings of IEEE International Conference on Image Processing (ICIP '05)*, pp. 914–917, Genova, Italy, September 2005.

[23] J. D. Gibbons, *Nonparametric Statistical Inference*, McGraw-Hill, New York, NY, USA, 1975.

[24] T. Ojala, T. Maenpaa, M. Pietikainen et al., "Outex—new framework for empirical evaluation of texture analysis algorithms," in *Proceedings of the 16th International Conference on Pattern Recognition*, vol. 1, pp. 701–706, 2002.

[25] P. J. Phillips, H. Wechsler, J. Huang, and P. J. Rauss, "The FERET database and evaluation procedure for face-recognition algorithms," *Image and Vision Computing*, vol. 16, no. 5, pp. 295–306, 1998.

[26] C. H. Chan, B. Goswami, J. Kittler, and W. Christmas, "Local ordinal contrast pattern histograms for spatiotemporal, lip-based speaker authentication," *IEEE Transactions on Information Forensics and Security*, vol. 7, no. 2, pp. 602–612, 2012.

10

A Robust Illumination Normalization Method Based on Mean Estimation for Face Recognition

Yong Luo,[1] **Ye-Peng Guan,**[1,2] **and Chang-Qi Zhang**[1]

[1] *School of Communication and Information Engineering, Shanghai University, 99 Shangda Road, Shanghai, China*
[2] *Key Laboratory of Advanced Displays and System Application, Ministry of Education, 99 Shangda Road, Shanghai, China*

Correspondence should be addressed to Ye-Peng Guan; ypguan@shu.edu.cn

Academic Editors: A. Bandera, O. Ghita, M. Leo, and S. Mattoccia

An illumination normalization method for face recognition has been developed since it was difficult to control lighting conditions efficiently in the practical applications. Considering that the irradiation light is of little variation in a certain area, a mean estimation method is used to simulate the illumination component of a face image. Illumination component is removed by subtracting the mean estimation from the original image. In order to highlight face texture features and suppress the impact of adjacent domains, a ratio of the quotient image and its modulus mean value is obtained. The exponent result of the ratio is closely approximate to a relative reflection component. Since the gray value of facial organs is less than that of the facial skin, postprocessing is applied to the images in order to highlight facial texture for face recognition. Experiments show that the performance by using the proposed method is superior to that of state of the arts.

1. Introduction

Face recognition is one of the most active research focuses due to its wide applications [1, 2]. Face recognition can be used in many areas including security access control, surveillance monitor, and intelligent human machine interface. The accuracy of face recognition is not ideal at present. Among numerous adverse factors for face recognition, appearance variation caused by illumination is one of the major problems which remain unsettled. Many approaches such as illumination cones method [3] and 9D linear subspace method [4] have been proposed to solve illumination problems and improve the face recognition. The main drawbacks of the approaches mentioned above are the need of knowledge about the light source or a large volume of training data. To overcome this demerit, region-based image preprocessing methods are proposed in [5–7]. These methods introduced some noise to make global illumination discontinuous.

Some illumination normalization methods are proposed to deal with the problem of varied lighting, which does not require training images with low computational complexity [8, 9], such as multiscale retinex (MSR) [10], wavelet-based normalization technique (WA) [11], and DCT-based

normalization technique (DCT) [12]. The extracted facial feature is poor and has messy histogram. In order to highlight facial texture features, some methods are proposed including adaptive nonlocal means (ANL) [13], DoG filtering (DOG) [14], steerable filter (SF) [15], and wavelet denoising (WD) [16]. Overall gray values after processing are different with varying degrees and partial facial feature information is removed in above methods. Retina modeling (RET) [17] is an improved method based on DOG [14]. Gradientfaces (GRF) [18] uses image gradient orientation to extract the illumination invariant feature. Weberfaces (WEB) [19] extracted the illumination invariant feature through computing relative gradient.

Aiming at improving some limits in illumination processing for face recognition, a new illumination normalization method has been proposed. Considering that the irradiation light is of little variation in a certain area, a mean estimation method is used to simulate the illumination component of a face image. Illumination component is removed by subtracting the mean estimation from the original image. In order to standardize the overall gray level of different facial images, a ratio matrix of the quotient image and its modulus mean value is obtained. The exponent result of the ratio is closely approximate to a relative reflection component. Since the gray value of facial organs is less than the facial skin, postprocessing is applied to the images to highlight facial texture for face recognition. The first contribution of the developed approach is that the performance is more robust in processing illumination variation for face recognition than that of state-of the arts. The second contribution is that the proposal can get some distinctive facial texture features for face recognition. The third contribution is to do fast illumination normalization in an ordinary hardware from a cluttered face image with some challenging illumination variations without any hypothesis for the face image contents in advance. The fourth contribution is to reduce the size of space required for image storage. Comparative study with some state of the arts has indicated the superior performance of the proposal.

The organization of the rest paper is as follows. In Section 2, mean estimation illumination normalization method is described. Some experimental results and comparisons are shown in Section 3. Some conclusions are given in Section 4.

2. Mean Illumination Estimation

Smoothing techniques are often used to estimate the illumination of the face image [13, 14]. According to the illumination-reflection model, the intension of a face image $f(x, y)$ can be described as

$$f(x, y) = r(x, y) i(x, y),\qquad(1)$$

where $r(x, y)$ is the reflection component and $i(x, y)$ is the illumination component.

Since $r(x, y)$ depends only on the surface material of an object, it is the intrinsic representation of a face image. Suppose $i(x, y)$ has little changed value in a small area when light source is remote. In order to separate the two components, logarithm transformation is applied to (1)

$$g(x, y) = \ln f(x, y)$$
$$= \ln r(x, y) + \ln i(x, y).\qquad(2)$$

The mean estimate of $g(x, y)$ is obtained as follows:

$$\hat{g}(x, y) = \frac{1}{n^2} \sum_{(s,t) \in w_{n \times n}} g(s, t)$$
$$= \frac{1}{n^2} \sum_{(s,t) \in w_{n \times n}} \ln r(s, t) + \frac{1}{n^2} \sum_{(s,t) \in w_{n \times n}} \ln i(s, t),\qquad(3)$$

where $w_{n \times n}$ is local neighborhood of the pixel (x, y) for image mean convolution processing, (s, t) is the locations of pixels in the neighborhood (x, y), and n is the length of $w_{n \times n}$ which will be discussed later.

The quotient image is computed from (2) and (3) to eliminate $i(x, y)$ as follows:

$$d(x, y) = g(x, y) - \hat{g}(x, y)$$
$$= \ln r(x, y) - \frac{1}{n^2} \sum_{(s,t) \in w_{n \times n}} \ln r(s, t) + \sigma,\qquad(4)$$

where $\sigma = \ln i(x, y) - (1/n^2) \sum_{(s,t) \in w_{n \times n}} \ln i(s, t)$.

The σ is a very small value which can be omitted. Equation (4) can be rewritten as

$$d(x, y) = g(x, y) - \hat{g}(x, y)$$
$$\approx \ln \frac{r(x, y)}{\left(\prod_{(s,t) \in w_{n \times n}} r(s, t)\right)^{1/n^2}},\qquad(5)$$

where $d(x, y)$ represents the ratio between the current point's reflectance and the $w_{n \times n}$ average reflectance.

It indicates the differences of materials between the point (x, y) and surrounding. When they are both the same kind of substance, the value of $d(x, y)$ is 0.

The reflectance of facial skin is usually greater than that of facial features. Consider

$$\alpha = \frac{1}{ab} \sum_{(x,y) \in f_{a \times b}} |d(x, y)|,\qquad(6)$$

where a is the number of rows in image, b is the number of columns in image, and $f_{a \times b}$ refers to the entire image range. α represents the average gray value ratio of the facial skin and facial features. The difference of the global gray level in processed images is reduced as

$$h(x, y) = \exp \frac{d(x, y)}{\alpha \cdot \beta},\qquad(7)$$

where β is a scaling tuning parameter and will be discussed later.

To suppress facial background noise and highlight facial texture features, the postprocessing is done as follows:

$$\hat{o}(x, y) = \begin{cases} h(x, y), & h(x, y) < 1, \\ 1, & h(x, y) \geq 1, \end{cases}$$
$$o(x, y) = \left[\frac{255 \times (\hat{o}(x, y) - c)}{1 - c} \right],\qquad(8)$$

where $o(x, y)$ is the final result image which is used to recognize face and c is the minimum value of $\hat{o}(x, y)$. $[\cdot]$ is rounded to the nearest integer operation. $o(x, y)$ refers to the relative reflection component of facial texture and skin. It can minimize the impact of illumination variations.

3. Experimental Results

To evaluate the performance of the proposed method, some challenging face databases with different illuminations are selected to test it. These face datasets include Yale B [20] and Extended Yale B [21], CMU-PIE [22], and CAS-PEAL-R1 [23]. Besides, some state of the arts including RET [17], GRF [18], and WEB [19] are selected to compare with the proposed method. Since PCA [24] and LDA [25] are highly sensitive to illumination variation, they are used to test illumination normalization in the same conditions.

In order to build a fair comparison with state of the arts, all these investigated methods are implemented with the parameters as the authors recommended.

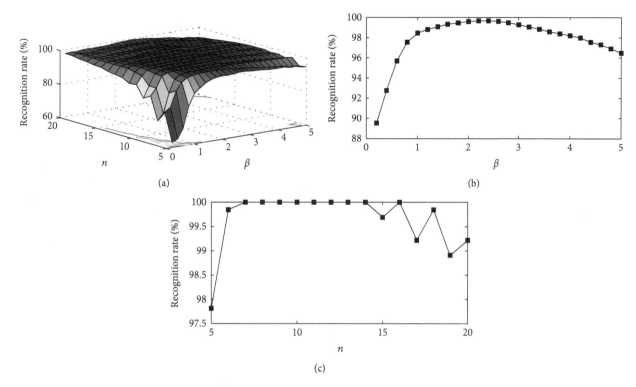

FIGURE 1: Face recognition results based on Yale B face database with different n and β. (a) 3D face recognition rate, (b) average face recognition rate with different β, and (c) face recognition rate with different n as β is 2.2.

TABLE 1: The statistical results of recognition rates on Yale B.

Recognition method	Average recognition rate (%)				Standard deviation of recognition rates ($\times 10^{-2}$)			
	RET [17]	GRF [18]	WEB [19]	Proposal	RET [17]	GRF [18]	WEB [19]	Proposal
PCA	96.60	87.44	88.21	**98.34**	3.11	7.57	6.43	**2.16**
LDA	98.11	93.11	97.33	**99.05**	1.98	7.11	1.97	**1.06**

3.1. Parameters Analysis. In order to get reasonable value for n and β, we select the Yale B face database to do face recognition. In Yale B face database, the frontally light face image (the light-source direction is $0°$) of each subject is selected as a training sample; the others are taken as a testing set. PCA is used to do face recognition.

Some experimental results are shown in Figure 1, where β is set from 0.2 to 5 at intervals of 0.2, n is set from 5 to 20 at intervals of 1. From Figure 1, the performance of face recognition is best when n is set 11 and β is 2.2, respectively.

The value of β will not be changed because the facial reflectance of different people varies little. The value of n will be changed according to the width of face variation:

$$n = \left[\frac{\text{wid}}{\text{wid}_0} n_0 \right], \quad (9)$$

where wid is the width of face. wid_0 is the width of face in Yale B face database and is set 168. n_0 is 11.

3.2. Comparisons on Yale B and Extended Yale B. Yale B face database includes 10 subjects under 64 illumination conditions. Yale B+ Extended Yale B face database includes 38 human subjects under 64 illumination conditions. The size of images is 168×192. The face images are numbered from 1 to 64 according to different illumination conditions. One illumination condition of each subject is selected randomly as a training sample; the others are taken as the testing set. Some experimental results after illumination normalization are shown in Figure 2.

The facial texture is highlighted if the proposal is adopted for illumination normalization in Figure 2. In order to evaluate quantitatively the performance among the investigated approaches, some experimental results on Yale B and Extended Yale B are shown in Figures 3~4, respectively. Face recognition results change acutely in some illuminations for RET [17], GRF [18], and WEB [19] in Figures 3~4. In order to further demonstrate the different performance of the investigated methods, some statistical results of face recognition are given in Tables 1~2, respectively.

One can note that the proposed method has the best performance for face recognition and the best stability in the experiments, and it is more robust than that of others at Yale B and Extended Yale B illuminations.

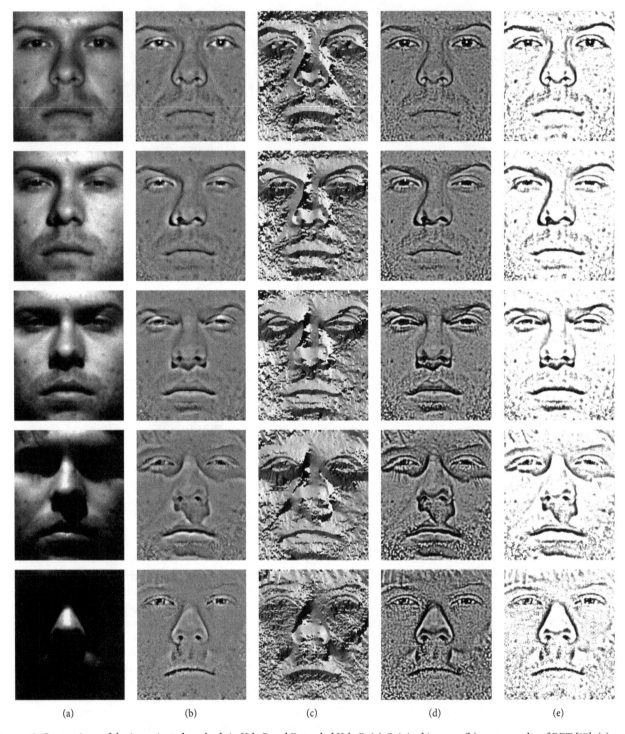

(a)   (b)   (c)   (d)   (e)

FIGURE 2: Comparison of the investigated methods in Yale B and Extended Yale B. (a) Original images, (b) some results of RET [17], (c) some results of GRF [18], (d) some results of WEB [19], and (e) some results of the proposal.

TABLE 2: The statistical results of recognition rates on Yale B+ Extended Yale B.

Recognition method	Average recognition rate (%)				Standard deviation of recognition rates ($\times 10^{-2}$)			
	RET [17]	GRF [18]	WEB [19]	Proposal	RET [17]	GRF [18]	WEB [19]	Proposal
PCA	88.89	66.86	64.67	**92.00**	4.93	14.34	12.73	**3.31**
LDA	93.08	81.38	89.79	**94.28**	2.56	12.36	3.43	**2.03**

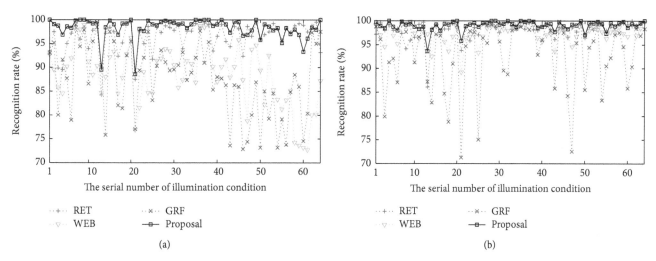

FIGURE 3: The experimental results on Yale B. (a) Some results of PCA and (b) some results of LDA.

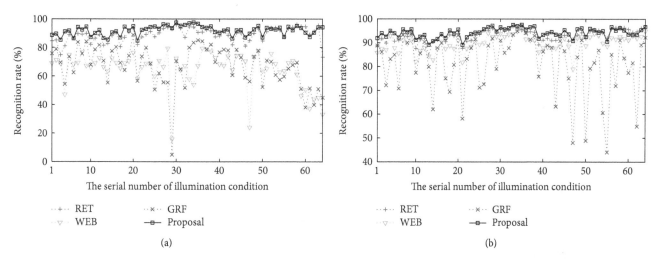

FIGURE 4: The experimental results on Yale B+ Extended Yale B. (a) Some results of PCA and (b) some results of LDA.

3.3. Comparisons on CMU-PIE. The CMU-PIE face database includes 68 subjects under 21 illuminations, in which the number of subjects is more than Yale B+ Extended Yale B. Some results for the same person under different illuminations are shown in Figure 5. The facial texture is highlighted also if the proposal is adopted for illumination normalization from Figure 5.

In order to evaluate quantitatively the performance among the investigated approaches, the face images from CMU-PIE face database are numbered from 1 to 21 according to different illuminations. One illumination of each subject is selected randomly as a training sample; the others are taken as the testing set. Some experimental results are shown in Figure 6.

Face recognition changes obviously in some illumination conditions for RET [17], GRF [18], and WEB [19] from Figure 6, while the face recognition is 100% if the proposal is used to normalize illumination.

Some statistical results of face recognition are given in Table 3 to further demonstrate the different performance of the investigated methods.

3.4. Comparisons on CAS-PEAL-R1. The illumination of CAS-PEAL-R1 face database is completely different from the ones mentioned above, in which the number of illumination conditions is not the same for each subject. Besides, it is more difficult for face recognition since the face image for the same person presents different poses and scale changes. Moreover, there exists illumination interference in this database; some examples for illumination interference are given in Figure 7.

If we take Figures 7(a) and 7(b) as a group of training samples set and Figures 7(c) and 7(d) are selected as a test set, there exist most matches in illumination condition between Figures 7(a) and 7(d). The same situation occurs to Figures 7(b) and 7(c). It indicates that the illumination interference leads to errors of face recognition easily.

In order to build a fair comparison among the investigated approaches, 233 subjects under 10 different illuminations are chosen, cropped, and resized to 168×192. One illumination of each subject is selected randomly as a training sample; and the others are taken as a testing set for face recognition. Some results for illumination normalization to

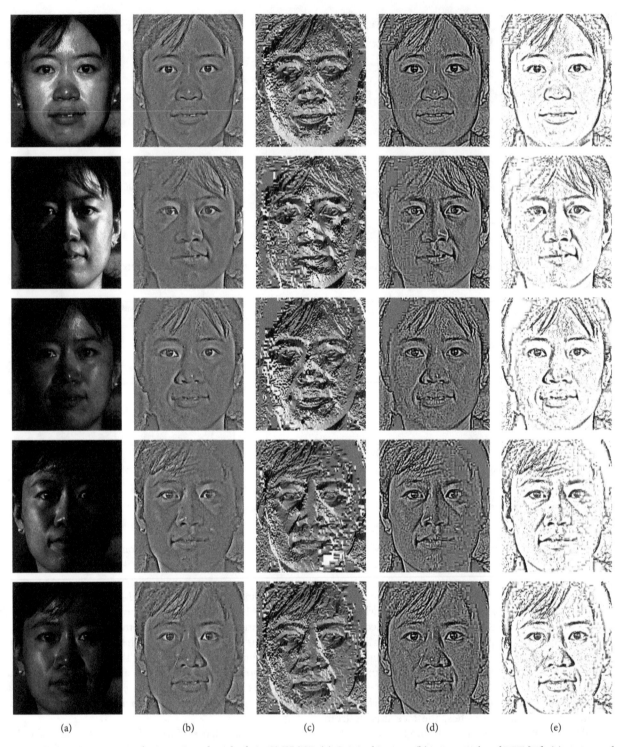

(a) (b) (c) (d) (e)

FIGURE 5: Comparisons among the investigated methods in CMU-PIE. (a) Original images, (b) some results of RET [17], (c) some results of GRF [18], (d) some results of WEB [19], and (e) some results of proposal.

TABLE 3: The statistical results of recognition rates on CMU-PIE.

Recognition method	Average recognition rate (%)				Standard deviation of recognition rates ($\times 10^{-2}$)			
	RET [17]	GRF [18]	WEB [19]	Proposal	RET [17]	GRF [18]	WEB [19]	Proposal
PCA	99.55	95.23	94.66	**100**	0.69	6.36	4.06	**0**
LDA	99.98	100	99.95	**100**	0.05	0	0.08	**0**

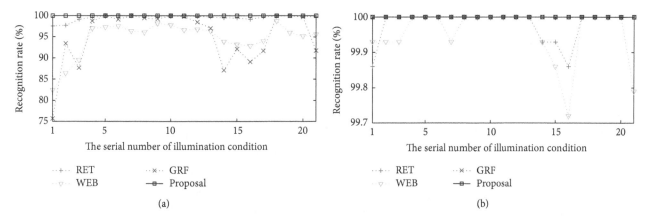

(a)

(b)

FIGURE 6: The experimental results on CMU-PIE. (a) Some results of PCA and (b) some results of LDA.

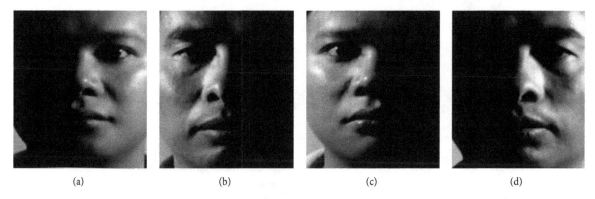

(a)   (b)   (c)   (d)

FIGURE 7: Some examples of illumination interference. (a) subject 11 under illumination condition no. 9, (b) subject 1 under illumination condition no. 9, (c) subject 11 under illumination condition no. 8, and (d) subject 1 under illumination condition no. 10.

the same person under different illuminations are shown in Figure 8.

One can find that the facial texture is highlighted if the proposal is adopted for illumination normalization in Figure 8.

Some quantitative results of face recognition among the investigated approaches are shown in Figure 9.

Face recognition changes acutely in some illumination conditions for RET [17], GRF [18], and WEB [19] in Figure 9, while the face recognition rate changes gently to the proposal.

Some statistical results of face recognition are given in Table 4 to further illuminate performance difference among the investigated methods.

Compared with other methods, the proposed method has superior performance for face recognition in the above experiments.

3.5. Running Time and Storage Space. From the above experiments compared with some state of the arts, the proposed method has superior performance for illumination normalization. In order to test its performance in real-time processing, we use all face images of Yale B and extended Yale B with size of 192×168 for testing. All the experiments are tested in Matlab7.10.0 at the PC with PIV 3.3 GHz CPU 3.41 GB RAM. In order to make a fair comparison, the dataset

is processed 10 times repeatedly. The average running times for different approaches are given in Table 5 which shows that the performance of the proposed method in real-time processing is better than that of RET [17] and WEB [19].

To test the size of required storage space, above face images are saved as TIF format based on LZW [26] compression algorithm. The size of required storage space for each subject including images formed under 64 different kinds of illumination conditions is shown in Table 6. The required storage space of the proposed method is the minimum.

From the above experiments, one can notice that performance of the proposed method in illumination normalization for face recognition is better than that of the state of the arts.

4. Conclusions

An illumination normalization method for face recognition is proposed. The proposed method can extract some distinct facial features for face recognition from face images under some challenging lighting conditions. The face texture features are highlighted and some adverse impacts of adjacent domains are suppressed which helps to improve face recognition. Experimental results show that the proposed method has much better performance than that of state of the arts by comparison.

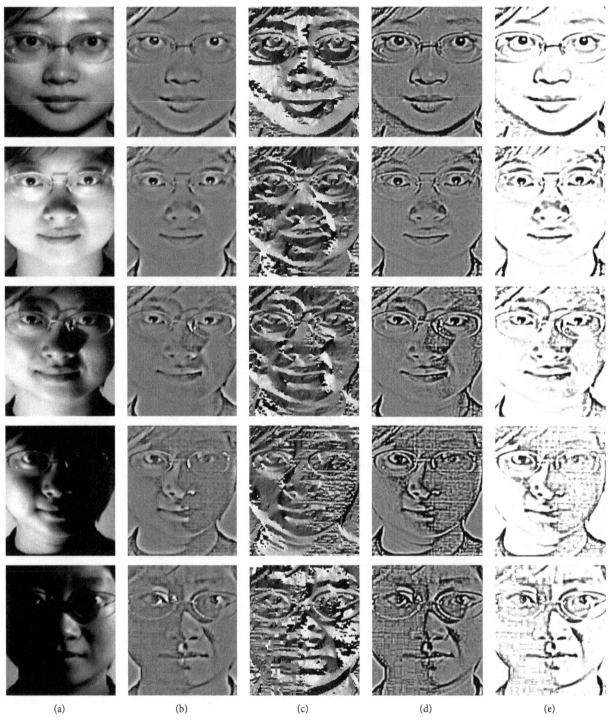

(a)   (b)   (c)   (d)   (e)

FIGURE 8: Comparisons of the investigated methods in CAS-PEAL-R1. (a) Original images, (b) some results of RET [17], (c) some results of GRF [18], (d) some results of WEB [19], and (e) some results of proposal.

TABLE 4: The statistical results of recognition rates on CAS-PEAL-R1.

Recognition method	Average recognition rate (%)				Standard deviation of recognition rates ($\times 10^{-2}$)			
	RET [17]	GRF [18]	WEB [19]	Proposal	RET [17]	GRF [18]	WEB [19]	Proposal
PCA	19.55	21.03	15.62	**23.21**	1.38	4.47	2.61	**2.23**
LDA	34.87	35.88	34.50	**41.36**	3.02	8.25	5.53	**2.96**

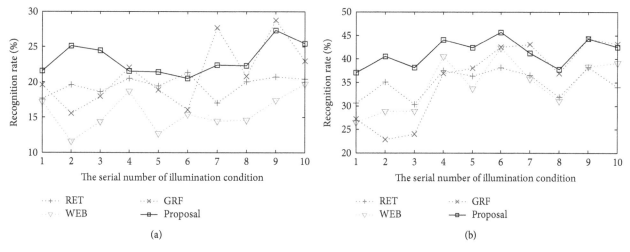

(a)

(b)

FIGURE 9: The experimental results on CAS-PEAL-R1. (a) Some results of PCA and (b) some results of LDA.

TABLE 5: The average running time per image in different methods.

	RET [17]	GRF [18]	WEB [19]	Proposal
Average running time (ms)	11	6	98	**9**

TABLE 6: The size of required storage space per subject in different methods.

	Original	RET [17]	GRF [18]	WEB [19]	Proposal
The size of required storage space (MB)	1.67	1.84	2.50	2.38	**1.30**

In the future, we will do more feature extraction to improve the performance of illumination normalization for face recognition.

Conflict of Interests

The authors declare that there is no conflict of interests regarding the publication of this paper.

Acknowledgments

This work is supported in part by the Natural Science Foundation of China (Grant nos. 11176016 and 60872117) and Specialized Research Fund for the Doctoral Program of Higher Education (Grant no. 20123108110014). The authors thank Vitomir Štruc for providing INface Matlab Toolbox for testing.

References

[1] J. Lu, Y. P. Tan, and G. Wang, "Discriminative multi-manifold analysis for face recognition from a single training sample per person," *IEEE Transactions on Pattern Analysis and Machine Intelligence*, vol. 35, no. 1, pp. 39–51, 2013.

[2] M. Matsumoto, "Cognition-based parameter setting of nonlinear filters using a face recognition system," *IET Image Processing*, vol. 6, no. 8, pp. 1057–1063, 2012.

[3] J. Ho, M.-H. Yang, J. Lim, K.-C. Lee, and D. Kriegman, "Clustering appearances of objects under varying illumination conditions," in *Proceedings of the IEEE Computer Society Conference on Computer Vision and Pattern Recognition*, pp. 11–18, Madison, Wis, USA, June 2003.

[4] R. Basri and D. W. Jacobs, "Lambertian reflectance and linear subspaces," *IEEE Transactions on Pattern Analysis and Machine Intelligence*, vol. 25, no. 2, pp. 218–233, 2003.

[5] G. An, J. Wu, and Q. Ruan, "An illumination normalization model for face recognition under varied lighting conditions," *Pattern Recognition Letters*, vol. 31, no. 9, pp. 1056–1067, 2010.

[6] S. Du and R. K. Ward, "Adaptive region-based image enhancement method for robust face recognition under variable illumination conditions," *IEEE Transactions on Circuits and Systems for Video Technology*, vol. 20, no. 9, pp. 1165–1175, 2010.

[7] P.-C. Hsieh and P.-C. Tung, "Illumination-robust face recognition using an efficient mirror technique," in *Proceedings of the 2nd International Congress on Image and Signal Processing (CISP '09)*, pp. 1–5, Taiwan, China, October 2009.

[8] V. Štruc and N. Pavešic, "Photometric normalization techniques for illumination invariance," in *Advances in Face Image Analysis: Techniques and Technologies*, Y. J. Zhang, Ed., pp. 279–300, IGI Global, 2011.

[9] V. Truc and N. Paveić, "Gabor-based kernel partial-least-squares discrimination features for face recognition," *Informatica*, vol. 20, no. 1, pp. 115–138, 2009.

[10] D. J. Jobson, Z.-U. Rahman, and G. A. Woodell, "A multiscale retinex for bridging the gap between color images and the human observation of scenes," *IEEE Transactions on Image Processing*, vol. 6, no. 7, pp. 965–976, 1997.

[11] S. Du and R. Ward, "Wavelet-based illumination normalization for face recognition," in *Proceedings of the IEEE International Conference on Image Processing (ICIP '05)*, vol. 2, pp. 954–957, Genova, Italy, September 2005.

[12] W. Chen, M. J. Er, and S. Wu, "Illumination compensation and normalization for robust face recognition using discrete cosine transform in logarithm domain," *IEEE Transactions on Systems, Man, and Cybernetics B*, vol. 36, no. 2, pp. 458–466, 2006.

[13] V. Štruc and N. Pavešic, *Illumination Invariant Face Recognition by Non-Local Smoothing*, Springer, Heidelberg, Germany, 2009.

[14] S. Nilufar, N. Ray, and H. Zhang, "Object detection with DoG scale-space: a multiple kernel learning approach," *IEEE Transactions on Image Processing*, vol. 21, no. 8, pp. 3744–3756, 2012.

[15] W. T. Freeman and E. H. Adelson, "The design and use of steerable filters," *IEEE Transactions on Pattern Analysis and Machine Intelligence*, vol. 13, no. 9, pp. 891–906, 1991.

[16] T. Zhang, B. Fang, Y. Yuan et al., "Multiscale facial structure representation for face recognition under varying illumination," *Pattern Recognition*, vol. 42, no. 2, pp. 251–258, 2009.

[17] N.-S. Vu and A. Caplier, "Illumination-robust face recognition using retina modeling," in *Proceedings of the IEEE International Conference on Image Processing (ICIP '09)*, pp. 3289–3292, Cairo, Egypt, November 2009.

[18] T. Zhang, Y. Y. Tang, B. Fang, Z. Shang, and X. Liu, "Face recognition under varying illumination using gradientfaces," *IEEE Transactions on Image Processing*, vol. 18, no. 11, pp. 2599–2606, 2009.

[19] B. Wang, W. Li, W. Yang, and Q. Liao, "Illumination normalization based on weber's law with application to face recognition," *IEEE Signal Processing Letters*, vol. 18, no. 8, pp. 462–465, 2011.

[20] A. S. Georghiades, P. N. Belhumeur, and D. J. Kriegman, "From few to many: illumination cone models for face recognition under variable lighting and pose," *IEEE Transactions on Pattern Analysis and Machine Intelligence*, vol. 23, no. 6, pp. 643–660, 2001.

[21] K.-C. Lee, J. Ho, and D. J. Kriegman, "Acquiring linear subspaces for face recognition under variable lighting," *IEEE Transactions on Pattern Analysis and Machine Intelligence*, vol. 27, no. 5, pp. 684–698, 2005.

[22] T. Sim, S. Baker, and M. Bsat, "The CMU pose, illumination, and expression database," *IEEE Transactions on Pattern Analysis and Machine Intelligence*, vol. 25, no. 12, pp. 1615–1618, 2003.

[23] W. Gao, B. Cao, S. Shan et al., "The CAS-PEAL large-scale chinese face database and baseline evaluations," *IEEE Transactions on Systems, Man, and Cybernetics A*, vol. 38, no. 1, pp. 149–161, 2008.

[24] M. A. Turk and A. P. Pentland, "Face recognition using eigenfaces," in *Proceedings of the IEEE Computer Society Conference on Computer Vision and Pattern Recognition*, pp. 586–591, June 1991.

[25] P. N. Belhumeur, J. P. Hespanha, and D. J. Kriegman, "Eigenfaces vs. fisherfaces: recognition using class specific linear projection," *IEEE Transactions on Pattern Analysis and Machine Intelligence*, vol. 19, no. 7, pp. 711–720, 1997.

[26] T. A. Welch, "A technique for high-performance data compression," *Computer*, vol. 17, no. 6, pp. 8–19, 1984.

11

Visible and Infrared Face Identification via Sparse Representation

Pierre Buyssens[1] and Marinette Revenu[2]

[1] *LITIS EA 4108-QuantIF Team, University of Rouen, 22 Boulevard Gambetta, 76183 Rouen Cedex, France*
[2] *GREYC UMR CNRS 6072 ENSICAEN-Image Team, University of Caen Basse-Normandie, 6 Boulevard Maréchal Juin, 14050 Caen, France*

Correspondence should be addressed to Pierre Buyssens; pierre.buyssens@gmail.com

Academic Editors: O. Ghita, D. Hernandez, Z. Hou, M. La Cascia, and J. M. Tavares

We present a facial recognition technique based on facial sparse representation. A dictionary is learned from data, and patches extracted from a face are decomposed in a sparse manner onto this dictionary. We particularly focus on the design of dictionaries that play a crucial role in the final identification rates. Applied to various databases and modalities, we show that this approach gives interesting performances. We propose also a score fusion framework that allows quantifying the saliency classifiers outputs and merging them according to these saliencies.

1. Introduction

Face recognition is a topic which has been of increasing interest during the last two decades due to a vast number of possible applications: biometrics, video surveillance, advanced HMI, or image/video indexation. Although considerable progress has been made in this domain, especially with the development of powerful methods (such as the Eigenfaces or the Elastic Bunch Graph Matching methods), automatic face recognition is not enough accurate in uncontrolled environments for a large use. Many factors can degrade the performances of facial biometric system: illumination variation creates artificial shadows, changing locally the appearance of the face; head poses modify the distance between localized features; facial expression introduces global changes; artefacts wearing, such as glasses or scarf, may hide parts of the face.

For the particular case of illumination, a lot of work has been done on the preprocessing step of the images to reduce the effect of the illumination on the face. Another approach is to use other imagery such as infrared, which has been showed to be a promising alternative. An infrared capture of a face is nearly invariant to illumination changes and allows a system to process in all the illumination conditions, including total darkness like night.

While visual cameras measure the electromagnetic energy in the visible spectrum (0.4–0.7 μm), sensors in the IR respond to thermal radiation in the infrared spectrum (0.7–14.0 μm). The infrared spectrum can mainly be divided into reflected IR (Figure 1(b)) and emissive IR (Figure 1(c)). Reflected IR contains near infrared (NIR) (0.7–0.9 μm) and short-wave infrared (SWIR) (0.9–2.4 μm). The thermal IR band is associated with thermal radiation emitted by the objects. It contains the midwave infrared (MWIR) (3.0–5.0 μm) and long-wave infrared (LWIR) (8.0–14.0 μm). Although the reflected IR is by far the most studied, we use thermal long-wave IR in this study.

Despite the advantages of infrared modality, infrared imagery has other limitations. Since a face captured under this modality renders its thermal patterns, a temperature screen placed in front of the face will totally occlude it. This phenomenon appears when a subject simply wears glasses. In this case, the captured face has two black holes, corresponding to the glasses, which is far more inconvenient than in the visible

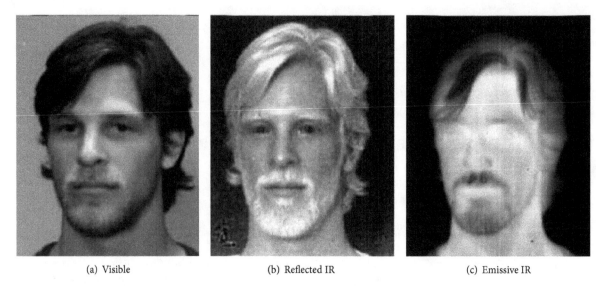

(a) Visible   (b) Reflected IR   (c) Emissive IR

FIGURE 1: A face captured under (a) visible spectrum, (b) reflected IR spectrum, and (c) emissive IR spectrum respectively.

modality. Moreover, thermal patterns can change due to external conditions such as weather. However, since these two modalities do not present the same advantages/limitations, using information of both can decrease the disadvantages of each and globally enhance the identification rates [1].

Two main schemes are considered in a biometric system [2].

(i) The verification (of authentication) aims to compare the unknown face with the one of a claimed identity. It is a one-to-one comparison scenario, which often involves a threshold step to accept/reject the probe.

(ii) The identification aims to find an unknown identity (probe) among a set of known identities (gallery).

Most of the approaches that have been proposed in the literature for the face recognition problem are built with the same three-step scheme:

(i) preprocessing of the images,

(ii) extraction of features from faces,

(iii) classification of these features.

Preprocessing Step. The first step intends to locate a face, resize it if necessary, and apply some algorithms to enhance the quality of the images. Illumination can also be corrected to simplify the features extraction.

Features Extraction Step. This second step consists in extracting salient features from faces. This strategy can globally be divided into two main approaches:

(i) the local approaches, which act locally on the face by extracting salient interest points (like eyes or mouths), and combine them into a global model;

(ii) the global approaches which often rely on a projection of the whole image onto a new low-dimensional space (these methods are then named Subspace methods).

Numerous local approaches based on geometrical features have been proposed in the literature [3–7].

The most popular local approach, named Elastic Bunch Graph Matching (EBGM) [8], consists in modeling the salient features (like nose, mouth, etc.) by a graph. To each node is associated a so-called jet which encodes the local appearance around the feature obtained via a Gabor filter. The classification of a probe graph involves then a specific algorithm that takes into account a geometric similarity measure and the appearance encoded by the jets.

The main advantages of these local approaches are their ability to deal with pose, illumination, or facial expression variations. Nevertheless, these approaches require a good localization of the discriminant features, which can be a difficult task in case of degradations of the image.

The global approaches often take the face image as a whole and perform a statistical projection of the images onto a face space. The most popular technique called Eigenfaces (first used by Turk and Pentland [9]) is based on a principal components analysis (PCA) of the faces. It has also been applied to infrared faces by Chen et al. [10]. Another popular technique is the *Fisherfaces* method based on a Linear Discriminant Analysis (LDA), which divides the face images into classes according to the Fisher criterion. It has been early applied by Kriegman et al. [11].

Note that the nonlinear versions Kernel-PCA and Kernel-LDA have been, respectively, applied in [12, 13].

The main drawback of the global approaches is their sensitivity to the illumination changes for the visible light modality and the thermal distribution of the face over time for the infrared modality. When the illumination (or the thermal distribution) of a face changes, its appearance undergoes a nonlinear transformation, and due to the linear projection often performed by these global approaches, the classification can fail. In the case of nonlinear projections, the choice of the kernel is critical and is a nontrivial problem. Moreover, as pointed out in [14], nonlinear dimensionality reduction methods can perform poorly on natural datasets.

Classification Step. The last step consists in classifying the extracted features. There are plenty of methods, simple ones based on distances between features via classification algorithms such as the Nearest Neighbor [15], others based on learning methods such as support vector machine [16] or neural networks [17]. However, these last methods have a significant drawback: they learn to recognize a fix number of identities, that is, classes. As the number of classes may vary by adding new identities to the system, for example, the design of the learning machine has to be updated and the learning recomputed. More recently, a seminal paper [18] has introduced a novel classification method relying on parsimony. The algorithm, named SRC for Sparse Representation-based Classification, decomposes in a sparse manner a probe feature vector $y \in \mathbb{R}^m$ onto a dictionary $A \in \mathbb{R}^{m \times n}$ composed of the n feature vectors of the gallery. As it mainly relies on a sparse decomposition problem, this algorithm requires $m < n$ in order to have an underdetermined system and a unique sparsest solution. More recent algorithms that use sparse decompositions have been proposed in the literature, such as robust sparse [19], group sparse [20], or structure sparse [21]. To ensure $m < n$, these algorithms first proceed to a dimension reduction via PCA (Eigenfaces) or other dimensionality reduction techniques. In our work, the extracted features of a face image are sparse and have a higher dimension than the images. Since the number of vectors of the gallery is less than the dimension of the vectors, such sparse-based classification algorithms cannot be used. Moreover, these classification algorithms make the assumption that a probe face lies onto a subspace specific to each individual. This assumption involves many faces of the same individual in the gallery, which is not the case of the databases used in our experiments. Finally, these algorithms are unusable in case of a one-to-one face comparison since the number of columns of A is 1. For all these reasons, this paper focuses on the feature extraction and makes use of the simple *Nearest Neighbor* algorithm as classifier.

This paper only considers the identification scheme. Assuming that the searched identity is always in the gallery, we focus on the rank-1 identification rates.

Contributions. This paper is a direct extension of our previous work [22]. A parameter exploration on the main parameters that pilot the dictionary design is presented. These learned dictionaries play a crucial role in the efficiency of the extracted features and then in the final identification rates. We propose also a framework for the fusion of different matchers at the score level. Based on a saliency function, it weights the outputs of a classifier without any assumptions.

The rest of the paper is organized as follows: Section 2 is dedicated to the proposed sparse features extraction method. Section 3 is devoted to the proposed score-based fusion method. Experimental results on various face datasets are presented in Section 4. Finally we present our conclusions and further work in Section 5.

2. Features Extraction

In this section, we present the proposed methodology for the features extraction and the fusion steps. After a brief recall of notations and definitions of the sparse decomposition theory, we detail the proposed scheme for the face features extraction and the fusion framework.

2.1. Notations and Definitions. An *atom* is an elementary basis element of a signal or an image. A collection of atoms (Φ_i) is called a dictionary Φ.

In this paper, the considered dictionaries are $N \times M$ matrices where the M columns represent the atoms (of size N) of the dictionary. When $r = M/N > 1$, the dictionary is overcomplete (with redundancy term r). In such a case, given a signal $\mathbf{x} \in \mathbb{R}^N$, the equation $\mathbf{x} = \Phi\lambda$ leads to an underdetermined system with an infinite set of solutions for λ.

2.1.1. Sparse Decomposition. Given a signal $x \in \mathbb{R}^N$ (or an image of size $\sqrt{N} \times \sqrt{N}$), we are looking for its decomposition according to a dictionary Φ composed of M vectors ϕ_m recovering $\mathbb{R}^N$. Let us define first the $\mathcal{L}_p$ norm of a vector $\mathbf{x}$

$$\|\mathbf{x}\|_p = \left(\sum_i |x_i|^p \right)^{1/p} \tag{1}$$

with the particular case of the "$\mathcal{L}_0$ norm" (defined as the number of nonzero elements of $\mathbf{x}$):

$$\|\mathbf{x}\|_0 = \sum_{0 \le i < N} a_i, \quad \text{where } a_i = \begin{cases} 1, & \text{if } x_i \ne 0, \\ 0, & \text{otherwise.} \end{cases} \tag{2}$$

When the dictionary is over-complete ($M > N$), there are an infinite set of coefficients α_i that may be used to decompose the signal onto the dictionary:

$$\mathbf{x} = \sum_{m=1}^{M} \alpha_m \phi_m. \tag{3}$$

In the sparse decomposition framework, the optimal solution is the one with the minimum of non-zeros elements (or the maximum of zeros elements). In this case, the problem is written:

$$\min_{\lambda} \|\lambda\|_0 \quad \text{such that } \mathbf{x} = \sum_{m=1}^{M} \lambda_m \phi_m. \tag{4}$$

Unfortunately, this problem is NP-hard.

Two approaches can be used to tackle this problem.

(i) The first one consists in a modification of the penalty term ($\|\mathbf{x}\|_0$) such that the problem becomes convex. Also known as Basis Pursuit (BP) [23] when turning the "$\mathcal{L}_0$" into an $\mathcal{L}_1$ norm, this approach gives equal results to the original problem under certain conditions (see [24] for more details). The problem becomes then

$$\min_{\lambda} \left(\left\| \mathbf{x} - \sum_{m=1}^{M} \lambda_m \phi_m \right\|_2^2 + \mu \|\lambda\|_1 \right). \tag{5}$$

Numerous algorithms have been developed for this problem resolution (also known under the name Lasso for Least Absolute Shrinkage and Selection Operator) based on the interior point method [25] or on iterative thresholding [26].

(ii) The second method usually used in the community is based on greedy algorithms that build iteratively a sparse representation of a signal [27]. The class of Matching Pursuit (MP) algorithms selects at each iteration the atom that minimizes the residual between the signal and the reconstruction obtained at the last iteration. More details on the well-known variant Orthogonal Matching Pursuit can be found in [28].

2.1.2. Dictionary Learning. An overcomplete dictionary Φ that leads to sparse representations can be chosen as a predefined set of functions adapted to the signal. For certain class of signals, this choice is appealing because it leads to simple and fast algorithms for the evaluation of the sparse decomposition. This is the case for overcomplete wavelets, curvelets, ridgelets, bandelets, Fourier transforms and more. Due to the morphological diversity contained in a natural image, it is often preferable to concatenate such basis to obtain the dictionary. Another way of constructing the dictionary is to learn it directly from data.

Many methods have been developed to perform this task such as those based on maximum likelihood [29–31], the one named Modeling of Optimal Directions (MOD) [32, 33], or those based on the a posteriori maximum [34, 35].

In this paper, we use the K-SVD algorithm proposed in [36] based on a singular value decomposition, which can be viewed as a generalization of the K-means, hence its name. Starting from a random initialization of the atoms, learning the dictionary proceeds in an iterative way, alternating the two steps:

(i) minimize (5) with respect to $\mathbf{x}$ keeping the dictionary elements ϕ_m constant;

(ii) update the atoms ϕ_m of the dictionary with $\mathbf{x}$ found at previous step.

2.2. Features Extraction Methodology. In this paper, we use sparse decompositions as features for the face identification. An appealing way would be to directly decompose faces onto a dictionary learned with a set of faces. This scheme is however impractical in practice for the following reasons.

(i) As a good sparse decomposition involves an overcomplete dictionary, one has to dispose of a dictionary whose size is at least equal to the signal dimension. As the signal (an image) is high-dimensional, the dictionary would be huge, and the decomposition would be very slow.

(ii) Because of the morphological diversity contained in the images of faces, a sparse decomposition would be more efficient when processed on a learned dictionary, which involves a number of training samples at least equal to the size of the dictionary.

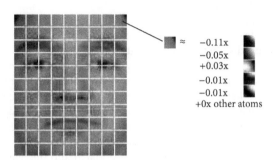

FIGURE 2: Schematic view of the feature extraction process.

For example, with images sizes of 40×50 (which is small for the face recognition task), the minimum number of atoms as well as the minimum number of training samples would be 2000. Moreover, within the K-SVD algorithm, one has to apply a singular value decomposition on matrices whose height is equal to the atoms dimension, which can be impractical in case of high-dimensional data. For these reasons, the sparse decomposition is processed on parts of the images.

Once the preprocessing is applied, the sparse features extraction of a face image acts in 3 steps:

(i) the image is splitted into n nonoverlapping square patches of size $\Gamma \times \Gamma$;

(ii) each patch is independently decomposed into a sparse vector $\mathbf{x}_k$ ($k \in \{1 \cdots K\}$) onto a dictionary Φ by minimizing (5);

(iii) the sparse vectors $\mathbf{x}_k$ are concatenated to form the final sparse feature vector $\mathbf{x}$ of the face.

A schematic view of the feature extraction process is shown in Figure 2.

In a first time, the dictionary used for the decomposition of the patches is learned from data with the algorithms OMP for the sparse code computation and K-SVD to update of the atoms.

In a second time, the features are computed with the algorithm FISTA proposed in [37] based on a two-step iterative soft-thresholding, which is a fast algorithm that solves (5).

Size of the Features. The size of the features depends on several parameters:

(i) the size Γ of the patches,

(ii) the redundancy r of the dictionary,

(iii) the size $w \times h$ of the image.

Since each extracted patch is decomposed onto the dictionary (composed of m atoms), and the feature vector is the concatenation of the p extracted patches, the size of a feature vector is computed as

$$\text{size} = p \times m, \tag{6}$$

where $m = r \times \Gamma^2$ and $p = \lceil (w/\Gamma) \times (h/\Gamma) \rceil$. If w (or h) is not divisible by Γ, the image is padded with zero. This padding

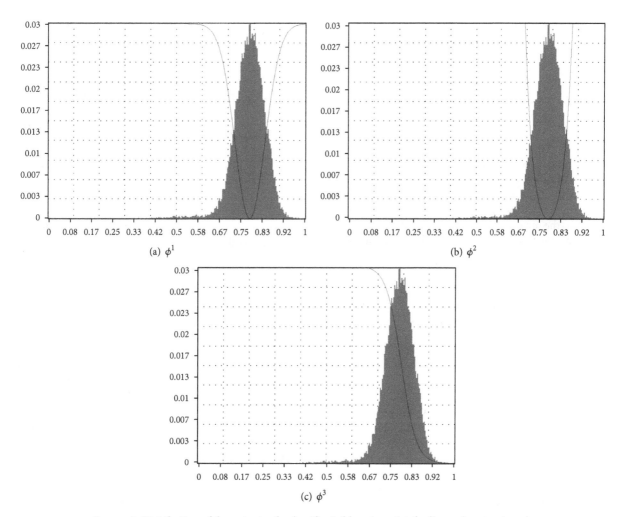

FIGURE 3: Distribution of the outputs of a classifier in blue. Associated saliency function in red.

has no effect on the recognition behavior since all the images are padded in the same way.

The dimension of the resulting feature vectors may be quite high (higher than the image dimension) but are very sparse, that is, containing few nonzero entries.

3. Score Fusion

Given classifiers that yield score rankings as results, we consider a fusion framework that weights the outputs of these classifiers without any assumptions.

Assuming that classifiers do not have the same accuracy, we propose a merging methodology that uses measures of saliency computed dynamically for each classifier. This fusion scheme can be divided into three steps:

(i) the scores produced by different classifiers may be heterogeneous, so a normalization step is required. Several normalization methods exist such as linear, logarithmic, or exponential normalizations;

(ii) a function of saliency is computed onto a score distribution according to some statistical measure, and a unique saliency value is attributed to each score;

(iii) final scores are computed as a weighted sum of the scores according to the saliencies.

Given a probe sample I, the distances to the labeled samples of the gallery $\mathbf{G}$ are computed giving a distribution of distances $\mathbf{D}$:

$$\mathbf{D} = \{d_k\},$$
$$d_k = \|I - \mathbf{G}_k\|,$$

(7)

where $\mathbf{G}_k$ is a feature vector of a gallery sample. After a normalization of $\mathbf{D}$, its mean μ and standard deviation σ are computed.

A saliency s_k is then given to each d_k according to a function depending on μ and σ:

$$s_k = \phi_{\mu,\sigma}(d_k).$$

(8)

In this work, we propose three saliency functions ϕ^1, ϕ^2, and ϕ^3 (Figure 3) that are of the form

$$\phi_{\mu,\sigma}^1 (d_k) = \frac{1}{\sigma\sqrt{2\pi}} \left(1 - e^{-(1/2)((d_k - \mu)/\sigma)^2}\right),$$

$$\phi_{\mu,\sigma}^2 (d_k) = \sigma\sqrt{2\pi} \frac{1}{e^{-(1/2)((d_k - \mu)/\sigma)^2}}, \qquad (9)$$

$$\phi_{\mu,\sigma}^3 (d_k) = \left(1 + \frac{1}{2}\tanh\left(\frac{1}{\sigma}(d_k - \mu)\right)\right)^{-1}.$$

This fusion scheme works with any 2-class classifiers that give a distance (or a similarity) measure as output. The saliency functions allow weighting the output of a classifier according to its response on a set of inputs (the gallery), without any ad hoc assumptions.

Note that the proposed functions deal with distances measures, but other functions can easily be used with similarity measures.

Saliency functions ϕ^1 and ϕ^2 tend to highly weight an uncommon measure, even if it is high (i.e., a probe sample far from any gallery samples). ϕ^3 specializes this idea by more penalizing higher distances than common distances and then favors small distances.

For a given classifier, this procedure then gives a distribution of distances which are weighted by their respective saliencies.

Given several classifiers C_i, the final fusion distances are computed as a weighted sum of the outputs:

$$d_k = \frac{\sum_i d_{k_i} \times s_{k_i}}{\sum_i s_{k_i}} \quad \forall k. \qquad (10)$$

As for the single-classifier experiments, the classification is performed via the *Nearest Neighbor* classifier.

4. Experiments and Results

In this section, we detail the experiments of both feature extraction performance and score fusion on different public databases. In all the experiments, the images are cropped to ensure that the eyes are roughly at the same position and scaled to the size 110×90.

4.1. Extended Yale B Database.
The extended Yale B database is composed of 2414 frontal-face images of 38 individuals [38]. Faces were captured under various laboratory-controlled lighting conditions. This experiment is mainly dedicated to show the effectiveness of the approach in term of recognition rates. The main parameters that pilot the dictionary learning are fixed to:

$$r = 2,$$

$$\Gamma = 10, \qquad (11)$$

$$n_{\text{OMP}} = 5.$$

With these parameters, the size of a face feature vector is $11 \times 9 \times 2 \times 10^2 = 19800$.

The dictionary is learned with a small number of images of the database. Figure 4 shows the atoms of the learned

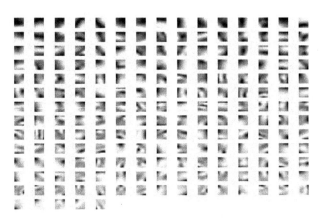

FIGURE 4: Learned atoms for $\Gamma = 10$ (patches size: 10×10) and $n_{\text{OMP}} = 5$ sorted by variance.

dictionary. One can see that some atoms encode low-frequency patterns, while others are more oriented edge selective. The database is then divided into disjoint training and testing parts (as in [18]), and face images are decomposed onto the dictionary following the methodology explained in Section 2.2. For the experiments, we randomly select 8, 16, and 32 images per individuals for training. Randomly dividing the database ensures that the results do not depend on a favorable choice of the training set. The mean rank-1 identification rates over 10 different executions are shown in Table 1. Identification rates are competitive with those given in [18], although our method performs the classification with a simple *Nearest Neighbor* classifier.

4.2. FERET Database.
The FERET database [39] is a well-known database composed of thousands of individuals. We focus on two subsets named *fa* and *fb*:

(i) *fa* contains 994 images of 994 individuals (one image per individual) and is used as gallery;

(ii) *fb* contains 992 images of 992 individuals (one image per individual) and is used as probe.

This experiment is mainly dedicated to evaluate the proposed score fusion methodology.

To this end, we extract simple random features from faces. Linear random projections are generated by Gaussian random matrices, hence the name of this technique Random-Faces [40]. A random projection matrix is extremely efficient to generate. Its entries are independently sampled from a zero-mean normal distribution, and each row is normalized to unit length.

In this experiment, we generate three different random projection matrices to map the faces to three random subspaces of dimension 50, 100, and 150.

Various normalization techniques and fusion methods have been implemented for comparison purposes. Normalization techniques used are the MinMax (MM), the Decimal Scaling (DeSc), the Z-Score (ZS), the Median Absolute Deviation (MAD), and the Hyperbolic Tangent (Tanh) techniques (see [41] for more details on these normalization techniques). Fusion methods used are classical ones of the literature [42]:

TABLE 1: Main results. (a) Identification rates on the extended Yale B database. (b) Identification rates for each random space on the FERET database and a comparison between different normalization and fusion techniques (best score per column in bold). (c) Identification rates on the Notre-Dame database obtained by score fusion of visible and infrared modalities (best score per column in bold).

(a)

Extended Yale B database			
Number of images	8	16	32
Identification rate %	88.39	95.74	98.04

(b)

FERET database					
Random subspace dimension			50	100	150
Identification rate %			67.43	73.28	74.69
	MM	DeSc	ZS	MAD	Tanh
PROD	68.95	77.92	77.92	77.92	78.12
SUM	78.02	73.18	78.12	78.12	78.12
MAX	77.21	67.64	0.10	0.10	75.30
MIN	68.95	**73.48**	74.19	74.29	74.19
ϕ^1	78.32	64.51	78.22	78.22	78.22
ϕ^2	76.00	13.91	74.79	74.39	74.79
ϕ^3	**78.42**	73.08	**78.42**	**78.42**	**78.42**

(c)

Notre-Dame database					
	MM	DeSc	ZS	MAD	Tanh
PROD	83.12	83.12	83.12	83.12	83.12
SUM	92.32	78.52	93.17	93.18	87.41
MAX	89.86	75.40	84.99	83.99	87.41
MIN	83.12	**87.41**	92.82	91.99	75.47
ϕ^1	85.86	11.19	91.80	91.15	57.77
ϕ^2	92.83	73.50	93.02	92.11	87.41
ϕ^3	**93.47**	51.71	**94.06**	**93.88**	**87.99**

the Product rule (PROD), the Sum rule (SUM), the Max rule (MAX), and the Min rule (MIN). Note that other score fusion methods exist such as the one based on a Gaussian Mixture Model [43], but they often rely on the need of several biometric samples from the same individual, which is not the case of our experiments.

Table 1 summarizes the identification rates of Random-Faces together with the different score fusion techniques. Despite the relative high number of individuals (about 1000), the difficult one-image-to-enroll scenario, and the simple extracted features, the identification rates are quite high (over 78%), and the proposed fusion scheme almost always outperforms the classical score fusion methods.

4.3. Notre-Dame Database. The database from the University of Notre-Dame (Collection $X1$) [42] is a public collection of 2D visible/thermal face images. This database has two advantages:

(i) a visible picture and its thermal counterpart are taken at the same time;

(ii) a well-defined test protocol is included with the database, which allows a fair comparison between previously published results on this database.

4.3.1. Details of the Database. The database is divided into two disjoints parts: the first one, named Train Set, is composed of 159 subjects. For each, one visible and one thermal images are available. The second part, named Test Set, is composed of 82 subjects. This set contains 2292 visible images and 2292 thermal images.

While the *Train Set* contains neither facial expressions nor illumination/thermal variations, the *Test Set* contains such variations.

Two experiments, named same session and time lapse, have been designed to test the facial identification algorithms across illumination variations and through time, respectively. In this work, we do not report identification rates on the same session experiment since it contains too few images and is too easy: most of the classical face recognition algorithms obtain identification rates close to 100%. We then report only the identification rates on the time lapse experiment which is a more challenging subdataset. The pictures have been taken within weeks/months which involves variations in faces appearance.

For this experiment, the test protocol consists in 16 subexperiments allowing picking galleries and probes of different facial expressions (neutral or smiling) and different lighting (FERET or Mugshot styles).

Note that each gallery contains only one image per subject (one-image-to-enroll scenario).

4.3.2. Details of the Experiment. Our experiment is mainly dedicated to a parameter exploration of the main parameters that pilot the dictionary design and to evaluate these parameters on the final identification rates.

The experiments have been conducted with different values of the considered hyperparameters: the size $\Gamma \times \Gamma$ of the square patches and the maximum number of atoms n_{OMP} allowed for the sparse decomposition within the algorithm OMP. These hyperparameters directly influence the learned dictionary, and then the extracted feature vectors. A grid search is performed onto these two parameters: Γ varies into $\{5, 10, 15, 20\}$ and n_{OMP} in $\{3, 4, 5, 6, 7, 8, 9, 10, 15, 20\}$. Note that each experiment is performed separately for the visible and infrared modality.

In order to learn the dictionary, for each couple $(\Gamma, n_{\mathrm{OMP}})$, 10000 patches of size $(\Gamma \times \Gamma)$ with sufficient standard deviation (to avoid too uniform patches) are randomly extracted from the Train Set. The maximum number of atoms allowed for the OMP algorithm is then fixed to n_{OMP}, which means that each training pattern is decomposed into a sum of n_{OMP} atoms, the coefficients of the other atoms being 0.

For all the experiments, the redundancy of the dictionary is set to 2 which means $2 \times \Gamma^2$ atoms to learn. The learning process is applied until convergence.

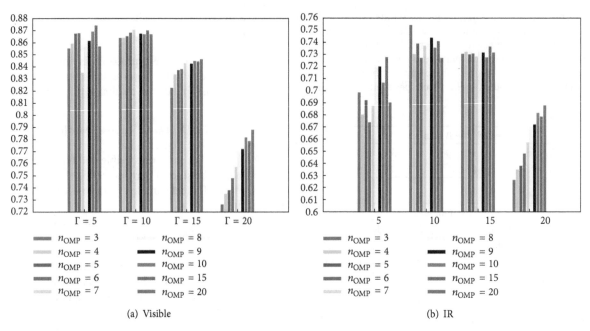

FIGURE 5: Rank-1 mean identification rates for different values of Γ and n_{OMP}. (a) Visible, (b) IR.

For each couple (Γ, n_{OMP}), a dictionary is learned, then the face features are extracted following the proposed scheme (Section 2).

4.3.3. Results. Figures 5(a) and 5(b) show the identification results at rank-1 for different values of Γ and n_{OMP} for the two modalities. For the sake of clarity, identification rates have been averaged: each bin represents the mean identification rate of the 16 subexperiments of the time lapse experiment.

Although the best identification rate for the visible modality (87.41%) is obtained with $\Gamma = 5$ and $n_{OMP} = 15$, one can see that identification rates for $\Gamma = 10$ are the most stable according to n_{OMP}, each bin exceeding 86%. Identification rates with $\Gamma = 15$ are worse, and those obtained with $\Gamma = 20$ are the worst.

Similar results can be observed with the infrared modality. Although identification rates seem more stable with $\Gamma = 15$, results with $\Gamma = 10$ are globally the better (73.60% avg.).

4.3.4. Modality Fusion. Identification rates obtained above show that visible modality performs better than LWIR modality. This result has already been showed in [42] or [44].

Best couples (Γ, n_{OMP}) for each modality found above are retained, and the fusion scheme presented in Section 3 is performed. As for the FERET database experiment, our score fusion scheme is compared with various normalization and fusion techniques. A summary the results and a comparison of identification rates previously published in the literature are shown in Table 2. Our method outperforms other methods in visible modality but gives lower identification rates in infrared. The lack of texture in this modality could explain that our sparse features approach gives such identification rates. Note that we previously published in [22] better identification rates with these sparse features conjointly

TABLE 2: Comparison of methods for the time-lapse experiment of the Notre-Dame database. Mean identification rates over the 16 subexperiments, standard deviation in parenthesis. Best score in bold.

| | Time lapse | | |
	[42]	[44]	This paper
Visible	82.66	72.50	**87.41**
	(7.75)	(4.01)	(4.32)
IR	**77.81**	40.06	75.40
	(3.31)	(3.47)	(2.60)
Fusion	92.5	80.12	**94.06**
	(2.71)	(4.13)	(2.08)

classified with the Sparse Representation-based Classification algorithm (SRC, [18]). Nevertheless, these results are not completely exact since the dimension of the features exceeds the number of elements of the gallery, which implies an overdetermined system within the SRC algorithm.

5. Conclusion and Future Work

We presented a facial feature extraction method based on sparse decompositions of patches of face images. It decomposes a face image onto a dictionary that has been learned from data. Applied to various databases and modalities, it offers comparable identification results to the state-of-the-art on the Notre-Dame database according to its specific protocol.

Modalities fusion offers an alternative to unimodal biometric systems. From the hypothesis that different modalities can offer complementary informations (which is often the case), fusion of these allows enhancing the reliability of a system.

We proposed a decision level fusion scheme based on a per-score measure of saliency. It does not depend on ad hoc assumptions and allows increasing rank-1 identification rates. Moreover, it is sufficiently general to be used with any number of features, biometrics, or classifiers.

Further work will involve the integration of our feature extraction scheme into a multiscale approach. A better selection could also enhance final decision scores. In this work, every patch is equally treated, even those containing hair, for example. This is obviously suboptimal and a selection or a weighting of discriminant patches will improve identification rates.

A limitation of our approach is also that faces have to be carefully aligned. The extracted features may not be robust to pose changes. However, recent works on the design of dictionaries that are robust to affine transformations could help to tackle this limitation. verification (of authentication) aims to compare the unknown face with the

References

[1] S. G. Kong, J. Heo, B. R. Abidi, J. Paik, and M. A. Abidi, "Recent advances in visual and infrared face recognition—a review," *Computer Vision and Image Understanding*, vol. 97, no. 1, pp. 103–135, 2005.

[2] A. K. Jain, A. Ross, and S. Prabhakar, "An introduction to biometric recognition," *IEEE Transactions on Circuits and Systems for Video Technology*, vol. 14, no. 1, pp. 4–20, 2004.

[3] R. Brunelli and T. Poggio, "Face recognition: features versus templates," *IEEE Transactions on Pattern Analysis and Machine Intelligence*, vol. 15, no. 10, pp. 1042–1052, 1993.

[4] Y. Gao and M. K. H. Leung, "Face recognition using line edge map," *IEEE Transactions on Pattern Analysis and Machine Intelligence*, vol. 24, no. 6, pp. 764–779, 2002.

[5] B. Heisele, P. Ho, J. Wu, and T. Poggio, "Face recognition: component-based versus global approaches," *Computer Vision and Image Understanding*, vol. 91, no. 1-2, pp. 6–21, 2003.

[6] J. R. Price and T. F. Gee, "Face recognition using direct, weighted linear discriminant analysis and modular subspaces," *Pattern Recognition*, vol. 38, no. 2, pp. 209–219, 2005.

[7] F. S. Samaria and A. C. Harter, "Parameterisation of a stochastic model for human face identification," in *Proceedings of the 2nd IEEE Workshop on Applications of Computer Vision*, pp. 138–142, December 1994.

[8] L. Wiskott, J. M. Fellous, N. Krüger, and C. D. Von Malsburg, "Face recognition by elastic bunch graph matching," *IEEE Transactions on Pattern Analysis and Machine Intelligence*, vol. 19, no. 7, pp. 775–779, 1997.

[9] M. A. Turk and A. P. Pentland, "Face recognition using eigenfaces," in *Proceedings of the IEEE Computer Society Conference on Computer Vision and Pattern Recognition*, pp. 586–591, June 1991.

[10] X. Chen, P. J. Flynn, and K. W. Bowyer, "PCA-based face recognition in infrared imagery: baseline and comparative studies," in *Proceedings of the IEEE International Workshop on Analysis and Modeling of Faces and Gestures*, pp. 127–134, IEEE Computer Society, 2003.

[11] D. J. Kriegman, J. P. Hespanha, and P. N. Belhumeur, "Eigenfaces vs. fisherfaces: recognition using class-specific linear projection," in *Proceedings of the European Conference on Computer Vision*, vol. 1, pp. 43–58, IEEE, 1996.

[12] B. Schölkopf, A. Smola, and K. R. Müller, "Nonlinear component analysis as a kernel eigenvalue problem," *Neural Computation*, vol. 10, no. 5, pp. 1299–1319, 1998.

[13] S. Mika, G. Ratsch, J. Weston, B. Scholkopf, and K. R. Muller, "Fisher discriminant analysis with kernels," in *Proceedings of the 9th IEEE Workshop on Neural Networks for Signal Processing (NNSP '99)*, pp. 41–48, August 1999.

[14] L. J. P. van der Maaten, E. O. Postma, and H. J. van den Herik, "Dimensionality reduction: a comparative review," Tech. Rep., 2009.

[15] S. Yang and C. Zhang, "Regression nearest neighbor in face recognition," in *Proceedings of the 18th International Conference on Pattern Recognition (ICPR '06)*, pp. 515–518, August 2006.

[16] H. J. Jia and A. M. Martinez, "Support vector machines in face recognition with occlusions," in *Proceedings of the IEEE Conference on Computer Vision and Pattern Recognition (CVPR '09)*, pp. 136–141, 2009.

[17] L. Bai and Y. Liu, "Neural networks and wavelets for face recognition," in *Proceedings of the 4th International Conference on Enterprise Information Systems (ICEIS '02)*, pp. 334–340, Ciudad Real, Spain, 2002.

[18] J. Wright, A. Y. Yang, A. Ganesh, S. S. Sastry, and Y. Ma, "Robust face recognition via sparse representation," *IEEE Transactions on Pattern Analysis and Machine Intelligence*, vol. 31, no. 2, pp. 210–227, 2009.

[19] M. Yang, L. Zhang, J. Yang, and D. Zhang, "Robust sparse coding for face recognition," in *Proceedings of the IEEE Conference on Computer Vision and Pattern Recognition (CVPR '11)*, pp. 625–632, IEEE, 2011.

[20] Y.-W. Chao, Y.-R. Yeh, Y.-W. Chen, Y.-J. Lee, and Y.-C. F. Wang, "Locality-constrained group sparse representation for robust face recognition," in *Proceedings of the 18th IEEE International Conference on Image Processing (ICIP '11)*, B. Macq and P. Schelkens, Eds., pp. 761–764, IEEE, Brussels, Belgium, 2011.

[21] E. Elhamifar and R. Vidal, "Robust classification using structured sparse representation," in *Proceedings of the IEEE Conference on Computer Vision and Pattern Recognition (CVPR '11)*, pp. 1873–1879, Providence, RI, USA, 2011.

[22] P. Buyssens and M. Revenu, "IR and visible identification via sparse representation," in *Biometrics: Theory, Applications and Systems*, IEEE, Was, USA, 2010.

[23] S. S. Chen, D. L. Donoho, and M. A. Saunders, "Atomic decomposition by basis pursuit," Tech. Rep., Department of Statistics, Stanford University, 1996.

[24] D. L. Donoho and M. Elad, "Maximal sparsity representation via l^1 minimization," *Proceedings of National Academy of Sciences*, vol. 100, pp. 2197–2202, 2003.

[25] C. Meszaros, "On the sparsity issues of interior point methods for quadratic programming," Tech. Rep., Laboratory of Operations Research and Decision Systems, Hungarian Academy of Sciences, 1998.

[26] M. J. Fadili and J.-L. Starck, "Sparse representation-based image deconvolution by iterative thresholding," *Astronomical Data Analysis*, vol. 6, 18, 2006.

[27] J. A. Tropp, "Greed is good: algorithmic results for sparse approximation," *IEEE Transactions on Information Theory*, vol. 50, no. 10, pp. 2231–2242, 2004.

[28] S. Mallat and Z. Zhang, "Matching pursuits with time-frequency dictionaries," Tech. Rep., inst-courant-cs, 1992.

[29] M. S. Lewicki, H. Hughes, and B. A. Olshausen, "A probabilistic framework for the adaptation and comparison of image codes," *Journal of the Optical Society of America*, vol. 16, no. 7, pp. 1587–1601, 1998.

[30] B. A. Olshausen and D. J. Field, "Sparse coding with an overcomplete basis set: a strategy employed by V1?" *Vision Research*, vol. 37, no. 23, pp. 3311–3325, 1997.

[31] K. Engan, S. O. Aase, and J. H. Husoy, "Multi-frame compression: theory and design," *Signal Processing*, vol. 80, no. 10, pp. 2121–2140, 2000.

[32] K. Engan, B. Rao, and K. Kreutz-Delgado, "Frame design using FOCUSS with method of optimized directions (MOD)," in *Proceedings of the Nordic Signal Processing Symposium*, pp. 65–69, Oslo, Norway, September 1999.

[33] K. Engan, S. O. Aase, and J. H. Husoy, "Frame based signal compression using method of Optimal Directions (MOD)," in *Proceedings of the 1999 IEEE International Symposium on Circuits and Systems (ISCAS '99)*, pp. V-1-V-4, Orlando, Fla, USA, June 1999.

[34] K. Kreutz-Delgado and B. D. Rao, "Focuss-based dictionary learning algorithms," in *Wavelet Applications in Signal and Image Processing*, vol. 41, pp. 19–53, IEEE, 2000.

[35] J. F. Murray and K. Kreutz-Delgado, "An improved focuss-based learning algorithm for solving sparse linear inverse problem," in *Proceedings of the International Conference on Signals, Systems and Computers*, vol. 41, pp. 19–53, 2001.

[36] M. Aharon, M. Elad, and A. Bruckstein, "K-svd: design of dictionaries for sparse representation," in *Proceedings of the Signal Processing with Adaptive Sparse Structured Representations (SPARS '5)*, vol. 5, pp. 9–12, 2005.

[37] A. Beck and M. Teboulle, "A fast iterative shrinkage-thresholding algorithm for linear inverse problems," *SIAM Journal on Imaging Sciences*, vol. 2, no. 1, pp. 183–202, 2009.

[38] A. S. Georghiades, P. N. Belhumeur, and D. J. Kriegman, "From few to many: illumination cone models for face recognition under variable lighting and pose," *IEEE Transactions on Pattern Analysis and Machine Intelligence*, vol. 23, no. 6, pp. 643–660, 2001.

[39] P. J. Phillips, H. Moon, S. A. Rizvi, and P. J. Rauss, "The FERET evaluation methodology for face-recognition algorithms," Tech. Rep., 1999.

[40] S. Kaski, "Dimensionality reduction by random mapping: fast similarity computation for clustering," in *Proceedings of the International Joint Conference on Neural Networks (IJCNN '98)*, vol. 1, pp. 413–418, 1998.

[41] A. Jain, K. Nandakumar, and A. Ross, "Score normalization in multimodal biometric systems," *Pattern Recognition*, vol. 38, no. 12, pp. 2270–2285, 2005.

[42] X. Chen, P. J. Flynn, and K. W. Bowyer, "IR and visible light face recognition," *Computer Vision and Image Understanding*, vol. 99, no. 3, pp. 332–358, 2005.

[43] J. Wang, Y. Li, X. Ao, C. Wang, and J. Zhou, "Multi-modal biometric authentication fusing iris and palmprint based on GMM," in *Proceedings of the IEEE/SP 15th Workshop on Statistical Signal Processing (SSP '09)*, pp. 349–352, September 2009.

[44] P. Buyssens, M. Revenu, and O. Lepetit, "Fusion of IR and visible light modalities for face recognition," in *Proceedings of the 3rd International Conference on Biometrics: Theory, Applications and Systems (BTAS '09)*, Wash, USA, September 2009.

12

Novel Approach for Rooftop Detection Using Support Vector Machine

Hayk Baluyan, Bikash Joshi, Amer Al Hinai, and Wei Lee Woon

Computing and Information Science, Masdar Institute of Science and Technology, Masdar City, Abu Dhabi, UAE

Correspondence should be addressed to Hayk Baluyan; bhayk@masdar.ac.ae

Academic Editors: A. Gasteratos, S.-J. Horng, J. M. Tavares, and C. S. Won

A new method for detecting rooftops in satellite images is presented. The proposed method is based on a combination of machine learning techniques, namely, k-means clustering and support vector machines (SVM). Firstly k-means clustering is used to segment the image into a set of rooftop candidates—these are homogeneous regions in the image which are potentially associated with rooftop areas. Next, the candidates are submitted to a classification stage which determines which amongst them correspond to "true" rooftops. To achieve improved accuracy, a novel two-pass classification process is used. In the first pass, a trained SVM is used in the normal way to distinguish between rooftop and nonrooftop regions. However, this can be a challenging task, resulting in a relatively high rate of misclassification. Hence, the second pass, which we call the "histogram method," was devised with the aim of detecting rooftops which were missed in the first pass. The performance of the model is assessed both in terms of the percentage of correctly classified candidates as well as the accuracy of the estimated rooftop area.

1. Introduction

Automatic rooftop detection from satellite/aerial images is an important task in a variety of applications. Interesting examples include change detection in urban monitoring, the production of digital maps, land use analysis, verification, and updating GIS databases and route planning [1, 2]. For example, accurate identification and localization of rooftops in urban images are a key step in territorial planning and city modeling. Similarly, knowledge of the location, profile, and density of buildings can be very useful in estimating the distribution of a city's population. In particular, rooftop detection can be used to analyze the size and location of human settlements in slums and other disorganized areas [2].

However, detecting rooftops from aerial or satellite images can be very challenging. One reason is that the images used often differ in terms of lighting conditions, quality, and resolution. Another reason is that buildings may have diverse and complicated shapes and structures and as such can be easily confused with similar objects such as cars, roads, and courtyards. The result of these complications is that there

are currently no algorithms or features that are universally applicable, that is, which can be used to detect roofs in all or even a majority of aerial and satellite images.

Much of the earlier work on rooftop detection has depended on computer vision and image processing techniques such as edge detection, corner detection, and image segmentation. One widely used approach is to first generate rooftop candidates using image segmentation techniques and then to identify the true rooftops within this set of candidates, where the latter process is performed using discriminative features such as intensity, shape, and area. Ren et al. and Nosrati and Saeedi [3, 4] proposed a technique for automatic polygonal rooftop extraction based on rooftop hypothesis generation and refinement. In the hypothesis generation step rooftop candidates are generated using edge and corner detection. The generated hypotheses are refined in the second step by using features that characterize rooftops such as the standard deviation of pixel intensities within rooftop candidates, relative gray level difference between rooftop surface points and outside points. In [5] a method for automatic building detection in aerial images using hierarchical feature based image segmentation is presented. In this approach the images are first segmented using the mean shift segmentation algorithm [6] to generate candidate building regions. In the subsequent step shadow information is used to determine if a candidate region is a rooftop. Jin and Davis [7] proposed a method based on differential morphological profile to generate building hypotheses with a verification process which used shadows and spectral information.

Many modern approaches have used machine learning to perform rooftop detection. In [8] a method is presented which used machine learning algorithms for selecting or rejecting candidate rooftops. Use of machine learning techniques facilitated better identification of true rooftops from the candidates even in the presence of noise and artifacts. In [9] a method for detecting building rooftops using LIDAR data was presented (LIDAR is a remote sensing technology that measures surface elevation using a laser). Mathematical morphological filtering is first used to separate ground and nonground objects in the image. Next, buildings and trees are classified from the nonground objects. An unbalanced support vector machine is used in the methodology since this reflects the characteristics of the data to be classified. For example, in urban areas the number of buildings in the image may be considerably more than the number of trees. Unbalanced SVM made the classification more accurate and automatic. Similarly a technique of detecting trees in urban areas has been presented in [10] using the aerial image LIDAR data. The detection of trees in urban areas is eventually used to exclude tree parts from the building rooftops for 3D city modeling. Firstly, segmentation is performed using a region growing algorithm and then trees are detected by performing classification on segments using SVM. Classification performance was assessed using ROC analysis. The performance of this methodology was then compared to other traditional approaches and was found to be better. In [11] a method is presented for detecting building damage in aerial images. The method used shadow information in addition to the spectral information to perform building damage detection. Images were first segmented using an improved watershed algorithm to produce multilevel image segments. An SVM was then used to classify the segments that were generated. It was observed that the accuracy of the presented methodology was significantly higher than the benchmark methodology which only used spectral information for classification.

Other studies have used both spectral and spatial features for the classification task (e.g., [12]). The main motivation for using both spatial and spectral features was that land cover types in urban areas are spectrally similar. So, the accuracy obtained using spectral features alone is comparatively low. It was observed that the use of spatial features along with the spectral features improved the accuracy of the building damage detection task considerably.

Based on our review of the literature, a new rooftop detection system which is novel in a number of key respects was developed. The proposed method has the following key characteristics.

(1) It uses only *panchromatic images*. In contrast, most of the approaches mentioned in the literature have used

LIDAR data [9, 10] and/or multispectral images [11, 12], both of which are more informative but also more difficult to obtain and expensive.

(2) It based on both *spectral and spatial features* extracted from the images.

(3) It utilizes *machine learning techniques*, namely, *k*-means clustering to segment the image into rooftop candidates and SVM to perform classification on these candidates.

(4) classification results obtained using the SVM are subjected to a *second-pass classification stage*. For easy reference we will refer to this as the "*histogram method*."

There do not seem to be any existing studies which combine all four characteristics above, and we believe that presented together these represent a significant improvement over existing methods for performing rooftop detection. The original motivation for this study was to assess the available rooftop area in Abu Dhabi, for the deployment of photovoltaics, as such images from this area are used to evaluate this method.

2. Proposed Method

The proposed rooftop detection system consists of the following three main steps.

(1) *Image Segmentation.* Each image is first divided into a set of candidate regions. This is done by first using *k*-means clustering, to divide pixels into a number of clusters based on colors and then using the flood-fill algorithm to group the pixels in each cluster into a set of connected components or regions. Each of these regions is now a rooftop *candidate*.

(2) *Feature Extraction and SVM Classification.* For each candidate, 8 features are extracted using MATLAB's *regionprops* method. These extracted features form the dataset, where each row represents a single candidate region. The SVM classifier is then trained to distinguish between rooftop regions and nonrooftop regions.

(3) *Histogram Method.* Although the trained SVM successfully detects many of the rooftops in the test images, in practice there were also many rooftop regions which were not detected (specific examples of these will be shown later). To detect initially rooftops that were missed initially, the histogram method was devised, which seeks to leverage the distribution of grayscale intensities of rooftop pixels that were correctly detected by the SVM. This method is based on the observation that rooftops which are in close proximity to one another also tend to have the same color.

The overall approach is shown in Figure 1. All the three steps listed above will now be discussed in greater detail.

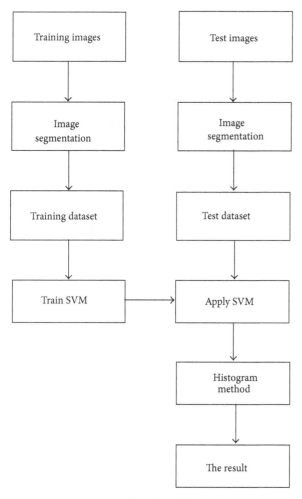

FIGURE 1: Diagram describing the overall model.

An important consideration is the choice of an appropriate value of k (the number of clusters). As is commonly done, a range of values were tested after which it was observed that $k = 4$ provided the best result (examples which illustrate this are shown later).

The result of applying the k-means algorithm is a labeling of each pixel in a given image into one of four different clusters (in cases where $k = 4$). The next step is to convert these labeled pixels into candidate rooftops, and this is achieved by grouping them into connected regions. For this purpose, the 4-connected flood fill algorithm is applied separately to pixels from each of the four clusters—the result is a set of regions where each pixel in a region is connected to at least one other pixel in the same region via one of the four principle directions. Another option was to use the 8-connected flood fill algorithm, which permits connections via any of the 8 pixels in the immediate neighborhood of a given pixel. In practice no significant difference was observed between these two methods (an example of this is shown in Figure 3) and as such the 4-connected flood fill algorithm was used as it was computationally less demanding [15].

2.2. Feature Extraction and SVM Model

2.2.1. Data Preparation. After dividing the training images into candidate regions (segments) as described in the previous section, the dataset was constructed, in which each row represents one of the segments. Eight features were extracted to describe each segment (this is discussed in more detail in the next section). Each row is manually labeled as "1" (if it corresponds to a rooftop) or "0" (if not).

2.2.2. Feature Extraction. Features are numerical attributes which characterize the object to be classified. So, the extracted features are those which hold properties which can help to distinguish rooftops and nonrooftops in an image [16]. In the proposed method eight features are considered which are highly relevant to the classification task at hand. These are as follows.

(1) *Area.* This is the area of a given segment in terms of the number of pixels. This feature can help filter out objects such as trees and cars which are simply too small to be a rooftop.

(2) *Ratio of Minor Axis to Major Axis Lengths.* This is the ratio of width to length of a given region. In Figure 4, the major and minor axes of a building are shown in red and blue, respectively. As can be seen the lengths of the minor and major axes of the highlighted building are comparable—in comparison, objects such as roads are elongated and have very low minor to major axis ratios.

(3) *Visible Vegetation Index (VVI).* The VVI gives an indication of the presence of vegetation in an image [10]. VVI is frequently calculated for multispectral

2.1. Image Segmentation.
The goal of image segmentation is to create a set of candidate regions (segments), each of which will later be classified as rooftop or nonrooftop. To divide an image into segments we use k-means clustering [13], to divide the pixels in an image into k clusters. The clustering is based on the *color* of the pixels, where each row presented to the k-means function represents a single pixel with 3 features: the red, green, and blue component intensities.

To improve the quality of the extracted segments bilateral filtering [14] is applied prior to clustering. Bilateral filtering is a preprocessing method which seeks to remove noise while preserving edge information. It combines two filtering approaches: domain filtering, which enforces closeness by weighing pixel values with coefficients that fall off with distance, and range filtering, which averages pixel values with weights that decay with dissimilarity. The result of the bilateral filtering is shown in Figure 2(b). In the same figure the results of the k-means clustering are shown both without and with bilateral filtering (Figures 2(c) and 2(d)). It can be observed that the use of bilateral filtering results in smoother and visually "cleaner" segments. In contrast, it can be seen that many segments obtained without the use of bilateral filtering contain noticeable levels of noise.

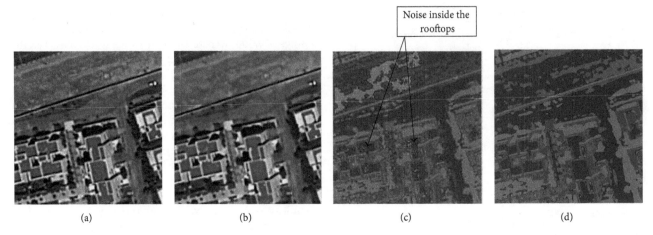

FIGURE 2: The original image (a). The result after applying bilateral filtering on the original image (b). The result of the k-means clustering with 4 clusters on the original image (c). The result of the k-means clustering with 4 clusters on the image obtained after bilateral filtering (d).

FIGURE 3: The original image (a). The result of 4-connected flood-fill algorithm (b). The result of 8-connected flood-fill algorithm (c).

images, but in the case of an RGB image it can be approximated using

VVI

$$= \left[\left(1 - \left|\frac{R - R_0}{R + R_0}\right|\right) \left(1 - \left|\frac{G - G_0}{G + G_0}\right|\right) \left(1 - \left|\frac{B - B_0}{B + B_0}\right|\right) \right]^{1/W}. \tag{1}$$

Here, R, G, and B denote the red, green, and blue intensities in the image, whereas R_0, B_0, and G_0 are the values of red, blue and green used to reference the green color. W is used to adjust the sensitivity of the scale and is known as weight component [17].

(4) *Solidity*. Solidity can be calculated as the ratio of the total area of a region to the area of the convex hull of the region [18]. Because most rooftops are rectangular in shape, rooftop-related regions in an image are likely to have higher values of solidity.

(5) *Mean Intensity*. This is the mean of all the grayscale intensity values present in a region [18]. Usually mean intensity values of the rooftops are similar. As in Figure 4 the rooftops are of similar intensity which is

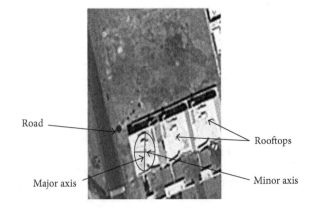

FIGURE 4: The image showing rooftop and nonrooftop objects together with the features.

different from that of other objects such as roads and vegetation.

(6) *Variance in Intensity*. This is the variance of the pixel intensities within a segmented region. A rooftop would tend to be fairly homogeneous in appearance, and as such the corresponding region would also have

a lower variance of intensity when compared to a nonrooftop region.

(7) *Extent.* The extent is the ratio of pixels in a given region to the total number of pixels of the bounding box. This is similar in concept to the solidity feature.

(8) *Eccentricity.* The value of eccentricity ranges from 0 to 1. A segment having eccentricity 0 is a circle whereas segment with eccentricity 1 is a line segment. This feature can help the classifier to reject objects which are overly elongated.

Each feature was normalized by subtracting the mean of the feature and dividing it by the standard deviation.

2.2.3. SVM Model. The support vector machine (SVM) is a machine learning technique which finds the decision boundary (or "hyperplane") that optimally separates the data points of one class from those of the other class, where a "hyperplane" is optimal if it maximizes the margin of separation between the two classes. Like most kernel methods, the performance of an SVM is heavily dependent on the choice of kernel function. Because of its good classification performance on our data, we used the Gaussian radial basis function kernel:

$$K(x, y) = e^{-(x-y)^2/2\sigma^2}. \tag{2}$$

Different values of sigma were tried and it was found that setting $\sigma = 1$ produced the best results (illustrative examples are shown later).

2.3. Histogram Method. As already mentioned, it is likely that the SVM will not be able to detect all the rooftop regions in an image. To help address this problem, color information from the detected rooftops was subsequently used to find the "missing" rooftops.

The main idea is to use the information from the regions which were classified by the SVM as rooftops in order to detect the misclassified segments. This is based on the observation that rooftops within a single image tend to have the same pixel intensities. Hence, the idea is to use the intensity information of the segments which were classified as rooftops by the SVM, to affect a "second-pass" of classification. An example is shown in Figure 5. In Figure 5(b) the segments which have been labeled black are the ones which were classified as rooftops by the SVM and the ones which were colored by black boundary are some of rooftop segments which were misclassified as nonrooftops. As can be seen, the grayscale intensities of these misclassified regions are similar of those of the detected rooftops, which suggest the histogram method could be very useful for these situations.

Two histograms were used: one for the intensities of pixels which were classified as rooftops and another for pixels which were classified as nonrooftops. Each histogram consisted of 10 bins, which represented a reasonable balance between computational requirements, good results, and adequate coverage of each bin (in terms of pixels). The two histograms are shown in Figures 5(c) and 5(d).

From the first distribution (shown in Figure 5(c)) 2 bins were chosen which contained the most number of pixels. At this point we applied the heuristic that misclassified rooftop pixels should fall into either of these two bins or into one of the immediate neighbors. In this way we ended up examining up to 6 bins out of 10 bins (in boundary cases this can be as low as 3 bins); thus the likelihood of the misclassified pixels falling into one of these 6 bins is very high.

Considering only 2 bins also avoids adding too much noise to the model, since considering too many bins can significantly increase both true positive and false positive rates. An example is shown in Figure 6, where it can be seen that taking 3 bins with the most number of pixels helps to detect brown rooftops; however it also resulted in an increase in false positives (Figure 6(c)).

Another issue related to the histogram method is having different objects (roads, cars, and so on), which are of the same color as the rooftops (as an example see Figure 7(a)). In such cases the histogram method cannot effectively distinguish nonrooftop from rooftop regions. A similar problem is encountered when there are no rooftops on the image at all (see Figure 7(b)). In such cases the histogram method will admit large numbers of false positives.

In order to avoid the situations discussed above a thresholding scheme was applied. The scheme adopted is based on the fact that the aim of the histogram method is to complement SVM classification; if the number of nondetected pixels in a bin is significantly higher than that of detected pixels in the same bin, there would be little sense in using that bin. For example, from Figure 5(d) it can be observed that there are 10000 nondetected pixels in the fifth bin; however from Figure 5(c) we have only less than 200 detected pixels in the fifth bin. Thus, the number of nonrooftop pixels (based on the SVM classification) is greater than the number of rooftop pixels by factor 50. It was found that applying a threshold to this ratio was very useful in avoiding cases like this. In our case setting a threshold of 15 proved to be the best choice for our datasets, though this remains as a tunable parameter which needs to empirically set when used with different datasets.

The results will be discussed in greater detail in the next section, but briefly our observation was that the "histogram" method performed very well for one of our datasets, where it resulted in a big increase in performance. Unfortunately for the second dataset this method did not perform as well; however, even in this case it still produced a slight improvement in performance. Suggested reasons for this will be presented later on in the paper.

3. Results and Discussion

3.1. Data. As explained earlier, one of the aims of research was for the proposed method to be able to work using only panchromatic data. Such data can be obtained from a variety of commercial sources, but for this study images that were manually collected from Google Maps were used. Since this paper was focused on finding the total amount of rooftop area for deployment of photovoltaics in Abu Dhabi, UAE, we use

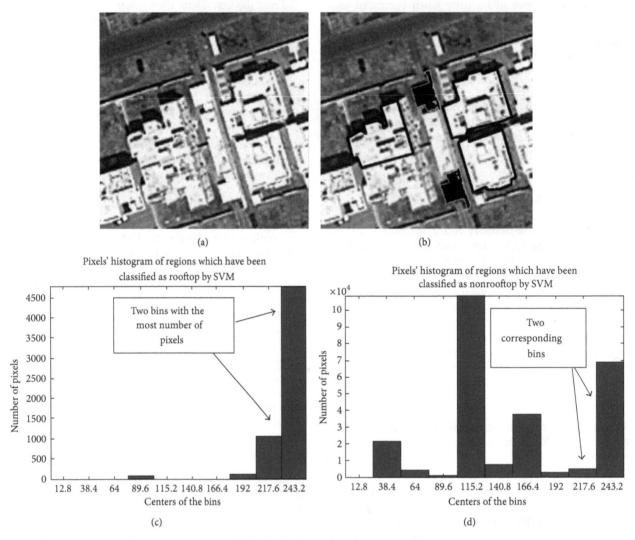

(a)

(b)

Pixels' histogram of regions which have been classified as rooftop by SVM

Two bins with the most number of pixels

(c)

Pixels' histogram of regions which have been classified as nonrooftop by SVM

Two corresponding bins

(d)

FIGURE 5: The original image (a) .The result after the SVM (b). The distribution of intensities of the detected rooftop pixels (c) .The distribution of intensities of the nondetected rooftop pixels (d).

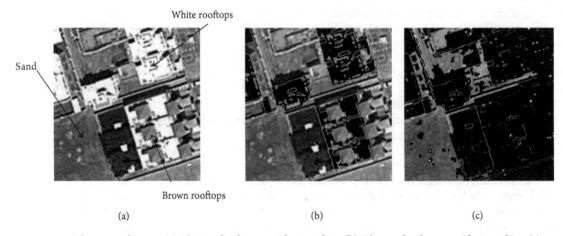

White rooftops

Sand

Brown rooftops

(a)   (b)   (c)

FIGURE 6: The original image (a). The result when considering 2 bins (b). The result when considering 3 bins (c).

images gathered from selected residential areas in Abu Dhabi city. To ensure the generality of our model, it was tested on two separate datasets, "Raha" and "Khalifa," which consist of images gathered from Al Raha Gardens and Khalifa City A.

For the segmentation process to work properly, the k-means algorithm had to be provided with images of an appropriate size. For this study, satellite images were divided into small tiles with 512×512 pixels, which corresponded to a plot of land measuring $70\,m \times 70\,m$. This size was chosen because it provided a pragmatic balance between being small enough such that the k-means algorithm could be effective, while still being large enough such that each tile typically contained a number of houses and hence roofs. The second issue was important as it meant that rooftops were rarely split between neighboring tiles.

14 such images were collected for each dataset, out of which 8 were used for training and the remaining 6 images were used for testing and validation. In addition rooftops in each of these images were manually labeled and these labels were subsequently used to label the regions extracted during the segmentation process, where each rooftop region is labeled "1" and nonrooftop regions "0."

Figure 8 shows examples of images from both datasets and also an example of a manually labeled image. As can be seen, many objects (such as cars and roads) have pixel intensities which are very similar to rooftops and as such our model needs to be able to distinguish these objects from true rooftops. For example for "Raha" images it is obvious that roads have almost the same color as most of the rooftops (see Figure 8(a)) and for "Khalifa" images there are many brown regions which look like rooftops; however they are not (see Figure 8(b)).

3.2. Experimental Results. Commonly adopted performance metrics were used to evaluate the performance of the system. These are Precision, Recall and F_1 score, which are defined as shown here:

$$\text{Precision} = \frac{\text{TP}}{\text{TP} + \text{FP}} * 100\%,$$

$$\text{Recall} = \frac{\text{TP}}{\text{TP} + \text{FN}} * 100\%, \tag{3}$$

$$F_1 = \frac{2 * \text{Precision} * \text{Recall}}{\text{Precision} + \text{Recall}} * 100\%.$$

Here TP, TN, FP, FN are, respectively, true positive, true negative, false positive, and false negative rates.

As mentioned, to determine the optimal value of σ, the performance in terms of F_1 score was calculated for a range of values of σ. Results for Raha and Khalifa datasets are shown in Figures 9(a) and 9(b). As we mentioned previously, it can be seen that $\sigma = 1$ results in the best performance.

As might be expected, it can be seen that the accuracy of the SVM grows with the size of the training dataset. The relationship between the F_1 score for the SVM on the training dataset and the number of training images used is shown in Figure 10.

TABLE 1: The results for trained SVM on Al Raha Gardens (a) and Khalifa City A (b) validation datasets.

(a)

Number of clusters	$k = 2$	$k = 3$	$k = 4$	$k = 5$	$k = 6$
Precision (%)	60.5	68.19	79.66	73.5	67.39
Recall (%)	86.62	84.9	83.71	72.4	68.22
F_1 score (%)	71.24	75.6	81.63	72.94	67.8

(b)

Number of clusters	$k = 2$	$k = 3$	$k = 4$	$k = 5$	$k = 6$
Precision (%)	64.5	68.2	77.2	75.5	69.12
Recall (%)	69.2	73.72	88.55	73.4	69.4
F_1 score (%)	66.76	70.85	82.48	74.43	69.25

TABLE 2: The numbers of detected rooftops before and after applying the histogram method.

	Before the histogram method	After the histogram method
Image 1 from Raha	12 out of 17	14 out of 17
Image 2 from Raha	9 out of 14	10 out of 14
Image 3 from Raha	7 out of 12	12 out of 12
Image 1 from Khalifa	4 out of 13	13 out of 13
Image 2 from Khalifa	6 out of 15	14 out of 15
Image 3 from Khalifa	4 out of 12	10 out of 12

While accuracy increases with the number of images used, this seems to level off after around 8 images and this was hence deemed to be sufficient amount of training data.

Finally, there was also the issue of the suitable value of k to be used when performing segmentation. As was already mentioned we have tried different values of k and found $k = 4$ to be the most suitable in our case. The performance of the SVM with parameter $\sigma = 1$ for different number of clusters on the validation dataset is shown in Table 1, where the best result (F_1 score equal 82%) for both validation sets can be seen.

We evaluate the overall performance of our method based on two criteria: the number of detected rooftops and the overall area covered by detected rooftops. We compare the results before and after applying the histogram method. In Table 2 the results for all 6 testing images are given.

It can be observed that the SVM performs quite well on "Raha" images even without using the histogram method. However for "Khalifa" images the performance of the basic SVM is weak and the histogram method produces a huge improvement for "Khalifa" datasets. One possible reason for this is that rooftops on "Raha" images are well separated from each other by white boundaries (see Figure 8(a)). Hence the image segmentation step often results in candidate regions which in general represent single rooftop. Since all rooftops

FIGURE 7: The image with roads of the same intensity as the rooftops (a). The image without any rooftop (b).

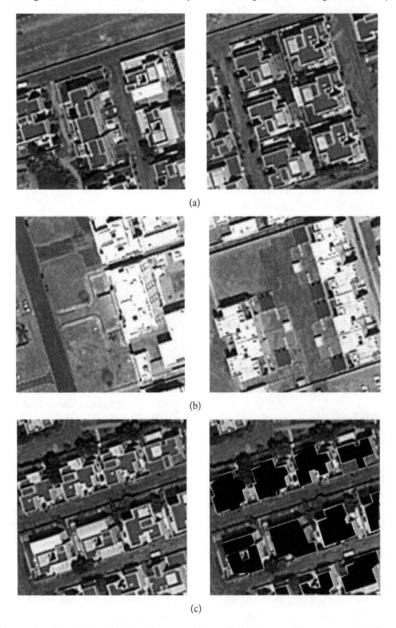

FIGURE 8: Sample images from Al Raha Gardens (a). Sample images from Khalifa City A (b). An example of a manually labeled image (c).

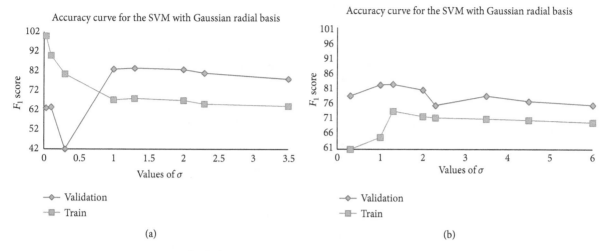

FIGURE 9: F_1 score for different values of sigma for "Raha" (a) and "Khalifa" datasets (b).

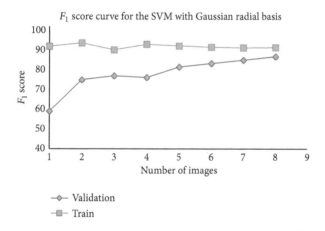

FIGURE 10: F_1 score for different number of training images for "Khalifa" dataset.

TABLE 3: The amount of detected rooftop pixels before and after applying the histogram method for Khalifa City A (a) and Al Raha Gardens test images (b).

(a)

	Before the histogram method	After the histogram method
Precision (%)	92.8	93.16
Recall (%)	52.4	70.01
F_1 score (%)	66.9	79.9

(b)

	Before the histogram method	After the histogram method
Precision (%)	88.5	97.6
Recall (%)	7.1	79.7
F_1 score (%)	13.1	87.7

have almost similar values for the extracted features, it makes the job of the SVM to make better classification easier.

In contrast in "Khalifa" images rooftops are not separated from each other very well (see Figure 8(b)); hence after the image segmentation step it is possible that 2 and more rooftops will be represented in a single candidate region, which forces the SVM to consider such candidate regions as outliers. Since rooftops in the Al Raha Gardens region have almost the same intensity as roads, cars, and other nonrooftop objects, the "histogram" method was frequently unable to detected rooftops that were not already detected using the other features. In contrast the rooftops in the Khalifa City A images are quite distinct in terms of the intensities of the corresponding regions, and this allowed the "histogram" method to make a significant contribution.

To better evaluate the overall performance of the model, results based on the correctly classified rooftop and non-rooftop pixels are presented in Table 3.

Again it can be observed that in contrast to the "Raha" dataset, the histogram method significantly improves the performance of the system on the "Khalifa" dataset (though we still see a slight improvement in the case of the "Raha" dataset).

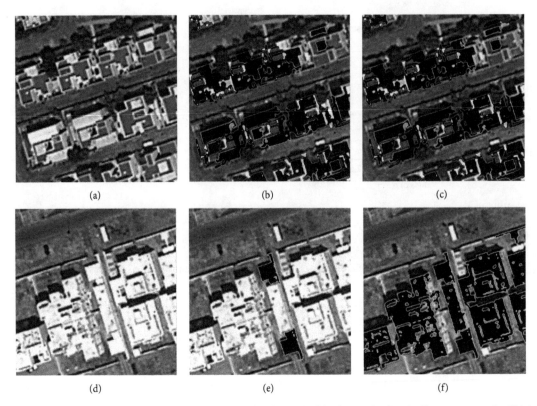

(a)   (b)   (c)

(d)   (e)   (f)

FIGURE 11: The original image from Raha Gardens (a). The result after the SVM (b). The result after the "histogram method" (c). The original image from Khalifa City A (d). The result after the SVM (e). The result after the "histogram method" (f).

More results of the performance of our model can be seen in Figure 11. It can be seen that there is not a big difference between Figures 11(b) and 11(c) since the basic SVM already performs well and the task of the histogram method in this case is to avoid the inclusion of additional noise. However a significant difference can be observed between Figures 11(e) and 11(f),which shows how the histogram method significantly improves the performance of the system.

4. Conclusion

The paper presented a new approach for detecting rooftops using machine learning techniques like k-means and SVM. While the results are still preliminary, we showed that the proposed method was able to retrieve a very high percentage of the rooftops present in an image while at the same time maintaining a low false positive rate. The method gives especially good results when all the rooftops in the image are of a similar color or gray level intensity. A unique feature of this method is its use of the "histogram method" to find rooftops which were initially missed by the SVM.

However there are still some situations in which the method does not perform well. For example rooftops which are very big relative to the image size were sometimes classified as nonrooftop by the SVM, which tended to consider such rooftops as outliers.

Another weakness of the method is poor performance when rooftops of many different colors are encountered. Also,

when there is a single "dominant" rooftop color, it renders the system less sensitive to rooftops with less common colors.

For future work we intend to extend the system along three main directions:

(1) improvements to the classification process via additional feature engineering to discover more informative features and screening and testing alternative classifiers, such as the unbalanced SVM used in [9];

(2) the addition of a higher-order classification stage. Rooftops which are in close proximity to each other tend to have similar characteristics (color, design, orientation, density, etc). While the histogram method is a step in this direction there are other characteristics beyond simply the grayscale intensity;

(3) testing and extension of the method to larger geographical areas.

References

[1] H. V. Guducu, "Building Detection from Satellite Images Using Shadow and Color Information," 2008.

[2] H. G. Akçay and S. Aksoy, "Building detection using directional spatial constraints," in *Proceedings of the 30th IEEE International Geoscience and Remote Sensing Symposium (IGARSS '10)*, pp. 1932–1935, July 2010.

[3] K. Ren, H. Sun, Q. Jia, and J. Shi, "Building recognition from aerial images combining segmentation and shadow," in *Proceedings of the IEEE International Conference on Intelligent*

Computing and Intelligent Systems (ICIS '09), pp. 578–582, chn, November 2009.

[4] M. S. Nosrati and P. Saeedi, "A novel approach for polygonal rooftop detection in satellite/aerial imageries," in *Proceedings of the 16th IEEE International Conference on Image Processing (ICIP '09)*, pp. 1709–1712, November 2009.

[5] M. Izadi and P. Saeedi, "Automatic building detection in aerial images using a hierarchical feature based image segmentation," in *Proceedings of the 20th International Conference on Pattern Recognition (ICPR '10)*, pp. 472–475, August 2010.

[6] D. Comaniciu and P. Meer, "Mean shift: a robust approach toward feature space analysis," *IEEE Transactions on Pattern Analysis and Machine Intelligence*, vol. 24, no. 5, pp. 603–619, 2002.

[7] X. Jin and C. H. Davis, "Automated building extraction from high-resolution satellite imagery in Urban areas using structural, contextual, and spectral information," *EURASIP Journal on Applied Signal Processing*, vol. 2005, no. 14, pp. 2196–2206, 2005.

[8] M. A. Maloof, P. Langley, T. O. Binford, R. Nevatia, and S. Sage, "Improved rooftop detection in aerial images with machine learning," *Machine Learning*, vol. 53, no. 1-2, pp. 157–191, 2003.

[9] W. Xin, "A new classification method for LIDAR data based on unbalanced support vector machine," in *Proceedings of the International Symposium on Image and Data Fusion (ISIDF '11)*, August 2011.

[10] J. Secord and A. Zakhor, "Tree detection in urban regions using aerial lidar and image data," *IEEE Geoscience and Remote Sensing Letters*, vol. 4, no. 2, pp. 196–200, 2007.

[11] P. Li, B. Song, and H. Xu, "Urban building damage detection from very high resolution imagery by One-Class SVM and shadow information," in *Proceedings of the IEEE International Geoscience and Remote Sensing Symposium (IGARSS '11)*, pp. 1409–1412, July 2011.

[12] P. Li, H. Xu, S. Liu, and J. Guo, "Urban building damage detection from very high resolution imagery using one-class SVM and spatial relations," in *Proceedings of the IEEE International Geoscience and Remote Sensing Symposium (IGARSS '09)*, pp. V112–V114, July 2009.

[13] K. Alsabti, S. Ranka, and V. Singh, "An efficient *k*-means clustering algorithm," in *Proceedings of the IPPS/SPDP Workshop on High Performance data Mining*, April 1998.

[14] C. Tomasi and R. Manduchi, "Bilateral filtering for gray and color images," in *Proceedings of the 1998 IEEE 6th International Conference on Computer Vision*, pp. 839–846, January 1998.

[15] A. H. Al-Fayadh, H. R. Mohamed, and R. S. Al-Shimsah, "CT angiography image segmentation by mean shift algorithm and contour with connected components image," *International Journal of Scientific and Engineering*, vol. 3, no. 8, pp. 4–9, 2012.

[16] Feature Selection, Wikipedia, 2013, http://en.wikipedia.org/wiki/Feature_selection.

[17] Visible Vegetation Index, http://phl.upr.edu/projects/visible-vegetation-index-vvi.

[18] Mathworks, 2013, http://www.mathworks.com/help/images/ref/regionprops.html#bqkf8jf.

13

Area Optimized FPGA-Based Implementation of The Sobel Compass Edge Detector

Sanjay Singh,[1] **Anil Kumar Saini,**[1] **Ravi Saini,**[1] **A. S. Mandal,**[1]
Chandra Shekhar,[1] **and Anil Vohra**[2]

[1] *CSIR-Central Electronics Engineering Research Institute (CSIR-CEERI), Pilani, Rajasthan 333031, India*
[2] *Electronic Science Department, Kurukshetra University, Kurukshetra, Haryana 136119, India*

Correspondence should be addressed to Sanjay Singh; sanjay.csirceeri@gmail.com

Academic Editors: V. Alchanatis and A. Nikolaidis

This paper presents a new FPGA resource optimized hardware architecture for real-time edge detection using the Sobel compass operator. The architecture uses a single processing element to compute the gradient for all directions. This greatly economizes on the FPGA resources' usages (more than 40% reduction) while maintaining real-time video frame rates. The measured performance of the architecture is 50 fps for standard PAL size video and 200 fps for CIF size video. The use of pipelining further improved the performance (185 fps for PAL size video and 740 fps for CIF size video) without significant increase in FPGA resources.

1. Introduction

Edge detection is one of the most important areas in lower level image processing. Quality of detected edges plays a very important role in realization of complex automated computer/machine vision systems [1]. Various edge detection algorithms are available in the literature and give different responses and details to the same input image. The Sobel edge detector is very popular than simple gradient operators due to its property to counteract the noise sensitivity and easier implementation [2]. The accuracy of the Sobel operator for edge detection is relatively low because it uses two masks which detect the edges in horizontal and vertical directions only. The accuracy can be enhanced by using the Sobel compass operator which uses a larger set of masks with narrowly spaced orientations [3, 4]. But use of the Sobel compass edge detector increases the computational complexity significantly for computing edges. It is hard to perform this computationally intensive task in real-time with serial processors. Alternative to this is design of specific hardware (ASICs or FPGAs) for the Sobel compass edge detector. The size and speed of current generation FPGAs are comparable to ASICs, but FPGAs provide the possibility to perform algorithm changes in later stages of the system development and reduce

the design cost and time [5]. This makes the FPGAs a suitable choice for such applications.

Some recent FPGA implementations are available in the literature for the Sobel compass edge detector. In [6, 7], the authors discussed the most obvious FPGA implementation of the Sobel compass edge detector, which uses multiple processing elements in parallel to compute gradient along each direction. This increased the FPGA resources. The hardware-software codesign-based approach has been discussed in [8] for Sobel compass operator implementation which uses eight processing elements in parallel. It is observed that, the main focus of most of existing FPGA-based implementations of the Sobel compass edge detector has been on achieving real-time performance by using highly parallel architecture and thus fully ignored the FPGA resources' optimizations. FPGA resource (area) optimization is important for edge detection as it is one of basic modules in the large automated video surveillance system (which uses many complex algorithms requiring large FPGA resources).

In this paper, an FPGA resource optimized hardware architecture for the Sobel compass edge detector for real-time video surveillance applications is investigated. We show that a single processing element is sufficient to compute the gradient along all directions in real-time. As the Sobel compass

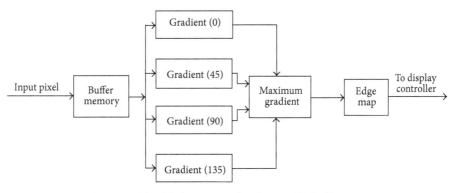

FIGURE 1: The Sobel compass edge detector block diagram.

edge detector is sliding window operator, smart buffer-based memory architecture is used to move the incoming pixels in computing window. The specific datapaths are designed, and controller is developed to perform the complete task. The design and simulation are done using VHDL and targeted to Xilinx ML510 (Virtex-5 FX130T) FPGA platform. Custom camera interface PCB is designed to interface Sony PTZ camera with ML510 FPGA platform. Complete system is tested for real-world scenario, and it robustly detects the edges in real-time for video sequences captured by camera.

2. The Sobel Compass Edge Detector

In this section, the used algorithm is briefly described, for a more detailed description we refer to [3, 4]. The Sobel operator is widely used for edge detection in images. It has advantage over simple gradient operators because of its property to counteract the noise sensitivity. It is based on computing an approximation of the gradient of the image intensity function. It uses two 3×3 spatial masks (Hx and Hy) which are convolved with the original image to calculate the approximations of the gradient. The Sobel operator uses two filters:

$$Hx = \begin{bmatrix} -1 & 0 & 1 \\ -2 & 0 & 2 \\ -1 & 0 & 1 \end{bmatrix}, \qquad Hy = \begin{bmatrix} -1 & -2 & -1 \\ 0 & 0 & 0 \\ 1 & 2 & 1 \end{bmatrix}. \quad (1)$$

These compute the average gradient components across the neighboring lines or columns, respectively. The local edge strength is defined as the gradient magnitude given by

$$GM(x, y) = \sqrt{Hx^2 + Hy^2}. \quad (2)$$

The accuracy of the Sobel operator for edge detection is relatively low because it uses two masks which detect the edges in horizontal and vertical directions only. This problem can be addressed by using the Sobel compass operator which uses a larger set of masks with narrowly spaced orientations. It uses eight masks ($H_0, H_{45}, H_{90}, H_{135}, H_{180}, H_{225}, H_{270}$, and

H_{315}) each providing edge strength along one of the eight possible directions of the compass:

$$H_0 = \begin{bmatrix} -1 & -2 & -1 \\ 0 & 0 & 0 \\ 1 & 2 & 1 \end{bmatrix}, \qquad H_{45} = \begin{bmatrix} -2 & -1 & 0 \\ -1 & 0 & 1 \\ 0 & 1 & 2 \end{bmatrix},$$

$$H_{90} = \begin{bmatrix} -1 & 0 & 1 \\ -2 & 0 & 2 \\ -1 & 0 & 1 \end{bmatrix}, \qquad H_{135} = \begin{bmatrix} 0 & 1 & 2 \\ -1 & 0 & 1 \\ -2 & -1 & 0 \end{bmatrix},$$

$$H_{180} = \begin{bmatrix} 1 & 2 & 1 \\ 0 & 0 & 0 \\ -1 & -2 & -1 \end{bmatrix}, \qquad H_{225} = \begin{bmatrix} 2 & 1 & 0 \\ 1 & 0 & -1 \\ 0 & -1 & -2 \end{bmatrix},$$

$$H_{270} = \begin{bmatrix} 1 & 0 & -1 \\ 2 & 0 & -2 \\ 1 & 0 & -1 \end{bmatrix}, \qquad H_{315} = \begin{bmatrix} 0 & -1 & -2 \\ 1 & 0 & -1 \\ 2 & 1 & 0 \end{bmatrix}. \quad (3)$$

Only the result of four (H_0, H_{45}, H_{90}, and H_{135}) of the above eight masks must actually be computed since the four others are identical except for the reversed sign. The edge strength E at position (x, y) is defined as the maximum of the eight masks output ($D_0, D_{45}, D_{90}, D_{135}, D_{180}, D_{225}, D_{270}$, and D_{315}), that is,

$$E_{xy} = \max\left(D_0, D_{45}, D_{90}, D_{135}, D_{180}, D_{225}, D_{270}, D_{315}\right). \quad (4)$$

Since $D_{180} = -D_0, D_{225} = -D_{45}, D_{270} = -D_{90}$, and $D_{135} = -D_{315}$, therefore, the above equation can be rewritten as

$$E_{xy} = \max\left(|D_0|, |D_{45}|, |D_{90}|, |D_{135}|\right). \quad (5)$$

Therefore, to find the edges in all possible directions, the four masks (H_0, H_{45}, H_{90}, and H_{315}) must be applied to each pixel of the input image. The Sobel compass edge detector has the advantage of not requiring the computation of squares and square roots (which are considered relatively expensive operations).

3. Proposed Architecture

This section describes the details of the proposed architecture for the Sobel compass edge detector. Figure 1 shows the basic

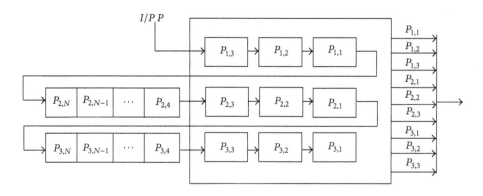

FIGURE 2: Buffer memory architecture.

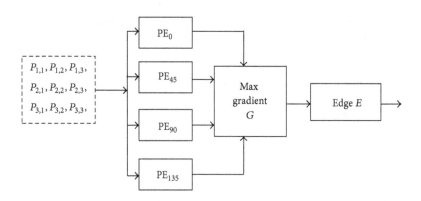

FIGURE 3: The standard Sobel compass edge detector architecture.

block level data flow diagram for computation of the Sobel compass edge detector. It consists of mainly four stages. In the first stage, the incoming pixel data from camera interface logic is stored in buffer memory. Four gradients along different directions are computed in the second stage. The maximum gradient is selected, and final edge map is computed by comparing the maximum gradient value with a threshold in the third and fourth stages, respectively.

In the Sobel compass operator, the 3×3 masks are used to compute gradient values along different directions over an input image. Therefore, it is necessary to store at least two rows of input image data in FPGA on-chip memory before the processing begins. To achieve this, we have used smart buffer-based memory architecture [9, 10] which utilizes two FIFOs and a set of registers in order to shift the image data into computing window (Figure 2). The length of the shift register depends on input image width.

The standard implementations of the Sobel compass edge detector [6, 7] use four processing elements in parallel for computing gradient along different directions. For comparison of results with our proposed architecture, we coded the standard architecture (Figure 3) in VHDL, synthesized using Xilinx ISE 10.3, and implemented on Xilinx ML510 (Virtex-5) FPGA board. The resulted maximum clock frequency for this architecture is 118.5 MHz.

It is observed that in the above implementation, each processing element (PE) performs the same set of operation

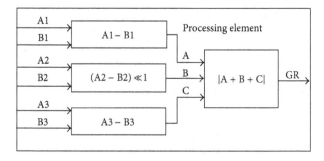

FIGURE 4: Processing element architecture.

(addition, subtraction, and multiplication by 2) on inputs applied to them. Processing element (PE) architecture for gradient computation is shown in Figure 4. The only difference for four gradient computation units (PE_0, PE_{45}, PE_{90}, and PE_{135}) is in inputs applied to them at a particular time. Therefore, by switching the inputs applied to anyone of processing element in appropriate manner, the same processing element can be used to compute all four gradients along different directions. This forms the basis for the proposed architecture.

For real-time video surveillance applications, the required frame rate is 25 fps (frames per second) for PAL size video (30 fps for NTSC size video). For high speed video surveillance application, for a frame rate of 50 fps for PAL size

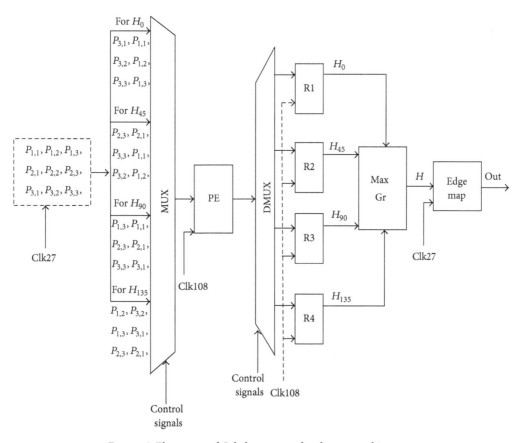

FIGURE 5: The proposed Sobel compass edge detector architecture.

video (60 fps for NTSC size video), clock frequency at which the image pixel data samples are available is 27 MHz. If the processing element is operated at 108 MHz (4 × 27 MHz), all the four gradients can be computed for available image pixel data before the arrival of next image pixel data using single processing element. The operating frequency of 108 MHz is well within the limits of maximum operating frequency (118.5 MHz) resulted from synthesis results. The digital clock managers available on FPGA are used to generate 108 MHz clock from 27 MHz pixel data clock.

Figure 5 shows the proposed architecture for real-time computation of edges in an image using the Sobel compass edge detector. Gradient computation for all directions is realized through single processing element (operating at 108 MHz). The PE is used in appropriate sequential order in different time slots for computing gradients along all directions. This architecture greatly economizes on the FPGA resources' usages (area) but needs storage elements to store results for future use and set of multiplexers for switching of inputs and outputs in different time slots. This architecture also requires a controller which insures proper functioning of complete design. Control signals for input selection multiplexer and output selection demultiplexer are generated at 108 MHz so that inputs to processing element can be switched and output can be stored properly. Image pixel data moves through computing window at 27 MHz. Gradient values for directions along 0 degree, 45 degree, 90 degree, and 135

degree are computed by processing element in 4 cycles at 108 MHz clock frequency, and the results are stored in R1, R2, R3, and R4 registers which works at 108 MHz frequency. Finally, the maximum gradient is selected by using the values stored in registers R1 to R4, and final edge map is computed by comparing the maximum gradient value with a threshold. Therefore, before the arrival of next image data samples (at 27 MHz), the final edge map of current pixel data is available.

The performance of the system is further improved by using a pipelined processing element (Figure 6) at the cost of area occupied by pipelined registers. Resulted maximum clock frequency is 405 MHz. Therefore, a frame rate of 185 fps can be achieved for standard PAL size video. The improvement in clock frequency in pipelined architecture is due to reduced maximum combinational path delay in processing element architecture.

4. Results

The proposed architecture has been designed using VHDL, simulated in ModelSim, and synthesized using Xilinx ISE 10.3. It has been implemented on Xilinx ML510 (Virtex-5) FPGA platform. It is capable of computing the edge map of an input image well within the real-time constraints while utilizing much less FPGA resources. The synthesis results (Table 1) reveal that the FPGA resources utilized by proposed edge detection architecture are more than 40% less as compared

TABLE 1: Comparison of synthesis results.

Synthesis parameters	Standard [6, 7] Figures 3–4	Proposed Figures 4 and 5 (percentage of reduction)	Proposed pipelined Figures 5–6 (percentage of reduction)
FPGA slices	67	40 (40.3%)	42 (37.3%)
Slice LUTs	222	109 (50.9%)	117 (47.3%)
LUT FF pairs	222	118 (46.8%)	133 (40.1%)
Slice register	2	40	95
Route-thrus	16	2 (87.5%)	2 (87.5%)

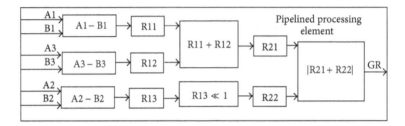

FIGURE 6: Pipelined processing element architecture.

FIGURE 7: Input test images and output images.

to the standard architecture. The synthesis parameters are number of FPGA slices used by the logic, number of slice LUTs (Look Up Tables), number of LUT Flip Flop Pairs (LUT Flip Flop pair represents one LUT paired with one Flip Flop within a slice), number of slice registers, and number of route-thrus (used for routing only). The resource reduction is not one-fourth of the resources utilized by standard architecture because of resource utilization by additional input and output switching logics. The measured performance of our system at 108 MHz operating frequency for PAL size video is 50 fps

(frames per second) and CIF size video is 200 fps. Pipelined implementation resulted in 185 fps frame rate for PAL size video and 740 fps for CIF size video. PAL size and CIF size images are most commonly used video formats for video surveillance cameras. Therefore, implemented system can easily detect edges for high frame rate surveillance applications while utilizing much less FPGA resources. The input test images (PAL size) taken from camera and output images produced by implemented system and displayed on monitor are shown in Figure 7.

5. Conclusion

In this paper, the hardware architecture for the Sobel compass edge detector, implemented on Xilinx ML510 FPGA platform, has been presented. This architecture greatly economizes on the FPGA resources' usages (area). The architecture used more than 40% less FPGA resources as compared to the standard implementations presented in the literature and maintained real-time constraints for video processing. The implemented architecture is integrated with camera and display monitor. The integrated system is tested for real-world scenario. It robustly detects the edge in real-time. It can be efficiently used as part of complex computer vision system without occupying much area.

Acknowledgment

S. Singh would like to thank Mr. Raj Singh, Group Leader, IC Design Group, for his constant guidance, suggestions, support, and encouragement.

References

[1] M. B. Ahmad and T. S. Choi, "Local threshold and boolean function based edge detection," *IEEE Transactions on Consumer Electronics*, vol. 45, no. 3, pp. 674–679, 1999.

[2] T. A. Abbasi and M. U. Abbasi, "A novel FPGA-based architecture for Sobel edge detection operator," *International Journal of Electronics*, vol. 94, no. 9, pp. 889–896, 2007.

[3] W. Burger and M. J. Burge, *Digital Image Processing: An Algorithmic Introduction Using Java*, Springer, New York, NY, USA, 2008.

[4] R. C. Gonzalez and R. E. Woods, *Digital Image Processing*, Pearson Education, New Delhi, India, 2009.

[5] H. Jiang, H. Ardö, and V. Öwall, "A hardware architecture for real-time video segmentation utilizing memory reduction techniques," *IEEE Transactions on Circuits and Systems for Video Technology*, vol. 19, no. 2, pp. 226–236, 2009.

[6] Z. Guo, W. Xu, and Z. Chai, "Image edge detection based on FPGA," in *Proceedings of the 9th International Symposium on Distributed Computing and Applications to Business, Engineering and Science*, pp. 169–171, August 2010.

[7] A. Nosrat and Y. S. Kavian, "Hardware description of multidirectional fast sobel edge detection processor by VHDL for implementing on FPGA," *International Journal of Computer Applications*, vol. 47, no. 25, pp. 1–7, 2012.

[8] K. C. Sudeep and J. Majumdar, "A novel architecture for real time implementation of edge detectors on FPGA," *International Journal of Computer Science Issues*, vol. 8, no. 1, pp. 193–202, 2011.

[9] Z. Vasicek and L. Sekanina, "Novel hardware implementation of adaptive median filters," in *Proceedings of the 11th IEEE Workshop on Design and Diagnostics of Electronic Circuits and Systems (DDECS '11)*, pp. 1–6, April 2008.

[10] C. Moore, H. Devos, and D. Stroobandt, "Optimizing the FPGA memory design for a sobel edge detector," in *Proceedings of the 20th Annual Workshop on Circuits, Systems and Signal Processing*, 2009.

14

Deformable Contour-Based Maneuvering Flying Vehicle Tracking in Color Video Sequences

Samira Sabouri,[1] **Alireza Behrad,**[2] **and Hassan Ghassemian**[3]

[1] *Department of Electrical Engineering, Science and Research Branch, Islamic Azad University, Tehran 14778-93855, Iran*
[2] *Faculty of Engineering, Shahed University, Tehran 18651-33191, Iran*
[3] *School of Electrical and Computer Engineering, Tarbiat Modares University, Tehran 14115-143, Iran*

Correspondence should be addressed to Alireza Behrad; behrad@shahed.ac.ir

Academic Editors: A. Gasteratos, C.-C. Han, D. P. Mukherjee, A. Prati, and J. M. Tavares

This paper presents a new method for the tracking of maneuvering flying vehicles using a deformable contour model in color video sequences. The proposed approach concentrates on targets with maneuvering motion in sky, which involves fundamental aspect change stemmed from 3D rotation of the target or video camera. In order to segment and track the aircraft in a video, at first, the target contour is initialized manually in a key frame, and then it is matched and tracked automatically in the subsequent frames. Generally active contour models employ a set of energy functions based on edge, texture, color, and shape features. Afterwards, objective function is minimized iteratively to track the target contour. In the proposed algorithm, we employ game of life cellular automaton to manage snake pixels' (snaxels') deformation in each epoch of minimization procedure. Furthermore, to cope with the large aspect change of aircraft, a Gaussian model has been taken into account to represent the target color in RGB space. To compensate for changes in luminance and chrominance ingredients of the target, the prior distribution function is dynamically updated during tracking. The proposed algorithm is evaluated using the collected dataset, and the expected probability of tracking error is calculated. Experimental results show positive results for the proposed algorithm.

1. Introduction

The video-based locating and tracking of flying vehicles is an interesting issue in the visual control of aerial systems, which may be employed in aerial surveillance, the navigation of flying robot, missile, microflying, unmanned aircraft, and so forth. In order to localize, track, and recognize flying vehicles, some approaches have been presented recently. In this context, four main state-of-the-art methodologies are well known and applicable including (1) invisible spectrum-based methods like radio detection and ranging (RADAR) or light detection and ranging (LIDAR); (2) visible spectrum-based approaches [1–8] such as existing algorithms in infrared and thermal imaging systems in the wavelength range of 380 nm to 780 nm and even more in far infrared case; (3) global positioning system (GPS-) based methods; and (4) combination of visible and invisible spectrum-based methods. Feasibility of these categories is mostly dependent upon the distance of the imaging system to the target of interest. Furthermore,

each flying vehicle has a set of flight specifications such as the minimum and maximum speed, maneuvering capability, flight board, and so on, whose data may help to estimate the position of the target accurately.

Irrespective of available information, the paper emphasizes on flying vehicle tracking (FVT) in color video sequences. In this domain, we concentrate especially on maneuvering aircraft with large aspect change, which is considered to be a challenging issue. Considering the high deformation of target contour in this application, utilizing deformable surfaces such as active contour [9–11] and active mesh [1, 12] models seems to be a proper choice.

1.1. Related Work. In [1], a method for flying vehicle tracking was introduced in monochrome video sequences. In this method, the incipient location of the target was determined manually; then, the target was tracked automatically by optimizing the mesh energy functions. In [2], a vision-based scheme for automatic locating of a flying vehicle was presented by means of extracting fuzzified edges features and matching edge pyramids as well as a motion flow vector classifier based on multilayer perceptrons (MLP) neural network. Ha et al. [3] introduced a method for real time tracking of flying targets via the combination of the geometric active contour model and optical flow algorithm. Haker et al. [4] used a segmentation method based on the adaptive thresholding and Bayesian statistic approach to identify and track target location. In [10], an active contour model for vehicle target tracking was utilized. To deal with the high aspect change problem, they handled the motion model around the vehicle to reduce the tracking error in monochrome video frames. Yilmaz [13] suggested an object tracking method based on an asymmetric kernel and mean shift approach in which the scale and the orientation of the kernel were changed adaptively. Molloy and Whelan [14] introduced an active mesh system for the motion tracking of rigid objects to alleviate one of the main problems in active contour models, that is, the snake initialization. Jian and Jie [15] proposed an approach to track small objects in infrared streams using the mean shift estimator algorithm. In [16], a method based on edge features extraction and matching as well as Kalman filter was suggested to detect and track mostly rigid objects like the land vehicles in video sequences grabbed by moving video cameras. Their method determined camcorder motion model by using the planar affine transformation. Lee et al. [17] suggested a deformable contour model based on frames difference map. In [18, 19], an approach for flying vehicle tracking based on the snake model was proposed. They utilized Kalman filter and an energy function the so-called electric fields, to handle large displacement of the target during tracking.

1.2. Motivation. Basically, target rotation around three roll, yaw, and pitch axes results in maneuvering motion of flying vehicle in sky. Additionally, the 3D rotation of aircraft or camera causes aspect change of the target during tracking process. Figure 1 shows aspect change problem in a typical video sequence. In the targets with aspect change some parts of the target appear during the video frames and some other parts disappear. The aspect change may create changes in the luminance and chrominance components of the target. Therefore, traditional optical flow approaches [20] or method based on feature matching [21] and model based approaches [16] fail in tracking targets with large aspect changes. Furthermore, because of maneuvering characteristics of the target, the path of target cannot be determined using algorithms based on estimation or data association [22]. In the paper, we focus on tracking aircraft targets with maneuvering motion and full aspect change and design a new scheme to alleviate general problems in this area.

Among different methods in literature for visual maneuvering aircraft locating and tracking, the approaches such as [10, 16] take into account partial aspect change. However, their efficiency was not proven for target with full aspect change where the target shape and view completely change. In this context, other issues such as different atmospheric conditions, change in luminance and chrominance, image noise, dynamic scene due to the motion of the camera,

FIGURE 1: Video streams of a typical aircraft with aspect change due to maneuvering motion of the target.

dwindling the size of target, and visibility reduction of the scene are challenging. Some of these problems like the change in luminance and chrominance and the size of the target are substantially originated due to the aspect change phenomenon.

To test the algorithm with video files in the mentioned situations and provide a standard and informative dataset, the collected dataset includes videos with various conditions in addition to the aspect change phenomenon.

To cope with these problems, we propose an algorithm based on the active contour model for tracking maneuvering target with full aspect change. The algorithm includes the following structural features.

(i) A deformable active contour model is designed to track maneuvering aircraft target with full aspect change.

(ii) A new set of external energy functions are defined in RGB color space to enhance tracking efficiency.

(iii) Game of life (GoL) cellular automaton is proposed to manage, arrange, and smooth snake pixels (snaxels) deformation in each epoch of minimization.

(iv) A parametric, multivariate, and unimodal Gaussian model is utilized to dynamically update color distribution of the target of interest in color video frames.

The rest of the paper is organized as follows: Section 2 summarizes the suggested method, and in its subsections, we discuss the deformable contour model, energy minimization and GoL-based contour updating, respectively. Experimental results appear in Section 3, and we conclude the paper in Section 4.

2. Proposed Method

Figure 2 depicts the block scheme of the proposed aircraft tracking algorithm. In the proposed algorithm, firstly the outer contour of the target is localized manually in the initial key frame. Then, a parametric, multivariate, and unimodal Gaussian model is calculated based on the central limit theorem (CLT) to represent target color distribution in RGB space. After contour initialization, the tracking algorithm starts by employing the parameters of the single gaussian model (SGM), that is, mean vector and covariance matrix, to find the location of the target contour in the current frame. Thereafter, the objective energy function is defined and optimized by means of a constrained greedy minimization procedure. To manage snaxels' deformation, we introduce a

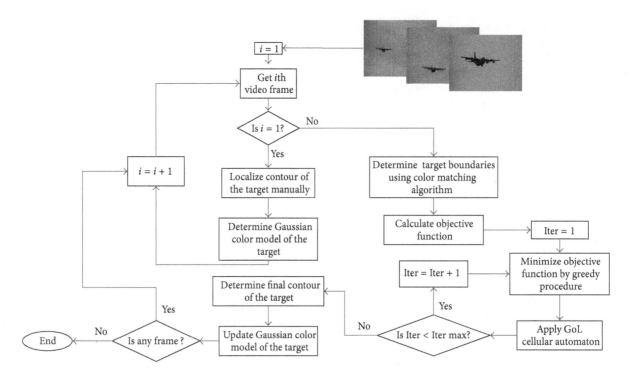

FIGURE 2: Block scheme of the proposed FVT in color video sequences.

GoL cellular automaton which is utilized in each epoch of the optimization routine. In order to deal with the aspect change phenomenon appropriately, the dynamic parametric model is updated after fixing control points and/or reaching the maximum number of iterations in each frame.

2.1. Determining Target Boundaries Using Color Matching Algorithm.

In the proposed method, a 2D active contour model is utilized to represent the outer boundary of the target during tracking algorithm. The structure of deformable contour is organized by superposition of predefined energy functions. These functions are minimized using an optimization algorithm.

One of the difficulties in tracking targets with high speed using active contour is the problem of local minimums in the energy minimization algorithm. Therefore, we utilize color distribution of the target to find the initial position of the target. For the first frame of the video, we localize the contour of the target manually. This leads to identify the region of interest (ROI) of the target. Figure 3 shows the ROI of a target and the histograms of color channels.

To determine the initial position of the contour in subsequent frames, a search region (SR) is defined to track the flying vehicle by matching and deforming the contour model. We consider the coordinates of SR as $(x_{\min} - dx, y_{\min} - dy)$ and $(x_{\max} + dx, y_{\max} + dy)$, where

$$
\begin{aligned}
x_{\min} &= \min_{\mathbf{x} \in \text{RoI}}(\mathbf{x}), & x_{\max} &= \max_{\mathbf{x} \in \text{RoI}}(\mathbf{x}), \\
y_{\min} &= \min_{\mathbf{y} \in \text{RoI}}(\mathbf{y}), & y_{\max} &= \max_{\mathbf{y} \in \text{RoI}}(\mathbf{y}).
\end{aligned}
\tag{1}
$$

The vector $(dx, dy)^T$ is a confident margin for the target displacement. This margin may be estimated based on the interframe motion of the target. It can be assumed constant, if the speed of aircraft is approximately uniform. In our simulations, we consider the confident margin as $(20, 20)$.

To determine the initial location of the contour in frame t, a parametric, unimodal Gaussian model is considered to represent color distribution of the target in RGB space. The color distribution of the target is represented by a multivariate SGM as

$$
p^t\left(\mathbf{F}^t(\mathbf{x})\right) = N\left(\mathbf{F}^t(\mathbf{x}); \boldsymbol{\mu}^{t-1}(\mathbf{x}); \boldsymbol{\Sigma}^{t-1}(\mathbf{x})\right), \tag{2}
$$

where $\mathbf{F}^t(\mathbf{x}) = [\mathbf{F}_R^t(\mathbf{x}), \mathbf{F}_G^t(\mathbf{x}), \mathbf{F}_B^t(\mathbf{x})]^T$ is the color vector, t is the frame index, $\mathbf{x}$ defines pixels coordinates, and the N function represents a multivariate normal distribution as follows:

$$
\begin{aligned}
& N\left(\mathbf{F}^t(\mathbf{x}); \boldsymbol{\mu}^{t-1}(\mathbf{x}); \boldsymbol{\Sigma}^{t-1}(\mathbf{x})\right) \\
& = c \exp\left(-\frac{1}{2}\left(\mathbf{F}^t(\mathbf{x}) - \boldsymbol{\mu}^{t-1}(\mathbf{x})\right)^T\right. \\
& \qquad \left. \times\left(\boldsymbol{\Sigma}^{t-1}(\mathbf{x})\right)^{-1}\left(\mathbf{F}^t(\mathbf{x}) - \boldsymbol{\mu}^{t-1}(\mathbf{x})\right)\right), \tag{3}
\end{aligned}
$$

$$
c = \frac{1}{\left((2\pi)^{d/2}\left|\boldsymbol{\Sigma}^{t-1}(\mathbf{x})\right|^{1/2}\right)}.
$$

Here d is the dimension of the color space, which is assumed to be 3 for RGB color space. The mean vector $\boldsymbol{\mu}^{t-1}(\mathbf{x})$ and covariance matrix $\boldsymbol{\Sigma}^{t-1}(\mathbf{x})$ are determined by the color

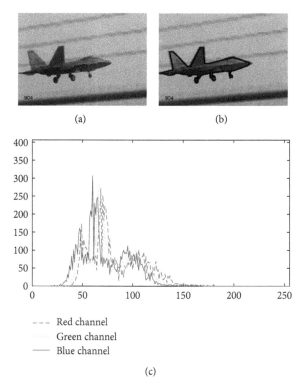

(a)   (b)

(c)

--- Red channel
..... Green channel
— Blue channel

FIGURE 3: Determining initial target contour manually: (a) an initial key frame, (b) target contour determined manually, and (c) histograms of color channels for ROI.

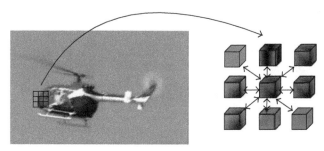

FIGURE 4: Moore 9-neighborhood for a typical snaxel.

information of pixels located inside the contour of the target in the frame $t - 1$ as

$$R = \left[\mathbf{F}_R^{t-1}(\mathbf{x}_1), \ldots, \mathbf{F}_R^{t-1}(\mathbf{x}_N) \right]^T,$$

$$G = \left[\mathbf{F}_G^{t-1}(\mathbf{x}_1), \ldots, \mathbf{F}_G^{t-1}(\mathbf{x}_N) \right]^T,$$

$$B = \left[\mathbf{F}_B^{t-1}(\mathbf{x}_1), \ldots, \mathbf{F}_B^{t-1}(\mathbf{x}_N) \right]^T,$$

$$\boldsymbol{\mu}^{t-1}(\mathbf{x}) = \begin{pmatrix} \mu_R \\ \mu_G \\ \mu_B \end{pmatrix}, \qquad \boldsymbol{\Sigma}^{t-1}(\mathbf{x}) = \begin{pmatrix} \sigma_R^2 & \sigma_{RG} & \sigma_{RB} \\ \sigma_{RG} & \sigma_G^2 & \sigma_{GB} \\ \sigma_{RB} & \sigma_{GB} & \sigma_B^2 \end{pmatrix}.$$

$$(4)$$

The initial location of the target contour in the current frame is determined using a color matching algorithm. The algorithm includes the following stages.

(1) Determine the color matching threshold, T_C, by means of prior color distribution as

$$T_C = \frac{\xi}{255} \left\lceil 255 \max \left(\boldsymbol{\lambda}^{1/2} \right) \right\rceil, \qquad \boldsymbol{\lambda} = \text{diag} \left(\boldsymbol{\Sigma}^{t-1}(\mathbf{x}) \right), \quad (5)$$

where the parameter ξ is a constant number in the range of $[0, 1]$, and the vector $\boldsymbol{\lambda}$ includes the diagonal elements of matrix $\boldsymbol{\Sigma}^{t-1}(\mathbf{x})$. The notation $\lceil \cdot \rceil$ denotes the ceiling function.

(2) Determine pixel color consistency for all pixels in SR in the current frame by measuring the Mahalanobis distance:

$$D_M(\mathbf{x}) = \left(\left(\mathbf{F}^t(\mathbf{x}) - \boldsymbol{\mu}^{t-1} \right)^T \left(\boldsymbol{\Sigma}^{t-1} \right)^{-1} \left(\mathbf{F}^t(\mathbf{x}) - \boldsymbol{\mu}^{t-1} \right) \right)^{1/2},$$

$$\mathbf{x} \in \text{SR}. \quad (6)$$

(3) Constitute binary color consistency image I_{CC}, by applying a threshold on $D_M(\mathbf{x})$:

$$I_{CC}(\mathbf{x}) = \begin{cases} 1, & D_M(\mathbf{x}) < T_C, \\ 0, & o.w., \end{cases} \quad (7)$$

where "1" values show image pixels, which are consistent with target color distribution.

(4) Suppress small regions in I_{CC} by applying a size-filtering algorithm. In the size filtering, distinct patches that have an area less than the threshold, T_A, are omitted:

$$T_A = \lceil \delta \cdot (h \times w) \rceil, \quad (8)$$

in which the factor δ is equal to 0.01, and the parameters h and w denote the height and width of SR, respectively.

(5) Extract the outer boundary of consistent pixel in I_{CC} as the initial contour position in the current frame. The final contour of the target is determined using 2D active contour model.

2.2. Active Contour Energy. The active contour model in the search region is considered as a closed contour with n-ordered snaxels, $\mathbf{V} = [\mathbf{v}_0, \ldots, \mathbf{v}_{n-1}]$, in which $\mathbf{v}_i = (x_i \quad y_i)^T$ denotes the ith control point or snaxel. The contour energy

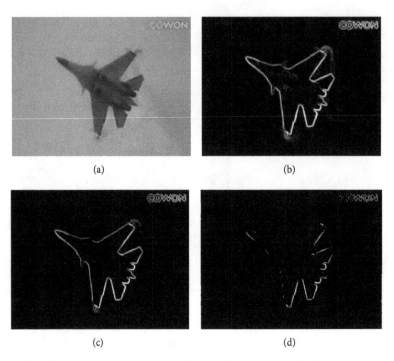

FIGURE 5: Edge energy function for different T_G values. (a) Original frame, (b) edge energy for $T_G = 0$, (c) edge energy for $T_G = 0.2$, and (d) edge energy for $T_G = 0.5$.

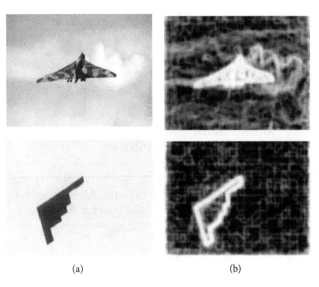

FIGURE 6: Color entropy of sample aircraft images. (a) Original images frames, (b) color entropy images.

in the active contour model is defined as the sum of energy functions for different snaxels of the contour:

$$E_{\text{contour}} = \sum_{i=0}^{n-1} E_{\text{contour}}\left(\mathbf{v}_i\right).$$ (9)

The snaxel energy consists of two parts including internal and external energies:

$$E_{\text{contour}}\left(\mathbf{v}_i\right) = E_{\text{internal}}\left(\mathbf{v}_i\right) + E_{\text{external}}\left(\mathbf{v}_i\right).$$ (10)

The internal energy function defines shape characteristics of the contour and is defined using the following [23]:

$$E_{\text{internal}}\left(\mathbf{v}_i\right) = E_{\text{co}}\left(\mathbf{v}_i\right) + E_{\text{cu}}\left(\mathbf{v}_i\right),$$ (11)

where $E_{\text{co}}(\mathbf{v}_i)$ and $E_{\text{cu}}(\mathbf{v}_i)$ are the normalized continuity and curvature energies for the snaxel $\mathbf{v}_i$, respectively. The continuity and curvature energy functions are defined as

$$E_{\text{co}}\left(\mathbf{v}_i\right) = \frac{\widetilde{E}_{\text{co}}\left(\mathbf{v}_i\right) - \min_{\mathbf{v}\in M}\left(\widetilde{E}_{\text{co}}\left(\mathbf{v}\right)\right)}{\max_{\mathbf{v}\in M}\left(\widetilde{E}_{\text{co}}\left(\mathbf{v}\right)\right) - \min_{\mathbf{v}\in M}\left(\widetilde{E}_{\text{co}}\left(\mathbf{v}\right)\right)},$$

$$\widetilde{E}_{\text{co}}\left(\mathbf{v}_i\right) = \left(\overline{h} - \left|\mathbf{v}_i - \mathbf{v}_{i-1}\right|\right)^2,$$

$$E_{\text{cu}}\left(\mathbf{v}_i\right) = \frac{\widetilde{E}_{\text{cu}}\left(\mathbf{v}_i\right) - \min_{\mathbf{v}\in M}\left(\widetilde{E}_{\text{cu}}\left(\mathbf{v}\right)\right)}{\max_{\mathbf{v}\in M}\left(\widetilde{E}_{\text{cu}}\left(\mathbf{v}\right)\right) - \min_{\mathbf{v}\in M}\left(\widetilde{E}_{\text{cu}}\left(\mathbf{v}\right)\right)},$$ (12)

$$\widetilde{E}_{\text{cu}}\left(\mathbf{v}_i\right) = \left|\left(\mathbf{v}_{i+1} - 2\mathbf{v}_i + \mathbf{v}_{i-1}\right)\right|^2.$$

Here, the domain M describes Moore 9-neighborhood as shown in Figure 4, and the parameter $\overline{h}$ is the average distance between two neighboring snaxels. The parameter is updated at the beginning of each epoch of energy minimization routine.

We define the external energy function based on image features such as edge, color, and texture to cope with the problem of large aspect change. Therefore, the external energy function for snaxel $\mathbf{v}_i$ is defined as

$$E_{\text{external}}\left(\mathbf{v}_i\right) = E_{\text{ed}}\left(\mathbf{v}_i\right) + E_{\text{si}}\left(\mathbf{v}_i\right) + E_{\text{te}}\left(\mathbf{v}_i\right).$$ (13)

The first term of external energy represents the edge energy. The edge energy attracts the target contour toward pixels with

```
(1) For Iter = 1 to Iter_max = 5
(2) For i = 0 to n − 1
        (i) Select ith snaxel of the deformable contour.
        (ii) Calculate energy function for the ith snaxel and its Moore 9-neighborhood.
        (iii) Find location with minimum energy if there is only one local minimum in Moore 9-neighborhood. Otherwise,
            find the point with shortest path. The path is measured based on Euclidian distance.
    End for i.
(3) Move snaxels to new locations.
(4) Apply the proposed GoL cellular automaton as it will be explained in the next subsection.
(5) Update characteristics of deformable contour including coordinates of new control points as well as the number of existing
        snaxels, n.
End for Iter.
```

PSEUDOCODE 1: The pseudo code for energy minimization algorithm and the proposed GoL cellular automaton.

TABLE 1: The probability of tracking error in terms of percent for four different approaches.

Video samples of MAVDB database	The proposed method		Method of [11]		Method of [17]		Method of [18]	
	AA	CM	AA	CM	AA	CM	AA	CM
Video number 2 (Figure 11(f))	6.42	0.49	12	0.71	10	0.45	7.33	0.42
Video number 16 (Figure 14(d))	25.07	0.98	5	0.36	6.5	0.16	6	0.22
Video number 33 (Figure 11(k))	3.17	0.34	12.65	0.92	33.3	1.4	45	1.56
Video number 46 (Figure 11(i))	7.26	0.55	30	1.8	23	0.89	16.4	0.77
Total videos	13.37	0.87	31.14	2.72	23.8	1.75	19.1	1.09

strong edges or pixels with large image gradients. In order to neglect noisy or weak edges, we define edge energy as

$$E_{\text{ed}}(\mathbf{v}_i) = \begin{cases} -\widetilde{E}_{\text{gr}}(\mathbf{v}_i), & \widetilde{E}_{\text{gr}}(\mathbf{v}_i) > T_G, \\ 0, & \widetilde{E}_{\text{gr}}(\mathbf{v}_i) \le T_G, \end{cases} \quad (14)$$

where $\widetilde{E}_{\text{gr}}(\mathbf{v}_i)$ defines the color gradient at the snaxel $\mathbf{v}_i$ and the gradient threshold $T_G = 0.2$ is employed to remove weak edges. To calculate color gradient, different color channels, $\mathbf{F}_L^t(\mathbf{x})$, for all $L \in \{R, G, B\}$, are smoothed using 2D Gaussian kernel, and image derivatives in x and y directions are calculated using Sobel operators. Then, we calculate the parameters of the color gradient as follows [24]:

$$g_{xx} = \left| \frac{\partial \mathbf{F}_R^t(\mathbf{x})}{\partial x} \right|^2 + \left| \frac{\partial \mathbf{F}_G^t(\mathbf{x})}{\partial x} \right|^2 + \left| \frac{\partial \mathbf{F}_B^t(\mathbf{x})}{\partial x} \right|^2,$$

$$g_{yy} = \left| \frac{\partial \mathbf{F}_R^t(\mathbf{x})}{\partial y} \right|^2 + \left| \frac{\partial \mathbf{F}_G^t(\mathbf{x})}{\partial y} \right|^2 + \left| \frac{\partial \mathbf{F}_B^t(\mathbf{x})}{\partial y} \right|^2,$$

$$g_{xy} = \frac{\partial \mathbf{F}_R^t(\mathbf{x})}{\partial x} \cdot \frac{\partial \mathbf{F}_R^t(\mathbf{x})}{\partial y} + \frac{\partial \mathbf{F}_G^t(\mathbf{x})}{\partial x} \cdot \frac{\partial \mathbf{F}_G^t(\mathbf{x})}{\partial y} \quad (15)$$

$$+ \frac{\partial \mathbf{F}_B^t(\mathbf{x})}{\partial x} \cdot \frac{\partial \mathbf{F}_B^t(\mathbf{x})}{\partial y},$$

$$\phi_1 = \frac{1}{2} \tan^{-1}\left(\frac{2g_{xy}}{g_{xx} - g_{yy}} \right), \qquad \phi_2 = \phi_1 + \frac{\pi}{2},$$

where $\partial \mathbf{F}_L^t(\mathbf{x})/\partial x$ and $\partial \mathbf{F}_L^t(\mathbf{x})/\partial y$, for all $L \in \{R, G, B\}$ define the derivatives of color components and φ_k, for all $k \in \{1, 2\}$ represents gradients directions.

We define normalized gradient energy, $\widetilde{E}_{\text{gr}}(\mathbf{v}_i)$, as

$$E_k' = \left(0.5 \left(\left(g_{xx} + g_{yy} \right) + \left(g_{xx} - g_{yy} \right) \cos\left(2\phi_k \right) \right. \right.$$

$$\left. \left. + 2g_{xy} \sin\left(2\phi_k \right) \right) \right), \quad \forall k \in \{1, 2\},$$

$$E_{\text{gr}}' = \max\left\{ E_1', E_2' \right\}, \quad (16)$$

$$\widetilde{E}_{\text{gr}}(\mathbf{v}_i) = \frac{E_{\text{gr}}'(\mathbf{v}_i) - \min_{\mathbf{v} \in M}\left(E_{\text{gr}}'(\mathbf{v}) \right)}{\max_{\mathbf{v} \in M}\left(E_{\text{gr}}'(\mathbf{v}) \right) - \min_{\mathbf{v} \in M}\left(E_{\text{gr}}'(\mathbf{v}) \right)}.$$

Figure 5 illustrates the results of the calculated edge energy image for different T_G values.

The second term of the external energy is the similarity energy, E_{si}. We define the similarity energy to attract a snaxel toward an image location with the same color distribution of the snaxel in the previous frame. To measure the similarity, the Mahalanobis distance in RGB color space is employed. We utilize the snaxel $\mathbf{v}_i$ and its Moore 9-neighborhood to calculate the color distribution of the snaxel. For the control point $\mathbf{v}_i$, the normalized similarity energy is obtained as

$$E_{\text{si}}(\mathbf{v}_i) = \frac{\widetilde{E}_{\text{si}}(\mathbf{v}_i) - \min_{\mathbf{v} \in M}\left(\widetilde{E}_{\text{si}}(\mathbf{v}) \right)}{\max_{\mathbf{v} \in M}\left(\widetilde{E}_{\text{si}}(\mathbf{v}) \right) - \min_{\mathbf{v} \in M}\left(\widetilde{E}_{\text{si}}(\mathbf{v}) \right)}, \quad (17)$$

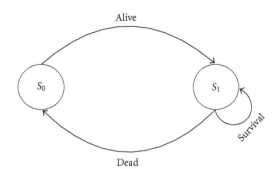

FIGURE 7: The state diagram of the proposed GoL cellular automaton.

where $\widetilde{E}_{si}(\mathbf{v}_i)$ is defined as

$$\widetilde{E}_{si}\left(\mathbf{v}_i\right) = \left(\left(\mathbf{F}^t\left(\mathbf{v}_i\right) - \boldsymbol{\mu}^{t-1}\right)^T\left(\boldsymbol{\Sigma}^{t-1}\right)^{-1}\left(\mathbf{F}^t\left(\mathbf{v}_i\right) - \boldsymbol{\mu}^{t-1}\right)\right)^{1/2}. \tag{18}$$

The third term of external energy, which is called texture energy, employs image texture to define energy function. This energy is based on the entropy of color channels. The entropy is a method to measure the content of information. Pixels in the target boundary have higher information content or entropy in comparison with pixels located inside the target or sky background in SR. Therefore, by utilizing the texture energy we aim at attracting contour snaxels toward points with higher information content.

To measure texture energy, we first calculate the entropy for each individual color channel using the following equation:

$$\mathbf{H}_L = \sum_{i=0}^{k-1} P_L\left(I_L^i\right) \log_2\left(\frac{1}{P_L\left(I_L^i\right)}\right), \quad \forall L \in \{R, G, B\}, \tag{19}$$

where I_L^i is a random variable representing ith intensity level in color channel L, and P_L denotes its probability mass function for color channel L which is determined using image histogram in Moore 9- neighborhood.

The normalized texture energy based on the entropy of color channels, for the snaxel $\mathbf{v}_i$, is defined as

$$E_{te}\left(\mathbf{v}_i\right) = \frac{\widetilde{E}_{te}\left(\mathbf{v}_i\right) - \min_{\mathbf{v}\in M}\left(\widetilde{E}_{te}\left(\mathbf{v}\right)\right)}{\max_{\mathbf{v}\in M}\left(\widetilde{E}_{te}\left(\mathbf{v}\right)\right) - \min_{\mathbf{v}\in M}\left(\widetilde{E}_{te}\left(\mathbf{v}\right)\right)}, \tag{20}$$

where color entropy image $\widetilde{E}_{te}(\mathbf{v}_i)$ is obtained as

$$\widetilde{E}_{te}\left(\mathbf{v}_i\right) = -\left(\mathbf{H}_R\left(\mathbf{v}_i\right) + \mathbf{H}_G\left(\mathbf{v}_i\right) + \mathbf{H}_B\left(\mathbf{v}_i\right)\right). \tag{21}$$

Here $\mathbf{H}_R(\mathbf{v}_i)$, $\mathbf{H}_G(\mathbf{v}_i)$, and $\mathbf{H}_B(\mathbf{v}_i)$ denote the entropy of R, G, and B color channels, respectively. The minus sign in (21) is used to minimize the texture energy in the areas with high information content.

Figure 6 illustrates two typical aircraft images and their color entropy images. As it is shown in the figure, the target area and its boundary reveal higher entropy values.

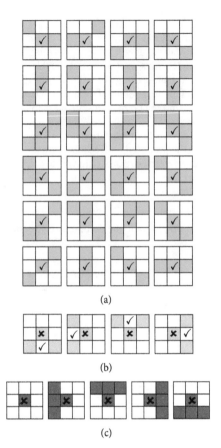

FIGURE 8: Defined structures and rules for the proposed GOL. (a) Continuance of life structures, (b) death and birth rules, and (c) death structures. Symbols √ and ✗ represent life and death at the next generation.

2.3. Energy Minimization. After defining energy function for the active contour, the objective energy function defined in (9) is minimized iteratively by means of a constrained greedy optimization routine in order to fit the deformable contour on the target precisely. Here, the constrained term denotes a set of conditions, which are applied during the minimization algorithm. The pseudocode of energy minimization procedure is given in Pseudocode 1 in which we apply the proposed GoL cellular automaton after each epoch of energy minimization algorithm.

2.4. Game-of-Life-Based Snaxel Updating. Both target and camera motion like 3D rotation and translation and zooming by the video camera result in changing shape and outer boundary of the aircraft. It is obvious that dynamic motion of snaxels toward the outer boundary of aircraft due to energy minimization routine causes some irregular deformation in the contour. Consequently, the number of control points should be changed. To regularize and smooth snaxels of the contour after energy minimization, we propose a GoL cellular automaton.

GoL cellular automata are substantially a type of two dimensional cellular automata [25]. Fundamentally,

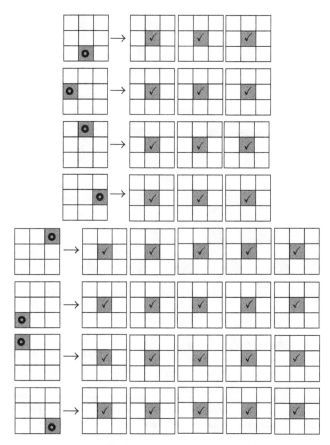

FIGURE 9: The rule of birth in the proposed GoL cellular automaton. The symbol ○ denotes cell that should be checked independently.

automata are simple agents with three main features including uniformity, synchronicity, and locality. Different cellular automata follow special rules to gain a distinct goal. Here, we design a set of rules for GoL to handle changes in snaxels of active contour model. According to the defined rules in the proposed automaton, some of snaxels, that is, alive cells, may be dead or remain without any change during evolution. It is also possible to create some new snaxels in the next generation. In the proposed cellular automaton, the neighborhood radius, r, is set to 1 with the 8-cell Moore neighborhood, and the number of generations, g, is considered to be 7. We consider two states, $N_Q = 2$, with the set of states $Q = \{S_0, S_1\}$, in which the states S_0 and S_1 represent dead and alive cells, respectively. Figure 7 shows the state diagram of the proposed cellular automaton. In the proposed GoL cellular automaton, the next state of a snaxel is determined based on the following rules.

(i) The rule of continuance of life: a live central cell will survive if its Moore 8-neighborhood is matched with one of the states in Figure 8(a).

(ii) The rule of death and birth: a live central cell dies, and its adjacent dead cell that is located between two alive cells becomes alive at the next generation when a correspondence to one of the states in Figure 8(b) is found.

(iii) The rule of death: a live central cell becomes dead if its Moore 8-neighborhood is matched with one of the states in Figure 8(c).

(iv) The rule of birth: a boundary dead cell with a live central cell that itself has one alive cell in its Moore 8-neighborhood will be checked for alive state. In this case, we check Moore 8-neighborhood of the dead cell; in the case of a match with one of the structures in Figure 9, the central dead cell is marked as alive in the next generation.

It is important to note that the total number of possible structure, N_s, for $N_Q = 2$, $r = 1$, and the Moore 9-neighborhood is determined as

$$N_s = \sum_{i=0}^{9} \binom{9}{i} \equiv N_Q^{(2r+1)^2} = 512. \tag{22}$$

In 2D active contour domain, it is not necessary to consider all the structure. Therefore, we define rules for only necessary structures.

Figure 10 shows simulation results for five initial states up to 6 generations. The results demonstrate that after maximum 4 generations, snaxels are stable. The cellular automaton in the first row of Figure 10 represents an ideal case for a contour whose shape is preserved during evolution; whereas other cellular automata have some irregularity and discontinuity because of the energy minimization algorithm. These contours are smoothed and regularized using the proposed GoL cellular automaton.

3. Experimental Results

The proposed FVT algorithm was implemented using a MATLAB program and tested using a Pentium-IV desktop Personal Computer (PC) with 2.8 GHz CPU and 512 MB RAM. For maneuvering aircraft tracking purposes, we provided an informative dataset called Maneuvering Aircraft Video DataBase (MAVDB). The database includes 72 video clips captured by diverse monocular, moving CCD camcorders. The dataset is freely available for academic application. Time duration of different videos in MAVDB varies from 1.2 s to 51.64 s with the frame rate of 15 Hz or 30 Hz. MAVDB include maneuvering targets in different conditions such as large aspect change, 3D rotation around different axis, targets with change in size, rigid or piecewise rigid flying vehicles, smoky aircrafts, cloudy atmospheric conditions, and illumination change.

Due to the presence of a relative similarity between noise and rain drops and/or ice crystals, we added Gaussian as well as salt and pepper noises to some video streams to simulate different atmospheric conditions especially rainy and snowy situations.

In Figure 11, the results of the proposed FVT algorithm on eleven sample video clips of MAVDB are shown.

Figure 12 depicts results of the proposed method on three noisy video clips. In Figures 12(a) and 12(b), we test our FVT under additive white Gaussian noise (AWGN) with normal distributions of $N(0, 0.01)$ and $N(0, 0.001)$,

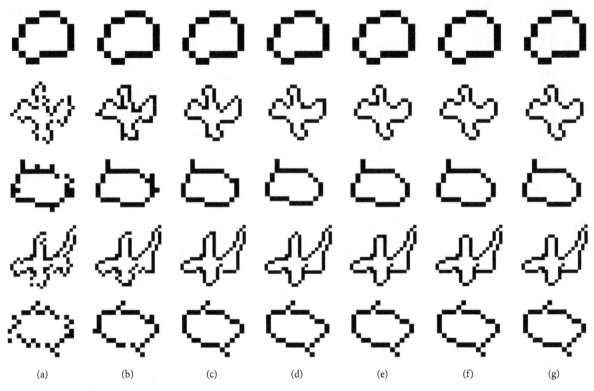

(a)   (b)   (c)   (d)   (e)   (f)   (g)

FIGURE 10: Simulation results of applying the proposed GoL cellular automaton on five initial states, (a) initial state which is obtained from energy minimization step, (b) the result of the first generation, (c) the result of the second generation, (d) the result of the third generation, (e) the result of the fourth generation, (f) the result of the fifth generation, and (g) the result of the sixth generation.

respectively. Figure 12(c) shows the results of the proposed tracking algorithm for video sequence with 12.5% additive salt and pepper noise (ASPN). The video sequence of Figure 12(a) shows a smoky fighter jet with maneuvering motion, and Figure 12(b) is a synthetic airplane video with large aspect change. In Figure 13, we have also plotted the trajectory for the true centroid (center of gravity (CoG)) and the tracked CoG of the target in Figure 12(a). These results demonstrate the robustness of our method in noisy video sequences.

Figure 14 depicts the results of the proposed FVT approach on four videos of MAVDB that seem to be more challenging than other videos. In the video sequences of Figure 14(a), a relatively abrupt change in statistical characteristics of color distribution exists. Figure 14(b) shows video sequence of a helicopter with two dominant red and black colors. In video sequence of Figure 14(c), the direct sunlight changes and saturates the intensity values for some parts of the target. The background of the video is also changed to be cloudy in some frames. Figure 14(d) shows the video sequence of an aircraft with textured surface. Obviously, in such situations, the probability of the tracking error increases and target contour fluctuates during tracking process. However instabilities are controlled and compensated because of the dynamic structure of the proposed tracking method as it is shown in Figure 14(d).

In order to measure the performance of the proposed FVT algorithm, we have measured the expected probability of the tracking error using two different methods based on

pixel-based performance evaluation (PE) algorithm. For this purpose, two criteria are considered and measured including alignment amount (AA) and confusion matrix (CM).

In order to measure the performance based on the AA criterion, we have defined the probability of error for a video frame as

$$P\,(\text{error}) = 1 - \frac{\bigcap_{i=1}^{2} \mathbf{F}_i}{\bigcup_{i=1}^{2} \mathbf{F}_i}, \tag{23}$$

where $\mathbf{F}_1$ and $\mathbf{F}_2$ are ground truth (GT) and predicted result (PR) frames, respectively. Therefore, in a video clip containing N_f frames, the mean error is calculated as follows:

$$\mu_e = E\,\{P\,(\text{error})\}$$
$$= 1 - \frac{1}{N_f} \sum_{n=1}^{N_f} \frac{P\,(\text{GT}_n, \text{PR}_n)}{P\,(\text{GT}_n) + P\,(\text{PR}_n) - P\,(\text{GT}_n, \text{PR}_n)}, \tag{24}$$

where the operator $E\{\cdot\}$ denotes the mathematical expectation.

The second performance evaluation method is based on a 2×2 confusion matrix, $\mathbf{C}$. To evaluate performance in a frame in this method, we construct the confusion matrix as follows:

$$\mathbf{C} = \begin{pmatrix} P\,(\text{OB}\mid\text{OB}) & P\,(\text{NO}\mid\text{OB}) \\ P\,(\text{OB}\mid\text{NO}) & P\,(\text{NO}\mid\text{NO}) \end{pmatrix} = \begin{pmatrix} \text{TP} & \text{FN} \\ \text{FP} & \text{TN} \end{pmatrix}, \tag{25}$$

where the notations OB and NO stand for object and non-object, respectively, and the elements TP, FP, FN, and TN

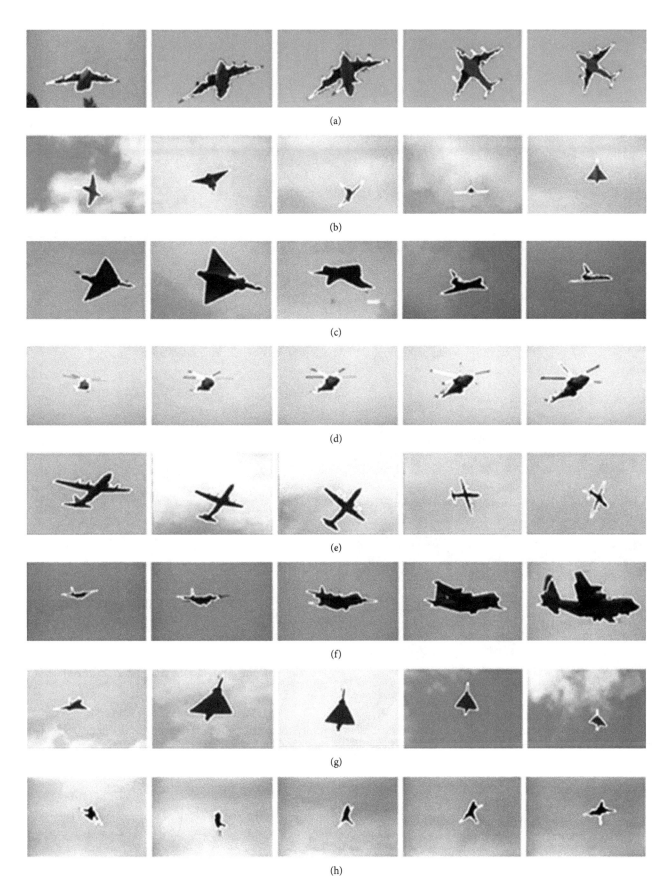

FIGURE 11: Continued.

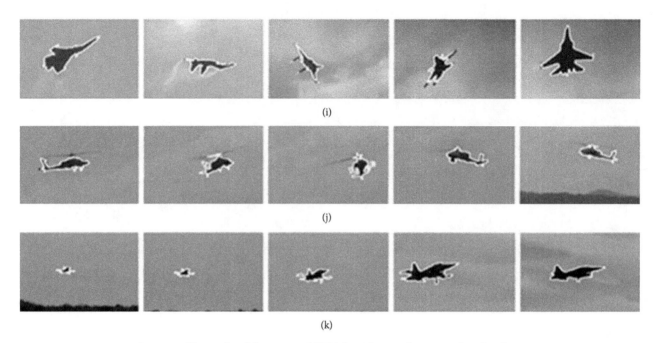

(i)

(j)

(k)

FIGURE 11: The results of the proposed FVT algorithm on eleven sample video clips.

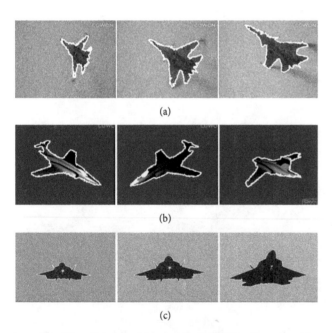

(a)

(b)

(c)

FIGURE 12: The efficiency of the proposed algorithm for noisy video sequences, (a) video clip with AWGN of $N(0, 0.01)$, (b) video clip with AWGN of $N(0, 0.001)$, and (c) video clip with ASPN and the density of 12.5%.

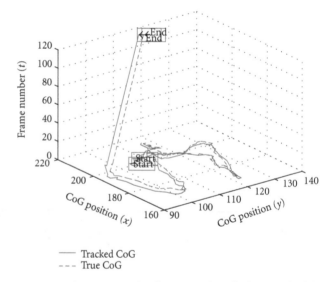

FIGURE 13: The trajectory for the true and tracked centroid of the video clip in Figure 12(a).

stand for true positive, false positive, false negative and true negative, respectively. In performance evaluation based on the confusion matrix, the expected probability of error for a video clip including N_f frames is determined as

$$\mu_e = E\{P(\text{error})\} = 1 - \frac{\sum_{i=1}^2 \mathbf{C}_t(i,i)}{\sum_{i=1}^2 \sum_{j=1}^2 \mathbf{C}_t(i,j)}, \quad (26)$$

where the total confusion matrix, $\mathbf{C}_t$, is calculated by using the following equation:

$$\mathbf{C}_t = \frac{1}{N_f \cdot (h_v \times w_v)} \cdot \begin{pmatrix} \sum_{n=1}^{N_f} \text{TP}_n & \sum_{n=1}^{N_f} \text{FN}_n \\ \sum_{n=1}^{N_f} \text{FP}_n & \sum_{n=1}^{N_f} \text{TN}_n \end{pmatrix}. \quad (27)$$

In the above equation h_v and w_v are the height and width of the video frames.

Figure 15 exemplifies the method to determine GT and PR in a typical video frame in order to measure the performance

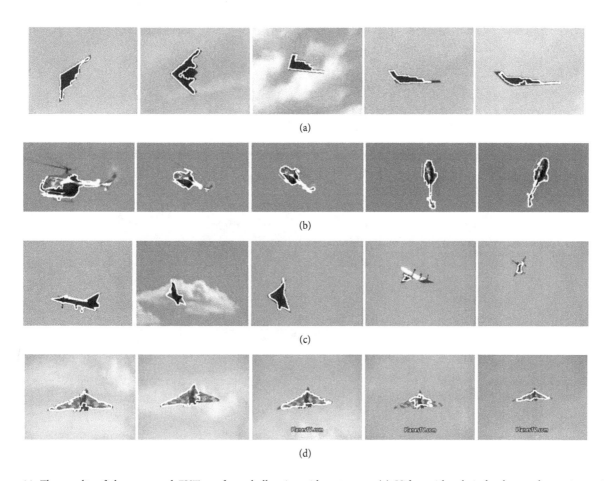

FIGURE 14: The results of the proposed FVT on four challenging video streams. (a) Video with relatively abrupt change in statistical characteristics of color distribution, (b) video sequence of a helicopter with two dominant red and black colors, (c) video with the direct sunlight which changes and saturates the intensity values for some parts of the target, and (d) video sequences of an aircraft with textured surface.

for both AA and CM methods. Considering high volume of frames in database, we calculate GT and PR with the interval of 10 frames in our experiments. Figure 16 illustrates the probability of error in terms of frame number for video streams shown in Figure 14(d) for $\xi = 0.13$. As it is shown in this figure, both curves show that the probability of error is not accumulative and is controlled during the tracking process. Figure 17 shows the expected probability of error in terms of ξ for video sequences shown in Figure 14(d).

To compare the results of the proposed algorithm with those of other methods, we also implemented the active contour method by Williams and Shah [11], parametric active contour method by Lee et al. [17], and the method presented by Torkan and Behrad [18, 19]. We implemented and tested different methods using the collected MAVDB dataset. Table 1 shows the expected probability of tracking error for different implemented algorithms using AA and CM methods. Table 1 shows that the expected probability of errors for the proposed algorithm using all videos in database are 13.37% and 0.87%, based on AA and CM methods, respectively. The table shows that the proposed algorithm has enhanced the accuracy up to 17.77% and 1.85% based on AA and CM methods, respectively.

4. Conclusions

In this paper, we presented a new algorithm for visual maneuvering aircraft tracking in sky based on the deformable contour model in color video sequences. The main aim of the algorithm is to cope with the maneuvering motion and large aspect change of targets stemmed from 3-D rotation of targets in sky or camera. Furthermore, we examined other challenging issues like noisy streams, different atmospheric conditions, and smoky aircraft. To test the proposed algorithm, we collected different video clips in a dataset called MAVDB. We implemented some existing method and tested the algorithm with the collected dataset. To evaluate performance of the proposed method, we measured the probability of tracking error based on two AA and CM criteria. The experimental results demonstrated that the proposed algorithm has reduced the probability of tracking error considerably. In error analysis for the proposed method, we perceived that, during tracking, most of the errors originated from changing the texture of target and its background. Fortunately, the dynamic update strategy in the proposed tracking method

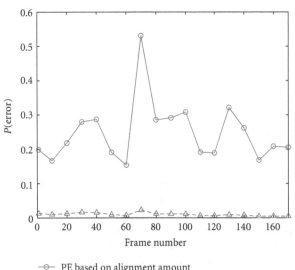

FIGURE 15: Calculation of PR and GT images. (a) Original frame, (b) GT of the original frame, (c) the contour obtained using the proposed FVT algorithm, and (d) the calculated PR image.

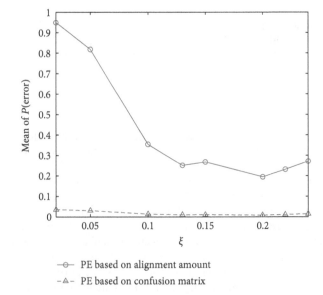

FIGURE 16: The plot of the probability of error in terms of frame number for video streams shown in Figure 14(d).

FIGURE 17: The plot of the expected probability of error in terms of ξ for video sequences shown in Figure 14(d).

Acknowledgment

The authors would like to sincerely thank A. Taimori, Ph.D. candidate of System Communication in the Tehran Science and Research Branch, Islamic Azad University, Iran, for his valuable suggestions that have helped the to improve the quality of this paper.

controls errors and prevent error accumulation as shown in Figure 14. For future works, we are going to focus on some other challenging issues such as occlusion, complex, and cluttered background, which may occur during take-off and landing.

References

[1] A. Taimori and S. Sabouri, "Vision based flying vehicle tracking," in *Proceedings of the IEEE International Conference on Systems, Man and Cybernetics (SMC '08)*, pp. 330–335, Singapore, October 2008.

[2] A. Taimori, A. Behrad, and S. Sabouri, "A new scheme for vision based flying vehicle detection using motion flow vectors classification," in *Proceedings of the 9th International Conference on Intelligent Systems Design and Applications (ISDA '09)*, pp. 175–180, Pisa, Italy, December 2009.

[3] J. Ha, C. Alvino, G. Pryor, M. Niethammer, E. Johnson, and A. Tannenbaum, "Active contours and optical flow for automatic tracking of flying vehicles," in *Proceedings of the American Control Conference (AAC '04)*, pp. 3441–3446, July 2004.

[4] S. Haker, G. Sapiro, A. Tannenbaum, and D. Washburn, "Missile tracking using knowledge-based adaptive thresholding," in *Proceedings of the IEEE International Conference on Image Processing (ICIP '01)*, pp. 786–789, October 2001.

[5] J. D. Redding, T. W. McLain, R. W. Beard, and C. N. Taylor, "Vision-based target localization from a fixed-wing miniature air vehicle," in *Proceedings of the American Control Conference (AAC '06)*, pp. 2862–2867, June 2006.

[6] J. J. Kehoe, R. S. Causey, A. Arvai, and R. Lind, "Partial aircraft state estimation from optical flow using non-model-based optimization," in *Proceedings of the American Control Conference (AAC '06)*, pp. 2868–2873, June 2006.

[7] Y. Jianchao, "A new scheme of vision based navigation for flying vehicles—concept study and experiment evaluation," in *Proceedings of the 7th International Conference on Control, Automation, Robotics and Vision (ICARC '02)*, pp. 643–648, December 2002.

[8] A. Betser, P. Vela, and A. Tannenbaum, "Automatic tracking of flying vehicles using geodesic snakes and kalman filtering," in *Proceedings of the 43rd IEEE Conference on Decision and Control (CDC '04)*, pp. 1649–1654, December 2004.

[9] M. Kass, A. Witkin, and D. Terzopoulos, "Snakes: active contour models," *International Journal of Computer Vision*, vol. 1, no. 4, pp. 321–331, 1989.

[10] B. Jamasbi, S. A. Motamedi, and A. Behrad, "Contour tracking of targets with large aspect change," *Journal of Multimedia*, vol. 2, no. 6, pp. 7–14, 2007.

[11] D. J. Williams and M. Shah, "A fast algorithm for active contours and curvature estimation," *CVGIP: Image Understanding*, vol. 55, no. 1, pp. 14–26, 1992.

[12] Y. Wang and O. Lee, "Active mesh—a feature seeking and tracking image sequence representation scheme," *IEEE Transactions on Image Processing*, vol. 3, no. 5, pp. 610–624, 1994.

[13] A. Yilmaz, "Object tracking by asymmetric kernel mean shift with automatic scale and orientation selection," in *Proceedings of the IEEE Computer Society Conference on Computer Vision and Pattern Recognition (CVPR '07)*, Minneapolis, Minn, USA, June 2007.

[14] D. Molloy and P. F. Whelan, "Active-Meshes," *Pattern Recognition Letters*, vol. 21, pp. 1071–1080, 2000.

[15] C. Jian and Y. Jie, "Real-time infrared object tracking based on mean shift," in *Proceedings of the 9th Iberoamerican Congress on Pattern Recognition (CIARP '04)*, pp. 45–52, Puebla, Mexico, 2004.

[16] A. Behrad and S. Ahmad Motamedi, "Moving target detection and tracking using edge features detection and matching,"

[17] B. H. Lee, I. Choi, and G. J. Jeon, "Motion-based boundary tracking of moving object using parametric active contour model," *IEICE Transactions on Information and Systems*, vol. E90-D, no. 1, pp. 355–363, 2007.

[18] S. Torkan and A. Behrad, "A new contour based tracking algorithm using improved greedy snake," in *18th Iranian Conference on Electrical Engineering (ICEE '10)*, pp. 150–155, Isfahan, Iran, May 2010.

[19] S. Torkan, *Aerial target tracking using energy minimization methods [M.S. thesis]*, Malek-e-Ashtar University of Technology, 2009.

[20] A. Verri and T. Poggio, "Motion field and optical flow: qualitative properties," *IEEE Transactions on Pattern Analysis and Machine Intelligence*, vol. v, pp. 490–498, 1992.

[21] G. Bradski and A. Kaehler, *Learning OpenCV*, O'Reilly Media, 2008.

[22] A. Yilmaz, O. Javed, and M. Shah, "Object tracking: a survey," *ACM Computing Surveys*, vol. 38, no. 4, 2006.

[23] E. Trucco and A. Verri, *Introductory Techniques For 3-D Computer Vision*, Prentice Hall, New York, NY, USA, 1998.

[24] S. Dizenzo, "A Note on the Gradient of a Multi-Image," *Computer Vision, Graphics, and Image Processing*, vol. 33, pp. 116–125, 1986.

[25] J. L. Schiff, *Cellular Automata a Discrete View of the World*, John Wiley & Sons, New York, NY, USA, 2008.

IEICE Transactions on Information and Systems, vol. E86-D, no. 12, pp. 2764–2774, 2003.

15

Vision Measurement Scheme Using Single Camera Rotation

Shidu Dong

College of Computer Science and Engineering, Chongqing University of Technology, Chongqing 400050, China

Correspondence should be addressed to Shidu Dong; shidu_dong@yahoo.com

Academic Editors: A. Nikolaidis and J. P. Siebert

We propose vision measurement scheme for estimating the distance or size of the object in static scene, which requires single camera with 3-axis accelerometer sensor rotating around a fixed axis. First, we formulate the rotation matrix and translation vector from one coordinate system of the camera to another in terms of the rotation angle, which can be figured out from the readouts of the sensor. Second, with the camera calibration data and through coordinate system transformation, we propose a method for calculating the orientation and position of the rotation axis relative to camera coordinate system. Finally, given the rotation angle and the images of the object in static scene at two different positions, one before and the other after camera rotation, the 3D coordinate of the point on the object can be determined. Experimental results show the validity of our method.

1. Introduction

Nowadays, digital camera or mobile phone with camera is very popular. It is appealing and convenient, if they are utilized to estimate the distance or size of an object. For this purpose, stereo images with disparity should be taken [1, 2]. One obvious method for the stereo image acquisition is using two cameras with different view angles. With two images of an object from two cameras and the relative orientation and position of the two different viewpoints, through the correspondence between image points in the two views, the 3D coordinates of the points on the object can be determined [3, 4]. But, in general, mobile phone or professional camera has only one camera and cannot acquire two images from different views simultaneously. Fortunately, there have been many methods for stereo vision system with single camera. The methods may be broadly divided into three categories. First, to obtain virtual images from different viewpoints, additional optical devices are introduced, such as two planar mirrors [5], a biprism [6], convex mirrors [1, 7], or the double lobed hyperbolic mirrors [8]. But these optical devices are expensive and space consuming. Second, 3D information of an object is inferred directly from a still image under the knowledge of some geometrical scene constraints such as planarity of points and parallelism of lines and planes [9–11] or prior knowledge about the scene obtained from

the supervised learning [12]. Nevertheless, these methods require constrained scenes or extra computation for training the depth models. Third, 3D information is extracted from sequential images with respect to camera movement, which is often adopted in robot area. Due to the uncertainties in the sequential camera position, however, it is difficult to get the accurate 3D information in that method [1].

In this paper, we propose a novel vision measurement method for estimating the distance or size of the object in static scene, which requires single camera with 3-axis accelerometer rotating around a fixed axis. Through the 3-axis accelerometer sensor, the slope angle of the camera relative to gravity direction can be obtained [13]. The angle can uniquely determine the position of the camera if the camera is rotated around a fixed axis which is not parallel to gravity. Moreover, the relative position and orientation of the camera between two positions, one before and the other after camera rotation, can be determined by the rotation angle. Therefore, at the given two positions, if the camera is calibrated, the classical binocular view methods [4] can be adopted to extract the 3D coordinates of the points on objects. Unfortunately, it is very difficult for the user to rotate the camera to the same slope angle as the calibrated one.

To deal with this problem, we firstly formulate the rotation matrix and translation vector from one coordinate system of the camera to another in terms of the rotation

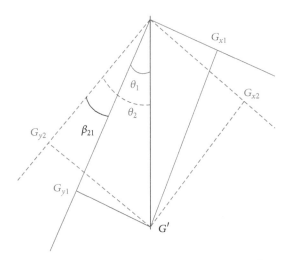

FIGURE 1: Position and rotation angle of the camera. G' denotes gravity division on the x-y plane of the sensor coordinate system. G_x and G_y denote the divisions of gravity on the x and y axes of the sensor coordinate system, respectively, and θ_1 and θ_2 denote the camera positions. β_{21} indicates the rotation angle.

angle. Then, with camera calibration data at various positions, we calculate the orientation and position of the rotation axis relative to the camera coordinate system. Accordingly, at given two positions, the rotation matrix and translation vector from one coordinate system of the camera to another can be calculated by rotation angle, and with the collected two images at the two positions, the 3D coordinate of the points on the object can be determined.

The paper is organized as follows: Section 2 provides a stereo vision system from single camera through rotation, and Section 3 indicates calculation method of the rotation matrix and translation vector from one coordinate system of the camera to another by the rotation angle. The calculation method for the position and orientation of rotation axis relative to the camera coordination system is proposed in Section 4, and the complete calibration and the 3D coordinate calculation of the point on an object are presented in Section 5. Experimental results are given in Section 6, and some conclusions and discussions are drawn in Section 7.

2. Stereo Vision through Camera Rotation

In what follows, we adopt the following hypotheses.

(H1) The camera is provided with a 3-axis accelerometer sensor, whose readouts, G_x, G_y, and G_z, are the divisions of gravity on the x, y, and z axes of the sensor coordinate system, respectively.

(H2) In calibration and measurement processes, the camera rotates around the fixed rotation axis which is parallel to the z axis of the sensor coordinate system and is not parallel to the direction of gravity.

Thus, in the course of the rotation, the readout G_z keeps steady. As a result, the division of gravity on the plane x-y of the sensor coordinate system G' also keeps steady

(see Figure 1). Therefore, the slope angle with respect to gravity division G' (position, for short) can be determined by

$$\theta = \arctan\left(\frac{G_x}{G_y}\right). \tag{1}$$

From position θ_1 to θ_2, the rotation angle of device β_{21} is governed by

$$\beta_{21} = \theta_2 - \theta_1. \tag{2}$$

Two images, I_1 and I_2, of an object are collected at the positions θ_1 and θ_2, respectively. O_1-xyz and O_2-xyz denote the camera coordinate systems at θ_1 and θ_2, respectively. (x_1, y_1, z_1) and (x_2, y_2, z_2) denote the coordinates of a point on the object relative to O_1-xyz and O_2-xyz, respectively, and (X_1, Y_1) and (X_2, Y_2) denote image coordinates of the point of the object on I_1 and I_2 (image coordinate for short), respectively.

The projection of object coordinates relative to O_1-xyz and O_2-xyz into image coordinates is summarized by the following forms:

$$s_1 \begin{bmatrix} X_1 \\ Y_1 \\ 1 \end{bmatrix} = \begin{bmatrix} f_x & 0 & c_x \\ 0 & f_y & c_y \\ 0 & 0 & 1 \end{bmatrix} \begin{bmatrix} x_1 \\ y_1 \\ z_1 \end{bmatrix},$$

$$s_2 \begin{bmatrix} X_2 \\ Y_2 \\ 1 \end{bmatrix} = \begin{bmatrix} f_x & 0 & c_x \\ 0 & f_y & c_y \\ 0 & 0 & 1 \end{bmatrix} \begin{bmatrix} x_2 \\ y_2 \\ z_2 \end{bmatrix}. \tag{3}$$

Let

$$\begin{bmatrix} x_2 \\ y_2 \\ z_2 \end{bmatrix} = \begin{bmatrix} R_{21} & T_{21} \end{bmatrix} \begin{bmatrix} x_1 \\ y_1 \\ z_1 \\ 1 \end{bmatrix} = \begin{bmatrix} r_1 & r_2 & r_3 & t_x \\ r_4 & r_5 & r_6 & t_y \\ r_7 & r_8 & r_9 & t_z \end{bmatrix} \begin{bmatrix} x_1 \\ y_1 \\ z_1 \\ 1 \end{bmatrix}, \tag{4}$$

where R_{21} and T_{21} denote rotation matrix and translation vector between O_2-xyz and O_1-xyz.

Substituting (3) into (4), we get

$$\rho_2 \begin{bmatrix} X_2 \\ Y_2 \\ 1 \end{bmatrix}$$

$$= \begin{bmatrix} f_x r_1 + c_x r_7 & f_x r_2 + c_x r_8 & f_x r_3 + c_x r_9 & f_x t_x + c_x t_z \\ f_y r_4 + c_y r_7 & f_y r_5 + c_y r_8 & f_y r_6 + c_y r_9 & f_y t_y + c_y t_z \\ r_7 & r_8 & r_9 & t_z \end{bmatrix}$$

$$\times \begin{bmatrix} (X_1 - c_x)\dfrac{z}{f_x} \\ (Y_1 - c_y)\dfrac{z}{f_y} \\ z_1 \\ 1 \end{bmatrix}. \tag{5}$$

Thus, the 3D coordinate of the point on the object relative to O_1-xyz (object coordinate) can be determined by

$$x_1 = (X_1 - c_x)\frac{z_1}{f_x},$$

$$y_1 = (Y_1 - c_y)\frac{z_1}{f_y},$$ (6)

$$z_1 = \frac{f_x f_y (f_x t_x + c_x t_z - X_2 t_z)}{B},$$

where

$$B = (X_2 - c_x)\left[r_7 f_y (X_1 - c_x) + r_8 f_x (Y_1 - c_y) + r_9 f_y f_x\right]$$
$$- f_x \left[f_y r_1 (X_1 - c_x) + f_x r_2 (Y_1 - c_y) + f_x r_3 f_y\right].$$ (7)

From (6), we can see that the object coordinate can be found provided that the intrinsic parameters f_x, f_y, c_x, and c_y, the rotation matrix R_{21}, and translation vector T_{21} are available.

With the camera calibration method proposed by Zhang [14], the camera intrinsic parameters and extrinsic parameters describing the camera motion around a static scene can be figured out. Let R_1 and T_1 denote the extrinsic parameters at θ_1 and R_2 and T_2 the extrinsic parameters at θ_2. For simplicity, $P_w = (x, y, z)$, $P_1 = (x_1, y_1, z_1)$, and $P_2 = (x_2, y_2,$ and $z_2)$ stand for the coordinates of the point on the object relative to the world coordinate system, O_1-xyz and O_2-xyz, respectively. Thus,

$$P_1 = R_1 P_w + T_1, \qquad P_2 = R_2 P_w + T_2.$$ (8)

From (8), we get

$$P_w = R_1^{-1} P_1 - R_1^{-1} T_1.$$ (9)

Substituting (9) into (8), we get

$$P_2 = R_2 R_1^{-1} P_1 - R_2 R_1^{-1} T_1 + T_2.$$ (10)

Equation (4) can be rewritten as

$$P_2 = R_{21} P_1 + T_{21}.$$ (11)

Thus,

$$R_{21} = R_2 R_1^{-1}, \qquad T_{21} = T_2 - R_2 R_1^{-1} T_1.$$ (12)

Based on the previous discussions, the object coordinate can be determined by the following process.

(1) The camera is calibrated, and the intrinsic parameters, f_x, f_y, c_x, and c_y, are obtained.

(2) At the positions θ_1 and θ_2, the camera is calibrated, and the corresponding extrinsic parameters, R_1, T_1, R_2, and T_2, are obtained. Then, R_{21} and T_{21} can be acquired from (12).

(3) In the course of measurement, the camera is rotated carefully to the positions θ_1 and θ_2. At these two positions, the two images of the object, I_1 and I_2, are collected. Once the image coordinates of the object, (X_1, Y_1) and (X_2, Y_2), are known, the object coordinate can be figured out by (6).

It should be noticed that it is rather difficult for the user to rotate the camera accurately to the positions θ_1 and θ_2, where camera is calibrated.

3. Calculation Method of Rotation Matrix and Translation Vector

Intuitively, the orientation and position of O_2-xyz relative to O_1-xyz, R_{21} and T_{21}, depend on the camera rotation angle, β_{21}. Thus, R_{21} and T_{21} may be figured out by β_{21}.

Let O_R-xyz be the coordinate system associated with the rotation axis, which is unit vector on the z axis of the coordinate system. Let R_x and T_x denote the orientation and position of O_R-xyz relative to O_1-xyz (orientation and position of the rotation axis). Its homogeneous matrix can be written as

$$M_X = \begin{bmatrix} R_X & T_X \\ 0 & 1 \end{bmatrix}.$$ (13)

The rotation matrix for the camera rotation around the z axis of O_R-xyz from θ_1 to θ_2 (device rotation matrix) can be modeled as

$$R_{\beta 21} = \begin{bmatrix} \cos\beta_{21} & -\sin\beta_{21} & 0 \\ \sin\beta_{21} & \cos\beta_{21} & 0 \\ 0 & 0 & 1 \end{bmatrix}.$$ (14)

Its homogeneous matrix can be written as

$$\text{Rot}(\beta_{21}) = \begin{bmatrix} R_{\beta 21} & 0 \\ 0 & 1 \end{bmatrix}.$$ (15)

The coordinate system transformation can be represented as a graph (Figure 2). A directed edge represents a relationship between two coordinate systems and is associated with a homogeneous transformation. From Figure 2, we can get

$$M_{21} M_X = M_X \text{Rot}(\beta_{21}),$$ (16)

where

$$M_{21} = \begin{bmatrix} R_{21} & T_{21} \\ 0 & 1 \end{bmatrix}.$$ (17)

Substituting (13), (15), and (17) into (16), we get

$$\begin{bmatrix} R_{21} & T_{21} \\ 0 & 1 \end{bmatrix}\begin{bmatrix} R_X & T_X \\ 0 & 1 \end{bmatrix} = \begin{bmatrix} R_X & T_X \\ 0 & 1 \end{bmatrix}\begin{bmatrix} R_{\beta 21} & 0 \\ 0 & 1 \end{bmatrix},$$ (18)

$$\begin{bmatrix} R_{21} R_X & R_{21} T_X + T_{21} \\ 0 & 1 \end{bmatrix} = \begin{bmatrix} R_X R_{\beta 21} & T_X \\ 0 & 1 \end{bmatrix},$$ (19)

$$R_{21} = R_X R_{\beta 21} R_X^{-1},$$ (20)

$$T_{21} = T_X - R_{21} T_X.$$ (21)

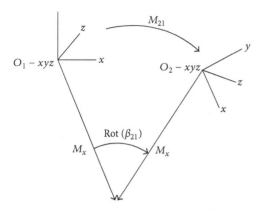

FIGURE 2: Coordinate system transformation represented by a graph.

From (20) and (21), we can see that the R_{21} and T_{21} can be calculated by the rotation angle β_{21} provided that R_x and T_x are available.

4. Calculation Method of Position and Orientation of Rotation Axis

4.1. Orientation of Rotation Axis. Suppose that the camera be calibrated at different positions. At position θ_i, we get camera calibration data. Let $\beta_{i1} = \theta_i - \theta_1$, and let $R_{\beta i1}$ denote the device rotation matrix with respect to rotation angle β_{i1}. R_{i1} and T_{i1} denote rotation matrix and translation vector between camera coordinate systems at the positions θ_i and θ_1. Equation (20) can be written as

$$R_{i1}R_X = R_X R_{\beta i1}. \tag{22}$$

When the rotation axis is fixed, R_x would be constant. Thus, given the values of R_{i1}, T_{i1}, and β_{i1}, we can solve (22) for R_x.

Using a normalized quaternion to define the rotation between two coordinate systems provides a simple and elegant way to formulate successive rotations [15–17]. Given rotation matrix

$$R = \begin{bmatrix} r_1 & r_2 & r_3 \\ r_4 & r_5 & r_6 \\ r_7 & r_8 & r_9 \end{bmatrix}, \tag{23}$$

it can be transformed to the quaternion with the following equation [18]:

$$q_0 = \sqrt{1 + r_1 + r_5 + r_9},$$

$$q_x = \frac{r_8 - r_6}{4 \times q_0}, \quad q_y = \frac{r_7 - r_3}{4 \times q_0}, \quad q_z = \frac{r_4 - r_2}{4 \times q_0}. \tag{24}$$

Similarly, the quaternion can be transformed to the rotation matrix with the following equation [18]:

$$R = \begin{bmatrix} q_0^2 + q_x^2 + q_y^2 + q_z^2 & 2\left(q_x q_y - q_0 q_z\right) & 2\left(q_x q_z + q_0 q_y\right) \\ 2\left(q_x q_y + q_0 q_z\right) & q_0^2 + q_y^2 - q_x^2 - q_z^2 & 2\left(q_y q_z - q_0 q_x\right) \\ 2\left(q_x q_z - q_0 q_y\right) & 2\left(q_y q_z + q_0 q_x\right) & q_0^2 + q_z^2 - q_x^2 - q_y^2 \end{bmatrix}. \tag{25}$$

Let q_{Ai}, q_X, and q_{Bi} denote the quaternion of R_{i1}, R_x, and $R_{\beta i1}$, respectively. With quaternion, the sequence of rotation can be formulated as an equation without involving rotation matrices [15]. As a result, the problem of solving $R_{i1}R_X = R_X R_{\beta i1}$ can be transformed into an equivalent problem involving the corresponding quaternion as follows [15]:

$$q_{Ai} \otimes q_X = q_X \otimes q_{Bi}. \tag{26}$$

Since the quaternion multiplication can be written in matrix form and with notations introduced in [19], we have the following [16]:

$$q_{Ai} \otimes q_X = Q(q_{Ai}) q_X, \qquad q_X \otimes q_{Bi} = W(q_{Bi}) q_X, \tag{27}$$

where, letting $q = [q_0, q_x, q_y, q_z]$,

$$Q(q) = \begin{bmatrix} q_0 & -q_x & -q_y & -q_z \\ q_x & q_0 & -q_z & q_y \\ q_y & q_z & q_0 & -q_x \\ q_z & -q_y & q_x & q_0 \end{bmatrix},$$

$$W(q) = \begin{bmatrix} q_0 & -q_x & -q_y & -q_z \\ q_x & q_0 & q_z & -q_y \\ q_y & -q_z & q_0 & q_x \\ q_z & q_y & -q_x & q_0 \end{bmatrix}. \tag{28}$$

Moreover, these two matrices are orthogonal [16], that is,

$$[Q(q)]^T Q(q) = [W(q)]^T W(q) = I. \tag{29}$$

Thus,

$$Q(q_{Ai}) q_X = W(q_{Bi}) q_X,$$

$$\left\| Q(q_{Ai}) q_X - W(q_{Bi}) q_X \right\|^2$$

$$= [Q(q_{Ai}) q_X - W(q_{Bi}) q_X]^T [Q(q_{Ai}) q_X - W(q_{Bi}) q_X]$$

$$= q_X^T \left\{ 2I - [Q(q_{Ai})]^T W(q_{Bi}) - [W(q_{Bi})]^T Q(q_{Ai}) \right\} q_X$$

$$= q_X^T [2I - C_i] q_X, \tag{30}$$

where

$$C_i = [Q(q_{Ai})]^T W(q_{Bi}) + [W(q_{Bi})]^T Q(q_{Ai}). \tag{31}$$

Thus, the total error function allowing us to compute q_X becomes

$$f(q_x) = \sum_{i=1}^{n} q_X^T [2I - C_i] q_X$$

$$= q_X^T \left[2nI - \sum_{i=1}^{n} C_i \right] q_X \tag{32}$$

$$= q_X^T [2nI - S] q_X,$$

where n is the number of positions of the camera:

$$S = \sum_{i=1}^{n} C_i, \qquad (33)$$

q_x is the unit quaternion. Therefore, q_x can be obtained by solving the following problem:

$$\min \quad f(q_X) = \min \left\{ q_X^T [2nI - S] q_X \right\} \qquad (34)$$
$$\text{s.t.} \quad q_X^T q_X = 1.$$

4.2. Position of Rotation Axis. At position θ_i, (21) can be written as

$$(I - R_{i1}) T_X = T_{i1}. \qquad (35)$$

When the rotation axis is fixed, T_x would be constant. Thus, given the values of R_{i1} and T_{i1}, we can solve (35) for T_X.

Let $E_i = [-T_{i1}, I - R_{i1}]$, $T_Y = [1, T_x^T]^T$, and thus

$$E_i T_Y = 0, \qquad (36)$$
$$\|E_i T_Y\|_2^2 = T_Y^T E_i^T E_i T_Y.$$

Let n denote the number of positions of the camera. The total error function is

$$g(T_Y) = \sum_{i=1}^{n} T_Y^T E_i^T E_i T_Y = T_Y^T \left[\sum_{i=1}^{n} E_i^T E_i \right] T_Y. \qquad (37)$$

Since the camera rotation axis is approximately vertical to T_X, the value of t_z approaches zero. Thus, $T_y = [t_{y0}, t_{y1}, t_{y2}, t_{y3}]$ can be obtained by solving the following problem:

$$\min \quad g(T_Y) = \min T_Y^T \left[\sum_{i=1}^{n} E_i^T E_i \right] T_Y \qquad (38)$$
$$\text{s.t.} \quad \begin{aligned} t_{y0} &= 1 \\ t_{y3} &< 1. \end{aligned}$$

5. Calculation of Position and Orientation of Rotation Axis and 3D Coordinate

5.1. Calculation of Position and Orientation of Rotation Axis. Based on the previous discussions, the complete process of calculation of position and orientation of rotation axis is outlined below:

(1) The chessboard (see Figure 3) is printed and plastered on plane. By rotating and moving the camera properly, a set of chessboard images is collected. Then, the values of the intrinsic parameters of the camera, f_x, f_y, c_x, and c_y, are obtained by calling the method proposed in [14].

FIGURE 3: Chessboard.

(2) The camera is fixed on a camera tripod, and the rotation axis of the camera, which is parallel to the z axis of the sensor coordinate system, lies in an approximately horizontal plane.

(3) By rotating the camera around the fixed axis to the different positions, another set of chessboard images are collected.

(4) The extrinsic parameters of the camera at the positions θ_i, R_i, and T_i are obtained by calling the function cvFindExtrinsicCameraParams2 in Opencv [20].

(5) The rotation matrix and translation vector between the camera coordinate systems at the positions θ_i and θ_1, R_{i1}, and T_{i1} are figured out by (12). The rotation angle β_{i1} and its corresponding rotation matrix $R_{\beta i1}$ are also calculated by (2) and (14).

(6) The R_{i1} and $R_{\beta i1}$ are converted into quaternions q_{Ai} and q_{Bi}, respectively, by using the method proposed by Bar-Itzhack [18].

(7) q_X is found by solving problem (34). As a result, the R_x can be obtained.

(8) T_X is obtained by solving problem (38).

5.2. 3D Coordinate Calculation. Based on the previous discussions, we present the complete process of 3D coordinate calculation as follows:

(1) The camera is fixed on a camera tripod whose rotation axis lies in an approximately horizontal plane.

(2) At certain position θ_1, the image of the object I_1 is collected.

(3) By rotating the camera on the fixed axis to another position θ_2, we get another image of the object I_2.

(4) The rotation angle β_{21} and its corresponding rotation matrix $R_{\beta 21}$ are figured out by (2) and (14).

(5) With $R_{\beta 21}$, R_{21} and T_{21} are calculated by (20) and (21).

(6) The image coordinate of the point of the object, (X_1, Y_1), on the image I_1 is appointed manually.

(7) The corresponding image coordinate in the image I_2, (X_2, Y_2), can be determined by stereo correspondence method, for example, the function FindStereoCorrespondenceBM in Opencv [20] or by manual.

(8) The 3D coordinate of the point on the object relative to O_1-xyz, (x_1, y_1, z_1), can be figured out by (6).

6. Experiments

Since digital camera with 3-axis accelerometer sensor is not available for us, IPhone 4, which has the sensor, is adopted. To simulate digital camera, the phone is placed in a box which is fixed on a camera tripod. And it is ensured that the z axis of the sensor (experiment results show that the axis is parallel to the optical axis of the camera) is parallel to the rotation axis of the camera tripod, so that the value of G_z keeps steady in the course of the rotation. In calibration course, the distance between the camera and the chessboard is about 1000 mm.

Figure 4 illustrates the curve of the quaternion of the rotation matrix between the camera coordinate systems at the ith position and 1st position, with respect to the rotation angle. The quaternion $q' = [q'_0, q'_x, q'_y, q'_z]$ was calculated by the proposed method with rotation angle, while $q = [q_0, q_x, q_y, q_z]$ was converted directly from rotation matrix R_{i1}, which was from calibration data. From the graph, one can see that the proposed method can calculate the rotation matrix by rotation angle.

Figure 5 plots the curve of translation vector between the camera coordinate systems at the ith position and 1st position, with respect to rotation angle. The vector $T' = [T'_x, T'_y, T'_z]$ was calculated by the proposed method with rotation angle, while $T = [T_x, T_y, T_z]$ was directly from calibration data T_{i1}. From the graphs, one can see that the proposed method can calculate effectively translation vector by rotation angle.

In order to estimate the accuracy of 3D coordinate calculated by the proposed method, the chessboard which has a bigger block than the one for calibration is printed. The width of the block is 46.6 mm, and the distance between the chessboard and the camera is about 1200 mm. The distance between two neighbor corners rather than the distance between the camera and the chessboard is calculated, because the measurement of the former by manual is easier. For simplicity, the corners of the blocks in images are automatically detected by calling the Opencv function "cvFindChessboardCorners" [19]. Figure 6 depicts the measurement error ratio of the distance between two corners with respect to rotation angle.

7. Conclusions

This paper proposed a stereo vision system with single camera, which requires digital camera with 3-axis accelerometer sensor rotating around the fixed axis which is parallel to the axis z of the sensor. Under these conditions, the slope angle relative to gravity, which can be figured out from the readouts of the sensor, can determine the camera position, and the rotation angle between two positions can determine the rotation matrix and translation vector from

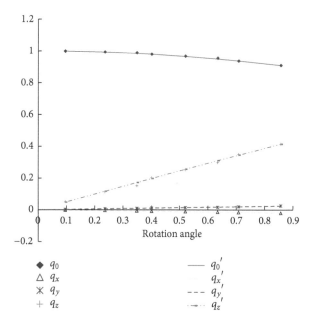

FIGURE 4: Curve of the quaternion of rotation matrix with respect to rotation angle; $q = [q_0, q_x, q_y, q_z]$ is converted from rotation matrix, and $q' = [q'_0, q'_x, q'_y, q'_z]$ is calculated by the proposed method.

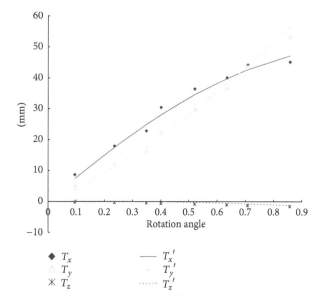

FIGURE 5: Curve of translation vector with respect to rotation angle; $T = [T_x, T_y, T_z]$ was directly from calibration data, and $T' = [T'_x, T'_y, T'_z]$ was calculated by (23) with rotation angle.

one coordinate system of the camera to another. Accordingly, given the rotation angle and the images of the object at two different positions, one before and the other after camera rotation, the 3D coordinates of the points on the object can be determined. Theoretical analysis and experimental results show the validity of our method.

It should be noticed that few digital cameras are provided with 3-axis accelerometer sensor. However, to obtain stereo vision, we believe that the inexpensive sensor embedded in

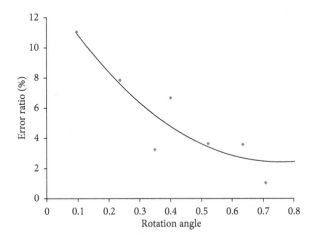

FIGURE 6: Measurement error ratio (%) of the distance between two corners with respect to rotation angle.

digital camera is worthy. Moreover, due to higher image quality and larger focus range, higher accuracy and larger range of measurement may be obtained. Furthermore, the smart phone which has the sensor is popular. If a mini fixed rotation axis is built in a corner of the phone and it does not move in the course of rotation, with the proposed method, the phone may estimate the size of the object being focused on and distance between the phone and the object.

Acknowledgment

This work is supported by Science and Technology Research Project of Chongqing's Education Committee (KJ110806).

References

[1] Y. Sooyeong and N. Ahuja, "An omnidirectional stereo vision system using a single camera," in *Proceedings of the 18th International Conference on Pattern Recognition (ICPR '06)*, pp. 861–865, August 2006.

[2] D. Marr and T. Poggio, "A computational theory of human stereo vision," *Proceedings of the Royal Society of London*, vol. 204, no. 1156, pp. 301–328, 1979.

[3] F. Tombari, S. Mattoccia, L. D. Stefano, and E. Addimanda, "Classification and evaluation of cost aggregation methods for stereo correspondence," in *Proceedings of the 26th IEEE Conference on Computer Vision and Pattern Recognition (CVPR '08)*, pp. 1–8, June 2008.

[4] H. C. Longuet-higgins, "A computer algorithm for reconstructing a scene from two projections," *Nature*, vol. 293, no. 5828, pp. 133–135, 1981.

[5] J. Gluckman and S. K. Nayar, "Catadioptric stereo using planar mirrors," *International Journal of Computer Vision*, vol. 44, no. 1, pp. 65–79, 2001.

[6] D. Lee and I. Kweon, "A novel stereo camera system by a biprism," *IEEE Transactions on Robotics and Automation*, vol. 16, no. 5, pp. 528–541, 2000.

[7] T. Svoboda and T. Pajdla, "Epipolar geometry for central catadioptric cameras," *International Journal of Computer Vision*, vol. 49, no. 1, pp. 23–37, 2002.

[8] D. Southwell, A. Basu, M. Fiala, and J. Reyda, "Panoramic stereo," *International Conference on Pattern Recognition*, vol. 1, pp. 378–382, 1996.

[9] A. Criminisi, I. Reid, and A. Zisserman, "Single view metrology," *International Journal of Computer Vision*, vol. 40, no. 2, pp. 123–148, 2000.

[10] A. Criminisi, "Single-view metrology: algorithms and applications," in *Proceedings of the 24th DAGM Symposium on Pattern Recognition*, vol. 2449 of *Lecture Notes in Computer Science*, pp. 224–239, 2002.

[11] G. Wang, Z. Hu, F. Wu, and H. Tsui, "Single view metrology from scene constraints," *Image and Vision Computing*, vol. 23, no. 9, pp. 831–840, 2005.

[12] A. Saxena, S. H. Chung, and A. Y. Ng, "3-D depth reconstruction from a single still image," *International Journal of Computer Vision*, vol. 76, no. 1, pp. 53–69, 2008.

[13] J. Rekimoto, "Tilting operations for small screen interfaces," in *Proceedings of the 9th ACM Annual Symposium on User Interface Software and Technology*, pp. 167–168, November 1996.

[14] Z. Zhang, "A flexible new technique for camera calibration," *IEEE Transactions on Pattern Analysis and Machine Intelligence*, vol. 22, no. 11, pp. 1330–1334, 2000.

[15] J. C. K. Chou and M. Kamel, "Finding the position and orientation of a sensor on a robot manipulator using quaternions," *International Journal of Robotics Research*, vol. 10, no. 3, pp. 240–254, 1991.

[16] F. Dornaika and R. Horaud, "Simultaneous robot-world and hand-eye calibration," *IEEE Transactions on Robotics and Automation*, vol. 14, no. 4, pp. 617–622, 1998.

[17] K. H. Strobl and G. Hirzinger, "Optimal hand-eye calibration," in *Proceedings of the IEEE/RSJ International Conference on Intelligent Robots and Systems (IROS '06)*, pp. 4647–4653, October 2006.

[18] I. Y. Bar-Itzhack, "New method for extracting the quaternion from a rotation matrix," *Journal of Guidance, Control, and Dynamics*, vol. 23, no. 6, pp. 1085–1087, 2000.

[19] M. W. Walker, L. Shao, and R. A. Volz, "Estimating 3-D location parameters using dual number quaternions," *Image Understanding*, vol. 54, no. 3, pp. 358–367, 1991.

[20] B. Gary and K. Adrian, *Learning OpenCV*, O'Reilly Media, 2008.

16

New Brodatz-Based Image Databases for Grayscale Color and Multiband Texture Analysis

Safia Abdelmounaime and He Dong-Chen

Centre for Research and Applications in Remote Sensing (CARTEL), Department of Geomatics, Sherbrooke University, QC, Canada J1K 2R1

Correspondence should be addressed to Safia Abdelmounaime; a.safia@usherbrooke.ca

Academic Editors: A. Nikolaidis and R. Schettini

Grayscale and color textures can have spectral informative content. This spectral information coexists with the grayscale or chromatic spatial pattern that characterizes the texture. This informative and nontextural spectral content can be a source of confusion for rigorous evaluations of the intrinsic textural performance of texture methods. In this paper, we used basic image processing tools to develop a new class of textures in which texture information is the only source of discrimination. Spectral information in this new class of textures contributes only to form texture. The textures are grouped into two databases. The first is the Normalized Brodatz Texture database (NBT) which is a collection of grayscale images. The second is the Multiband Texture (MBT) database which is a collection of color texture images. Thus, this new class of textures is ideal for rigorous comparisons between texture analysis methods based only on their intrinsic performance on texture characterization.

1. Introduction

It has long been argued that texture plays a key role in computer-based pattern recognition. Texture can be the only effective way to discriminate between different surfaces that have similar spectral characteristics [1–6].

Texture was early recognized as mainly a spatial distribution of tonal variations in the same band [7]. Different grayscale texture methods have been proposed based on different techniques [7–12]. For an objective and rigorous comparison between different texture analysis methods, it is important to use standard databases [13, 14]. The standard Brodatz grayscale texture album [15] has been widely used as a validation dataset [16, 17]. It is composed of 112 grayscale images representing a large variety of natural grayscale textures. This database has been used with different levels of complexity in texture classification [18], texture segmentation [19], and image retrieval [20]. A rotation invariant version of the Brodatz database was also proposed [21] and used for texture classification and retrieval [22, 23].

Recently, we have seen a growing interest in color texture [24]. This is a natural evolution of the field of texture, from grayscale to color texture. The use of color in texture analysis showed several benefits [25–27]. In color texture, efforts have been made to find efficient methods to combine color and texture features [24]. Consequently, the evaluation of color texture methods requires images in which color and texture information are both sources of discriminative information. Many color texture databases have been proposed for the evaluation of color texture methods. The VisTex database from the MIT Media Lab, the Corel Stock Photo Library, the color Outex database [21], and the CUReT database [28] are the most widely used. Images from these databases have rich textural and chromatic content and are ideal for color texture methods.

In this paper, we examine the validation of texture methods from a different point of view. We start from a simple observation: an image has spectral and textural information, and both can be used in image description [7]. The spectral information can affect the performance of texture characterization due to the differences in the mathematical concept of these methods. A good example is the cooccurrence matrices method [7] and the texture spectrum method [8]. The first is more sensitive to spectral information because it uses the spectral values as they appear in the images while the second uses the relative spectral values [29]. A rigorous evaluation of texture methods, without the influence of spectral information, requires images with texture as the only source of discrimination. The use of such images will guarantee that texture methods are compared on the same basis of textural performance.

Here, we propose a new texture database in which images do not have discriminative spectral information. The aim is to provide the pattern recognition community new images that allow validation of texture analysis methods based only on texture information. To do so, we used basic yet efficient image processing techniques to produce texture images without any pure spectral informative content. The first database is the Normalized Brodatz Texture (NBT) database, which is a collection of grayscale textures derived from the Brodatz album. Images from the NBT database have the rich textural content of the original Brodatz textures. At the same time, their spectral content is uninformative. The second database is the Multiband Texture (MBT) database. This database is a collection of color images. The color of these images contributes only to form texture and does not have any discriminative value if used as pure spectral information. Images from these databases have different levels of complexity in terms of their intraband and interband spatial distributions. This allows developing texture characterization problems with various degrees of difficulty. The proposed databases along with the existing databases form a more complete dataset for the evaluation of texture methods.

The paper is organized as follows. In Section 2, we present the normalized grayscale Brodatz textures. Section 3 presents a comprehensive analysis of the chromatic and textural content of some color texture images from the VisTex database. Section 4 illustrates the concept of multiband texture using astronomical and remote sensing satellite images. In Section 5, a new multiband texture database is presented and analyzed. Section 6 presents experiments on multiband texture database. Conclusions are drawn in Section 7.

2. Normalized Grayscale Textures

This section presents the first texture category: grayscale texture. A good example of this type of texture is the 112 texture images of the Brodatz album. This album provides a very useful natural texture database, which has been widely used to evaluate texture discrimination methods [30–33]. Texture from this album can be digitized into different gray-level intervals resulting in different background intensities. In Figure 1 we give an example of six different Brodatz textures organized into two sets: D32, D28, and D10 (top row); and D64, D95, and D75 (bottom row). For example, D32 has a black background while D28 and D10 have gray and white backgrounds, respectively. This background effect introduces discriminative information to these images, in addition to their initial texture content. Indeed, as shown in Figure 2, these textures have localized modes, and it is possible to discriminate between them with significant accuracy using

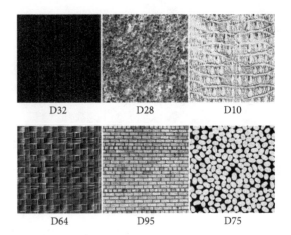

FIGURE 1: Samples of Brodatz grayscale textures.

only their histograms (i.e., background intensity, without using texture information).

It would be interesting to compare all texture analysis methods using images with the same gray-level interval so that the background intensity does not interfere in the texture discrimination process. Various simple, and yet efficient, techniques can be used to perform this task. In this paper we used linear stretching [34], histogram equalization [35], and contrast limited adaptive histogram equalization [34].

We removed the background effect of the Brodatz textures by normalizing them to the same eight-bit (256 gray levels) intensity interval. A good normalization algorithm needs to preserve the visual appearance of the texture of the original image, while redistributing the image gray levels in order to occupy the whole 256 intensity interval. To do so, the histograms of all the 112 Brodatz images were generated and visually analyzed. Then, different normalization techniques were tested on each image, and the one that redistributed the images' gray values with the least visual alteration of the texture was selected. Figures 3 and 4 show the normalized images in Figure 1 and their corresponding histograms, respectively. Unlike the original images, the gray values of the normalized images occupy the whole 256 gray-level range and, consequently, it is not possible to discriminate between them using only first-order statistics. The use of texture information is necessary to discriminate between these normalized texture images.

We produced a new database called the Normalized Brodatz Texture (NBT) database, which is available online (http://pages.usherbrooke.ca/asafia/mbt/) to allow the validation of texture analysis methods based only on texture information.

3. Colored Textures

This section presents the second texture category referred to as colored texture. A representative example of this category is the VisTex database. It can be seen as a generalization of the Brodatz database from grayscale to color texture. In this

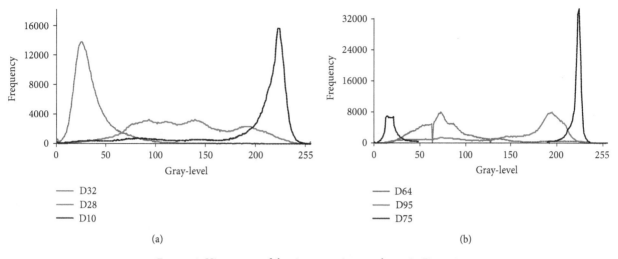

(a)   (b)

FIGURE 2: Histograms of the six texture images shown in Figure 1.

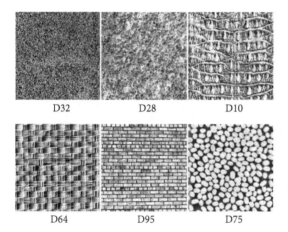

FIGURE 3: Normalized textures in Figure 1.

TABLE 1: Correlation coefficients between the three RGB channels of three images from the VisTex database.

	$r_{(R,G)}$	$r_{(R,B)}$	$r_{(G,B)}$
Fabric.0001	0.998	0.923	0.953
Wood.0002	0.964	0.909	0.972
Water.0005	0.979	0.932	0.914

TABLE 2: Correlation coefficients for the textural content of the three channels of the Fabric.0001 image.

	$r_{(R,G)}$	$r_{(R,B)}$	$r_{(G,B)}$
Contrast	0.997	0.960	0.975
Dissimilarity	0.998	0.972	0.982

section we will analyze the chromatic and textural content of some images from this database.

3.1. Chromatic Content Analysis. Figure 5 presents three typical natural color texture images (i.e., Fabric.0001, Wood.0002, and Water.0005; each image is 512 by 512 pixels) from the VisTex database. From a chromatic viewpoint, each texture image in Figure 5 has a predominantly monotone color: brown, brown-gray, and blue-green (from left to right). This monotone color is the result of the gray-level distribution of each of the three RGB (red, green, blue) channels shown in Figure 6. The histograms of these channels show well-localized peaks, and the differences between the three histograms of each texture are mainly attributed to shifts in the pixel intensities along the x-axis without a significant change in the histogram shape. The well-localized peaks produce the same background as for Brodatz images (Section 2). On the other hand, the correlation coefficients between the three RGB channels in each texture image show that they were strongly correlated ($r > 0.909$, see Table 1).

3.2. Textural Content Analysis. In Figure 7 the three RGB channels of the Fabric.0001 texture image are presented separately. These three channels contain the same texture with different dominant gray-level intensities. In order to provide quantitative measurements of the texture similarity of these three RGB channels, cooccurrence matrix features (contrast and dissimilarity) were estimated separately for each channel using a moving window of five by five pixels and a displacement vector of one pixel in the horizontal direction (0°). Six textural channels (i.e., two features for each of the three channels) were generated and organized into two triplets (i.e., one triplet for each texture feature). The correlation coefficient (r) was then calculated for the three textural channels of each triplet in order to analyze the variation of texture between the three channels. As shown in Table 2, the texture features of the same image were highly correlated with $r \geq 0.960$.

In order to provide more detailed evaluation measures, these correlations were also estimated between the rows of the three channels. The results are summarized in Figure 8. For a fixed texture feature, this figure gives the correlation coefficient (y-axis) between the ith row (i is the index in the x-axis) of this texture feature image estimated in a fixed

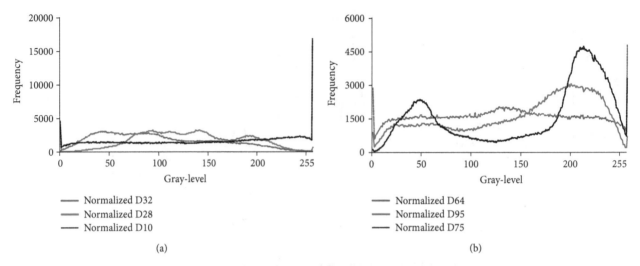

(a)   (b)

FIGURE 4: Histograms of the six textures shown in Figure 3.

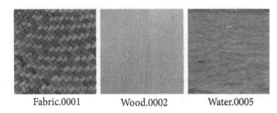

FIGURE 5: Examples of color texture images from the VisTex database.

channel and the ith row of the same texture feature image estimated in a different channel. This figure can be interpreted as correlation profiles along the row dimension of the texture feature images.

As shown in Figure 8, an important correlation exists between the texture information for the three channels of the Fabric.0001 texture. For both texture features (i.e., contrast and dissimilarity), the maximum correlation was recorded between the R and G channels (r close to 1). For the six correlation profiles, the minimum recorded correlation was 0.881, confirming that, just as for the chromatic content, the texture content of the three Fabric.0001 channels was highly correlated. Similar results were obtained for other VisTex images. This high similarity explains why methods using only one band to estimate texture are successful.

3.3. Colored Brodatz Texture Database. Given the strong chromatic content and the high textural similarity of VisTex images, it was possible to transform grayscale Brodatz images to color images similar to VisTex images. To do so, for each Brodatz image, two additional channels were generated to form pseudo-RGB color texture images by a simple gray-level shift. This produced color Brodatz texture images (Figure 9) with richly textured content (the same as the original Brodatz textures) and high informative color content similar to VisTex images. This process produced a gradient of colors (e.g., D44 and D95) that gave these images a natural appearance, while

preserving the original Brodatz texture. The entire grayscale Brodatz album (112 images) was generalized from grayscale to color texture by random histogram shifting. We call this database the Colored Brodatz Texture (CBT) database, and it is available online (http://pages.usherbrooke.ca/asafia/mbt/).

4. Multiband Texture

This section presents the third category of texture referred to as multiband texture. A good example of this category is astronomical and remote sensing images. This section presents an analysis of the chromatic and textural content of some of these images.

4.1. Chromatic Content Analysis. Figure 10 presents three images where the first two are astronomical images from the Spitzer and Hubble NASA telescopes, and the third is from a remote sensing earth satellite. These images were taken with instruments having relatively high spatial resolutions (e.g., ~1.8 m for WorldView-2). This produces contrasting bands because it is possible to detect small details in the observed object. Indeed, as shown in Figure 11, the histograms of these images covered the whole 256 gray-level range. This is in contrast with images in Figure 6. On the other hand, the wavelengths depicted in each of the three-color composites are very different: for example, for the Tarantula Nebula image, emission at 775 nm is depicted in green and 0.826 nm in blue. This produces RGB bands that are less correlated compared with images with closer wavelengths, such as natural images taken in the visible spectrum domain. As shown in Table 3, the correlation coefficients between their RGB channels are relatively small compared with those of VisTex images given in Table 2 (e.g., $r = -0.108$ and $r = 0.390$ between the red and blue bands of the WorldView-2 and Tarantula Nebula images, resp.). These two characteristics related to the spatial resolution and the wavelength contribute to the formation of images with rich color content.

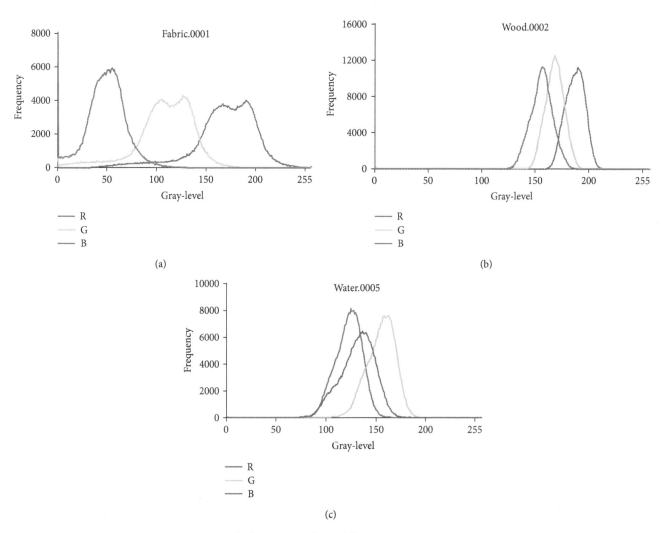

(a)

(b)

(c)

FIGURE 6: RGB histograms of two of the texture images in Figure 5.

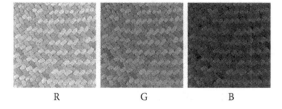

FIGURE 7: RGB channels of the Fabric.0001 texture image.

TABLE 3: Correlation coefficients between the three RGB channels for the images in Figure 10.

	$r_{(R,G)}$	$r_{(R,B)}$	$r_{(G,B)}$
Galaxy IC-342	0.842	0.766	0.751
Tarantula Nebula	0.869	0.390	0.710
WorldView-2	0.606	−0.108	0.643

Quantitative measures of the color distribution of images in Figure 10 were carried out based on the histogram of the hue component of the HSI transform [36]. Figures 12(a) and 12(b) give the results obtained for the two images: Galaxy IC-342 and the portion of the WorldView-2 image showing a quarry. The x-axis represents colors ranging from hue = $0°$ to hue = $360°$ and the y-axis is the frequency of the corresponding color. These two figures show that the images in Figure 10 have a large color range instead of a specific localized color range, as was the case for VisTex images (Figures 12(c) and 12(d)). In these images, there is no color background; consequently, it is not possible to discriminate between these images based only on their color.

4.2. Textural Content Analysis. Cooccurrence-matrix-based features (contrast and dissimilarity) were estimated and analyzed (as described in Section 3) for two images in Figure 10 (Galaxy IC-342 and WorldView-2). The correlation coefficient (r) was then calculated between the three textural channels of these two images as described in Section 3. Results are summarized in Table 4. Overall, the comparison with Table 2 showed that images from this category of texture have less correlated textural content than images from the

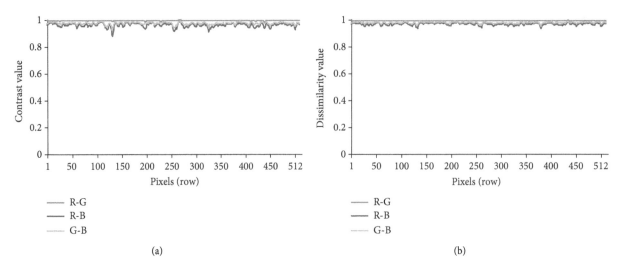

(a)   (b)

FIGURE 8: Per-row correlation coefficient profile of the cooccurrence matrix features of the Fabric.0001 image.

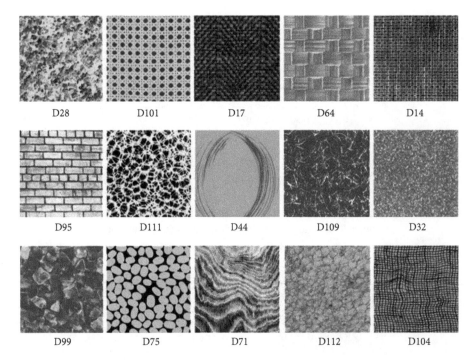

FIGURE 9: Texture samples from the Colored Texture Brodatz (CBT) database.

colored texture category (Table 2). The textural content of Galaxy IC-342 bands is less correlated than that of the WorldView-2 image. The textural content of some bands in WorldView-2 showed a very small correlation. This was the case, for example, for the dissimilarity of the red and blue channels ($r = 0.087$).

For a detailed analysis of the textural content of images in Figure 13, per-row correlation coefficient (r) profiles were also estimated as described in Section 3. Except for two correlation profiles estimated between the red and the green bands of the WorldView-2 image, the ten other profiles showed small correlations. This means that the bands of these

two images possess different textural content, which was in contrast with the VisTex images (Figure 8).

Given the low informative value of the chromatic content of these images, and the low correlation between the textural content of their spectral bands, we can conclude that, for these images, the most discriminative information is texture. This includes intraband and interband texture information. It would be useful to have a standard database in which images have the same characteristics as those studied in this section. A standard database would be useful for the validation of methods focusing only on the texture of color images because the color information has low informative content.

TABLE 4: Correlation coefficients for the textural content of the three channels of the images in Figure 10.

	Galaxy IC-342			WorldView-2		
	$r_{(R,G)}$	$r_{(R,B)}$	$r_{(G,B)}$	$r_{(R,G)}$	$r_{(R,B)}$	$r_{(G,B)}$
Contrast	0.544	0.402	0.494	0.768	0.431	0.728
Dissimilarity	0.634	0.502	0.540	0.794	0.087	0.365

Galaxy IC-342   Tarantula Nebula   WorldView-2

FIGURE 10: Three multiband textures. Galaxy IC-342: NASA Spitzer Space Telescope. Red = 24.0 μm, green = 5.8 μm and 8.0 μm, and blue = 3.6 μm and 4.5 μm. Tarantula Nebula: red = 4.5 μm, 5.8 μm, and 8.0 μm (all from Spitzer IRAC), green = 775 nm from Hubble ACS Telescope and from Hubble WFC3 Telescope, and blue = 0.826 nm from Chandra Telescope ACIS. WorldView-2: red = 427 nm, green = 724 nm, and blue = 949 nm.

5. Developing the Multiband Texture (MBT) Database

We developed a new texture database for the validation of methods focusing on intraband and interband texture. It is referred to as the Multiband Texture (MBT) database. The key concept was to combine three different grayscale textures to form a new three-channel color texture. These grayscale textures were taken from the proposed NBT database (Section 2). As NBT textures do not have pure spectral discriminative information, the chromatic content of the resulting three-channel texture images do not have discriminative value. In addition, as each image in the NBT has rich texture content, the resulting color textures from the MBT have important intraband and interband discriminative textural content.

To have a clear idea of the visual appearance of images from this new database, Figure 14 presents a set of 15 images. The names of the three original NBT textures that form each multiband texture are indicated at the bottom of each image. For example, the D28D92D111 multiband texture indicates that the D28 Brodatz texture was used for the red channel, D92 for the green, and D111 for the blue. This figure shows that multiband textures have a wide variety of textures, including coarse and fine textures, such as D31D99D108 and D4D16D17, respectively; in addition, they have directional and random textures, such as D51D83D85 and D109D110D112, respectively.

We analyzed the chromatic and textural content of some images from the MTB database, exactly as was done in the previous sections. As shown in Figure 15, MBT images have rich color content with an almost flat hue histogram (Figures 15(a) and 15(b)). In addition, the correlation coefficients between the three RGB channels of these multiband textures were very small ($r \leq 0.183$). This demonstrates that the chromatic information has no discriminative value.

The per-row correlation of the textural content of multiband images showed a very low correlation (Figures 15(c) and 15(d)). The average of the 9 × 640 per-row correlation measures was 0.36 with a standard deviation of 0.088, whereas it was 0.99 with a standard deviation of 0.018 for the VisTex images.

The chromatic and textural content of the MBT images is similar to that of the astronomical and remote sensing images. However, some improvement over these latter images was found as the color distribution of the MBT images is richer (almost uniform color distribution) and their textural content is less correlated.

When we focus on studying only the textural content (intraband and interband spatial interactions) of color images, without being influenced by pure color information, MTB images are ideal. The color of MBT images is an intrinsic part of the texture itself. This color is the result of texture variations within and between the different spectral channels. The complete characterization of MBT images can only be achieved by the simultaneous analysis of the texture of its three channels.

The proposed MTB database can be seen as a generalization of the study of Rosenfeld et al. [37] in which the authors worked on a single multiband texture image generated artificially by introducing a spatial shift between the different bands. The spatial shift was used to amplify the differences between textures of the different bands. The MBT database shows more diversity in the visual appearance of texture and it has different complexity levels. The MBT is not totally new to the image processing community because it was developed from the well-documented Brodatz album. Previously acquired knowledge from the analysis of texture in the Brodatz album can therefore be useful for the analysis of MBT images.

Textures are usually classified as artificial for computer-generated textures and genuine for textures found in human surroundings [38]. Textures from the MBT have both aspects. The three channels of each multiband texture are real textures from the Brodatz album. At the same time, as the three channels of each multiband texture do not come from the same surface, multiband images are also artificial. Here we propose a new category of texture called hybrid texture—textures from the MBT database are from this new category. The visual appearance of the 154 textures composing this new database is very diverse: fine, medium, coarse, random and directional, and so forth. In addition, the texture of the three bands of each color image from the MBT database has different levels of similarity. This provides different levels of difficulty for characterizing interband texture information. This database is available online (http://pages.usherbrooke.ca/asafia/mbt/).

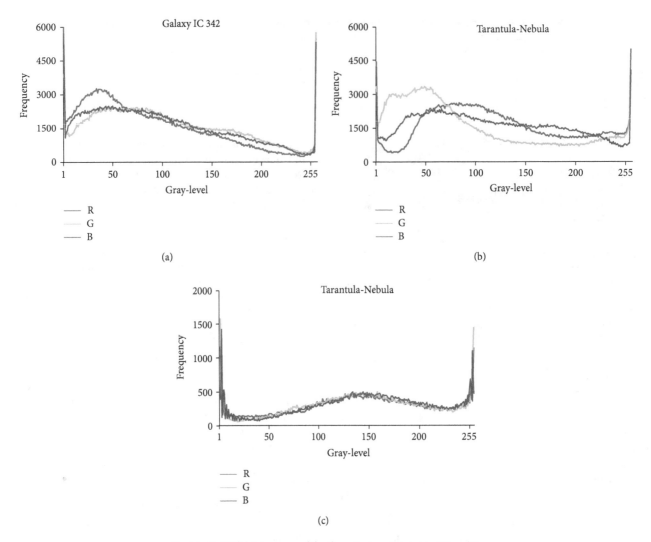

FIGURE 11: RGB histograms of the three texture images in Figure 10.

Based on our results, multiband texture can be defined by extending the definition proposed by Haralick et al. [7] for grayscale texture: the texture of color (or, in general, multiband) images is formed by the spatial distribution of the tonal variations in the same band plus the spatial distribution of the tonal variations across different bands. The first distribution in the proposed definition defines the grayscale texture, defined by Haralick in [7]. The second one defines the part of texture resulting from interband spatial variation. These two types of distributions define multiband texture. Both spatial distributions contribute in different amounts to form the whole texture of the color or multiband image.

An important aspect of this definition is that it clearly identifies a certain part of color as an intrinsic part of the texture. Indeed, gray-level variation across the different bands produces color and, when this variation is the result of interband texture differences, it is identified as part of texture. Consequently, this definition introduces a distinction between this chromatic part of texture and the pure chromatic image content that does not possess texture values.

6. Experiments on MBT Database

Section 5 showed that images from the MBT database have almost the same chromatic content and also have important intraband and interband spatial variations. This has two important implications. The first is that it is not possible to discriminate between MBT images using only chromatic information. The second is that it is not possible to discriminate between MBT images using only intraband texture characterization as it is usually the case for existing color texture databases. In this section we tested the validity of these two observations in the context of texture classification. For that, we carry out two independent classifications. The first used only spectral information (RGB values) and the second used only intraband texture information. We used a mosaic of eight textures (Figure 16) from the MBT database. Figures 17(a) and 17(b) indicate the names of the MBT images according to their relative positions in the mosaic and the three textures from the Normalized Brodatz Texture (Section 2) that were used to generate each MBT image.

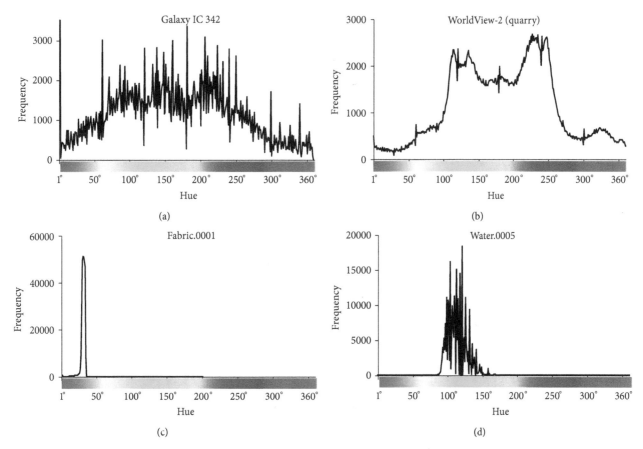

FIGURE 12: Color content comparison between multiband textures (a and b) and VisTex color textures (c and d). The well-localized peaks in Fabric.0001 and Water.0005 (bottom row) indicate the presence of a dominant color tone, whereas the flat histograms in Galaxy IC 342 and WorldView-2 (top row) indicate a wide range of color content.

6.1. Spectral Classification. The mosaic in Figure 16 was classified using several benchmark spectral-based algorithms including K-means [39], Isodata [39], maximum likelihood [35], and mean-shift [40]. The results for all of the tested algorithms showed that none of them were able to identify the eight textures. For the first three classification algorithms, for example, the results showed that all eight textures were almost evenly distributed over the entire area of the mosaic. This supported the observation in Section 5 related to the quasi-uniform distribution of the color content in MTB images. For the mean-shift segmentation algorithm, the boundaries of the detected regions were totally different from those of the eight textures. This result provides clear evidence that color texture images from the MBT database do not possess pure chromatic informative content. The highest overall classification rate for the spectral classifications was 12.5%.

6.2. Textural Extraction and Classification. Among the existing texture analysis methods, we selected the wavelet transform [35]. This transform is a powerful technique for the analysis and decomposition of images at multiple resolutions and different frequencies [35]. This property makes it especially suitable for the segmentation and classification of texture [9, 41, 42]. We used as texture feature the local energy measure

of each wavelet subband [9] which has proven to be efficient in texture classification [9, 43, 44]:

$$E = \frac{1}{N^2} \sum_{\Re} W(i, j)^2, \tag{1}$$

where E is the energy estimated using a neighborhood $\Re$ of size N, W is the wavelet coefficient, and (i, j) gives the spatial position.

The resulting output for a transformed single band at a fixed level is one approximate subband and three detail subbands (i.e., horizontal, vertical, and diagonal). For texture analysis, only the detail subbands were used [45]. As a result, the energy feature was estimated using only the three detail subbands separately. The choice of the wavelet function is a crucial step in texture analysis [46]. It is beyond the scope of this paper to present a detailed study of the effect of wavelet function characteristics on multiband texture discrimination. For the purposes of this study, different wavelet functions were tested. The best combination of wavelet function and moving window for energy feature calculation was the biorthogonal spline function and a moving window of 33 by 33. This was fixed empirically based on the overall classification accuracy of the mosaic in Figure 16.

We used one-level wavelet decomposition because more decomposition levels did not bring significant improvement.

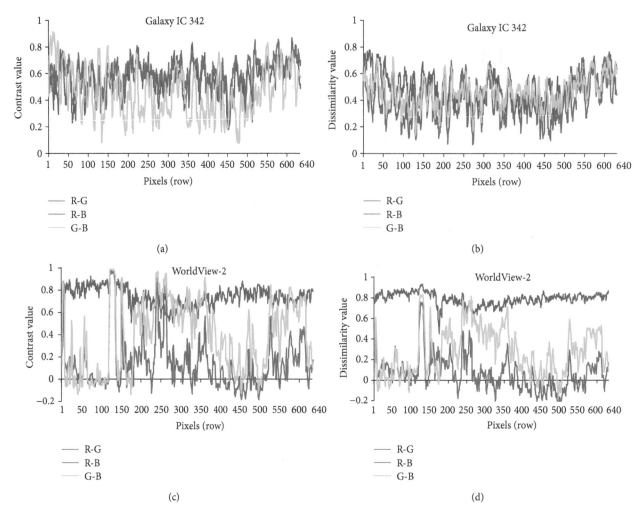

FIGURE 13: Per-row correlation coefficient profile of the cooccurrence matrix for the Galaxy IC-342 (a and b) and WorldView-2 (c and d) images.

Consequently, the classification process used three texture feature images as input in the case of the *intensity* band and nine in the case of the three-band analysis.

Many classification processes have been proposed by the pattern recognition community in the literature. For our experiments, a simple minimum distance classifier scheme based on the Euclidean distance was used in order to test the discrimination power of texture features using a basic classifier. Training samples of 50 by 50 pixels each were selected from the center of each of the eight textures in Figure 16 to serve as reference data. The size of 50 by 50 pixels was first determined by evaluating the accuracy of the classifier with different sample sizes ranging from 10×10 to 100×100 pixels.

In color images, texture is usually extracted either in the *intensity* image component [47–50] or in each of the three RGB bands separately [51–53]. Both of the two strategies were tested in two different classifications. The first classification related to the first strategy used three texture bands (3 details subbands). The second one used nine texture bands (3 details bands × 3 spectral bands).

TABLE 5: Classification results for the three texture analysis methods comparing one-band and three-band texture analysis.

	Intensity	Three band
Overall classification rate	22.6	46.8

The classification results are summarized in Table 5. We can notice that that the *intensity* component did not preserve multiband texture. It only provided an overall classification rate of 22.6%. The three-band strategy provided better results with an overall classification rate of 46.8%. This means that for MBT images, the analysis of each band separately preserves better texture than the use of the *intensity* image component. However, none of the two strategies was able to achieve satisfactory classification rate of the MBT mosaic. This means that texture of this mosaic cannot be simplified into three independent texture plans or as one intensity component. Texture of MBT should be analyzed as a whole by considering the intraband and the interband spatial interactions.

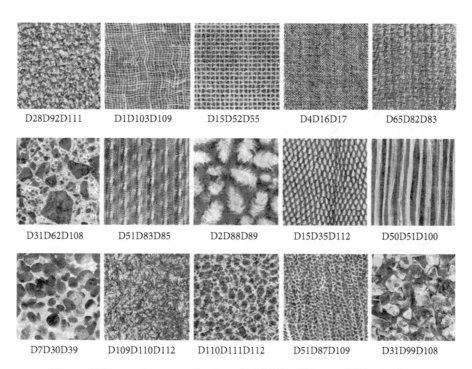

FIGURE 14: Texture image samples from the Multiband Texture (MBT) database.

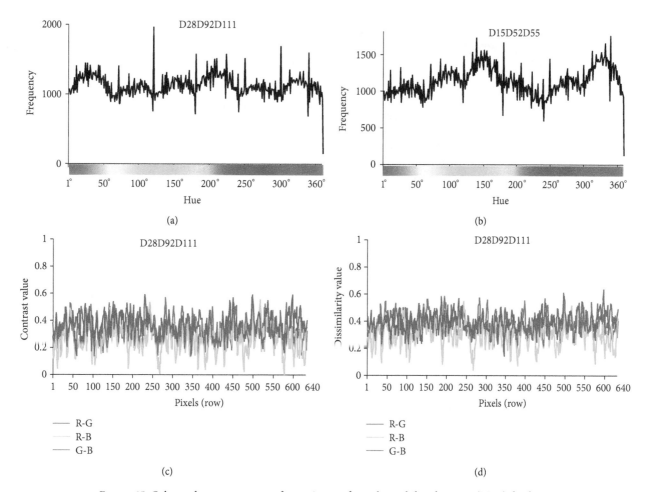

FIGURE 15: Color and texture content of some images from the multiband texture (MBT) database.

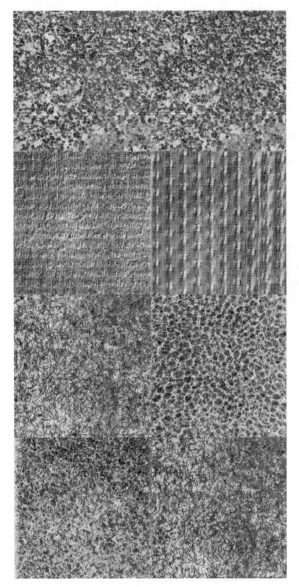

FIGURE 16: Mosaic of eight textures from the MBT database.

Dz87	Dz107
Dz141	Dz9
Dz97	Dz154
Dz105	Dz153

(a)

D19D54D93	D33D54D57
D67D80D103	D1D83D104
D28D110D111	D110D111D112
D32D33D54	D109D110D112

(b)

FIGURE 17: (a) Names and position of the eight MBT images in Figure 16. (b) Names of the three textures from the NBT database (Section 2) used to form each texture MBT in (a).

has the advantage of both preserving the rich textural content of the original Brodatz images and also having a wide variety of color content.

We introduced the concept of multiband texture to describe texture resulting from the combined effects of intra-band and interband spatial variations. We showed that this type of texture exists in images with high spatial resolution and/or images with spectral channels having very different wavelengths. To study multiband textures, we proposed a new database referred to as the Multiband Texture (MBT) database. Images from this database have two important characteristics. First, their chromatic content—even if it is rich—does not have discriminative value, yet it contributes to form texture. Second, their textural content is characterized by high intraband and interband variation. These two characteristics make this database ideal for the texture analysis of color images without the influence of color information. It fills the gap for databases suitable for the analysis of generalized spatial interactions in multiband space. The classification results of the eight textures from the MBT database confirmed that this database can be used to develop intraband and interband texture-based analysis methods.

Acknowledgments

The authors are grateful to the Natural Sciences and Engineering Research Council of Canada (NSERC) for sponsoring this research through the Postgraduate Scholarship (PhD) awarded to S. Abdelmounaime and the Discovery Grant awarded to H. Dong-Chen.

7. Conclusion

This paper examined various fundamental issues of texture information in grayscale, color, and multiband images.

For grayscale texture, we showed that pure spectral information can have a discriminative role. To make texture the main discriminative source of information, we presented an improvement over the Brodatz texture database by normalizing it, in order to eliminate the grayscale background effect. This new database is referred to as the Normalized Brodatz Texture (NBT) database.

For color images, we introduced the concept of colored texture to identify the category of textures in which color is a background with important informative value that is dissociated from texture. Based on this concept, we proposed the Colored Brodatz Texture (CBT) database, which is an extension of the Brodatz texture database. This new database

References

[1] L. R. Sarker and J. E. Nichol, "Improved forest biomass estimates using ALOS AVNIR-2 texture indices," *Remote Sensing of Environment*, vol. 115, no. 4, pp. 968–977, 2011.

[2] X. Wang, N. D. Georganas, and E. M. Petriu, "Fabric texture analysis using computer vision techniques," *IEEE Transactions on Instrumentation and Measurement*, vol. 60, no. 1, pp. 44–56, 2011.

[3] A. Kassnera and R. E. Thornhilla, "Texture analysis: a review of neurologic MR imaging applications," *American Journal of Neuroradiology*, vol. 31, no. 5, pp. 809–816, 2010.

[4] J. R. Smith, C. Y. Lin, and M. Naphade, "Video texture indexing using spatio-temporal wavelets," in *Proceedings of the International Conference on Image Processing (ICIP '02)*, vol. 2, pp. II/437–II/440, September 2002.

[5] W. Phillips III, M. Shah, and N. D. Lobo, "Flame recognition in video," *Pattern Recognition Letters*, vol. 23, no. 1–3, pp. 319–327, 2002.

[6] R. C. Nelson and R. Polana, "Qualitative recognition of motion using temporal texture," *CVGIP—Image Understanding*, vol. 56, no. 1, pp. 78–89, 1992.

[7] R. M. Haralick, K. Shanmugam, and I. Dinstein, "Textural features for image classification," *IEEE Transactions on Systems, Man and Cybernetics*, vol. 3, no. 6, pp. 610–621, 1973.

[8] D. C. He and L. Wang, "Texture unit, texture spectrum, and texture analysis," *IEEE Transactions on Geoscience and Remote Sensing*, vol. 28, no. 4, pp. 509–512, 1990.

[9] A. Laine and J. Fan, "Texture classification by wavelet packet signatures," *IEEE Transactions on Pattern Analysis and Machine Intelligence*, vol. 15, no. 11, pp. 1186–1191, 1993.

[10] A. C. Bovik, M. Clark, and W. S. Geisler, "Multichannel texture analysis using localized spatial filters," *IEEE Transactions on Pattern Analysis and Machine Intelligence*, vol. 12, no. 1, pp. 55–73, 1990.

[11] H. Xin, Z. Liangpei, and W. Le, "Evaluation of morphological texture features for mangrove forest mapping and species discrimination using multispectral IKONOS imagery," *IEEE Geoscience and Remote Sensing Letters*, vol. 6, no. 3, pp. 393–397, 2009.

[12] A. Voisin, V. A. Krylov, G. Moser, S. B. Serpico, and J. Zerubia, "classification of very high resolution SAR images of urban areas using copulas and texture in a hierarchical Markov random field model," *IEEE Geoscience and Remote Sensing Letters*, vol. 10, no. 1, pp. 96–100, 2013.

[13] R. M. Haralick, "Performance characterization in computer vision," *CVGIP—Image Understanding*, vol. 60, no. 2, pp. 245–249, 1994.

[14] P. J. Phillips and K. W. Bowyer, "Empirical evaluation of computer vision algorithms," *IEEE Transactions on Pattern Analysis and Machine Intelligence*, vol. 21, no. 4, pp. 289–290, 1999.

[15] P. Brodatz, *Textures: A Photographic Album for Artists & Designers*, Dover, New York, NY, USA, 1966.

[16] L. Liu and P. Fieguth, "Texture classification from random features," *IEEE Transactions on Pattern Analysis and Machine Intelligence*, vol. 34, no. 3, pp. 574–586, 2012.

[17] J. Yang, Y. Zhuang, and F. Wu, "ESVC-based extraction and segmentation of texture features," *Computers & Geosciences*, vol. 49, pp. 238–247, 2012.

[18] F. M. Khellah, "Texture classification using dominant neighborhood structure," *IEEE Transactions on Image Processing*, vol. 20, no. 11, pp. 3270–3279, 2011.

[19] B. M. Carvalho, T. S. Souza, and E. Garduno, "Texture fuzzy segmentation using adaptive affinity functions," in *Proceedings of the 27th Annual ACM Symposium on Applied Computing*, pp. 51–53, Trento, Italy, March 2012.

[20] I. J. Sumana, G. Lu, and D. Zhang, "Comparison of curvelet and wavelet texture features for content based image retrieval," in *Proceedings of the IEEE International Conference on Multimedia and Expo (ICME '12)*, pp. 290–295, July 2012.

[21] T. Ojala, T. Maenpaa, M. Pietikainen, J. Viertola, J. Kyllonen, and S. Huovinen, "Outex–new framework for empirical evaluation of texture analysis algorithms," in *Proceedings of the 16th International Conference on Pattern Recognition (ICPR '02)*, vol. 1, pp. 701–706, August 2002.

[22] T. Ojala, M. Pietikainen, and T. Maenpaa, "Multiresolution gray-scale and rotation invariant texture classification with local binary patterns," *IEEE Transactions on Pattern Analysis and Machine Intelligence*, vol. 24, no. 7, pp. 971–987, 2002.

[23] P. Janney and Z. Yu, "Invariant features of local textures—a rotation invariant local texture descriptor," in *Proceedings of the IEEE Computer Society Conference on Computer Vision and Pattern Recognition (CVPR '07)*, June 2007.

[24] D. E. Ilea and P. F. Whelan, "Image segmentation based on the integration of colourtexture descriptors—a review," *Pattern Recognition*, vol. 44, no. 10-11, pp. 2479–2501, 2011.

[25] Y. Deng and B. S. Manjunath, "Unsupervised segmentation of color-texture regions in images and video," *IEEE Transactions on Pattern Analysis and Machine Intelligence*, vol. 23, no. 8, pp. 800–810, 2001.

[26] G. Paschos, "Perceptually uniform color spaces for color texture analysis: an empirical evaluation," *IEEE Transactions on Image Processing*, vol. 10, no. 6, pp. 932–937, 2001.

[27] F. Bianconi, A. Fernández, E. González, D. Caride, and A. Calviño, "Rotation-invariant colour texture classification through multilayer CCR," *Pattern Recognition Letters*, vol. 30, no. 8, pp. 765–773, 2009.

[28] K. J. Dana, B. van Ginneken, S. K. Nayar, and J. J. Koenderink, "Reflectance and texture of real-world surfaces," *ACM Transactions on Graphics (TOG)*, vol. 18, no. 1, pp. 1–34, 1999.

[29] L. Wang and D. He, "A new statistical approach for texture analysis," *PE&RS*, vol. 56, no. 1, pp. 61247–61266, 1990.

[30] H. Weschsler and M. Kidode, "A random walk procedure for texture discrimination," *IEEE Transactions on Pattern Analysis and Machine Intelligence*, vol. 1, no. 3, pp. 272–280, 1979.

[31] L. M. Kaplan, "Extended fractal analysis for texture classification and segmentation," *IEEE Transactions on Image Processing*, vol. 8, no. 11, pp. 1572–1585, 1999.

[32] J. Melendez, M. A. Garcia, D. Puig, and M. Petrou, "Unsupervised texture-based image segmentation through pattern discovery," *Computer Vision and Image Understanding*, vol. 115, no. 8, pp. 1121–1133, 2011.

[33] K. I. Kilic and R. H. Abiyev, "Exploiting the synergy between fractal dimension and lacunarity for improved texture recognition," *Signal Processing*, vol. 91, no. 10, pp. 2332–2344, 2011.

[34] K. Zuiderveld, "Contrast limited adaptive histogram equalization," in *Graphics Gems IV*, pp. 474–485, Morgan Kaufmann, Burlington, Mass, USA, 1994.

[35] *Digital Image Processing*, R. C. Gonzalez and R. E. Woods Eds., Prentice Hall, Upper Saddle River, NJ, USA, 2008.

[36] A. Drimbarean and P. F. Whelan, "Experiments in colour texture analysis," *Pattern Recognition Letters*, vol. 22, no. 10, pp. 1161–1167, 2001.

[37] A. Rosenfeld, C. Y. Wang, and A. Y. Wu, "Multispectral texture," *IEEE Transactions on Systems, Man and Cybernetics*, vol. 12, no. 1, pp. 79–84, 1982.

[38] A. Stolpmann and L. S. Dooley, "Genetic algorithms for automized feature selection in a texture classification system," in *Proceedings of the 4th International Conference on Signal Processing Proceedings (ICSP '98)*, vol. 2, pp. 1229–1232, October 1998.

[39] J. T. Tou and R. C. Gonzalez, *Pattern Recognition Principles*, vol. 7, Image Rochester, New York, NY, USA, 1974.

[40] D. Comaniciu and P. Meer, "Mean shift: a robust approach toward feature space analysis," *IEEE Transactions on Pattern Analysis and Machine Intelligence*, vol. 24, no. 5, pp. 603–619, 2002.

[41] M. Unser, "Texture classification and segmentation using wavelet frames," *IEEE Transactions on Image Processing*, vol. 4, no. 11, pp. 1549–1560, 1995.

[42] Y. Dong and J. Ma, "Wavelet-based image texture classification using local energy histograms," *IEEE Signal Processing Letters*, vol. 18, no. 4, pp. 247–250, 2011.

[43] M. Acharyya, R. K. De, and M. K. Kundu, "Extraction of features using M-band wavelet packet frame and their neuro-fuzzy evaluation for multitexture segmentation," *IEEE Transactions on Pattern Analysis and Machine Intelligence*, vol. 25, no. 12, pp. 1639–1644, 2003.

[44] A. Safia, M. F. Belbachir, and T. Iftene, "A wavelet transformation for combining texture and color: application to the combined classification of the HRV SPOT images," *International Journal of Remote Sensing*, vol. 27, no. 18, pp. 3977–3990, 2006.

[45] G. van de Wouwer, P. Scheunders, S. Livens, and D. van Dyck, "Wavelet correlation signatures for color texture characterization," *Pattern Recognition*, vol. 32, no. 3, pp. 443–451, 1999.

[46] A. Mojsilovic, D. Rackov, and M. Popovic, "On the selection of an optimal wavelet basis for texture characterization," in *Proceedings of the International Conference on Image Processing (ICIP '98)*, vol. 3, pp. 678–682, October 1998.

[47] G. Paschos and K. P. Valavanis, "A color texture based visual monitoring system for automated surveillance," *IEEE Transactions on Systems, Man and Cybernetics C*, vol. 29, no. 2, pp. 298–307, 1999.

[48] C. Garcia and G. Tziritas, "Face detection using quantized skin color regions merging and wavelet packet analysis," *IEEE Transactions on Multimedia*, vol. 1, no. 3, pp. 264–277, 1999.

[49] J. Chen, T. N. Pappas, A. Mojsilović, and B. E. Rogowitz, "Adaptive perceptual color-texture image segmentation," *IEEE Transactions on Image Processing*, vol. 14, no. 10, pp. 1524–1536, 2005.

[50] X. Y. Wang, T. Wang, and J. Bu, "Color image segmentation using pixel wise support vector machine classification," *Pattern Recognition*, vol. 44, no. 4, pp. 777–787, 2011.

[51] A. Sengur, "Wavelet transform and adaptive neuro-fuzzy inference system for color texture classification," *Expert Systems with Applications*, vol. 34, no. 3, pp. 2120–2128, 2008.

[52] A. Y. Yang, J. Wright, Y. Ma, and S. S. Sastry, "Unsupervised segmentation of natural images via lossy data compression," *Computer Vision and Image Understanding*, vol. 110, no. 2, pp. 212–225, 2008.

[53] A. Emran, M. Hakdaoui, and J. Chorowicz, "Anomalies on geologic maps from multispectral and textural classification: the bleida mining district (Morocco)," *Remote Sensing of Environment*, vol. 57, no. 1, pp. 13–21, 1996.

17

Local Stereo Matching Using Adaptive Local Segmentation

Sanja Damjanović, Ferdinand van der Heijden, and Luuk J. Spreeuwers

Signals and Systems Group, Department of EEMCS, University of Twente, Hallenweg 15, 7522 NH Enschede, The Netherlands

Correspondence should be addressed to Sanja Damjanović, s.damjanovic@ewi.utwente.nl

Academic Editors: A. Bandera, E. Davies, B. K. Gunturk, S. Mattoccia, and Y. Zhuge

We propose a new dense local stereo matching framework for gray-level images based on an adaptive local segmentation using a dynamic threshold. We define a new validity domain of the frontoparallel assumption based on the local intensity variations in the 4 neighborhoods of the matching pixel. The preprocessing step smoothes low-textured areas and sharpens texture edges, whereas the postprocessing step detects and recovers occluded and unreliable disparities. The algorithm achieves high stereo reconstruction quality in regions with uniform intensities as well as in textured regions. The algorithm is robust against local radiometrical differences and successfully recovers disparities around the objects edges, disparities of thin objects, and the disparities of the occluded region. Moreover, our algorithm intrinsically prevents errors caused by occlusion to propagate into nonoccluded regions. It has only a small number of parameters. The performance of our algorithm is evaluated on the Middlebury test bed stereo images. It ranks highly on the evaluation list outperforming many local and global stereo algorithms using color images. Among the local algorithms relying on the frontoparallel assumption, our algorithm is the best-ranked algorithm. We also demonstrate that our algorithm is working well on practical examples as for disparity estimation of a tomato seedling and a 3D reconstruction of a face.

1. Introduction

Stereo matching has been a popular topic in computer vision for more than three decades, ever since one of the first papers appeared in 1979 [1]. Stereo images are two images of the same scene taken from different viewpoints. Dense stereo matching is a correspondence problem with the aim to find for each pixel in one image the corresponding pixel in the other image. A map of all pixel displacements in an image is a disparity map. To solve the stereo correspondence problem, it is common to introduce constraints and assumptions, which regularize the stereo correspondence problem.

The most common constraints and assumptions for stereo matching are the epipolar constraint, the constant brightness or the Lambertian assumption, the uniqueness constraint, the smoothness constraint, the visibility constraint and the ordering constraint [2–4]. Stereo correspondence algorithms belong to one of two major groups, local or global, depending on whether the constraints are applied to a small local region or propagated throughout the whole image. Local stereo methods estimate the correspondence using a local support region or a window [5, 6]. Local algorithms generally rely on an approximation of the smoothness constraint assuming that all pixels within the matching region have the same disparity. This approximation of the smoothness constraint is known as the frontoparallel assumption. However, the frontoparallel assumption is not valid for highly curved surfaces or around disparity discontinuities. Global stereo methods consider stereo matching as a labeling problem where the pixels of the reference image are nodes and the estimated disparities are labels. An energy functional embeds the matching assumptions by its data, smoothness, and occlusion terms and propagates them along the scan line or through the whole image. The labeling problem is solved by energy functional minimization, using dynamic programming, graph cuts, or belief propagation [7–9]. A recent review of both local and global stereo vision algorithms can be found in [10].

Algorithms based on rectangular window matching give an accurate disparity estimation provided the majority of the window pixels belong to the same smooth object surface with only a slight curvature or inclination relative to the image plain. In all other cases, window-based matching produces an incorrect disparity map: the discontinuities are smoothed, and the disparities of the high-textured surfaces are propagated into low-textured areas [11]. Another restriction of window-based matching is the size of objects of which the disparity is to be determined. Weather the disparity of a narrow object can be correctly estimated depends mostly on the similarity between the occluded background, visible background, and object [12]. Algorithms which use suitably shaped matching areas for cost aggregation result in a more accurate disparity estimation, [13–18]. The matching region is selected using pixels within certain fixed distances in RGB, CIELab color space, and/or Euclidean space.

To alleviate the frontoparallel assumption, some approaches allow the matching area to lie on the inclined plane, such as in [19, 20]. The alternative to the idea that properly shaped areas for cost aggregation can result in more accurate matching results is to allocate different weights to pixels in the cost aggregation step. In [21], the pixels closer in the color space and spatially closer to the central pixel are given proportionally more significance, whereas, in [22], the additional assumption of connectivity plays a role during weight assignment.

Our stereo algorithm belongs to the group of local stereo algorithms. Within the stereo framework, we rely on some standard and some modified matching constraints and assumptions. We use the epipolar constraint to convert the stereo correspondence into a one-dimensional problem. However, we modify the interpretation of the frontoparallel assumption and the Lambertian constraint. A novel interpretation of the frontoparallel assumption is based on local intensity variations. By adaptive local segmentation in both matching windows, we constrain the frontoparallel assumption only to the intersection of the central matching segments of the initial rectangular window. This mechanism prevents the propagation of the matching errors caused by occlusion and enables an accurate disparity estimation for narrow objects. The algorithm estimates correctly disparities of both textured as well as textureless surfaces, and disparities around depth discontinuities, disparities of the small as well as large objects independently of the initial window size. We apply the Lambertian constraint to local intensity differences and not to the original gray values of the pixels in the segment. In the postprocessing step, we apply the occlusion constraint without imposing the ordering constraint, which enables successful disparity estimation for narrow objects. Also, our stereo algorithm is suitable for a fast real-time implementation, because it is local algorithm for gray-valued images which uses a local segmentation and only a small subset of window pixels for cost calculation.

Our main contribution is the introduction of the relationship between the frontoparallel assumption and the local intensity variation and its applications to the stereo matching. In addition, we introduce a preprocessing step that smoothes low-textured areas and sharpens texture edges producing the image more favorable for a proper local adaptive segmentation.

The paper is organized as follows: in Section 2, we explain our stereo matching framework: the preprocessing step, the adaptive local segmentation, the matching region selection, the stereo matching, and the postprocessing step;

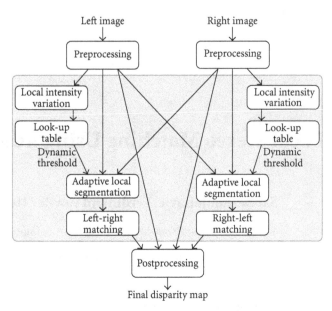

FIGURE 1: Flow chart of the local stereo matching algorithm using adaptive local segmentation.

in Section 3, we show and discuss the results of our algorithm on different stereo images; in Section 4, we draw conclusions.

2. Stereo Algorithm

Our algorithm consists of three steps: a preprocessing step, a matching step, and a postprocessing step. The flow chart of the algorithm is shown in Figure 1. Input to the algorithm is a pair of rectified stereo images I_l and I_r, where one of them, for instance I_l, is considered as the reference image. For each pixel in the reference image, we perform matching along the epipolar line for each integer-valued disparity within the disparity range. Firstly, the input images are preprocessed, as explained in Section 2.1. The preprocessing step is applied to each image individually. Next, we calculate the local intensity variations maps for the preprocessed images and used them to determine the dynamic threshold for adaptive local segmentation, and elaborated in Section 2.2. Further, the stereo matching comprises a final region selection from segments, a matching cost calculation for all disparities from the disparity range and disparity estimation by a modification of the winner-take-all estimation method, see Section 2.3. The result of the matching is two disparity maps, D_{LR} and D_{RL}, corresponding to the left and right images of the stereo pair. Finally, postprocessing step calculates the final disparity map corresponding to the reference image as described in Section 2.4.

2.1. Preprocessing. We apply a nonlinear intensity transformation to the input images in order to make them more suitable for adaptive local segmentation. The presence of the Gaussian noise and the sampling errors in image can produce erroneous segments for matching. The noise is dominant in the low-textured and uniform regions, while the sampling errors are pronounced in the high-textured

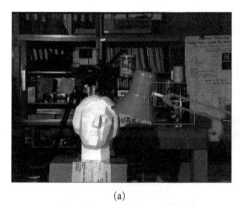
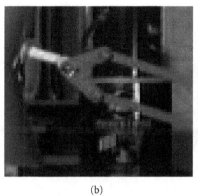
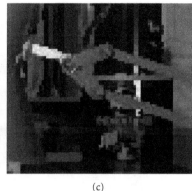

(a)   (b)   (c)

FIGURE 2: Illustration of the preprocessing step for one image from *Tsukuba* stereo pair: (a) original image, (b) detail of the original image, and (c) detail of the original image after the preprocessing step is applied.

image regions. The sampling effects can be tackled by choosing a cost measure insensitive to sampling as in [23], or by interpolating the cost function as in [24]. We handle these problems differently and within the preprocessing step. The applied transformation suppresses the noise in low-textured regions while simultaneously suppressing the sampling effects in the high-textured regions.

The transformation is based on the interpolated subpixel samples by bicubic transform in the 4 neighborhoodS and by consistently replacing the central pixel value by maximum or by minimum value of the set, depending on the relation between the mean and the median of the set. We form a set of samples of the observed pixel at the position (x, y) and the intensities in horizontally and vertically interpolates image at the subpixel level at δ_i:

$$\delta_i = -\frac{7}{8} + i \cdot \frac{1}{8}, \quad i \in \{0, 1, \ldots, 14\},$$

$$v = \{I(x - \delta_i, y), I(x, y - \delta_i) \mid \forall i \in \{0, 1, \ldots, 14\}\}. \tag{1}$$

The intensity transformation is performed by replacing the intensity $I(x, y)$ with the new intensity as

$$I(x, y) = \begin{cases} \max\{v\}: & \text{if median}\{v\} > \text{mean}\{v\} \\ \min\{v\}: & \text{otherwise} \end{cases} . \tag{2}$$

All intensity values are corrected in the same manner. If the pixel intensity differs significantly from its four neighbors, as in the high-textured regions, it will be replaced by the maximum value in the interpolated subpixel set v, resulting in the sharpening effect. On the other hand, in low-textured regions, the intensity change is small, and replacing the initial intensity value systematically with the minimum value of the interpolated subpixel set v, it produces the favorable denoising effect. These positive effects originate from the image resampling done by bicubic interpolation, because the bicubic interpolation exhibits overshoots at locations with large differences between adjacent pixels, see Chapter 4.4 in [25] and Chapter 6.6 in [26]. These favorable effects are lacking if the interpolation method is linear.

We illustrate the effect of the preprocessing step for an image from a stereo pair from the Middlebury evaluation

database in Figure 2. Therefore, the preprocessing step modifies regions with high-intensity variations and results in the sharper image. Further, in Section 3, we show the influence of this step to overall algorithm score.

2.2. Adaptive Local Segmentation. Adaptive local segmentation establishes a new relationship between the local intensity variation and the frontoparallel assumption applied to stereo matching. Adaptive local segmentation selects a central subset of pixels from a large rectangular window for which we assume that the frontoparallel assumption holds for the segment. The segment contains the central window pixel and pixels, spatially connected to the central pixel, whose intensities lie within the dynamic threshold from the intensity of the central window. Starting from the segment, we form a final region selection for matching, see Section 2.3.

The idea behind the adaptive local segmentation is to prevent that the matching region contains the pixels with significantly different disparities prior to actually estimating disparity. We accomplish this aim by conveniently choosing threshold for segmentation based on the local texture. If local texture is uniform with local intensity variations caused only by the Gaussian noise, we opt for a small threshold value. In this way, because the intensity variations are small, the segment will comprise the whole uniform region. We assume that these pixels originate from the smooth surface of one object and therefore that the frontoparallel assumption holds for the segment. On the other hand, if the window is textured, that is, intensity variations are significantly larger than the noise level, it is not possible to distinguish based only on the pixel intensities and prior to matching, whether the pixels originate from one textured object or from several different objects at different distances from the camera. In this case, relying on the high texture for an accurate matching result, it is good to select small segment in order to assure that the segment contains pixels from only one object and does not contain depth discontinuity. Due to the high local intensity variations, this is achieved by large threshold.

We introduce local intensity variation measure in order to determine the level of local texture and subsequently the dynamic threshold. We define the local intensity variation

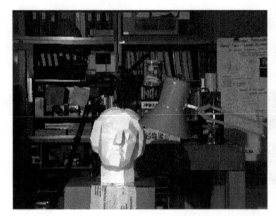 

FIGURE 3: Left image from *Tsukuba* stereo pair with a color-coded local intensity variations levels: the lowest local intensity variation is in red, and in the ascending order follow orange, green; the highest local intensity variations are in blue.

measure as a sharpness of local edges in the 4 neighborhoods of the central window pixel. The sharper local edges are, the larger is the local intensity variation. We calculate the local intensity variation using the maximum of the first derivatives in the horizontal and the vertical directions at the half-pixel interpolated image by benefiting again from overshooting effect of the bicubic interpolation. The horizontal central difference for a pixel at the position (x, y) in image I is calculated as

$$H = \left| I\left(x - \frac{1}{2}, y\right) - I\left(x + \frac{1}{2}, y\right) \right|, \qquad (3)$$

where $I(x - 1/2, y)$ and $I(x + 1/2, y)$ are horizontal half-pixel shifts of image I to the left and to the right. The vertical central difference for a pixel at the position (x, y) in image I is calculated as

$$V = \left| I\left(x, y - \frac{1}{2}\right) - I\left(x, y + \frac{1}{2}\right) \right|, \qquad (4)$$

where $I(x, y - 1/2)$ and $I(x, y + 1/2)$ are vertical half-pixel shifts of image I. We define the intensity variation measure as

$$M_t(x, y) = \max(V, H). \qquad (5)$$

We divide local intensity variations into four ranges based on the preselected constant T and define a dynamic threshold for each range by a look-up table:

$$T_d(x, y) = \begin{cases} \dfrac{T}{2}: & M_t(x, y) \in \left[0, \dfrac{T}{4}\right) \\[2mm] \dfrac{3 \cdot T}{4}: & M_t(x, y) \in \left[\dfrac{T}{4}, \dfrac{T}{2}\right) \\[2mm] T: & M_t(x, y) \in \left[\dfrac{T}{2}, T\right) \\[2mm] 2 \cdot T: & M_t(x, y) \in [T, \infty) \end{cases} \qquad (6)$$

Figure 3 shows a color-coded dynamic threshold map, or equivalently local intensity variation ranges, for the left image from *Tsukuba* stereo pair from the Middlebury stereo evaluation set [27].

Step 1: Dynamic thresholding
for $i = 1$ to W **do**
    for $j = 1$ to W **do**
        if $|p_{l/r}^{i,j} - c_{l/r}| < T_d(x, y)$ **then**
            set $\mathbf{B}_{l/r}^{i,j}$ to 1
        end if
    end for
end for
Step 2: Dilation
Dilate $\mathbf{B}_{l/r}$ with 3×3 squared structured element
Step 3: Imposing connectivity
for $i = 1$ to W **do**
    for $j = 1$ to W **do**
        if $\mathbf{B}_{l/r}^{i,j} = 1$ and not connected to $\mathbf{B}_{l/r}^{w+1,w+1}$ **then**
            set $\mathbf{B}_{l/r}^{i,j}$ to 0
        end if
    end for
end for

ALGORITHM 1: Adaptive local segmentation for reference pixel $I_l(x, y)$.

The dynamic threshold $T_d(x, y)$ defined by (6) for the reference pixel in the reference image is also used for the adaptive local segmentation in the nonreference image for all potentially corresponding pixels from the disparity range.

The adaptive local segmentation pseudocode for the reference pixel $I_l(x, y)$ in the left image is given by Algorithm 1. The segmentation is performed for reference and nonreference windows independently using the same threshold $T_d(x, y)$. Thus, in the $W \times W$ window, where $W = 2 \cdot w + 1$, around the pixel at the position (x, y) in the reference image, we declare that the pixel at (i, j) position, where $i, j = 1, \ldots, W$ in the reference window, belongs to the segment if its gray value $p_l^{i,j}$ differs from the central pixel's gray value $c_l = p_l^{w+1, w+1}$ for less than the dynamic threshold $T_d(x, y)$. The segment pixels in the nonreference window are chosen in similar way using the same threshold $T_d(x, y)$. Next, the central 8-connected components in the

```
for i = 1 to W do
    for j = 1 to W do
        if B_l^{i,j} ∧ B_r^{i,j} then
            set B^{i,j} to 1
        end if
    end for
end for
```

ALGORITHM 2: The final binary map calculation.

dilated masks are selected. The final segments are defined by the binary $W \times W$ maps, B_l and B_r, with ones if the pixels belong to the segment. Dilation is performed by 3×3 squared structured element to include additional neighbor pixels into segments and to merge isolated but close-selected pixels.

2.3. Stereo Correspondence. The matching region is defined by the overlap of the adaptive local segments in the reference and nonreference windows. Thus, the matching region is defined by binary map B, which has ones if and only if both binary maps, B_l and B_r, have ones at the same positions, as given in Algorithm 2.

We assume that the corresponding pixels have similar intensities and that the differences exist only due to the Gaussian noise with the variance σ_n^2. One-dimensional vectors, $\mathbf{z}_l$ and $\mathbf{z}_r$, are formed from the pixels from the left and right matching window at positions of ones within the binary map $\mathbf{B}$. Besides the noise, differences between vectors can occur due to different offsets and due to occlusion. To make the matching vectors insensitive to local different offsets, we subtract the central pixel values c_l and c_r from vectors $\mathbf{z}_l$ and $\mathbf{z}_r$, given by Algorithm 3. In this way, the intensity information is transformed from the absolute intensities to the differences of intensities with respect to the central window pixels. Further, we impose the Lambertian assumption on the pixels after the central pixel subtraction and not on the original pixel intensities. To prevent the occlusion influence in matching we eliminate the occlusion outliers by keeping only the coordinates of vectors which differ for less than threshold T as given by Algorithm 4.

We calculate the matching cost using the sum of squared differences (SSDs) [7, 28]. To compare the costs with different length of vectors $\mathbf{z}_l$ and $\mathbf{z}_r$ for different disparities, we introduce the normalized SSD:

$$C_{nSSD}(d) \propto \frac{1}{N_p} \cdot \frac{\|\mathbf{z}_l - \mathbf{z}_r\|^2}{4 \cdot \sigma_n^2}, \quad (7)$$

where N_p is the length of vectors $\mathbf{z}_l$ and $\mathbf{z}_r$ for disparity d.

The *winner-take-all* (WTA) method selects the disparity with the minimal cost for the observed reference pixel. In our algorithm, besides the cost, the number of pixels participating in the cost calculation is also an indication of a correspondence. This ordinal measure cannot be used directly in the disparity estimation, because it is not always a reliable indication of the correspondence as in the case of occlusion. If the number of pixels used in the cost calculation

is very low, it may be due to occlusion. However, a reliable match has a substantial ordinal support.

We combine the cost and the number of participating pixels in the disparity estimation and introduce a hybrid WTA; we consider only disparities supported by a sufficient number of pixels as potential candidates for a disparity estimate. Thus, the final disparity estimate is chosen from a subset of the all possible disparities from the disparity range. We term these disparity candidates as the reliable disparity candidates [13, 29].

The reliable disparity candidates have at least $N_s = K_p \cdot \max\{N_p^{x,y}\}$ supporting pixels, where $N_p^{x,y}$ is a set containing the number of pixels participating in the cost aggregation step for each possible disparity value from the disparity range $[D_{min}, D_{max}]$. K_p is the ratio coefficient $0 < K_p \leq 1$. The estimated disparity $d(x, y)$ is

$$d(x, y) = \underset{d_i \in \{D_{min}, \ldots, D_{max}\}}{\text{argmin}} \left\{ C_{nSSD}^{x,y}(d_i) \mid N_p^{x,y}(d_i) > N_s \right\}, \quad (8)$$

where $x = 1, \ldots, R$ and $y = 1, \ldots, C$, for image of the dimension $R \times C$ pixels, and d_i belongs to the set of all possible disparities from the disparity range $[D_{min}, D_{max}]$.

The final result of the hybrid WTA is the disparity map D

$$D = \{d(x, y) \mid \forall x \in [1, R] \land \forall y \in [1, C]\}. \quad (9)$$

We calculate two disparity maps, one disparity map, D_{LR}, with the left image I_l as the reference, and the other, D_{RL}, as the right image I_r as the reference.

2.4. Postprocessing. In the postprocessing, we detect the disparity errors and correct them. There are some areas of incorrect disparity values caused by low-textured areas larger than the initial window. There are some isolated disparity errors with significantly different disparity from the neighborhood disparities, so called outliers, caused by isolated pixels or groups of several pixels if the adaptive local segmentation did not result in sufficiently large segment due to high local intensity variation. Also, there are disparity errors caused by occlusion. Although the matching procedure is the same for both occluded and nonoccluded pixels, our stereo matching algorithm does not propagate error caused by occlusions because the boundaries of objects are taken into account by both the adaptive local segmentation and the final matching region selection. However, occluded pixels do not have corresponding pixels, and the estimated disparities for the occluded pixels are incorrect.

The postprocessing consists of several steps including median filtering of the initial disparity maps, disparity refinement of the individual disparity maps, consistency check, and propagation of the reliable disparities.

First, we apply $L \times L$ *median filter* to both disparity maps, D_{LR} and D_{RL}, and eliminate disparity outliers. Second, we refine the filtered disparity maps individually to correct low-textured areas with erroneous disparities, in an iterative procedure. The refinement step propagates disparities by histogram voting to the regions with close intensities defined by a look-up table given in (10) across the whole image as

N'_p is the length of the vectors $\mathbf{z}_l$ and $\mathbf{z}_r$
c_l and c_r are the central intensities in the left and in the right window
for $i = 1$ to N'_p **do**
    $\mathbf{z}_l(i) = \mathbf{z}_l(i) - c_l$
    $\mathbf{z}_r(i) = \mathbf{z}_r(i) - c_r$
end for

ALGORITHM 3: Offset neutralization.

TABLE 1: x_{tmp} and y_{tmp} values for histogram calculation in (11).

	Direction	x_{tmp}	y_{tmp}	Condition
1	Up	$x - i_u$	y	$i_u = \{1 \text{ to } x - 1 \mid x - 1 > 0\}$
2	Up-right	$x - i_{ur}$	$y + i_{ur}$	$i_{ur} = \{1 \text{ to } \min(x - 1, C - y) \mid \min(x - 1, C - y) > 0\}$
3	Right	x	$y + i_r$	$i_r = \{1 \text{ to } C - y \mid C - y > 0\}$
4	Down-right	$x + i_{dr}$	$y + i_{dr}$	$i_{dr} = \{1 \text{ to } \min(R - x, C - y) \mid \min(R - x, C - y) > 0\}$
5	Down	$x + i_d$	y	$i_d = \{1 \text{ to } R - x \mid R - x > 0\}$
6	Down-left	$x + i_{dl}$	$y - i_{dl}$	$i_{dl} = \{1 \text{ to } \min(R - x, y - 1) \mid \min(R - x, y - 1) > 0\}$
7	Left	x	$y - i_l$	$i_l = \{1 \text{ to } y - 1 \mid y - 1 > 0\}$
8	Up-left	$x - i_{ul}$	$y - i_{ul}$	$i_{ul} = \{1 \text{ to } \min(x - 1, y - 1) \mid \min(x - 1, y - 1) > 0\}$

N'_p is the length of the initial vectors $\mathbf{z}_l$ and $\mathbf{z}_r$
$k = 0$
for $i = 1$ to N'_p **do**
    if $|\mathbf{z}_l(i) - \mathbf{z}_r(i)| \geq T$ **then**
        Remove $\mathbf{z}_l(i)$ and $\mathbf{z}_r(i)$
    end if
end for
N_p is the length of the final vectors $\mathbf{z}_l$ and $\mathbf{z}_r$

ALGORITHM 4: Elimination of the outliers.

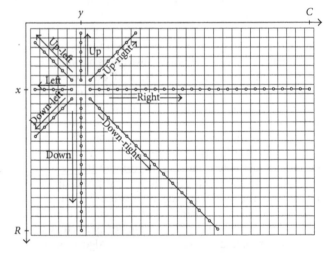

FIGURE 4: Propagation scheme.

illustrated in propagation scheme in Figure 4. Some similar notions to this approach appear separately in the literature, [18, 30], and we were inspired by them. In [30], the cost aggregation is done along the 16 radial directions in disparity space, while in [18], histogram voting is used within the segment for disparity refinement. We refine our disparity maps by histogram voting of accumulating disparities along 8 radial directions across the whole disparity map with constraint of the maximum allowed intensity difference with the pixel being refined. The maximum intensity difference is defined by a dynamic threshold T_p with the same logic behind as in local intensity variation measure in Section 2.2, with the difference that here we distinguish three ranges of intensity differences. Thus, the histogram is formed using disparities of the pixels with close intensities along 8 radial directions, see Figure 4 and Table 1. The pixels are close in intensities, and their disparities are taken into account in histogram forming if they lie within the threshold T_p from

the intensity of the pixel at the observed position (x, y). The threshold $T_p(x, y)$ is selected based on a look-up table:

$$T_p(x, y) = \begin{cases} \dfrac{T}{2}: & M_t(x, y) \in \left[0, \dfrac{T}{2}\right) \\[2mm] \dfrac{3T}{4}: & M_t(x, y) \in \left[\dfrac{T}{2}, \dfrac{3 \cdot T}{4}\right). \\[2mm] T: & M_t(x, y) \in \left[\dfrac{3 \cdot T}{4}, \infty\right) \end{cases} \quad (10)$$

The histogram H with a number of bins equal to the number of disparities within the disparity range is formed by counting the disparities along 8 radial directions for the pixels whose intensity is within threshold $T_p(x, y)$:

$$H\left(d\left(x_{\text{tmp}}, y_{\text{tmp}}\right)\right) = H\left(d\left(x_{\text{tmp}}, y_{\text{tmp}}\right)\right) + 1$$

$$\text{if } \left| I\left(x_{\text{tmp}}, y_{\text{tmp}}\right) - I(x, y) \right| < T_p(x, y), \tag{11}$$

where x_{tmp} and y_{tmp} are given by Table 1.

We calculate disparity d_h as a disparity of the normalized histogram maximum:

$$h(i) = \frac{H(i)}{\sum_i H(i)}, \quad i = D_{\min} \text{ to } D_{\max}, \tag{12}$$

$$d_h = \arg\max_i h(i), \quad i = D_{\min} \text{ to } D_{\max}. \tag{13}$$

The initial disparity $d(x, y)$ is replaced by the new value d_h if it is significantly supported, that is, if the normalized histogram value $h(d_h)$ is greater than α; otherwise, it is left unchanged:

$$d(x, y) = \begin{cases} d_h: & \text{if } |d_h - d(x, y)| > 1 \land h(d_h) > \alpha \\ d(x, y): & \text{otherwise} \end{cases}, \tag{14}$$

where α, $0 \leq \alpha < 1$, is a significance threshold. The steps given by (11), (12), (13), and (14) are repeated iteratively until there are no more updates to disparities in the map.

Next, we detect *occluded disparities* by the consistency check between two disparity maps:

$$\left| D_{\text{RL}}(x, y - D_{\text{LR}}(x, y)) - D_{\text{LR}}(x, y) \right| \leq 1. \tag{15}$$

If the condition in (15) is not satisfied for disparity $D_{\text{LR}}(x, y)$, we declare it as inconsistent and eliminate it from the disparity map. The missing disparities are filled in by an iterative refinement procedure similar to the previously applied procedure for the disparity propagation by histogram voting. In the iterative step to fill in the inconsistent disparities, we use the threshold look-up table (10) as in the disparity refinement step. We calculate the histogram h of the consistent disparities with close intensities along 8 radial directions as given by (11) and (12). The missing disparity is filled in with the disparity d_h with the largest support in the histogram, provided that the histogram is not empty. The remaining unfilled inconsistent disparities, and we fill in by the disparity of the nearest neighbor with known disparities with the smallest intensity differences. As a last step in the postprocessing, we apply $L \times L$ *median filter* to obtain the final disparity map.

3. Experiments and Discussion

We have used the Middlebury stereo benchmark [4] to evaluate the performance of our stereo matching algorithm. The parameters of the algorithm are fixed for all four stereo pairs as required by the benchmark. There are five free parameters in our algorithm. The threshold value is set to $T = 12$. The half-window size is $w = 15$, and the window size

TABLE 2: Evaluation results based on the online Middlebury stereo benchmark [4]: the errors are given in percentages for the nonoccluded (NONOCC) region, the whole image (ALL), and discontinuity (DISC) areas. The numbers within brackets indicate the ranking in the Middlebury table.

Images	Nonocc	All	Disc
Tsukuba	**1.33 (37)**	1.82 (32)	7.19 (46)
Venus	**0.32 (39)**	0.79 (46)	4.5 (58)
Teddy	**5.32 (17)**	11.9 (40)	14.5 (19)
Cones	**2.73 (14)**	9.69 (53)	7.91 (21)

is $W \times W$ where $W = 31$. The noise variance σ_n^2 is a small and constant scaling factor in (7). The ratio coefficient in hybrid WTA is $K_p = 0.5$. In the postprocessing step, the median filter parameter is $L = 5$, and the significance threshold in histogram voting is $\alpha = 0.45$.

Figure 5 shows results for all four stereo pairs from the Middlebury stereo evaluation database: *Tsukuba*, *Venus*, *Teddy*, and *Cones*. The leftmost column contains the left images of the four stereo pairs. The ground truth (GT) disparity maps are shown in the second column, the estimated disparity maps are shown in the third column, and the error maps are shown in the forth column. In the error maps, the white regions denote correctly calculated disparity values which do not differ for more than 1 from the ground truth. If the estimated disparity differs for more than 1 from the ground truth value, it is marked as an error. The errors are shown in black and gray, where black represents the errors in the nonoccluded regions, and gray represents errors in the occluded regions. The quantitative results in the Middlebury stereo evaluation framework are presented in Table 2.

The results show that our stereo algorithm preserves disparity edges. It estimates successfully the disparities of thin objects and successfully deals with subtle radiometrical differences between images of the same stereo pair. Occlusion errors are not propagated, and occluded disparities are successfully filled in the postprocessing step. A narrow object is best visible in the *Tsukuba* disparity map (the lamp construction) and in *Cones* disparity map (pens in a cup in the lower right corner). Our algorithm correctly estimates disparities of both textureless and textured surfaces, for example, the examples of large uniform surfaces in stereo pairs *Venus* and *Teddy* are successfully recovered.

The images in the Middlebury database have different sizes, different disparity ranges, and different radiometric properties. The stereo pairs *Tsukuba*, 384×288 pixels, and *Venus*, 434×383 pixels, have disparity ranges from 0 to 15 and from 0 to 19. The radiometric properties of the images in these stereo pairs are almost identical, and the offset compensation given by Algorithm 3 is not significant for these two example pairs, as we demonstrated in [13]. As required by the Middlebury evaluation framework, we apply the offset compensation to all four stereo pairs. The stereo pairs *Teddy*, 450×375 pixels, and *Cones*, 450×375 pixels, have disparity ranges from 0 to 59. The images of these stereo pairs are not radiometrically identical, and the offset

FIGURE 5: Disparity results for the stereo pairs (1st row: *Tsukuba*, 2nd row: *Venus*, 3rd row: *Teddy*, and 4th row: *Cones*) from the Middlebury testbed database. The columns show, from left to the right, the left image, ground truth, result computed by our stereo algorithm, and disparity error map larger than 1 pixel. The nonoccluded regions errors with ranking are, respectively, *Tsukuba* 1.33% (37), *Venus* 0.32% (39), *Teddy* 5.32% (17), and *Cones* 2.73% (14).

compensation successfully deals with these radiometrical differences [13].

The error percentages together with ranking in the Middlebury evaluation online list are given in Table 2. The numbers show error percentages for nonoccluded regions (NONOCC), discontinuity regions (DISC), and the whole (ALL) disparity map. The overall ranking of our algorithm in the Middlebury evaluation table of stereo algorithms is the 28th place out of 123 evaluated algorithms. Thus, our stereo algorithm outperforms many local as well as global algorithms. Among the algorithms ranked in the Middlebury stereo evaluation, there are only two local algorithms ranked higher than our algorithm, but both of them do not impose the frontoparallel assumption strictly: a local matching method using image geodesic-supported weights *GeoSup* [5] and a matching approach with slanted support windows *PatchMatch* [31]. Both of these algorithms use colored images, while our algorithm works with intensity images and

achieves comparable results. Although these approaches have better general ranking in the Middlebury stereo evaluation list, our approach with matching based on frontoparallel regions outperforms the *PatchMatch* algorithm for *Tsukuba* stereo pair, and the *GeoSup* algorithm for *Tsukuba*, *Teddy*, and *Cones* stereo pairs. Thus, our approach with region selection by threshold produces more accurate disparity maps for cluttered scenes than *GeoSup* algorithm with region selection using geodesic support weights.

To investigate the contribution of the preprocessing and the postprocessing steps to the overall result, we show in Table 3 the results we obtained on the benchmark stereo pairs with or without the preprocessing and the postprocessing steps in the algorithm. We show the results if neither, only one, and both steps are applied. If our postprocessing step was omitted, the $L \times L$ median filter was applied. From the results in Table 3, we conclude that both steps, if individually applied, improve the qualities of the final disparity maps.

TABLE 3: Comparison of results with (+) or without (−) preprocessing (preP) and postprocessing (postP) steps.

PreP	PostP	Tsukuba			Venus			Teddy			Cones		
		Nonocc	All	Disc	Nonocc	All	Disc	Nonocc	All	Disc	Nonocc	All	Disc
−	−	3.6	5.41	10.04	2.76	4.38	13.18	8.11	17.42	19.73	4.77	15.04	12.33
+	−	2.74	4.50	10.11	0.62	1.63	7.95	7.52	16.82	19.41	3.98	14.37	11.27
−	+	2.45	3.05	7.31	1.53	2.11	5.75	6.11	12.49	15.20	3.20	9.30	9.14
+	+	1.33	1.82	7.19	0.32	0.79	4.5	5.32	11.90	14.50	2.73	9.69	7.91

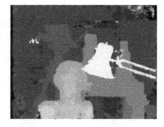

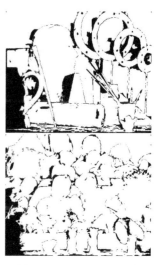

FIGURE 6: Disparity results for the stereo pair *Tsukuba*: (a) without preprocessing and without postprocessing, (b) without preprocessing and with postprocessing, (c) with preprocessing and without postprocessing, and (d) with preprocessing and with postprocessing.

FIGURE 7: Disparity results for the stereo pairs (1st row: *Art*, 2nd row: *Dolls*) from the Middlebury database of the stereo images. Size of each image is 370 × 463 pixels. Disparity range in both stereo pair is 0 to 75. The columns show, from left to the right, the left image, the ground truth, the result computed by our stereo algorithm, and the disparity error map larger than 1 pixel.

If we apply both steps, the accuracy of the disparity maps is the highest. Furthermore, the improvement contribution of the preprocessing step is greater than the postprocessing step only for *Venus* stereo pair. This is because the sampling effects were most pronounced in *Venus* scene. In addition, we show in Figure 6 the disparity maps for *Tsukuba* stereo pair for all four combinations: if the preprocessing and the postprocessing steps are included or not in the algorithm. We conclude that the preprocessing step plays a significant role in accurate disparity estimation of textureless areas, while the postprocessing step especially helps in an accurate estimation of disparity discontinuities.

To illustrate the subtle features of our algorithm not captured in the standard test bed images, and we apply our stereo algorithm, while retaining the parameter values, on some other images from the Middlebury site in Figure 7. For

two other stereo pairs, *Art* and *Dolls*, we show the left images of two stereo pairs in the leftmost column. The ground truth (GT) disparity maps are in the second column. The third column shows our estimation of the disparity maps. The fourth column shows the error maps with regard to the ground truth. The algorithm successfully recovers the disparities of very narrow structures as in *Art* disparity map. The disparity of the cluttered scene is successfully estimated, as in *Dolls* disparity map.

Next, we demonstrate that the presented local stereo algorithm works well on practical problems. Examples of disparity map estimation and 3D reconstruction of a face are shown for stereo pair *Sanja* in Figure 8. The disparity map estimation of a plant in stereo pair *Tomato seedling* is shown in Figure 9. The parameters of the algorithm are kept the same as in the previous examples. Thus, our algorithm

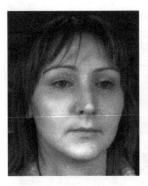
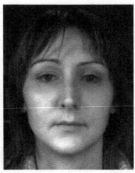
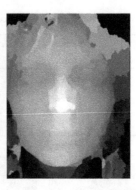
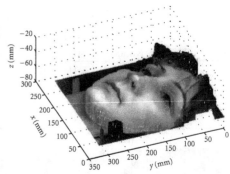

FIGURE 8: Disparity results for the stereo pair *Sanja*, taken at the vision laboratory of Signals and Systems Group, University of Twente. Size of each image is 781×641 pixels. Disparity range is 0 to 40. (a) Left stereo image, (b) right stereo image, (c) disparity map corresponding to the right image, and (d) depth map with texture overlay.

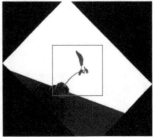

FIGURE 9: Disparity results for the stereo pair *Tomato seedling*, taken within MARVIN project at the vision laboratory of Intelligent System Group, Wageningen UR-Food and Biobased Research. Size of the region of interest in each image is 300×310 pixels. Disparity range is 0 to 90. (a) Left stereo image, (b) right stereo image, (c) region of interest in the left image, and (d) disparity map corresponding to the left image.

successfully estimates the disparity of the smooth low-textured objects and is suitable also for application to 3D face reconstruction, Figure 8(d). Our algorithm also successfully estimated the disparity map of the tomato seedling. *Tomato seedling* stereo images represent a challenging task for a stereo matching algorithm in general, because the viewpoints significantly differ and the structure of the plant is narrow, that is, much smaller than the window dimension.

As far as the initial window size is concerned, our algorithm is not influenced by the window size above certain size. In principle, we could apply our algorithm using the whole image as the initial window around the reference pixel. This would result in a sufficiently large region selection for uniform regions in the image and make the ordinal measure within the hybrid WTA more reliable. On the other hand, in matching windows with high local intensity variations, the selected region is always significantly smaller than the window and does not change if the window is enlarged because of the connectivity constraint with the reference central pixel.

4. Conclusion

In our local stereo algorithm, we have introduced a new approach for stereo correspondence based on the adaptive local segmentation by a dynamic threshold so that the frontoparallel assumption holds for a segment. Further, we have established a relationship among the local intensity variation in an image and the dynamic threshold. We have applied the novel preprocessing procedure on both stereo images to eliminate the influence of noise and sampling artifacts. The mechanism for the final matching region selection prevents error propagation due to disparity discontinuities and occlusion. In the postprocessing step, we introduce a new histogram voting procedure for disparity refinement and for filling in the eliminated inconsistent disparities. Although the starting point in matching is the large rectangular window, disparity of narrow structures is accurately estimated.

We evaluated our algorithm on the stereo pairs from the Middlebury database. It ranks highly on the list, outperforming many local and global algorithms that use color information while we use only intensity images. Our algorithm is the best performing algorithm in the class of local algorithms which use intensity images and the frontoparallel assumption without weighting the intensities of the matching region. Furthermore, our algorithm matches textureless as well as textured surfaces equally well, handles well the local radiometric differences, preserves edges in disparity maps, and successfully recovers the disparity of thin objects and the disparities of the occluded regions. We demonstrated the performance of our algorithm on two additional examples from the Middlebury database and on two practical examples. The results on this additional examples show that the disparity maps of scenes of different natures are successfully estimated: smooth low-textured objects as well as textured cluttered scenes, narrow structures, and textureless surfaces. Moreover, our algorithm has also other positive aspects making it suitable for real-time implementation: it is local; it has just five parameters; intensity variations are locally calculated, and there is no global segmentation algorithm involved.

References

[1] D. Marr and T. Poggio, "A computational theory of human stereo vision," *Proceedings of the Royal Society of London*, vol. 204, no. 1156, pp. 301–328, 1979.

[2] M. Z. Brown, D. Burschka, and G. D. Hager, "Advances in computational stereo," *IEEE Transactions on Pattern Analysis and Machine Intelligence*, vol. 25, no. 8, pp. 993–1008, 2003.

[3] O. D. Faugeras, *Three-Dimensional Computer Vision: A Geometric Viewpoint*, MIT Press, 1993.

[4] D. Scharstein and R. Szeliski, "A taxonomy and evaluation of dense two-frame stereo correspondence algorithms," *International Journal of Computer Vision*, vol. 47, no. 1–3, pp. 7–42, 2002.

[5] A. Hosni, M. Bleyer, M. Gelautz, and C. Rhemann, "Local stereo matching using geodesic support weights," in *Proceedings of the IEEE International Conference on Image Processing (ICIP '09)*, pp. 2093–2096, November 2009.

[6] K. Zhang, J. Lu, and G. Lafruit, "Cross-based local stereo matching using orthogonal integral images," *IEEE Transactions on Circuits and Systems for Video Technology*, vol. 19, no. 7, pp. 1073–1079, 2009.

[7] P. N. Belhumeur, "A bayesian approach to binocular stereopsis," *International Journal of Computer Vision*, vol. 19, no. 3, pp. 237–260, 1996.

[8] Y. Boykov, O. Veksler, and R. Zabih, "Fast approximate energy minimization via graph cuts," *IEEE Transactions on Pattern Analysis and Machine Intelligence*, vol. 23, no. 11, pp. 1222–1239, 2001.

[9] J. Sun, N. N. Zheng, and H. Y. Shum, "Stereo matching using belief propagation," *IEEE Transactions on Pattern Analysis and Machine Intelligence*, vol. 25, no. 7, pp. 787–800, 2003.

[10] N. Lazaros, G. C. Sirakoulis, and A. Gasteratos, "Review of stereo vision algorithms: from software to hardware," *International Journal of Optomechatronics*, vol. 2, no. 4, pp. 435–462, 2008.

[11] C. Lawrence Zitnick and T. Kanade, "A cooperative algorithm for stereo matching and occlusion detection," *IEEE Transactions on Pattern Analysis and Machine Intelligence*, vol. 22, no. 7, pp. 675–684, 2000.

[12] H. Hirschmüller, P. R. Innocent, and J. Garibaldi, "Real-time correlation-based stereo vision with reduced border errors," *International Journal of Computer Vision*, vol. 47, no. 1–5, pp. 229–246, 2002.

[13] S. Damjanović, F. van der Heijden, and L. J. Spreeuwers, "Sparse window local stereo matching," in *Proceedings of the International Conference on Computer Vision Theory and Application (VISAPP '11)*, pp. 689–693, March 2011.

[14] R. K. Gupta and S. Y. Cho, "Real-time stereo matching using adaptive binary window," in *Proceedings of the 5th International Symposium on 3D Data Processing, Visualization and Transmission (3DPVT '10)*, 2010.

[15] F. Tombari, S. Mattoccia, L. D. Stefano, and E. Addimanda, "Classification and evaluation of cost aggregation methods for stereo correspondence," in *Proceedings of the 26th IEEE Conference on Computer Vision and Pattern Recognition (CVPR '08)*, pp. 1–8, June 2008.

[16] X. Sun, X. Mei, S. Jiao, M. Zhou, and H. Wang, "Stereo matching with reliable disparity propagation," in *Proceedings of the IEEE International Conference on 3D Digital Imaging, Modeling, Processing, Visualisation and Transmittion (3DIMPVT '11)*, 2011.

[17] K. Zhang, J. Lu, and G. Lafruit, "Scalable stereo matching with locally adaptive polygon approximation," in *Proceedings of the IEEE International Conference on Image Processing (ICIP '08)*, pp. 313–316, October 2008.

[18] K. Zhang, J. Lu, G. Lafruit, R. Lauwereins, and L. Van Gool, "Accurate and efficient stereo matching with robust piecewise voting," in *Proceedings of the IEEE International Conference on Multimedia and Expo (ICME '09)*, pp. 93–96, IEEE Press, Piscataway, NJ, USA, July 2009.

[19] M. Bleyer, C. Rother, and P. Kohli, "Surface stereo with soft segmentation," in *Proceedings of the IEEE Computer Society Conference on Computer Vision and Pattern Recognition (CVPR '10)*, pp. 1570–1577, June 2010.

[20] H. Tao, H. S. Sawhney, and R. Kumar, "A global matching framework for stereo computation," in *Proceedings of the 8th International Conference on Computer Vision*, pp. 532–539, July 2001.

[21] K. J. Yoon and I. S. Kweon, "Adaptive support-weight approach for correspondence search," *IEEE Transactions on Pattern Analysis and Machine Intelligence*, vol. 28, no. 4, pp. 650–656, 2006.

[22] A. Hosni, M. Bleyer, M. Gelautz, and C. Rhemann, "Geodesic adaptive support weight approach for localstereo matching," in *Proceedings of the Computer Vision Winter Workshop*, pp. 60–65, 2010.

[23] S. Birchfield and C. Tomasi, "Depth discontinuities by pixel-to-pixel stereo," *International Journal of Computer Vision*, vol. 35, no. 3, pp. 269–293, 1999.

[24] R. Szeliski and D. Scharstein, "Sampling the Disparity Space Image," *IEEE Transactions on Pattern Analysis and Machine Intelligence*, vol. 26, no. 3, pp. 419–425, 2004.

[25] Q. Wu, F. A. Merchant, and K. R. Castleman, *Microscope Image Processing*, Academic Press, 2008.

[26] R. C. Gonzalez, R. E. Woods, and S. L. Eddins, *Digital Image Processing Using MATLAB*, Gatesmark Publishing, 2nd edition, 2009.

[27] Middlebury stereo, March 2012, http://vision.middlebury.edu/stereo/.

[28] I. J. Cox, "Maximum likelihood N-camera stereo algorithm," in *Proceedings of the IEEE Computer Society Conference on Computer Vision and Pattern Recognition*, pp. 733–739, June 1994.

[29] S. Damjanović, F. Van Der Heijden, and L. J. Spreeuwers, "Sparse window local stereo matching," in *Proceedings of the International Workshop on Computer Vision Applications (CVA '11)*, pp. 83–86, 2011.

[30] H. Hirschmüller, "Stereo processing by semiglobal matching and mutual information," *IEEE Transactions on Pattern Analysis and Machine Intelligence*, vol. 30, no. 2, pp. 328–341, 2008.

[31] B. Bleyer, C. Rhemann, and C. Rother, "Patchmatch stereo—stereo matching with slanted support windows," in *Proceedings of the British Machine Vision Conference*, 2011.

Permissions

The contributors of this book come from diverse backgrounds, making this book a truly international effort. This book will bring forth new frontiers with its revolutionizing research information and detailed analysis of the nascent developments around the world.

We would like to thank all the contributing authors for lending their expertise to make the book truly unique. They have played a crucial role in the development of this book. Without their invaluable contributions this book wouldn't have been possible. They have made vital efforts to compile up to date information on the varied aspects of this subject to make this book a valuable addition to the collection of many professionals and students.

This book was conceptualized with the vision of imparting up-to-date information and advanced data in this field. To ensure the same, a matchless editorial board was set up. Every individual on the board went through rigorous rounds of assessment to prove their worth. After which they invested a large part of their time researching and compiling the most relevant data for our readers. Conferences and sessions were held from time to time between the editorial board and the contributing authors to present the data in the most comprehensible form. The editorial team has worked tirelessly to provide valuable and valid information to help people across the globe.

Every chapter published in this book has been scrutinized by our experts. Their significance has been extensively debated. The topics covered herein carry significant findings which will fuel the growth of the discipline. They may even be implemented as practical applications or may be referred to as a beginning point for another development. Chapters in this book were first published by Hindawi Publishing Corporation; hereby published with permission under the Creative Commons Attribution License or equivalent.

The editorial board has been involved in producing this book since its inception. They have spent rigorous hours researching and exploring the diverse topics which have resulted in the successful publishing of this book. They have passed on their knowledge of decades through this book. To expedite this challenging task, the publisher supported the team at every step. A small team of assistant editors was also appointed to further simplify the editing procedure and attain best results for the readers.

Our editorial team has been hand-picked from every corner of the world. Their multi-ethnicity adds dynamic inputs to the discussions which result in innovative outcomes. These outcomes are then further discussed with the researchers and contributors who give their valuable feedback and opinion regarding the same. The feedback is then collaborated with the researches and they are edited in a comprehensive manner to aid the understanding of the subject.

Apart from the editorial board, the designing team has also invested a significant amount of their time in understanding the subject and creating the most relevant covers. They scrutinized every image to scout for the most suitable representation of the subject and create an appropriate cover for the book.

The publishing team has been involved in this book since its early stages. They were actively engaged in every process, be it collecting the data, connecting with the contributors or procuring relevant information. The team has been an ardent support to the editorial, designing and production team. Their endless efforts to recruit the best for this project, has resulted in the accomplishment of this book. They are a veteran in the field of academics and their pool of knowledge is as vast as their experience in printing. Their expertise and guidance has proved useful at every step. Their uncompromising quality standards have made this book an exceptional effort. Their encouragement from time to time has been an inspiration for everyone.

The publisher and the editorial board hope that this book will prove to be a valuable piece of knowledge for researchers, students, practitioners and scholars across the globe.

List of Contributors

Amioy Kumar, M. Hanmandlu and Hari M. Gupta
Biometrics Research Laboratory, Department of Electrical Engineering, Indian Institute of Technology Delhi, Hauz Khas, New Delhi 110 016, India

Fabrizio Russo
Department of Engineering and Architecture, University of Trieste, Via A. Valerio 10, 34127 Trieste, Italy

Christopher Kanan
Jet Propulsion Laboratory, California Institute of Technology, Pasadena, CA 91109, USA

Samy Sadek
Department of Mathematics and Computer Science, Faculty of Science, Sohag University, 82524 Sohag, Egypt

Ayoub Al-Hamadi, Gerald Krell and Bernd Michaelis
Institute for Information Technology and Communications (IIKT), Otto von Guericke University Magdeburg, 39106 Magdeburg, Germany

Christophe Soares and Rui S. Moreira
INESC TEC, FEUP, University of Porto, Porto, Portugal

José M. Torres and Pedro Sobral
ISUS Group, FCT, University Fernando Pessoa, Porto, Portugal

Ruan Lakemond, Clinton Fookes and Sridha Sridharan
Image and Video Research Laboratory, Queensland University of Technology, GPO Box 2434, 2 George Street, Brisbane, QLD 4001, Australia

Ricardo Omar Chávez, Hugo Jair Escalante, Manuel Montes-y-Gómez and Luis Enrique Sucar
Department of Computer Sciences, Instituto Nacional de Astrofssica, Optica y Electronica, Luis Enrique Erro No. 1, 72840 Tonantzintla, PUE, Mexico

Olli Lahdenoja, Jonne Poikonen and Mika Laiho
Business and Innovation Development BID Technology, University of Turku, 20014 Turku, Finland

Ye-Peng Guan
School of Communication and Information Engineering, Shanghai University, 99 Shangda Road, Shanghai, China
Key Laboratory of Advanced Displays and System Application, Ministry of Education, 99 Shangda Road, Shanghai, China

Yong Luo and Chang-Qi Zhang
School of Communication and Information Engineering, Shanghai University, 99 Shangda Road, Shanghai, China

Pierre Buyssens
LITIS EA 4108-QuantIF Team, University of Rouen, 22 Boulevard Gambetta, 76183 Rouen Cedex, France

Marinette Revenu
GREYC UMR CNRS 6072 ENSICAEN-Image Team, University of Caen Basse-Normandie, 6 Boulevard Marechal Juin, 14050 Caen, France

Hayk Baluyan, Bikash Joshi, Amer Al Hinai and Wei Lee Woon
Computing and Information Science, Masdar Institute of Science and Technology, Masdar City, Abu Dhabi, UAE

Sanjay Singh, Anil Kumar Saini, Ravi Saini, A. S. Mandal and Chandra Shekhar
CSIR-Central Electronics Engineering Research Institute (CSIR-CEERI), Pilani, Rajasthan 333031, India

Anil Vohra
Electronic Science Department, Kurukshetra University, Kurukshetra, Haryana 136119, India

Samira Sabouri
Department of Electrical Engineering, Science and Research Branch, Islamic Azad University, Tehran 14778-93855, Iran

Alireza Behrad
Faculty of Engineering, Shahed University, Tehran 18651-33191, Iran

Hassan Ghassemian
School of Electrical and Computer Engineering, Tarbiat Modares University, Tehran 14115-143, Iran

Shidu Dong
College of Computer Science and Engineering, Chongqing University of Technology, Chongqing 400050, China

Safia Abdelmounaime and He Dong-Chen
Centre for Research and Applications in Remote Sensing (CARTEL), Department of Geomatics, Sherbrooke University, QC, Canada

Sanja Damjanovic, Ferdinand van der Heijden and Luuk J. Spreeuwers
Signals and Systems Group, Department of EEMCS, University of Twente, Hallenweg 15, 7522 NH Enschede, The Netherlands